PHP for the Web

Fifth Edition

LARRY ULLMAN

 Peachpit Press

Visual QuickStart Guide
PHP for the Web, Fifth Edition
Larry Ullman

Peachpit Press
1301 Sansome Street
San Francisco, CA 94111

Find us on the web at: www.peachpit.com
To report errors, please send a note to: errata@peachpit.com
Peachpit Press is a division of Pearson Education.

Copyright © 2016 by Larry Ullman

Senior Editor: Karyn Johnson
Development Editor: Robyn G. Thomas
Copyeditor: Liz Welch
Technical Reviewer: Paul Reinheimer
Proofreader: Scout Festa
Production Coordinator: David Van Ness
Compositor: WolfsonDesign
Indexer: Valerie Haynes Perry

Notice of Rights

Notice of Liability

Trademarks

ISBN-13: 978-0-134-29125-3
ISBN-10: 0-134-29125-5

2   16

Printed and bound in the United States of America

Dedication

For Jessica, Gina, and Rich, with gratitude for all their love and support.

Special Thanks to:

Many, many thanks to everyone at Peachpit Press for their assistance and hard work, especially:

Robyn Thomas, for managing the project adeptly, and for knowing when to push and poke.

Liz Welch, for fine-tuning my prose with her copyediting skills.

Paul Reinheimer, for the superlative technical review, keeping me honest, and finding things to improve even in a fifth edition.

Scout Festa, for the sharp proofreading eye.

David Van Ness, who takes a bunch of disparate stuff and turns it into a book.

Thanks for doing what's required to create, publish, distribute, market, sell, and support these books.

My sincerest thanks to the readers of the other editions of this book and my other books. Thanks for your feedback and support and for keeping me in business.

Rasmus Lerdorf (who got the PHP ball rolling), the people at PHP.net and Zend.com, those who frequent the various newsgroups and mailing lists, and the greater PHP and open source communities for developing, improving upon, and supporting such wonderfully useful technology.

Zoe and Sam, for continuing to be the kid epitome of awesomeness.

Jessica, for doing everything you do and everything you can.

Table of Contents

Introduction

When I began the first edition of this book in 2000, PHP was a little-known *open source* project. It was adored by technical people in the know but not yet recognized as the popular choice for web development that it is today. When I taught myself PHP, very little documentation was available on the language—and that was my motivation for writing this book in the first place.

Today things are different. The Internet has gone through a boom and a bust and has righted itself. Furthermore, PHP is now the reigning king of dynamic web design tools and has expanded somewhat beyond the realm of just web development. But despite PHP's popularity and the increase in available documentation, sample code, and examples, a good book discussing the language is still relevant. Although PHP is in the beginnings of its sixth major release, a book such as this—which teaches the language in simple but practical terms— can still be your best guide in learning the information you need to know.

This book will teach you PHP, providing both a solid understanding of the fundamentals and a sense of where to look for more advanced information. Although it isn't a comprehensive programming reference, this book, through demonstrations and real-world examples, provides the knowledge you need to begin building dynamic websites and web applications using PHP.

What Is PHP?

PHP originally stood for *Personal Home Page*. It was created in 1994 by Rasmus Lerdorf to track the visitors to his online résumé. As its usefulness and capabilities grew (and as it began to be utilized in more professional situations), PHP came to mean *PHP: Hypertext Preprocessor*. The definition basically means that PHP handles data before it becomes HTML—which stands for Hypertext Markup Language.

According to the official PHP website, found at www.php.net 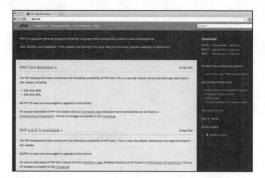, PHP is "a popular general-purpose scripting language that is especially suited to web development." More specifically, PHP is a scripting language commonly embedded within HTML. Let's examine what this means in more detail.

To say that PHP *can be embedded into HTML* means that PHP code can be written within your HTML code—HTML being the language with which all web pages are built. Therefore, programming with PHP starts off as only slightly more complicated than hand-coding HTML.

Also, PHP is a *scripting language*, as opposed to a *compiled language*. This means that PHP is designed to do something *only after an event occurs*—for example, when a user submits a form or goes to a URL (Uniform Resource Locator—the technical term for a web address). Another popular example of a scripting language is JavaScript, which commonly handles events that occur within the browser. Both PHP and JavaScript can also be described as *interpreted*, because the code must be run through an executable, such as the PHP module or the browser's JavaScript component. Conversely, compiled languages such as C and C++ can be used to write stand-alone applications that can act independently of any event.

Ⓐ As of this writing, this is the appearance of the official PHP website, located at www.php.net. Naturally, this should be the first place you look to address most of your PHP questions and curiosities.

PHP 6?

Yes, as of this writing, the current versions of PHP were 5 and 7, but not 6! There's a long and amusing story here, but the short version is that PHP 6 was actively developed for a while. After hitting many snags, the development was halted and the created work was rolled into PHP 5.

When it became time to work on the next major version, after much debate it was decided that that version would be named PHP 7. So although there was once a beta version of PHP 6, no final release ever saw the light of day.

B This Zend website contains useful software as well as a code gallery and well-written tutorials.

What PHP Is Not

The thing about PHP that confuses most new learners is what PHP can't do. Although you can use the language for an amazing array of tasks, its main limitation is that PHP cannot be used for client-side features found in some websites.

Using a client-side technology like JavaScript, you can create a new browser window, make pop-up dialogs, dynamically generate and alter forms, and much more. None of these tasks can be accomplished using PHP because PHP is server-side, whereas those are client-side issues. But you can use PHP to create JavaScript, just as you can use PHP to create HTML.

When it comes time to develop your own PHP projects, remember that you can use PHP only to send information (HTML and such) to the browser. You can't do anything else within the browser until another request from the server has been made (a form has been submitted or a link has been clicked).

You should also understand that PHP is a *server-side* technology. This refers to the fact that everything PHP does occurs on the server (as opposed to on the *client*, which is the computer being used by the person viewing the website). A *server* is just a computer set up to provide the pages you see when you go to a web address with your browser. I'll discuss this process in more detail later in this introduction (see "How PHP Works").

Finally, PHP is *cross-platform*, meaning that it can be used on machines running Unix, Windows, Macintosh, and other operating systems. Again, we're talking about the *server's* operating system, not the client's. Not only can PHP run on almost any operating system, but, unlike many other programming languages, it enables you to switch your work from one platform to another with few or no modifications.

As of this writing, PHP is simultaneously in versions 5.5.35, 5.6.21, and 7.0.6. (There are slight differences between versions 5.5 and 5.6, so 5.5 continues to be supported for a while.) Although I wrote this book using a stable version of PHP 7, all of the code is backward compatible, at least to PHP version 5.*x*. In a couple of situations where a feature requires a more current version of PHP, or where older versions might have slight variations, a note in a sidebar or a tip will indicate how you can adjust the code accordingly.

More information can be found at PHP.net and Zend (www.zend.com), a key company involved with PHP development **B**.

Why Use PHP?

Put simply, PHP is better, faster, and easier to learn than the alternatives. All websites must begin with just HTML, and you can create an entire site using a number of static HTML pages. But basic HTML is a limited approach that does not allow for flexibility or dynamic behavior. Visitors accessing HTML-only sites see simple pages with no level of customization or dynamic behavior. With PHP, you can create exciting and original pages based on whatever factors you want to consider. PHP can also interact with databases and files, handle email, and do many other things that HTML alone cannot.

Web developers learned a long time ago that HTML alone won't produce enticing and lasting websites. Toward this end, server-side technologies such as PHP have become the norm. These technologies allow developers to create web applications that are dynamically generated, taking into account whichever elements the programmer desires. Often database-driven, these advanced sites can be updated and maintained more readily than static HTML pages.

When it comes to choosing a server-side technology, the primary alternatives 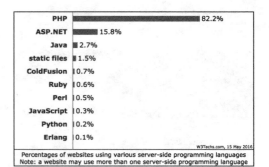 to PHP are: ASP.NET (Active Server Pages), JSP (JavaServer Pages), Ruby (through the Rails or Sinatra frameworks), and some newer server-side JavaScript options such as Node.js.

PHP	82.2%
ASP.NET	15.8%
Java	2.7%
static files	1.5%
ColdFusion	0.7%
Ruby	0.6%
Perl	0.5%
JavaScript	0.3%
Python	0.2%
Erlang	0.1%

W3Techs.com, 15 May 2016

Percentages of websites using various server-side programming languages
Note: a website may use more than one server-side programming language

A The Web Technology Surveys site says that PHP is running on 82 percent of all websites (http://w3techs.com/technologies/overview/programming_language/all).

So the question is, why should a web developer use PHP instead of ASP.NET, Node.js, or whatever else to make a dynamic website?

- **PHP is much easier to learn and use.** People—perhaps like you—without any formal programming training can write PHP scripts with ease after reading this one book. In comparison, ASP.NET requires an understanding of Visual Basic, C#, or another language; Node.js requires JavaScript. These are more complex languages and are much more difficult to learn.

- **PHP was written specifically for dynamic web page creation.** Perl, VBScript, Java, and Ruby were not, and this fact suggests that, by its very intent, PHP can do certain tasks faster and more easily than the alternatives. I'd like to make it clear, however, that although I'm suggesting that PHP is *better for certain things*—specifically those it was created to do, PHP isn't a "better" programming language than JavaScript or C#—they can do things PHP can't.

- **PHP is both free and cross-platform.** Therefore, you can learn and use PHP on nearly any computer and at no cost. Furthermore, its open source nature means that PHP's users are driving its development, not some corporate entity.

- **PHP is the most popular tool available for developing dynamic websites.** As of this writing, PHP is in use on over 82 percent of all websites Ⓐ and is the sixth most popular programming language overall Ⓑ. Many of the biggest websites—Yahoo, Wikipedia, and Facebook, just to name three—and content management tools, such as WordPress, Drupal, Moodle, and Joomla, use PHP. By learning this one language, you'll provide yourself with either a usable hobby or a lucrative skill.

May 2016	May 2015	Change	Programming Language	Ratings	Change
1	1		Java	20.956%	+4.09%
2	2		C	13.223%	-3.62%
3	3		C++	6.698%	-1.18%
4	5	⌃	C#	4.481%	-0.78%
5	6	⌃	Python	3.789%	+0.06%
6	9	⌃	PHP	2.992%	+0.27%
7	7		JavaScript	2.340%	-0.79%
8	15	⌃⌃	Ruby	2.338%	+1.07%
9	11	⌃	Perl	2.326%	+0.51%
10	8	⌄	Visual Basic .NET	2.325%	-0.64%

Ⓑ The Tiobe Index (www.tiobe.com/tiobe_index) uses a combination of factors to rank the popularity of programming languages.

How PHP Works

PHP is a server-side language, which means the code you write in PHP resides on a host computer that serves web pages to browsers. When you go to a website (www.LarryUllman.com, for example), your Internet service provider (ISP) directs your request to the server that holds the www.LarryUllman.com information. That server reads the PHP code and processes it according to its scripted directions. In this example, the PHP code tells the server to send the appropriate web page data to your browser in the form of HTML **A**. In short, PHP creates an HTML page on the fly based on parameters of your choosing.

This differs from an HTML-generated site in that when a request is made, the server merely sends the HTML data to the browser—no server-side interpretation occurs **B**. Hence, to the end user's browser, there may or may not be an obvious difference between what **home.html** and **home.php** look like, but how you arrive at that point is critically altered. The major difference is that by using PHP, you can have the server *dynamically* generate the HTML code. For example, different information could be presented if it's Monday as opposed to Tuesday or if the user has visited the page before. Dynamic web page creation sets apart the less appealing, static sites from the more interesting, and therefore more visited, interactive ones.

The central difference between using PHP and using straight HTML is that PHP does everything on the server and then sends the appropriate information to the browser. This book covers how to use PHP to send the right data to the browser.

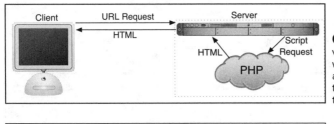

A This graphic demonstrates (albeit in very simplistic terms) how the process works between a client, the server, and a PHP module (an application added to the server to increase its functionality) to send HTML back to the browser.

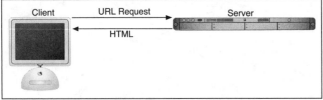

B Compare this direct relationship of how a server handles basic HTML to **A**. This is also why HTML pages can be viewed in your browser from your own computer—they don't need to be "served," but dynamically generated pages need to be accessed through a server that handles the processing.

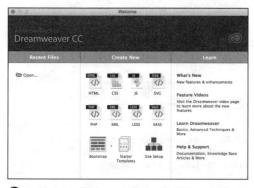

A The popular Dreamweaver application supports PHP development, among other server-side technologies.

What You'll Need

The most important requirement for working with PHP—because it's a server-side scripting language—is access to a PHP-enabled server. Considering PHP's popularity, your web host most likely has this option available to you on their servers. You'll need to contact them to see what technology they support.

Your other option is to install PHP and a web server application (like Apache) on your own computer. Users of Windows, Mac OS X, or Linux can easily install and use PHP for no cost. Directions for installing PHP are available in Appendix A, "Installation and Configuration." If you're up to the task of using your own PHP-installed server, you can take some consolation in knowing that PHP is available for free from the PHP website (www.php.net) and comes in easy-to-install packages. If you take this approach, and I recommend that you do, then your computer will act as both the client and the server.

The second requirement is almost a given: You must have a text editor on your computer. Atom, Notepad++, UltraEdit, and similar freeware applications are all sufficient for your purposes, and TextMate, SublimeText, and other commercial applications offer more features that you may appreciate. If you're accustomed to using a graphical interface (also referred to as WYSIWYG—What You See Is What You Get) such as Adobe Dreamweaver **A** or Aptana Studio, you can consult that application's manual to see how to program within it.

continues on next page

Third, you need a method of getting the scripts you write to the server. If you've installed PHP on your own computer, you can save the scripts to the appropriate directory. However, if you're using a remote server with a web host, you'll need an SFTP (Secure File Transfer Protocol) program to send the script to the server. There are plenty of SFTP applications available; for example, in Chapter 1, "Getting Started with PHP," I use the free FileZilla (http://filezilla-project.org ).

Ⓑ The FileZilla application can be used on many different operating systems to move PHP scripts and other files to a remote server.

Finally, if you want to follow the examples in Chapter 12, "Intro to Databases," you need access to MySQL (www.mysql.com Ⓒ). MySQL is available in a free version that you can install on your own computer.

Ⓒ MySQL's website (as of this writing).

This book assumes only a basic knowledge of HTML, although the more comfortable you are handling raw HTML code *without* the aid of a WYSIWYG application such as Dreamweaver, the easier the transition to using PHP will be. Every programmer will eventually turn to an HTML reference at some time or other, regardless of how much you know, so I encourage you to keep a good HTML book by your side. One such introduction to HTML is Elizabeth Castro and Bruce Hyslop's *HTML, XHTML, and CSS: Visual QuickStart Guide* (Peachpit Press, 2014).

Previous programming experience is certainly not required. However, it may expedite your learning because you'll quickly see numerous similarities between, for example, Perl and PHP or JavaScript and PHP.

Script i.1 A sample PHP script, with line numbers and bold emphasis on a specific section of code.

```
1    <!doctype html>
2    <html lang="en">
3    <head>
4        <meta charset="utf-8">
5        <title>Hello, World!</title>
6    </head>
7    <body>
8    <?php print "Hello, world!"; ?>
9    </body>
10   </html>
```

About This Book

This book attempts to convey the fundamentals of programming with PHP while hinting at some of the more advanced features you may want to consider in the future, without going into overwhelming detail. It uses the following conventions to do so.

The step-by-step instructions indicate what coding you're to add to your scripts and where. The specific text you should type is printed in a unique type style to separate it from the main body text. For example:

`<?php print "Hello, World!"; ?>`

The PHP code is also written as its own complete script and is numbered by line for reference (**Script i.1**). You shouldn't insert these line numbers yourself, because doing so will render your work inoperable.

I recommend using a text editor that automatically displays the line numbers for you—the numbers will help when you're debugging your work. In the scripts, you'll sometimes see particular lines highlighted in bold, in order to draw attention to new or relevant material.

What's New in This Book?

I would consider this fifth edition to be a modest revision of an already solid book. The biggest changes are

- All examples now use HTML5.

- The MySQL code uses the most current version of PHP's MySQL extension.

- We cover PHP 7, as applicable.

Finally, I tweaked some of the examples mostly to satisfy my own drive for perfection. No content from the previous edition has been removed.

Because of the nature of how PHP works, you need to understand that there are essentially three views of every script: the PHP code (e.g., Script i.1), the code that's sent to the browser (primarily HTML), and what the browser displays to the end user. Where appropriate, sections of, or all of, the browser window are revealed, showing the result of the exercise **A**. Occasionally, you'll also see an image displaying the HTML source that the browser received **B**. You can normally access this view by choosing View Source or View Page Source from the appropriate browser menu. To summarize, **B** displays the HTML the browser receives, and **A** demonstrates how the browser interprets that HTML. Using PHP, you'll create the HTML that's sent to the browser.

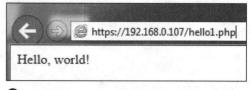

Hello, world!

A This is a sample view you'll see of the browser window. For the purposes of this book, it won't make any difference which browser or operating system you use.

```
F12    DOM Explorer        Console        Debugger

<!DOCTYPE html>
<html lang="en">
    <head>
        <meta charset="utf-8"></meta>
        <title>Hello, World!</title>
    </head>
    <body>
        Hello, world!
    </body>
</html>
```

B By viewing the source code received by the browser, you can see the HTML created by PHP and sent by the server.

Because the columns in this book are narrower than the common text editor screen, sometimes lines of PHP code printed in the steps have to be broken where they would not otherwise break in your editor. A small gray arrow indicates when this kind of break occurs. For example:

```php
print "This is going to be a longer
→ line of code.";
```

You should continue to use one line in your scripts, or else you'll encounter errors when executing them. (The gray arrow isn't used in scripts that are numbered.)

While demonstrating new features and techniques, I'll do my best to explain the why's and how's of them as I go. Between reading about and using a function, you should clearly comprehend it. Should something remain confusing, though, this book contains a number of references where you can find answers to any questions (see Appendix B, "Resources and Next Steps"). If you're confused by a particular function or example, your best bet will be to check the online PHP manual or the book's supporting website (and its user support forum).

Companion Website

While you're reading this book, you may also find it helpful to visit the *PHP for the Web: Visual QuickStart Guide, 5th Edition* website, found within www.LarryUllman.com. There you'll find every script in this book available in a downloadable form. However, I strongly encourage you to type the scripts yourself in order to become more familiar with the structure and syntax of PHP. The site also provides an errata page listing any mistakes made in this text.

What many users find most helpful, though, is the book's supporting forum, found through the website or more directly at www.LarryUllman.com/forums/. Using the forum, you can

- Find answers to problems you're having

- Receive advice on how to approach an idea you have

- Get debugging help

- See how changes in the technologies have affected the examples in the book

- Learn what other people are doing with PHP

- Confirm the answers to review questions

- Receive a faster reply from me than if you send me a direct email

Which Book Is Right for You?

This is the fifth edition of my first book on PHP. Like the original, it's written with the beginner or nonprogrammer in mind. If you have little or no programming experience, prefer a gentler pace, or like to learn things in bite-sized pieces, this is the book for you. Make no mistake: This book covers what you need to know to begin developing dynamic websites and uses practical examples, but it does so without any in-depth theory or advanced applications.

Conversely, if you pick up new technologies really quickly or already have some experience developing websites, you may find this to be too basic. In that case, you should consider my *PHP and MySQL for Dynamic Web Sites: Visual QuickPro Guide* instead (Peachpit Press, 2012). It discusses SQL and MySQL in much greater detail and goes through several more complex examples, but it does so at a quick jog.

Questions, comments, or suggestions?

If you have a PHP-specific question, there are newsgroups, mailing lists, and question-and-answer sections available on PHP-related websites for you to turn to. These are discussed in more detail in Appendix B. Browsing through these references or searching the Internet will almost always provide you with the fastest answer.

You can also direct your questions, comments, and suggestions to me. You'll get the fastest reply using the book's corresponding forum; I always answer those questions first. If you'd rather email me, you can do so through the contact page on the website. I do try to answer every email I receive, but it will probably take a week or two (whereas you'll likely get a reply in the forum within a couple of days).

For more tips and an enlightening read, see the sidebar on this page and Eric Steven Raymond's "How to Ask Questions the Smart Way," at www.catb.org/~esr/faqs/smart-questions.html. The 10 minutes you spend on it will save you hours in the future. Those people who will answer your questions, like myself, will be most appreciative!

Getting Started with PHP

When learning any new programming language, always begin with an understanding of the basic syntax and functionality, which is what you'll learn in this chapter. The focus here is on the fundamentals of HTML and PHP, and how the two languages work together. The chapter also covers some recommended programming and debugging techniques, the use of which will greatly ease the learning process.

If you've never programmed before, a focused reading of this chapter will start you on the right track. If you have some programming experience, you'll be able to breeze through these pages, gaining a perspective for the book's remaining material. By the end of this chapter you will have successfully written and executed your first PHP scripts and be on your way to developing dynamic web applications.

In This Chapter

Basic HTML Syntax

All web pages are made using HTML (Hypertext Markup Language). Every web browser, be it Google's Chrome, Mozilla's Firefox, Microsoft's Internet Explorer and Edge, or Apple's Safari, turns HTML code—

```
<h1>Hello, World!</h1>
I just wanted to say <em>Hello</em>.
```

—into the web page presented to the user **A**.

As of this writing, the current version of HTML is 5, which should remain the norm for some time to come (it was officially standardized in 2014). HTML5 is a solid and practical version of the language, well suited for today's web.

Before getting into the syntax of PHP, let's create one simple but valid HTML document that can act as a template for many of this book's examples.

Hello, World!

I just wanted to say *Hello*.

A How one web browser renders the HTML code.

Basic CSS

HTML elements define a page's content, but formatting the look and behavior of such content is left to CSS (Cascading Style Sheets). As with HTML, this book does not teach CSS in any detail, but because some of the book's code uses CSS, you should be familiar with its basic syntax.

You can add CSS to a web page in a couple of ways. The first, and easiest, method is to use HTML style tags:

```
<style type="text/css">
/* rules */
</style>
```

The CSS rules are defined between the opening and closing style tags.

You can also use the **link** HTML tag to incorporate CSS rules defined in an external file:

```
<link href="styles.css" rel="stylesheet" type="text/css">
```

That file would contain only the rules, without the style tags.

CSS rules are applied to combinations of general page elements, CSS classes, and specific items:

```
img { border: 0px; }
.error { color: red; }
#about { background-color: #ccc; }
```

The first rule applies to every image tag. The second applies to any element that has a class of **error**:

```
<p class="error">Error!</p>
```

The third rule applies only to the specific element that has an **id** value of **about**:

```
<p id="about">About...</p>
```

(Not all elements need to have an **id** attribute, but no two elements should have the same **id** value.)

For the most part, this book uses CSS only to do simple things, such as changing the color or background color of an element or some text.

For more on CSS, search the web or see a dedicated book on the subject.

To create an HTML page:

1. Open your text editor or integrated development environment (IDE).

   You can use pretty much any application to create HTML and PHP pages. Popular choices include

   - Adobe's Dreamweaver (www.adobe.com)
   - Aptana Studio (www.aptana.com)
   - PhpStorm (www.jetbrains.com)
   - Sublime Text (www.sublimetext.com)
   - Atom (https://atom.io)

   The first three are IDEs, making them more complicated to use but also more powerful. The last two are text editors. All these programs run on most common operating systems.

2. Choose File > New to create a new, blank document.

   Some text editors allow you to start by creating a new document of a certain type—for example, a new HTML file . If your application has this option, use it!

3. Start with the HTML header lines (**Script 1.1**):

   ```
   <!doctype html>
   <html lang="en">
   ```

   A valid HTML5 document begins with these lines. They tell the web browser what type of document to expect. For this template, and in this entire book, *HTML5* pages will be created. One of the niceties of HTML5 is its minimal doctype and syntax.

B PhpStorm and most other web development applications can create the basics of an HTML document for you.

Script 1.1 This simple document contains the basics of an HTML5 page.

```
1   <!doctype html>
2   <html lang="en">
3   <head>
4      <meta charset="utf-8">
5      <title>Welcome to this Page!</title>
6   </head>
7   <body>
8   <h1>This is a basic HTML page!</h1>
9   <br>
10  <p>Even with <em>some</em> decoration,
    it's still not very exciting.</p>
11  </body>
12  </html>
```

Understanding Encoding

Encoding is a huge subject, but what you most need to understand is this: *The encoding you use in a file dictates what characters can be represented* (and therefore, what written languages you can use). To select an encoding, you must first confirm that your text editor or IDE can save documents using that encoding. Some applications let you set the encoding in the preferences or options area; others set the encoding when you save the file.

To indicate the encoding to the browser, there's a corresponding **meta** tag:

```
<meta charset="utf-8">
```

The **charset=utf-8** part says that UTF-8 (short for 8-bit Unicode Transformation Format) encoding is being used. Unicode is a way of reliably representing every symbol in every alphabet. Version 8.0.0 of Unicode—the current version as of this writing—supports over 120,000 characters! The most commonly used Unicode encoding is UTF-8.

If you want to create a multilingual web page, UTF-8 is the way to go, and it'll be used in this book's examples. You don't have to, of course. But whatever encoding you do use, make sure the encoding indicated by the HTML page matches the actual encoding used by the text editor or IDE. If you don't, you'll likely see odd characters when viewing the page in a web browser.

4. Create the head section of the page:

```
<head>
   <meta charset="utf-8">
   <title>Welcome to this Page!
 → </title>
</head>
```

The head of an HTML page should include the **charset** meta tag. The "Understanding Encoding" sidebar discusses what this means in more detail.

The head also contains the page's title, which appears at the top of the browser window or tab, as well as in the browser's bookmarks and history. You can also place JavaScript and CSS references in the head.

5. Create the body section:

```
<body>
<h1>This is a basic HTML page!
 → </h1>
<br>
<p>Even with <em>some</em>
 → decoration, it's still not
 → very exciting.</p>
</body>
```

The page's content—what is shown in the browser—goes between opening and closing **body** tags.

6. Complete the page with a closing HTML tag:

```
</html>
```

continues on next page

7. Choose File > Save As. In the dialog box that appears, choose Text Only (or ASCII) for the format, if you're given the option.

   HTML and PHP documents are just plain text files (unlike, for example, a Microsoft Word document, which is stored in a proprietary, binary format). You may also need to indicate the encoding (**utf-8**) when you save the file (again, see the "Understanding Encoding" sidebar).

8. Navigate to the location where you wish to save the script.

   You can place this script anywhere you'd like on your computer, although using one dedicated folder for every script in this book, perhaps with sub-folders for each chapter, makes sense.

9. Save the file as **welcome.html**.

   HTML5 pages use the standard **.html** extension.

10. Test the page by viewing it in your browser **C**.

    Unlike with PHP scripts (as you'll soon discover), you can test HTML pages by opening them directly in a browser.

C The HTML page, as interpreted by the browser.

> **TIP** Search the web or use the book's support forum (www.LarryUllman.com/forums/) to find a good HTML and PHP editor or IDE.

> **TIP** For more information on HTML, check out Elizabeth Castro and Bruce Hyslop's excellent book *HTML and CSS, Eighth Edition: Visual QuickStart Guide* (Peachpit Press, 2014).

Basic PHP Syntax

Now that you've seen how HTML will be handled in this book, it's time to begin PHP scripting. To create a PHP page, you'll start exactly as you would if you were creating an HTML document from scratch. Understanding the reason for this is vitally important: Web browsers are client applications that understand HTML; *PHP is a server-side technology* that cannot run in the client. To bridge this gap, PHP is used on the server to generate HTML that's run in a browser (refer to the section "How PHP Works" in this book's "Introduction" for a visual representation of this relationship).

There are three main differences between a standard HTML page and a PHP script. First, PHP scripts should be saved with the `.php` file extension (for example, `index.php`). Second, you place PHP code within `<?php` and `?>` tags, normally within the context of some HTML:

```
...
<body><h1>This is HTML.</h1>
<?php PHP code! ?>
<p>More HTML</p>
...
```

The PHP tags indicate the parts of the page to be run through the PHP processor on the server. This leads to the third major difference: *PHP scripts must be run on a PHP-enabled web server* (whereas HTML pages can be viewed on any computer, directly in a browser). This means that *PHP scripts must always be run through a URL* (for example, http://example.com/page.php). If you're viewing a PHP script in a web browser and the address does not begin with *http*, the PHP script will not work.

To make this first PHP script do something without too much programming fuss, you'll use the **phpinfo()** function. This function, when called, sends a table of information to the web browser. That table lists the specifics of the PHP installation on that particular server. It's a great way to test your PHP installation and has a high "bang for your buck" quality.

However, the **phpinfo()** function not only outputs a table of information, it also creates a complete HTML page for you. So this first PHP script does not require the standard HTML code, although subsequent scripts in this chapter will.

To create a new PHP script on your computer:

1. Create a new PHP document in your text editor or IDE, to be named **phpinfo.php** (Script 1.2).

   For this specific case, you'll start with a blank file. But if your text editor or IDE has PHP file templates for you, you can certainly start with one of those.

2. Begin the page with **<?php** on its own line.

   This opening PHP tag tells the server that the following code is PHP and should be handled as such.

   If your application has a PHP template for you, it may have created the PHP tags already.

Script 1.2 This first PHP script invokes a single PHP function.

```
1    <?php
2    phpinfo();
3    ?>
```

3. Add the following on the next line:

```
phpinfo();
```

The syntax will be explained in detail later, but in short, this is just a call to an existing PHP function named *phpinfo*. You must use the opening and closing parentheses, with nothing between them, and the semicolon.

4. Type `?>` on its own line, as the last line.

The closing PHP tag tells the server that the PHP section of the script is over. Again, because the `phpinfo()` function generates a complete HTML page for you, no HTML tags are needed.

5. Save the script as `phpinfo.php`.

Not to overstate the point, but remember that PHP scripts must use a valid file extension. Most likely you'll have no problems if you save your files as *filename*`.php`.

You also need to be certain that the application or operating system is not adding a hidden extension to the file. Notepad on Windows, for example, attempts to add `.txt` to uncommon file extensions, which renders the PHP script unusable. (Generally speaking, do not use Notepad.)

TIP Just as a file's extension on your computer tells the operating system in what application to open the file, a web page's extension tells the server how to process the file: *file*`.php` goes through the PHP module, *file*`.aspx` is processed as ASP.NET, and *file*`.html` is a static HTML document (normally). The extension associations are determined by the web server's settings.

TIP If you're developing PHP scripts for a hosted website, check with your hosting company to learn which file extensions you can use for PHP documents. In this book you'll see `.php`, the most common extension.

TIP You'll occasionally see PHP's *short tags*—simply `<?` and `?>`—used in other people's scripts, although I recommend sticking with the formal tags: `<?php` and `?>`. Support for the short tags must be enabled on a server, and using them makes your code less portable.

TIP You'll find it handy to have a copy of the `phpinfo.php` file around. As you'll soon see, this script reports upon PHP's capabilities, settings, and other features of your server. In fact, this book frequently suggests you return to this script for those purposes.

TIP PHP scripts can also be executed without a web browser, using a command-line interface and a standalone PHP executable. But that topic is well outside the scope of this book (and it's a much less common use of PHP regardless).

Using SFTP

Unlike HTML, which can be tested directly in a browser, PHP scripts need to be run from a PHP-enabled server in order to see the results. Specifically, PHP is run through a *web server application*, such as Apache (http://httpd.apache.org), Nginx (www.nginx.com), or Internet Information Server (IIS; www.iis.net).

You can obtain a PHP-enabled server in one of two ways:

- Install the software on your own computer.
- Acquire web hosting.

PHP is open source software (meaning, in part, that it's free) and is generally easy to install (with no adverse effect on your computer). If you want to install PHP and a web server on your computer, follow the directions in Appendix A, "Installation and Configuration." Once you've done so, you can skip ahead to the next section of the chapter, where you'll learn how to test your first PHP script.

If you're not running PHP on your own computer, you'll need to transfer your PHP scripts to the PHP-enabled server using SFTP (Secure File Transfer Protocol). The web hosting company or server's administrator will provide you with SFTP access information, which you'll enter into an SFTP client. Many SFTP client applications are available; this next sequence of steps uses the free FileZilla (http://filezilla-project.org), which runs on many operating systems.

To SFTP your script to the server:

1. Open your SFTP application.

2. In the application's connection window, enter the information provided by your web host **A**.

   SFTP access requires a host (for example, the domain name or an IP address), username, and password.

3. Click Quickconnect (or your SFTP client's equivalent).

   If you've provided the correct information, you should be able to connect. If not, you'll see error messages at the top of the FileZilla window **B**.

A The connection section of FileZilla's main window (as it appears on the Mac).

B The reported error says that the connection attempt was refused.

4. Navigate to the proper directory for your web pages (for example, **www**, **htdocs**, or **httpdocs**).

The SFTP application won't necessarily drop you off in the appropriate directory. You may need to do some navigation to get to the *web document root*. The web document root is the directory on the server to which a URL directly points (for example, www.larryullman.com, as opposed to www.larryullman.com/somedir/). If you're unsure of what the web document root is for your setup, see the documentation provided by the hosting company (or ask them for support).

In FileZilla, the right column represents the files and directories on the server; the left column represents the files and directories on your computer **C**. Just double-click folders to open them.

5. Upload your script—**phpinfo.php**—to the server.

To do this in FileZilla, drag the file from the left column—your computer—to the right column—the server.

> **TIP** Some text editors and IDEs have built-in SFTP capability, allowing you to save your scripts directly to the server. Other applications can run PHP scripts without leaving the application at all.

> **TIP** You can also transfer files to your web server using version control software, such as Git (https://git-scm.com). Although this is an excellent route, it's well beyond the scope of a beginner's guide to PHP.

Local site: /Users/larry/Sites/				Remote site:		/html
▶ Library				▼ html		
▶ Movies				? css		
Music				? downloads		

Filename ^	Filesize	Filetype	Last modified		Filename ^	Filesize	Filetype	Last modifi
..					..			
phpinfo.php	19	PHP	01/17/16 16:01:50		css		Directory	01/08/16 2
					downl...		Directory	01/08/16 2
					forums		Directory	01/10/16 1(
					images		Directory	01/08/16 2

C I've successfully connected to the remote server and navigated into the **html** directory (aka the web document root).

Testing Your Script

Testing a PHP script is a two-step process. First, you must put the PHP script in the appropriate directory for the web server. Second, you run the PHP script in your web browser by loading the correct URL.

If you're using a separate web server, like one provided by a hosting company, you just need to use an SFTP application to upload your PHP script to it (as in the previous steps). If you have installed PHP on your personal computer, then you can test your PHP scripts by saving them in, or moving them to, the web document root. This is normally

- `~/Sites` for Mac OS X users (where ~ stands for your home directory; this is no longer created automatically on newer versions of Mac OS X, but you can make one)

- `C:\Inetpub\wwwroot` for Windows users running IIS

- `C:\xampp\htdocs` for Windows users running XAMPP (www.apachefriends.org)

- `/Applications/MAMP/htdocs` for Mac users running MAMP (www.mamp.info)

If you're not sure what the web document root for your setup is, see the documentation for the web server application or operating system (if the web server application is built in).

Once you've got the PHP script in the right place, use your browser to execute it.

To test your script in the browser:

1. Open your favorite web browser.

   For the most part, PHP doesn't behave differently on different browsers (because PHP runs on the server), so use whichever browser you prefer. In this book, you'll see that I primarily use Chrome, regardless of the operating system.

2. In the browser's address bar, enter the URL of the site where your script has been saved.

   In my case, I enter www.larryullman.com, but your URL will certainly be different.

   If you're running PHP on your own computer, the URL is http://localhost (Windows); or http://localhost/ *~username* (Mac OS X), where you should replace *username* with your username. Some all-in-one packages, such as MAMP and XAMPP, may also use a *port* as part of the URL: http://localhost:*8888*.

   If you're not sure what URL to use, see the documentation for the web server application you installed.

3. Add **/phpinfo.php** to the URL.

   If you placed the script within a subdirectory of the web document root, you would add that subdirectory name to the URL as well (for example, **/ch01/phpinfo.php**).

4. Press Return/Enter to load the URL.

   The page should load in your browser window **A**.

continues on next page

PHP Version 7.0.2

php-osx.liip.ch by Liip (originally developed by www.local.ch)

System	Darwin Larrys-iMac.local 15.2.0 Darwin Kernel Version 15.2.0: Fri Nov 13 19:56:56 PST 2015; root:xnu-3248.20.55~2/RELEASE_X86_64 x86_64
Build Date	Jan 8 2016 10:12:25
Configure Command	'./configure' '--prefix=/usr/local/php5' '--with-apxs2=/usr/sbin/apxs' '--with-config-file-scan-dir=/usr/local/php5/php.d' '--with-libxml-dir=shared,/usr' '--with-openssl=/usr' '--with-zlib=/usr' '--with-zlib-dir=/usr' '--with-gd' '--with-ldap' '--with-xmlrpc' '--enable-exif' '--enable-soap' '--enable-wddx' '--enable-ftp' '--enable-sockets' '--with-bz2=/usr' '--enable-zip' '--enable-shmop' '--enable-sysvsem' '--enable-sysvshm' '--enable-sysvmsg' '--enable-mbstring' '--enable-bcmath' '--enable-calendar' '--with-mhash' '--enable-fpm' '--with-mysql=mysqlnd' '--with-mysqli=mysqlnd' '--with-pdo-mysql=mysqlnd' '--enable-pcntl' '--enable-dtrace' '--disable-phpdbg' '--enable-opcache' '--with-icu-dir=/usr/local/php5' '--with-xsl=shared,/usr/local/php5' '--with-imap=shared,../imap-2007f' '--with-kerberos=/usr' '--with-imap-ssl=/usr' '--with-gettext=/usr/local/php5' '--with-curl=shared,/usr/local/php5' '--with-png-dir=/usr/local/php5' '--with-jpeg-dir=/usr/local/php5' '--enable-gd-native-ttf' '--with-freetype-dir=/usr/local/php5' '--with-pgsql=shared,/usr/local/php5' '--with-pdo-pgsql=shared,/usr/local/php5' '--with-mcrypt=shared,/usr/local/php5' '--with-tidy=/usr/local/php5' '--with-gmp=shared,/usr/local/php5' '--with-readline=shared,/usr/local/php5' 'CC=cc '-L/usr/local/php5/lib' '-I/usr/local/php5/include' '-I/usr/include/libxml2' '-I/usr/local/php5/include/tidy' '-DENTROPY_CH_RELEASE=1' 'CFLAGS=-g '-O' '-mmacosx-version-min=10.10' '-I/usr/local/php5/include' '-arch' '-no-cpp-precomp' '-DENTROPY_CH_ARCHS="i386/x86_64"' '-DENTROPY_CH_RELEASE=1" 'LDFLAGS=-L/usr/local/php5/lib '-arch' 'YACC=/usr/local/Cellar/bison/3.0.2/bin/bison '-y" 'CXXFLAGS=-arch
Server API	Apache 2.0 Handler
Virtual Directory Support	disabled
Configuration File (php.ini) Path	/usr/local/php5/lib
Loaded Configuration File	/usr/local/php5/lib/php.ini
Scan this dir for additional .ini files	/usr/local/php5/php.d
Additional .ini files parsed	/usr/local/php5/php.d/10-extension_dir.ini, /usr/local/php5/php.d/20-extension-opcache.ini, /usr/local/php5/php.d/50-extension-apcu.ini, /usr/local/php5/php.d/50-extension-curl.ini, /usr/local/php5/php.d/50-extension-gmp.ini, /usr/local/php5/php.d/50-extension-imap.ini, /usr/local/php5/php.d/50-extension-intl.ini, /usr/local/php5/php.d/50-extension-mcrypt.ini, /usr/local/php5/php.d/50-extension-mssql.ini, /usr/local/php5/php.d/50-extension-pdo_pgsql.ini, /usr/local/php5/php.d/50-extension-pgsql.ini, /usr/local/php5/php.d/50-extension-readline.ini, /usr/local/php5/php.d/50-extension-xdebug.ini, /usr/local/php5/php.d/50-extension-xsl.ini, /usr/local/php5/php.d/99-liip-developer.ini
PHP API	20151012
PHP Extension	20151012
Zend Extension	320151012
Zend Extension Build	API320151012,NTS
PHP Extension Build	API20151012,NTS
Debug Build	no
Thread Safety	disabled
Zend Signal Handling	disabled

A If the script executed correctly, the browser result should look like this (woohoo!).

If you see the PHP code **B** or a blank page, it could mean many things:

- You are not loading the PHP script through a URL (that is, the address does not begin with *http*). Note that you may need to click the address bar to view the full URL, including the *http*, because many of today's browsers hide this by default.

- PHP has not been enabled on the server.

- You are not using the proper extension.

If you see a *file not found* or similar error **C**, it could be because

- You entered the incorrect URL.

- The PHP script is not in the proper directory.

- The PHP script does not have the correct name or extension.

TIP It's very important to remember that you can't open a PHP file directly in a browser as you would open HTML pages or files in other applications. PHP scripts must be processed by the web server, which means you must access them via a URL (an address that starts with *http://*).

TIP Even if you aren't a seasoned computer professional, you should consider installing PHP on your computer. Doing so isn't too difficult, and PHP is free. Again, see Appendix A for instructions.

```
<?php
phpinfo();
?>
```

B If you see the raw PHP code, then the PHP code is not being executed.

Not Found

The requested URL /phpinf.php was not found on this server.

C This server response indicates a mismatch between the URL attempted and the files that actually exist on the server.

Sending Text to the Browser

PHP wouldn't be very useful if all you could do was see that it works (although that confirmation is critical). You'll use PHP most frequently to send information to the browser in the form of plain text and HTML tags. To do so, use **print**:

```
print "something";
```

Just type the word **print**, followed by what you want to display: a simple message, the value of a variable, the result of a calculation, and so forth. In that example, the message is a string of text, so it must be surrounded with quotation marks.

PHP is case-insensitive when it comes to calling functions, such as **phpinfo()** and **print**. Using **print**, **Print**, and **PRINT** nets the same results. Later in the book, you'll see examples where case makes a crucial difference.

To be clear, **print** doesn't actually *print* anything; it just outputs data. When a PHP script is run through a browser, that PHP output is received by the browser itself as if it were content from a static HTML file.

Also note that the line is terminated by a semicolon (**;**). Every statement in PHP code must end with a semicolon, and forgetting this requirement is a common cause of errors. A *statement* in PHP is an executable line of code, like

```
print "something";
```

or

```
phpinfo();
```

Conversely, comments, PHP tags, control structures (for example, conditionals and loops), and certain other constructs discussed in this book don't require semicolons.

Finally, you should know about a minor technicality: Whereas `phpinfo()` is a *function*, `print` is actually a *language construct*. Although it's still standard to refer to `print` as a function, because `print` is a language construct, no parentheses are required when using it, as in the `phpinfo()` example.

To print a simple message:

1. Begin a new HTML document in your text editor or IDE, to be named `hello1.php` (Script 1.3):

   ```
   <!doctype html>
   <html lang="en">
   <head>
     <meta charset="utf-8">
     <title>Hello, World!</title>
   </head>
   <body>
   <p>The following was created by
   → PHP:
   ```

   Most of this code is the standard HTML. The last line will be used to distinguish between the hard-coded HTML and the PHP-generated HTML.

2. On the next line, type `<?php` to create the initial PHP tag.

3. Add

   ```
   print "Hello, world!";
   ```

   Printing the phrase *Hello, world!* is the first step most programming references teach. Even though it's a trivial reason to use PHP, you're not really a programmer until you've made at least one *Hello, world!* application.

Script 1.3 By putting the `print` statement between the PHP tags, the server will dynamically send the *Hello, world!* greeting to the browser.

```
1    <!doctype html>
2    <html lang="en">
3    <head>
4        <meta charset="utf-8">
5        <title>Hello, World!</title>
6    </head>
7    <body>
8    <p>The following was created by PHP:
9    <?php
10   print "Hello, world!";
11   ?>
12   </p>
13   </body>
14   </html>
```

Ⓐ A simple **Hello, world!** example: your first foray into PHP programming.

4. Close the PHP section and complete the HTML page:

```
?>
</p>
</body>
</html>
```

5. Save the file as **hello1.php**, place it on your PHP-enabled server, and test it in your browser **Ⓐ**.

If you're running PHP on your own computer, remember that you can save the file to the proper directory and access the script via http://localhost/.

If you see an error or a blank page instead of the results shown in the figure, review the "Testing Your Script" section, or skip ahead to the "Basic Debugging Steps" section at the end of this chapter.

TIP You can use other functions to send text to the browser, including `echo` and `printf()`, but this book primarily uses `print`.

TIP You can—and commonly will—use `print` over multiple lines:

```
print "This is a longer
sentence of text.";
```

The closing quotation mark terminates the message being printed, and the semicolon is placed only at the end of that line.

Using the PHP Manual

The PHP manual—accessible online at www.php.net/manual—lists every function and feature of the language. The manual discusses general concepts (installation, syntax, variables) first and ends with the functions by topic (MySQL, string functions, and so on).

To quickly look up any function in the PHP manual, go to www.php.net/*functionname* in your web browser (for example, www.php.net/print).

To understand how functions are described, look at the start of the **print** function's page **A**.

The first line is the name of the function itself, followed by the versions of PHP in which it's available. As the language grows, new functions are added and, occasionally, older functions are removed. Then there's a textual description of the function along with the function's basic usage. The usage is the most important and confusing part.

In this example, the first value—**int**—says that **print** returns an integer value (specifically, **print** returns 1, always). Within the parentheses, **string $arg** states that the function takes one required argument, which should be in the form of a string. You've already seen this in action.

A The PHP manual's page for the **print** language construct.

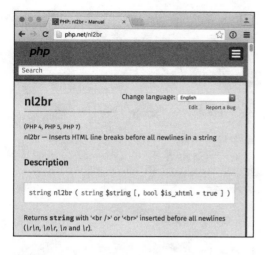

B The PHP manual's page for the `nl2br()` function.

As a comparison, check out the manual's listing for the `nl2br()` function **B**. This function converts newlines found within text (the equivalent of pressing Return/Enter) into HTML break tags. This function, which returns a string, takes a string as its first argument and an optional Boolean (TRUE/FALSE) as its second. The square brackets indicate optional arguments, which are always listed last. When a function takes multiple arguments, they are separated by commas. Hence, this function can be called like so:

```
nl2br("Some text");
nl2br("Some text", false);
```

As the definition also indicates, the second argument has a default value of **true**, meaning it'll create **
** tags (which is XHTML compliant) unless the function is passed a second argument value of **false**. In that case, the function will create **
** tags instead.

The most important thing to remember about the PHP manual is that it exists! If you're ever confused by a function or how it is properly used, check the PHP manual's reference page for it.

To look up a function definition:

1. Go to www.php.net/*functionname* in your web browser.

   If the PHP manual doesn't have a matching record for the function you tried, check the spelling or look at the recommended alternatives that the manual presents **C**.

2. Compare the versions of PHP that the function exists in with the version of PHP you're using.

   Use the **phpinfo()** function, already demonstrated, to know for certain what version of PHP you are running. If a function was added in a later version of PHP, you'll need to either upgrade the version you have or use a different approach.

3. Examine what type of data the function returns.

   Sometimes you may be having a problem with a function because it returns a different type of value than you expect it to.

4. Examine how many and what types of arguments the function requires or can take.

   The most common mistake when using functions is sending the wrong number or type of arguments when the function is called.

5. Read the user comments, when present, to learn more.

   Sometimes the user comments can be quite helpful (other times not).

TIP If you see a message saying that a function has been deprecated **D**, that means the function will be dropped from future versions of PHP, and you should start using the newer, better alternative (there is almost always a better alternative identified).

C The manual will present alternative functions if the entered URL doesn't exactly match a reference.

D Deprecated functions should be avoided in your code.

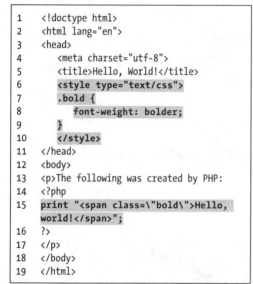

```
(!) Parse error: syntax error, unexpected 'page'
(T_STRING) in /Users/larry/Sites/test.php on line 11
```

A Attempting to print double quotation marks will create errors, because they conflict with the **print** statement's primary double quotation marks.

Script 1.4 Using **print**, you can send HTML tags along with text to the browser, where the formatting will be applied.

```
1    <!doctype html>
2    <html lang="en">
3    <head>
4        <meta charset="utf-8">
5        <title>Hello, World!</title>
6        <style type="text/css">
7        .bold {
8            font-weight: bolder;
9        }
10       </style>
11   </head>
12   <body>
13   <p>The following was created by PHP:
14   <?php
15   print "<span class=\"bold\">Hello,
     world!</span>";
16   ?>
17   </p>
18   </body>
19   </html>
```

Sending HTML to the Browser

As those who first learned HTML quickly discovered, viewing plain text in a web browser leaves a lot to be desired. Indeed, HTML was created to make plain text more appealing and useful. Because HTML works by adding tags to text, you can use PHP to also send HTML tags to the browser, along with other data:

```
print "<b>Hello, world!</b>";
```

There is one situation where you have to be careful, though. HTML tags that require double quotation marks, like **<a href="page.php">link</a>**, will cause problems when printed by PHP, because the **print** function uses quotation marks as well **A**:

```
print "<a href="page.php">link</a>";
```

One workaround is to *escape* the quotation marks within the HTML by preceding them with a backslash (****):

```
print "<a href=\"page.php\">link</a>";
```

By escaping each quotation mark within the **print** statement, you tell PHP to print the mark itself instead of treating the quotation mark as either the beginning or the end of the string to be printed.

To send HTML to the browser:

1. Open the **hello1.php** script (Script 1.3) in your text editor or IDE, if it is not already open.

2. Within the HTML head, declare a CSS class (**Script 1.4**):

   ```
   <style type="text/css">
   .bold {
     font-weight: bolder;
   }
   </style>
   ```

continues on next page

This CSS code declares a class named *bold*, which will be used to add emphasis to text. This is obviously a fairly trivial use of CSS, but by declaring this as a class, it can easily be updated, perhaps to change the color of the text or the size, along with its weight.

3. Edit the *Hello, world!* message by adding HTML tags, making it read as follows:

```
print "<span class=\"bold\">
→ Hello, world!</span>";
```

To make the PHP-generated part of the message stand out, CSS styling will bold the greeting. For this to work, you must escape the quotation marks within the span tag so they don't conflict with the **print** statement's quotation mark.

4. Save the script as **hello2.php**, place it on your PHP-enabled server, and run the page in your browser **B**.

The following was created by PHP: **Hello, world!**

B The new version of the *Hello, world!* page, with a little more decoration and appeal.

Using White Space

When programming in PHP, white space is generally (but not universally) ignored. Any blank line (just one or several in a row) in PHP code is irrelevant to the end result. Likewise, tabs and spaces are normally inconsequential to PHP. And because PHP code is not visible in the browser (unless there's a problem with the server), white space in your PHP files has no impact on what the end user sees.

The spacing of HTML code shows up in the HTML source of a web page but has only a minimal effect on what's viewed in the browser. For example, all of a page's HTML source code could be placed on one line without changing what the end user sees. If you had to hunt for a problem in the HTML source, however, you would not like the long, single line of HTML.

You can affect the spacing of dynamically generated HTML code by printing it in PHP over multiple lines, or by using the newline character (**\n**) within double quotation marks:

```
print "Line 1\nLine 2";
```

Again, use of the newline character affects the *HTML source code* of the web page, not what the end user sees rendered in the browser.

To adjust the spacing in the rendered web page, you'll use CSS, plus paragraph, div, and break tags, among others.

5. View the HTML page source to see the code that was sent to the browser .

How you do this depends on the browser: Select View > Developer > View Source in Chrome, View > Page Source in Firefox, or View > Source in Internet Explorer.

This is a step you'll want to be in the habit of taking, particularly when problems occur. Remember that PHP is primarily used to generate HTML, sent to and interpreted by the browser. Often, confirming what was sent to the browser (by viewing the source) will help explain the problem you're seeing in the browser's interpretation (or visible result).

TIP Understanding the role of quotation marks and how to escape problematic characters is crucial to programming with PHP. These topics will be covered in more detail in the next two chapters.

TIP The HTML you send to the web browser from PHP doesn't need to be this simple. You can create tables, JavaScript, and much, much more.

TIP Remember that any HTML outside the PHP tags will automatically go to the browser. Within the PHP tags, `print` statements are used to send HTML to the web browser.

```
1  <!doctype html>
2  <html lang="en">
3  <head>
4          <meta charset="utf-8">
5          <title>Hello, World!</title>
6          <style type="text/css">
7          .bold {
8                  font-weight: bolder;
9          }
10         </style>
11 </head>
12 <body>
13 <p>The following was created by PHP:
14 <span class="bold">Hello, world!</span></p>
15 </body>
16 </html>
```

C The resulting HTML source code of **hello2.php** **B**.

Adding Comments to Scripts

Comments are integral to programming, not because they do anything but because they help you remember why *you* did something. The computer ignores these comments when it processes the script. Furthermore, PHP comments are never sent to the browser, remaining your secret.

PHP supports three ways of adding comments. You can create a single-line comment by putting either **//** or **#** at the beginning of the line you want ignored:

```
// This is a comment.
```

You can also use **//** or **#** to begin a comment at the end of a PHP line, like so:

```
print "Hello"; // Just a greeting.
```

Although it's largely a stylistic issue, **//** is much more commonly used in PHP than **#**.

You can create a multiline comment using **/*** to begin the comment and ***/** to conclude it:

```
/* This is a
multi-line comment. */
```

Some programmers prefer this comment style because it contains both open and closing "tags," providing demarcation for where the comment begins and ends.

```
1    <!doctype html>
2    <html lang="en">
3    <head>
4        <meta charset="utf-8">
5        <title>Hello, World!</title>
6        <style type="text/css">
7        .bold {
8            font-weight: bolder;
9        }
10       </style>
11   </head>
12   <body>
13   <p>The following was created by PHP:
     <br>
14   <?php
15   /*
16    * Filename: hello3.php
17    * Book reference: Script 1.5
18    * Created by: Larry Ullman
19    */
20
21   //print "<span class=\"bold\">Hello,
     world!</span>";
22
23   ?>
24   <!-- This is an HTML comment. -->
25   </p>
26   </body>
27   </html>
```

To add comments to a script:

1. Open the **hello2.php** created earlier (Script 1.4) in your text editor or IDE.

2. After the initial PHP tag, add some comments to your script (**Script 1.5**):

   ```
   /*
    * Filename: hello3.php
    * Book reference: Script 1.5
    * Created by: Larry Ullman
    */
   ```

   This is just a sample of the kind of comments you can write. You should document what the script does, what information it relies on, who created it, when, and so forth. Stylistically, such comments are often placed at the top of a script (as the first thing within the PHP section, that is), using formatting like this. The extra asterisks aren't required; they just draw attention to the comments.

3. On line 21, in front of the **print** statement, type **//**.

   By preceding the **print** statement with two slashes, you ensure that the function call is "commented out," meaning it will never be executed.

4. After the closing PHP tag (on line 23), add an HTML comment:

   ```
   <!-- This is an HTML comment. -->
   ```

   This line of code will help you distinguish among the different comment types and where they appear. This comment will appear only within the HTML source code.

   continues on next page

5. Save the script as **hello3.php**, place it on your PHP-enabled server, and run the page in your web browser 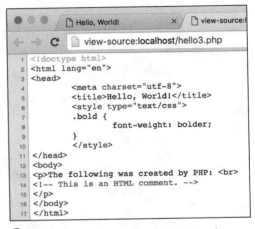.

6. View the source of the page to see the HTML comment **B**.

TIP You can comment out just one line of code or several using the /* and */ method. With // or #, you can negate only one line at a time.

TIP Different programmers prefer to comment code in different ways. The important thing is to find a system that works for you and stick to it.

TIP Note that you cannot use HTML comment characters (<!-- and -->) within PHP to comment out code. You could have PHP print those tags to the browser, but in that case you'd create a comment that appeared in the HTML source code on the client's computer (but not in the browser window). PHP comments never make it as far as a user's computer.

TIP Despite my strong belief that you can't over-comment your scripts, the scripts in this book aren't as documented as they should be, in order to save space. But the book will document each script's name and number, for cross-reference purposes.

TIP When you change a script's code, be certain to update its comments as well. It's quite confusing to see a comment that suggests a script or a line of code does something other than what it actually does.

A With the **print** statement commented out, the page looks just as it would if the **print** call weren't there.

```
1  <!doctype html>
2  <html lang="en">
3  <head>
4      <meta charset="utf-8">
5      <title>Hello, World!</title>
6      <style type="text/css">
7      .bold {
8          font-weight: bolder;
9      }
10     </style>
11 </head>
12 <body>
13 <p>The following was created by PHP: <br>
14 <!-- This is an HTML comment. -->
15 </p>
16 </body>
17 </html>
```

B HTML comments don't appear in the web browser but are in the HTML source. PHP comments remain in the PHP script on the server, not visible inside the HTML source.

Basic Debugging Steps

Debugging is by no means a simple concept to grasp, and unfortunately, it's one that is only truly mastered by doing. The next 50 pages could be dedicated to the subject and you'd still merely pick up a fraction of the debugging skills that you'll eventually acquire and need.

The reason I introduce debugging in this harrowing way is that it's important not to enter into programming with delusions. Sometimes code won't work as expected, you'll inevitably create careless errors, and some days you'll want to pull your hair out, even when using a comparatively user-friendly language such as PHP. In short, *prepare to be perplexed and frustrated at times*. I've been coding in PHP since 1999, and occasionally I still get stuck in the programming muck. But debugging is a very important skill to have, and one that you will eventually pick up out of necessity and experience. As you begin your PHP programming adventure, I offer the following basic but concrete debugging tips.

To debug a PHP script:

- Make sure you're always running PHP scripts through a URL!

  This is perhaps the most common beginner's mistake. PHP code must be run through the web server application, which means it must be requested through http://*something*. When you see actual PHP code instead of the result of that code's execution, most likely you're not running the PHP script through a URL.

- Know what version of PHP you're running.

  Some problems arise from the version of PHP in use. Before you ever use any PHP-enabled server, run the **phpinfo.php** file (Script 1.2) to confirm the version of PHP in use.

- Make sure **display_errors** is on.

  This is a basic PHP configuration setting (discussed in Appendix A). You can confirm this setting by executing the **phpinfo()** function (just use your browser to search for **display_errors** in the resulting page). For security reasons, PHP may not be set to display the errors that occur. If that's the case, you'll end up seeing blank pages when problems occur. To debug most problems, you'll need to see the errors, so turn this setting on while you're learning. You'll find instructions for doing so in Appendix A and Chapter 3, "HTML Forms and PHP."

- Check the HTML source code.

  Sometimes the problem is hidden in the HTML source of the page. In fact, sometimes the PHP error message can be hidden there!

- Trust the error message.

  Another very common beginner's mistake is to not fully read or trust the error that PHP reports. Although an error message can often be cryptic and may seem meaningless, it can't be ignored. At the very least, PHP is normally correct as to the line on which the problem can be found. And if you need to relay that error message to someone else (like when you're asking me for help), do include the entire error message!

- Take a break!

  So many of the programming problems I've encountered over the years, and the vast majority of the toughest ones, have been solved by stepping away from my computer for a while. It's easy to become frustrated and confused, and in such situations, any further steps you take are likely to make matters only worse.

TIP These are just some general debugging techniques, specifically tailored to the beginning PHP programmer. They should suffice for now, because the examples in this book are relatively simple. More complex coding requires more advanced debugging techniques, so my *PHP and MySQL for Dynamic Web Sites: Visual QuickPro Guide, Fourth Edition* (Peachpit Press, 2012) dedicates a whole chapter to this subject.

Review and Pursue

Each chapter in this book ends with a "Review and Pursue" section. In these sections you'll find:

- Questions regarding the material just covered
- Prompts for ways to expand your knowledge and experience on your own

If you have any problems with these sections, in either answering the questions or pursuing your own endeavors, turn to the book's supporting forum (www.LarryUllman.com/forums/).

Review

- What is HTML? What is the current version of HTML?
- What encoding is your text editor or IDE set to use? Does that match the encoding specified in your generated HTML pages? Why does the encoding matter?
- What is CSS and what is it used for?
- What file extension should PHP scripts have for your particular server?
- What is meant by "web root directory"? What is the web root directory for your server?
- How do you test PHP scripts? What happens when PHP scripts are not run through a URL?
- Name two ways comments can be added to PHP code. Identify some reasons to use comments.

Pursue

- If you have access to more than one server, confirm what version of PHP is running on another server.

- Create a static HTML page that displays some information. Then replace some of the static content with content created by PHP.

- Create a template to use for your own work. The template should contain the HTML shell, the opening and closing PHP tags, and some basic comments.

- Confirm, using the `phpinfo()` function, that `display_errors` is enabled on your server. If it's not, change your server's configuration to enable it (see Chapter 3 and Appendix A).

- In subsequent chapters, occasionally check the PHP manual's page when a new function is mentioned in the book.

Variables

The previous chapter covered how to use PHP to send simple text and HTML to a web browser—in other words, something for which you don't need PHP at all! Don't worry, though; this book will teach you how to use **print** in conjunction with other PHP features to do great and useful things with your website.

To make the leap from creating simple, static pages to dynamic web applications and interactive websites, you need variables. Understanding what variables are, the types of variables that a language supports, and how to use them is critical.

This chapter introduces the fundamentals of variables in PHP, and later chapters cover the different types in greater detail. If you've never dealt with variables before, this chapter will be a good introduction. If you're familiar with the concept, then you should be able to work through this chapter with ease.

What Are Variables?

A *variable* is a container for data. Once data has been stored in a variable (or, stated more commonly, once a variable has been assigned a value), that data can be altered, printed to the browser, saved to a database, emailed, and so forth.

Variables in PHP are, by their nature, flexible: You can put data into a variable, retrieve that data from it (without affecting the value of the variable), put new data in it, and continue this cycle as many times as necessary. But variables in PHP are largely temporary: *Most only exist*—that is, they only have a value—*for the duration of the script's execution on the server*. Once the execution of the script completes (often when the final closing PHP tag is encountered), those variables cease to exist. Furthermore, after users click a link or submit a form, they are taken to a new page that may have an entirely separate set of variables.

Before getting too deep into the discussion of variables, let's write a quick script that reveals some of PHP's *predefined* variables. These are variables that PHP automatically creates when a script runs. Over the course of the book, you'll be introduced to many different predefined variables. This particular example looks at the predefined **$_SERVER** variable. It contains lots of information about the computer on which PHP is running.

The **print_r()** function offers an easy way to display any variable's value:

```
print_r($variable_name);
```

Just provide the name of the variable you'd like to inspect as a single argument to the **print_r()** function. (You'll learn more about a variable's syntax throughout this chapter.)

Script 2.1 This script uses the `print_r()` function to show the values stored in the `$_SERVER` predefined variable.

```
1   <!doctype html>
2   <html lang="en">
3   <head>
4       <meta charset="utf-8">
5       <title>Predefined Variables</title>
6   </head>
7   <body>
8   <pre>
9   <?php // Script 2.1 - predefined.php
10
11  // Show the value of the $_SERVER
    variable:
12  print_r($_SERVER);
13
14  ?>
15  </pre>
16  </body>
17  </html>
```

To print PHP's predefined variables:

1. Create a new PHP script in your text editor or IDE, to be named **predefined.php** (Script 2.1).

2. Create the initial HTML tags:

   ```
   <!doctype html>
   <html lang="en">
   <head>
     <meta charset="utf-8">
     <title>Predefined Variables
     → </title>
   </head>
   <body>
   <pre>
   ```

   This code repeats the HTML template created in the preceding chapter. Within the body of the page, the `<pre>` tags are being used to make the generated PHP information more legible. Without using the `<pre>` tags, the `print_r()` function's output would be difficult to read in a browser.

3. Add the PHP code:

   ```
   <?php // Script 2.1 -
   → predefined.php
   print_r($_SERVER);
   ?>
   ```

   The PHP code contains just one function call. The function should be provided with the name of a variable.

   In this example, the variable is **$_SERVER**, which is special in PHP. **$_SERVER** stores all sorts of data about the server: its name and operating system, the name of the current user, information about the web server application (Apache, Nginx, IIS, and so on), and more. It also reflects the PHP script being executed: its name, where it's stored on the server, and so forth.

   continues on next page

Note that you must type **$_SERVER** exactly as it is here, in all upper-case letters.

4. Complete the HTML page:

```
</pre>
</body>
</html>
```

5. Save the file as **predefined.php**, upload it to your server (or save it to the appropriate directory on your computer), and test it in your browser **Ⓐ**.

   Once again, remember that you must run all PHP scripts through a URL (that is, http://*something*).

6. If possible, transfer the file to another computer or server running PHP and execute the script in your browser again **Ⓑ**.

TIP Printing out the value of any variable as you've done here is one of the greatest debugging tools. Scripts often don't work as you expect them to because one or more variables do not have the values you assume they should, so confirming their actual values is extremely helpful.

TIP If you don't use the HTML <pre></pre> tags, the result will be like the jumble of information in **Ⓒ**.

```
Predefined Variables                    ×

← → C    localhost/predefined.php              ☆  ⓘ  ≡

Array
(
    [HTTP_HOST] => localhost
    [HTTP_CONNECTION] => keep-alive
    [HTTP_ACCEPT] => text/html,application/xhtml+xml,applicati
    [HTTP_UPGRADE_INSECURE_REQUESTS] => 1
    [HTTP_USER_AGENT] => Mozilla/5.0 (Macintosh; Intel Mac OS )
    [HTTP_ACCEPT_ENCODING] => gzip, deflate, sdch
    [HTTP_ACCEPT_LANGUAGE] => en-US,en;q=0.8
    [PATH] => /usr/bin:/bin:/usr/sbin:/sbin
    [SERVER_SIGNATURE] =>
    [SERVER_SOFTWARE] => Apache/2.4.16 (Unix) PHP/7.0.2
    [SERVER_NAME] => localhost
    [SERVER_ADDR] => ::1
    [SERVER_PORT] => 80
    [REMOTE_ADDR] => ::1
    [DOCUMENT_ROOT] => /Users/larry/Sites
    [REQUEST_SCHEME] => http
    [CONTEXT_PREFIX] =>
    [CONTEXT_DOCUMENT_ROOT] => /Users/larry/Sites
    [SERVER_ADMIN] => you@example.com
    [SCRIPT_FILENAME] => /Users/larry/Sites/predefined.php
    [REMOTE_PORT] => 49176
    [GATEWAY_INTERFACE] => CGI/1.1
    [SERVER_PROTOCOL] => HTTP/1.1
    [REQUEST_METHOD] => GET
    [QUERY_STRING] =>
    [REQUEST_URI] => /predefined.php
    [SCRIPT_NAME] => /predefined.php
    [PHP_SELF] => /predefined.php
    [REQUEST_TIME_FLOAT] => 1453769830.966
    [REQUEST_TIME] => 1453769830
)
```

Ⓐ The **$_SERVER** variable, as printed out by this script, is a master list of values pertaining to the server and the PHP script.

```
Array
(
    [HTTP_HOST] => ████████████
    [HTTP_CONNECTION] => keep-alive
    [HTTP_ACCEPT] => text/html,application/xhtml+xml,application/xm
    [HTTP_UPGRADE_INSECURE_REQUESTS] => 1
    [HTTP_USER_AGENT] => Mozilla/5.0 (Macintosh; Intel Mac OS X 10_
    [HTTP_ACCEPT_ENCODING] => gzip, deflate, sdch
    [HTTP_ACCEPT_LANGUAGE] => en-US,en;q=0.8
    [PATH] => /usr/local/sbin:/usr/local/bin:/usr/sbin:/usr/bin:/sk
    [SERVER_SIGNATURE] =>
Apache/2.4.7 (Ubuntu) Server at ████████████ Port 80

    [SERVER_SOFTWARE] => Apache/2.4.7 (Ubuntu)
    [SERVER_NAME] => ████████████
    [SERVER_ADDR] => ████████████
    [SERVER_PORT] => 80
    [REMOTE_ADDR] => 73.230.80.44
    [DOCUMENT_ROOT] => /var/www/████████████/html
    [REQUEST_SCHEME] => http
    [CONTEXT_PREFIX] =>
    [CONTEXT_DOCUMENT_ROOT] => /var/www/████████████/html
    [SERVER_ADMIN] => ████████████
    [SCRIPT_FILENAME] => /var/www/████████████/html/predefined.php
    [REMOTE_PORT] => 49237
    [GATEWAY_INTERFACE] => CGI/1.1
    [SERVER_PROTOCOL] => HTTP/1.1
    [REQUEST_METHOD] => GET
    [QUERY_STRING] =>
    [REQUEST_URI] => /predefined.php
    [SCRIPT_NAME] => /predefined.php
    [PHP_SELF] => /predefined.php
    [REQUEST_TIME_FLOAT] => 1453769900.813
    [REQUEST_TIME] => 1453769900
)
```

B With the **predefined.php** page, different servers will generate different results (compare with Ⓐ).

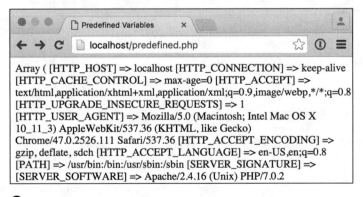

Array ([HTTP_HOST] => localhost [HTTP_CONNECTION] => keep-alive [HTTP_CACHE_CONTROL] => max-age=0 [HTTP_ACCEPT] => text/html,application/xhtml+xml,application/xml;q=0.9,image/webp,*/*;q=0.8 [HTTP_UPGRADE_INSECURE_REQUESTS] => 1 [HTTP_USER_AGENT] => Mozilla/5.0 (Macintosh; Intel Mac OS X 10_11_3) AppleWebKit/537.36 (KHTML, like Gecko) Chrome/47.0.2526.111 Safari/537.36 [HTTP_ACCEPT_ENCODING] => gzip, deflate, sdch [HTTP_ACCEPT_LANGUAGE] => en-US,en;q=0.8 [PATH] => /usr/bin:/bin:/usr/sbin:/sbin [SERVER_SIGNATURE] => [SERVER_SOFTWARE] => Apache/2.4.16 (Unix) PHP/7.0.2

C With large, complex variables such as **$_SERVER**, not using the HTML preformatting tags with **print_r()** creates an incomprehensible mess (compare to Ⓐ Ⓑ).

Variable Syntax

Now that you've had a quick dip in the variable pool, it's time to swim a bit deeper. In the preceding example, the script printed out the value of PHP's predefined **$_SERVER** variable. You can also create your own variables, once you understand the proper syntax. To create appropriate variable names, you must follow these rules:

- All variable names must be preceded by a dollar sign (**$**).

- Following the dollar sign, the variable name must begin with either a letter (A–Z, a–z) or an underscore (_). A number cannot immediately follow the dollar sign.

- The rest of the variable name can contain any combination of letters, underscores, and numbers.

- You may not use spaces within the name of a variable. (Instead, the underscore is commonly used to separate words.)

- Each variable must have a unique name.

- Variable names are *case-sensitive*! Consequently, **$variable** and **$Variable** are two different constructs, and it would be a bad idea to use two variables with such similar names.

This last point is perhaps the most important: Variable names in PHP are case-sensitive. Using the wrong letter case is a very common cause of bugs. (If you used, for example, **$_server** or **$_Server** in the previous script, you'd see either an error message or nothing at all **A**.)

(!) Notice: Undefined variable: _server in /Users/larry/Sites/predefined.php on line *11*				
Call Stack				
#	**Time**	**Memory**	**Function**	**Location**
1	0.0002	361080	{main}( )	.../predefined.php:0

A Misspelling a variable's name, including its case, will create undesired and unpredictable results.

Script 2.2 Properly documenting the purposes of variables, along with using meaningful names, is a hallmark of a professional programmer.

```
1    <!doctype html>
2    <html lang="en">
3    <head>
4        <meta charset="utf-8">
5        <title>Variables and Comments</title>
6    </head>
7    <body>
8    <?php // Script 2.2
9
10   // Define my variables....
11   $year = 2016; // The current year.
12   $june_avg = 88; // The average
     temperature for the month of June.
13   $page_title = 'Weather Reports'; //
     A title for the page.
14
15   // ... and so forth.
16   ?>
17   </body>
18   </html>
```

TABLE 2.1 Valid Variables in PHP

Name
$first_name
$person
$address1
$_SERVER

TABLE 2.2 Invalid Variables in PHP

Name	Reason
$first name	Has a space
$first.name	Has a period
first_name	Does not begin with $
$1address	A number cannot follow $

To help minimize bugs, I recommend the following policies:

- Always use all lowercase variable names.
- Make your variable names descriptive (for example, **$first_name** is better than **$fn**).
- Use comments to indicate the purpose of variables (**Script 2.2**), redundant as that may seem.
- Above all, be consistent with whatever naming convention you choose!

Table 2.1 lists some sample valid variables; **Table 2.2** lists some invalid variables and the rules they violate.

TIP Unlike some other languages, PHP doesn't require you to *declare* or *initialize* a variable prior to use, although PHP does issue warnings when you do. In other words, you *can* refer to variables without first defining them. But it's best not to do that; try to write scripts so that every variable is defined or validated before use.

TIP There are two main variable naming conventions, determined by how you delineate words. These are the so-called *camel-hump* or *camel-case* (named because of the way capital letters break up the word—for example, $FirstName) and *underscore* ($first_name) styles. This book uses the latter convention.

Types of Variables

This book covers three common PHP variable types: *numbers*, *strings*, and *arrays*. This chapter introduces them quickly, and later chapters discuss them in more detail:

- Chapter 4, "Using Numbers"
- Chapter 5, "Using Strings"
- Chapter 7, "Using Arrays"

A fourth variable type, *objects*, is introduced in Appendix B, "Resources and Next Steps," but isn't covered in this book. That particular subject is just too advanced for a beginner's guide—in fact, basic coverage of the subject in my *PHP Advanced and Object-Oriented Programing: Visual QuickPro Guide, Third Edition* (Peachpit Press, 2013) requires over 150 pages!

Numbers

Technically speaking, PHP breaks numbers into two types: *integers* and *floating-point* (also known as *double-precision floating-point* or *doubles*). Due to the lax way PHP handles variables, it largely won't affect your programming to group the two categories of numbers into one all-inclusive membership, at least when you're just starting out. Still, let's briefly discuss the differences between the two, to be precise.

The first type of numbers—*integers*—is also known as *whole numbers*. They can be positive or negative but include neither fractions nor decimals. Numbers that use a decimal point (even something like 1.0) are *floating-point* numbers, also known as *floats*. You use floating-point numbers to refer to fractions, because the only way to express a fraction in PHP is to convert it to its decimal equivalent. Hence, 1¼ is written as 1.25. **Table 2.3** lists some sample valid numbers and their formal type; **Table 2.4** lists invalid numbers and the rules they violate.

TIP As you'll soon see, you add quotation marks around invalid numbers to turn them into valid strings.

TABLE 2.3 Valid Numbers in PHP

Number	Type
1	Integer
1.0	Floating-point
1972	Integer
19.72	Floating-point
−1	Integer
−1.0	Floating-point

TABLE 2.4 Invalid Numbers in PHP

Number	Reason
1/3	Contains a slash
1996a	Contains a letter
08.02.06	Contains multiple decimals

Strings

A string is any number of characters enclosed within a pair of either single (') or double (") quotation marks. Strings can contain any combination of characters that exist: letters, numbers, symbols, and spaces. Strings can also contain variables.

Here are examples of valid string values:

```
"Hello, world!"
"Hello, $first_name!"
"1/3"
'Hello, world! How are you today?'
"08.02.06"
"1996"
''
```

That last example is an *empty string*—a string that contains no characters.

To create a string, just wrap 0 or more characters within quotation marks. There are cases, however, where you may run into problems. For example:

```
"I said, "How are you?""
```

This string will be tricky. Chapter 1, "Getting Started with PHP," hinted at the same problem with respect to printing HTML code. When PHP hits the second quotation mark in the example, it assumes the string ends there; the continuing text (*How...*) causes an error. To use a quotation mark within a string you *escape* the quotation mark by putting a backslash (\) before it:

```
"I said, \"How are you?\""
```

The backslash tells PHP to treat each escaped quotation mark as part of the *value* of the string, rather than using it as the string's opening or closing indicators.

You can similarly circumvent this problem by using different quotation mark types:

```
'I said, "How are you?"'
"I said, 'How are you?'"
```

TIP Notice that "1996" converts an integer into a string, simply by placing the number within quotes. Essentially, the string contains the characters *1996*, whereas the number (a nonquoted value) would be equal to 1996. It's a fine distinction, and one that won't matter in your code, because PHP lets you perform mathematical calculations with the string *1996* just as you can with the number.

TIP Chapter 1 also demonstrated how to create a new line by printing the \n character within double quotation marks. Although escaping a quotation mark prints the quotation mark, escaping an *n* prints a new line, escaping an *r* creates a carriage return, and escaping a *t* creates a tab.

TIP Understanding strings, variables, and the single and double quotation marks is critical to programming with PHP. For this reason, a section at the end of this chapter is dedicated to the subject.

Arrays

Arrays are covered more thoroughly in Chapter 7, but let's look at them briefly here. Whereas a string or a number contains a single value (both are said to be *scalar*), an array can have more than one value assigned to it. You can think of an array as a list or table of values: You can put multiple strings and/or numbers into one array.

Arrays use *keys* to create and retrieve the values they store. The resulting structure—a list of key-value pairs—is similar to a two-column spreadsheet. Unlike arrays in other programming languages, the array structure in PHP is so flexible that it can use either numbers or strings for both the keys and the values. The array doesn't even need to be consistent in this respect. (All of this will make more sense in Chapter 7, when you start working with specific examples.)

PHP supports two kinds of arrays, based on the format of the keys. If the array uses numbers for the keys (**Table 2.5**), it's known as an *indexed* array. If it uses strings for the keys (**Table 2.6**), it's an *associative* array. In either case, the values in the array can be of any variable type (string, number, and so on).

TIP The array's key is also referred to as its *index*. You'll see these two terms used interchangeably.

TIP An array can, and frequently will, contain other arrays, creating what is called a *multi-dimensional* array.

TIP What PHP refers to as an *associative array* is known as a *hash* in Perl and Ruby, among other languages.

TABLE 2.5 Indexed Array

Key	Value
0	Dev
1	Rachel
2	Denise
3	Arnold

TABLE 2.6 Associative Array

Key	Value
VT	Vermont
NH	New Hampshire
IA	Iowa
PA	Pennsylvania

```
Number is 1

String is Hello, world!
```

The result of printing the values of two variables.

```
⚠ Notice: Array to string conversion in /Users/larry/Sites/test.php on line 14
Call Stack
#  Time      Memory     Function    Location
1  0.0001       362008  {main}( )    .../test.php:0
_SERVER is Array
```

Ⓑ Using the **print** statement on a complex variable type, such as an array, will not have the results you desire.

Variable Values

To assign a value to a variable, regardless of the variable type, you use the equals sign (=). Therefore, the equals sign is known as the *assignment operator*, because it assigns the value on the right to the variable on the left. For example:

```
$number = 1;
$floating_number = 1.2;
$string = "Hello, world!";
```

Each of these lines represents a complete statement (that is, an executable action), so each concludes with a semicolon.

To print the value of a variable, use the **print** function:

```
print $number;
print $string;
```

If you want to print a variable's value within a context, you can place the variable's name in the printed string, as long as you use double quotation marks Ⓐ:

```
print "Number is $number";
print "String is $string";
```

Using **print** in this way works for the scalar (single-valued) variable types—numbers and strings. For complex variable types—arrays and objects—you cannot just use **print** Ⓑ:

```
print "_SERVER is $_SERVER";
```

As you've already seen, **print_r()** can handle these nonscalar types, and you'll learn other approaches later in the book.

Whether you're dealing with scalar or nonscalar variables, don't forget that printing out their values is an excellent debugging technique when you're having problems with a script.

Because variable types aren't locked in (PHP is referred to as a *weakly typed* language), they can be changed on the fly:

```
$variable = 1;
$variable = "Greetings";
```

If you were to print the value of **$variable** now, the result would be *Greetings*. The following section better demonstrates the concept of assigning values to variables and then accessing those values.

To assign values to and access variables:

1. Create a new PHP script in your text editor or IDE, to be named **variables.php** (Script 2.3).

2. Create the initial HTML tags:

```
<!doctype html>
<html lang="en">
<head>
   <meta charset="utf-8">
   <title>Variables</title>
</head>
<body>
```

3. Begin the PHP code:

```
<?php // Script 2.3 -
→ variables.php
```

4. Define some number and string variables:

```
$street = "100 Main Street";
$city = "State College";
$state = "PA";
$zip = 16801;
```

These lines create four different variables of both string and number types. The strings are defined using quotation marks, and each variable name follows the syntactical naming rules.

Script 2.3 Some basic variables are defined and their values printed by this script.

```
1    <!doctype html>
2    <html lang="en">
3    <head>
4       <meta charset="utf-8">
5       <title>Variables</title>
6    </head>
7    <body>
8    <?php // Script 2.3 - variables.php
9
10   // An address:
11   $street = "100 Main Street";
12   $city = "State College";
13   $state = "PA";
14   $zip = 16801;
15
16   // Print the address:
17   print "<p>The address is:<br>$street
        <br>$city $state $zip</p>";
18
19   ?>
20   </body>
21   </html>
```

The address is:
100 Main Street
State College PA 16801

C Some variables are assigned values, and then printed within a context.

> **(!)** Parse error: syntax error, unexpected 'print' (T_PRINT) in /Users/larry/Sites/variables.php on line *17*

D Parse errors are the most common type of PHP error, as you'll discover. They're frequently caused by missing semicolons or mismatched quotation marks or parentheses.

> **(!)** Notice: Undefined variable: Street in /Users/larry/Sites/variables.php on line *17*
>
> **Call Stack**
>
> | # | Time | Memory | Function | Location |
> |---|--------|---------|----------|-------------------|
> | 1 | 0.0001 | 362024 | {main}( ) | .../variables.php:0 |
>
> The address is:
>
> State College PA 16801

E The *Undefined variable* error indicates that you used a variable with no value (it hasn't been defined). This can happen with misspellings and capitalization inconsistencies.

Remember that each statement must conclude with a semicolon and that the variable names are case-sensitive.

5. Print out the values of the variables within some context:

```
print "<p>The address is:
→ <br>$street <br>$city $state
→ $zip</p>";
```

Here a single **print** statement references all the variables. The entire string to be printed (consisting of text, HTML tags, and variables) is enclosed within double quotation marks. The HTML **
** tags make the text flow over multiple lines in the browser.

6. Complete the PHP section and the HTML page:

```
?>
</body>
</html>
```

7. Save the file as **variables.php**, upload it to your server (or save it to the appropriate directory on your computer), and test it in your browser **C**.

> **TIP** If you see a parse error **D** when you run this script, you probably either omitted a semicolon or have an imbalance in your quotation marks. In such particular cases, the mistake itself is likely on the previous line of code (than reported in the error message) but wasn't caught by PHP until the next line.

> **TIP** If one of the variable's values isn't printed out or you see an *Undefined variable* error **E**, you most likely failed to spell a variable name the same way twice.

> **TIP** If you see a blank page, you most likely have an error but PHP's display_errors configuration is set to off. See Chapter 3, "HTML Forms and PHP," for details.

Understanding Quotation Marks

Now that you know the basics of variables and how to create them, let's do an exercise to make sure you completely understand how to properly use quotation marks. PHP, like most programming languages, allows you to use both double (") and single (') quotation marks—but they give vastly different results. It's critical that you comprehend the distinction, so the next example will run tests using both types just to emphasize the different behaviors.

The rule to remember is: *Items within single quotation marks are treated literally; items within double quotation marks are extrapolated.* This means that within double quotation marks, a variable's name is replaced with its value, as in Script 2.3, but the same is not true for single quotation marks.

This rule applies anywhere in PHP you might use quotation marks, including uses of the **print** function and the assignment of values to string variables. An example is the best way to demonstrate this critical concept.

This script simply demonstrates how the type of quotation mark you use with variables affects the result.

```
1    <!doctype html>
2    <html lang="en">
3    <head>
4        <meta charset="utf-8">
5        <title>Quotes</title>
6    </head>
7    <body>
8    <?php // Script 2.4 - quotes.php
9
10   // Single or double quotation marks
     won't matter here:
11   $first_name = 'Larry';
12   $last_name = "Ullman";
13
14   // Single or double quotation marks DOES
     matter here:
15   $name1 = '$first_name $last_name';
16   $name2 = "$first_name $last_name";
17
18   // Single or double quotation marks DOES
     matter here:
19   print "<h1>Double Quotes</h1>
20   <p>name1 is $name1 <br>
21   name2 is $name2</p>";
22
23   print '<h1>Single Quotes</h1>
24   <p>name1 is $name1 <br>
25   name2 is $name2</p>';
26
27   ?>
28   </body>
29   </html>
```

To use quotation marks:

1. Begin a new PHP script in your text editor or IDE, to be named **quotes.php** (**Script 2.4**).

2. Create the initial HTML tags:

   ```
   <!doctype html>
   <html lang="en">
   <head>
       <meta charset="utf-8">
       <title>Quotes</title>
   </head>
   <body>
   ```

3. Begin the PHP code:

   ```
   <?php // Script 2.4 - quotes.php
   ```

4. Create two string variables:

   ```
   $first_name = 'Larry';
   $last_name = "Ullman";
   ```

   It doesn't matter whether you use single or double quotation marks for these two variables, because each string can be treated literally. However, if you're using your own name here (and feel free to do so) and it contains an apostrophe, you'll need to either use double quotation marks or escape the apostrophe within single quotation marks:

   ```
   $last_name = "O'Toole";
   $last_name = 'O\'Toole';
   ```

   continues on next page

5. Create two different *name* variables, using the existing **first_** and **last_name** variables:

```
$name1 = '$first_name
→$last_name';
$name2 = "$first_name
→$last_name";
```

In these lines, it makes a huge difference which quotation marks you use. The **$name1** variable is now literally equal to **$first_name $last_name**, because no extrapolation occurs. Conversely, **$name2** is equal to *Larry Ullman*, presumably the intended result.

6. Print out the variables using both types of quotation marks:

```
print "<h1>Double Quotes</h1>
<p>name1 is $name1 <br>
name2 is $name2</p>";
print '<h1>Single Quotes</h1>
<p>name1 is $name1 <br>
name2 is $name2</p>';
```

Again, the quotation marks make all the difference here. The first **print** statement, using double quotation marks, prints out the values of the **$name1** and **$name2** variables, whereas the second, using single quotation marks, prints out **$name1** and **$name2** literally.

The HTML in the **print** statements makes them more legible in the browser. Each statement is executed over three lines of PHP code for additional readability, which is perfectly acceptable.

Double Quotes

name1 is $first_name $last_name
name2 is Larry Ullman

Single Quotes

name1 is $name1
name2 is $name2

Ⓐ The different quotation marks (single versus double) dictate whether the variable's name or value is printed.

7. Complete the PHP section and the HTML page:

```
?>
</body>
</html>
```

8. Save the file as **quotes.php**, upload it to your server (or save it to the appropriate directory on your computer), and test it in your browser Ⓐ.

TIP If you're still confused about the distinction between the two types of quotation marks, always stick with double quotation marks and you'll be safer.

TIP Arguably, using single quotation marks when you can is marginally preferable, because PHP won't need to search the strings looking for variables, resulting in better performance. But, at best, this is a minor optimization.

TIP The shortcuts for creating newlines (\n), carriage returns (\r), and tabs (\t) must be used within double quotation marks to have the desired effect. Within single quotes, each of those is treated literally.

TIP Remember that you don't always need to use quotation marks at all. When assigning a numeric value or when only printing a variable, you can omit them:

```
$num = 2;
print $num;
```

Review and Pursue

If you have any problems with the review questions or the pursue prompts, turn to the book's supporting forum (www.LarryUllman.com/forums/).

Review

- What kind of variable is **$_SERVER** an example of?

- What character must all variables begin with?

- What characters can be used in a variable's name (after the required initial character)? What other characters can be used in a variable's name, after the first character?

- Are variable names case-sensitive or case-insensitive?

- What does it mean to say that a variable is *scalar*? What are examples of scalar variable types? What is an example of a nonscalar variable type?

- What is the assignment operator?

- What great debugging technique—with respect to variables—was introduced in this chapter?

- What is the difference between using single and double quotation marks?

Pursue

- Create another PHP script that defines some variables and prints their values. Try using variables of different scalar types.

- Create a PHP script that prints the value of some variables within some HTML. More sophisticated practice might involve using PHP and variables to create a link or image tag.

HTML Forms and PHP

The previous chapter provided a brief introduction to the topic of variables. Although you'll commonly create your own variables, you'll also frequently use variables in conjunction with HTML forms. Forms are a fundamental unit of websites, enabling such features as registration and login systems, search capability, and online shopping. Even the simplest site will find logical reasons to incorporate HTML forms. And with PHP, it's stunningly simple to receive and handle data generated by them.

With that in mind, this chapter will cover the basics of creating HTML forms and explain how the submitted form data is available to a PHP script. This chapter will also introduce several key concepts of real PHP programming, including how to manage errors in your scripts.

In This Chapter

Creating a Simple Form

For the HTML form example in this chapter, you'll create a feedback page that takes the user's salutation (or title), name, email address, response, and comments **A**. The code that generates a form goes between opening and closing form tags:

```
<form>
form elements
</form>
```

The form tags dictate where a form begins and ends. Every element of the form must be entered between these two tags. The opening form tag should also contain an **action** attribute. It indicates the page to which the form data should be submitted. This value is one of the most important considerations when you're creating a form. In this book, the **action** attributes will always point to PHP scripts:

```
<form action="somepage.php">
```

Before creating this next form, let's briefly revisit the topic of HTML5. HTML5 introduces some new form element types, such as *email*, *number*, and *url*. These types, which are generally well supported by current browsers, provide additional benefits over a simple text input, including:

- Built-in browser-based validation (for example, the browser will check that entered text is a syntactically valid email address or URL).

- Better user experience (for example, an email address-specific keyboard presented to mobile users).

HTML5 also introduces a **required** attribute that prevents a form from being submitted without a value entered or selected **B**.

A The HTML form that will be used in this chapter's examples.

B The **required** attribute validates—in the browser—that a selection was made or content was entered.

```
1   <!doctype html>
2   <html lang="en">
3   <head>
4       <meta charset="utf-8">
5       <title>Feedback Form</title>
6   </head>
7   <body>
8   <!-- Script 3.1 - feedback.html -->
9   <div><p>Please complete this form to
    submit your feedback:</p>
10
11  <form action="handle_form.php">
12
13      <p>Name: <select name="title"
        required>
14      <option value="Mr.">Mr.</option>
15      <option value="Mrs.">Mrs.</option>
16      <option value="Ms.">Ms.</option>
17      </select> <input type="text"
        name="name" size="20" required>
        </p>
18
19      <p>Email Address: <input
        type="email" name="email"
        size="20" required></p>
20
21      <p>Response: This is...
22      <input type="radio"
        name="response" value="excellent"
        required> excellent
23      <input type="radio"
        name="response" value="okay"> okay
24      <input type="radio"
        name="response" value="boring">
        boring</p>
25
26      <p>Comments: <textarea
        name="comments" rows="3" cols="30"
        required></textarea></p>
27
28      <input type="submit" name="submit"
        value="Send My Feedback">
29
30  </form>
31  </div>
32  </body>
33  </html>
```

As a final note, give each form element its own unique name. Stick to a consistent naming convention when naming elements, using only letters, numbers, and the underscore (_). The result should be names that are also logical and descriptive.

To create a basic HTML form:

1. Begin a new document in your text editor or IDE, to be named **feedback.html** (Script 3.1):

   ```
   <!doctype html>
   <html lang="en">
   <head>
      <meta charset="utf-8">
      <title>Feedback Form</title>
   </head>
   <body>
   <!-- Script 3.1 - feedback.html
   ⇥ -->
   <div><p>Please complete this
   ⇥ form to submit your feedback:
   ⇥ </p>
   ```

2. Add the opening form tag:

   ```
   <form action="handle_form.php">
   ```

   The form tag indicates that this form will be submitted to the page **handle_ form.php**, found within the same directory as this HTML page. You can use a full URL to the PHP script, if you'd prefer to be explicit (for example, **http:// www.example.com/handle_form.php**).

   continues on next page

3. Add a select menu plus a text input for the person's name:

```
<p>Name: <select name="title"
→ required>
<option value="Mr.">Mr.</option>
<option value="Mrs.">Mrs.
→ </option>
<option value="Ms.">Ms.</option>
</select> <input type="text"
→ name="name" size="20" required>
→ </p>
```

The inputs for the person's name will consist of two elements Ⓐ. The first is a drop-down menu of common titles: *Mr.*, *Mrs.*, and *Ms.* Each option listed between the select tags is an answer the user can choose Ⓒ. The second element is a basic text box for the person's full name. Arguably, this list should be expanded, or you could use a text input to let users enter their preferred title.

Every form element, except for the submit button, will have the **required** attribute.

4. Add a text input for the user's email address:

```
<p>Email Address: <input type=
→ "email" name="email" size="20"
→ required></p>
```

The email input type is new in HTML5. On browsers that support it—all the most recent ones—client-side validation is automatic Ⓓ.

Please complete this form to submit your feedback:

Name ✓ Mr.
      Mrs.
Email Ms.

Ⓒ The select element creates a drop-down menu of options.

Email Address: invalid email address

Response: This is... ◯ ❗ Please include an '@' in the email address. 'invalid email address' is missing an '@'.

Ⓓ The email input type, new in HTML5, validates the syntax of the entered text against what's required for email addresses.

5. Add radio buttons for a response:

```
<p>Response: This is...
<input type="radio"
→ name="response"
→ value="excellent" required>
→ excellent
<input type="radio"
→ name="response" value="okay">
→ okay
<input type="radio"
→ name="response"
→ value="boring"> boring</p>
```

This HTML code creates three radio buttons (clickable circles, Ⓐ). Because they all have the same value for the **name** attribute, only one of the three can be selected at a time. Adding the **required** attribute to any one of them makes selection of one of them a requirement.

6. Add a **textarea** to record the comments:

```
<p>Comments: <textarea
→ name="comments" rows="3"
→ cols="30" required>
→ </textarea></p>
```

A textarea gives users more space to enter their comments than a text input would. However, the text input lets you limit how much information users can enter, which you can't do with the textarea (not without using JavaScript, that is). When you're creating a form, choose input types appropriate to the information you wish to retrieve from the user.

Note that a textarea *does* have a closing tag, unlike the text input type.

7. Add the submit button:

```
<input type="submit"
→ name="submit" value="Send My
→ Feedback">
```

The **value** attribute of a submit input is what appears on the button in the browser Ⓐ. You could also use *Go!* or *Submit*, for example.

8. Close the form:

```
</form>
```

9. Complete the page:

```
</div>
</body>
</html>
```

10. Save the page as **feedback.html**, and view it in your browser.

Because this is an HTML page, not a PHP script, you could view it in your browser directly from your computer.

> **TIP** Note that feedback.html uses the HTML extension because it's a standard HTML page (not a PHP script). You could use the .php extension without a problem, even though there's no actual PHP code. (Remember that in a PHP page, anything not within the PHP tags—<?php and ?>—is assumed to be HTML.)

> **TIP** Be certain that your action attribute correctly points to an existing file on the server, or your form won't be processed properly. In this case, the form will be submitted to handle_form.php, to be located in the same directory as the feedback.html page.

> **TIP** In this example, an HTML form is created by hand-coding the HTML, but you can do this in a webpage application (such as Adobe Dreamweaver) if you're more comfortable with that approach.

Choosing a Form Method

The experienced HTML developer will notice that the feedback form just created is missing one thing: The initial form tag has no **method** attribute. The **method** attribute tells the server how to transmit the data from the form to the handling script.

You have two choices with **method**: GET and POST. With respect to forms, the difference between using GET and POST is squarely in how the information is passed from the form to the processing script. The GET method sends all the gathered information along as part of the URL. The POST method transmits the information invisibly to the user. For example, upon submitting a form, if you use the GET method, the resulting URL will be something like

```
http://example.com/page.php?var=
→ value&age=20&...
```

Following the name of the script, `page.php`, is a question mark, followed by one *name=value* pair for each piece of data submitted.

When using the POST method, the end user will only see

```
http://example.com/page.php.
```

Ⓐ If users refresh a PHP script that data has been sent to via the POST method, they will be asked to confirm the action (the specific message will differ depending on the browser).

When deciding which method to use, keep in mind these four factors:

- With the GET method, a limited amount of information can be passed.

- The GET method sends the data to the handling script publicly (which means, for example, that a password entered in a form would be viewable by anyone within eyesight of the browser, creating a larger security risk).

- A page generated by a form that used the GET method can be bookmarked, but one based on POST can't be.

- Users will be prompted if they attempt to reload a page accessed via POST **Ⓐ**, but will not be prompted for pages accessed via GET.

Generally speaking, GET requests are used when asking for information from the server. Search pages almost always use GET (check out the URLs the next time you use a search engine), as do sites that paginate results (like the ability to browse categories of products). POST is normally used to trigger a server-based action. This might be the submission of a contact form (result: an email gets sent) or the submission of a blog's comment form (result: a comment is added to the database and therefore the page).

This book uses POST almost exclusively for handling forms, although you'll also see a useful technique involving the GET method (see "Manually Sending Data to a Page" at the end of this chapter).

To add a method to a form:

1. Open **feedback.html** (Script 3.1) in your text editor or IDE, if it is not already open.

2. Within the initial **form** tag, add **method="post"** (Script 3.2, line 11).

   The form's **method** attribute tells the browser how to send the form data to the receiving script. Because there may be a lot of data in the form's submission (including the comments), and because it wouldn't make sense for the user to bookmark the resulting page, POST is the logical method to use.

3. Save the script and reload it in your browser.

   It's important that you get in the habit of reloading pages in the browser after you make changes. It's quite easy to forget the reloading step and find yourself flummoxed when your changes are not being reflected.

Script 3.2 Adding a **method** attribute with a value of *post* completes the form.

```
1    <!doctype html>
2    <html lang="en">
3    <head>
4        <meta charset="utf-8">
5        <title>Feedback Form</title>
6    </head>
7    <body>
8    <!-- Script 3.2 - feedback.html -->
9    <div><p>Please complete this form to
     submit your feedback:</p>
10
11   <form action="handle_form.php"
     method="post">
12
13       <p>Name: <select name="title"
         required>
14       <option value="Mr.">Mr.</option>
15       <option value="Mrs.">Mrs.</option>
16       <option value="Ms.">Ms.</option>
17       </select> <input type="text"
         name="name" size="20" required></p>
18
19       <p>Email Address: <input type="email"
         name="email" size="20" required></p>
20
21       <p>Response: This is...
22       <input type="radio" name="response"
         value="excellent" required> excellent
23       <input type="radio" name="response"
         value="okay"> okay
24       <input type="radio" name="response"
         value="boring"> boring</p>
25
26       <p>Comments: <textarea
         name="comments" rows="3" cols="30"
         required></textarea></p>
27
28       <input type="submit" name="submit"
         value="Send My Feedback">
29
30   </form>
31   </div>
32   </body>
33   </html>
```

4. View the source of the page to make sure all the required elements are present and have the correct attributes **B**.

TIP In the discussion of the methods, GET and POST are written in capital letters to make them stand out. However, the form in the script uses post. Don't worry about this inconsistency (if you caught it at all)—the method will work regardless of case.

```
1  <!doctype html>
2  <html lang="en">
3  <head>
4          <meta charset="utf-8">
5          <title>Feedback Form</title>
6  </head>
7  <body>
8  <!-- Script 3.2 - feedback.html -->
9  <div><p>Please complete this form to submit your feedback:</p>
10
11 <form action="handle_form.php" method="post">
12
13         <p>Name: <select name="title" required>
14         <option value="Mr.">Mr.</option>
15         <option value="Mrs.">Mrs.</option>
16         <option value="Ms.">Ms.</option>
17         </select> <input type="text" name="name" size="20" required></p>
18
19         <p>Email Address: <input type="email" name="email" size="20" required></p>
20
21         <p>Response: This is...
22         <input type="radio" name="response" value="excellent" required> excellent
23         <input type="radio" name="response" value="okay"> okay
24         <input type="radio" name="response" value="boring"> boring</p>
25
26         <p>Comments: <textarea name="comments" rows="3" cols="30" required></textarea></p>
27
28         <input type="submit" name="submit" value="Send My Feedback">
29
30 </form>
31 </div>
32 </body>
33 </html>
```

B With forms, much of the important information, such as the **action** and **method** values or element names, can be seen only within the HTML source code.

Receiving Form Data in PHP

Now that you've created a basic HTML form capable of taking input from a user, you need to write the PHP script that will receive and process the submitted form data. For this example, the PHP script will simply repeat what the user entered into the form. In later chapters, you'll learn how to take this information and store it in a database, send it in an email, write it to a file, and so forth.

To access the submitted form data, you need to refer to a particular *predefined variable*. Chapter 2, "Variables," already introduced one predefined variable: **$_SERVER**. When it comes to handling form data, the specific variable the PHP script would refer to is either **$_GET** or **$_POST**. If an HTML form uses the GET method, the submitted form data will be found in **$_GET**. When an HTML form uses the POST method, the submitted form data will be found in **$_POST**.

$_GET and **$_POST**, besides being predefined variables (that is, ones you don't need to create), are *arrays*, a special variable type (**$_SERVER** is also an array). This means that both **$_GET** and **$_POST** may contain numerous values, making the printing of those values more challenging. You cannot treat arrays like so:

```
print $_POST; // Will not work!
```

(Also see **B** under "Variable Values" in Chapter 2 for the result of the previous code.)

Instead, to access a specific value, you must refer to the array's *index* or *key*. Chapter 7, "Using Arrays," goes into this subject in detail, but the premise is simple. Start with a form element whose **name** attribute has a value of **address**:

```
<input type="text" name="address" />
```

Then, assuming that the form uses the POST method, the value entered into that form element would be available in **$_POST['address']**:

```
print $_POST['address'];
```

Unfortunately, there is one little hitch here: When used within double quotation marks, the single quotation marks around the key will cause parse errors **A**:

```
print "You provided your address as:
→ $_POST['address']";
```

You can avoid this problem in a couple of ways. This chapter will use the solution that's syntactically the simpler of the two: just assign the particular **$_POST** element to another variable first:

```
$something = $_POST['something'];
→ print "Thanks for saying:
→ $something";
```

In Chapter 7 you'll learn another approach.

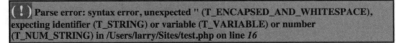

⚠ Parse error: syntax error, unexpected '' (T_ENCAPSED_AND_WHITESPACE), expecting identifier (T_STRING) or variable (T_VARIABLE) or number (T_NUM_STRING) in /Users/larry/Sites/test.php on line *16*

A This ugly parse error is created by attempting to use **$_POST['address']** within double quotation marks.

```
1    <!doctype html>
2    <html lang="en">
3    <head>
4        <meta charset="utf-8">
5        <title>Your Feedback</title>
6    </head>
7    <body>
8    <?php // Script 3.3 handle_form.php
9
10   // This page receives the data from
     feedback.html.
11   // It will receive: title, name, email,
     response, comments, and submit in
     $_POST.
12
13   // Create shorthand versions of the
     variables:
14   $title = $_POST['title'];
15   $name = $_POST['name'];
16   $response = $_POST['response'];
17   $comments = $_POST['comments'];
18
19   // Print the received data:
20   print "<p>Thank you, $title $name,
     for your comments.</p>
21   <p>You stated that you found this
     example to be '$response' and
     added:<br>$comments</p>";
22
23   ?>
24   </body>
25   </html>
```

Two final notes before implementing this information in a new PHP script: First, as with all variables in PHP, **$_POST** is case sensitive; it must be typed exactly as you see it here (a dollar sign, one underscore, then all capital letters). Second, the indexes in **$_POST**—*something* in the preceding example—must exactly match the values of the **name** attributes in the corresponding form element.

To handle an HTML form:

1. Begin a new document in your text editor or IDE, to be named **handle_form.php** (Script 3.3):

   ```
   <!doctype html>
   <html lang="en">
   <head>
       <meta charset="utf-8">
       <title>Your Feedback</title>
   </head>
   <body>
   ```

2. Add the opening PHP tag and any comments:

   ```
   <?php // Script 3.3
   → handle_form.php
   // This page receives the data
   → from feedback.html.
   // It will receive: title, name,
   → email, response, comments, and
   → submit in $_POST.
   ```

   Comments are added to make the script's purpose clear. Even though the **feedback.html** page indicates where the data is sent (via the **action** attribute), a comment here indicates the reverse (where this script is getting its data). It also helps to spell out the exact form element names, in a case-sensitive manner.

   continues on next page

3. Assign the received data to new variables:

```
$title = $_POST['title'];
$name = $_POST['name'];
$response = $_POST['response'];
$comments = $_POST['comments'];
```

Again, since the form uses the POST method, the submitted data can be found in the **$_POST** array. The individual values are accessed using the syntax **$_POST['*name_attribute_value*']**. This works regardless of the form element's type (input, email, select, checkbox, etc.).

To make it easier to use these values in a **print** statement in Step 4, each value is assigned to a new variable in this step. Neither **$_POST['email']** nor **$_POST['submit']** is being addressed, but you can create variables for those values if you'd like.

4. Print out the user information:

```
print "<p>Thank you, $title
→ $name, for your comments.</p>
<p>You stated that you found
→ this example to be '$response'
→ and added:<br>$comments</p>";
```

This one **print** statement uses the four variables within a context to show the user what data the script received.

5. Close the PHP section, and complete the HTML page:

```
?>
</body>
</html>
```

Please complete this form to submit your feedback:

Name: [Mr. ▾] [Larry Ullman]

Email Address: [larry@example.net]

Response: This is... ⦿ excellent ○ okay ○ boring

Comments: [No problems so far!]

[Send My Feedback]

B Whatever the user enters into the HTML form should be printed out to the browser by the `handle_form.php` script **C**.

Thank you, Mr. Larry Ullman, for your comments.

You stated that you found this example to be 'excellent' and added: No problems so far!

C This is another application of the `print` statement discussed in Chapter 1, but it constitutes your first dynamically generated web page.

Thank you, Mr. , for your comments.

D Notices like these occur when a script refers to a variable that doesn't exist. In this particular case, the cause is erroneously referring to `$_POST['Name']` when it should be `$_POST['name']`.

6. Save the script as **handle_form.php**.

Note that the name of this file must exactly match the value of the **action** attribute in the form.

7. Upload the script to the server (or store it in the proper directory on your computer if you've installed PHP), making sure it's saved in the same directory as **feedback.html**.

8. Load **feedback.html** in your browser through a URL (*http://something*).

You must load the HTML form through a URL so that when it's submitted to the PHP script, that PHP script is also run through a URL. *PHP scripts must always be run through a URL!*

Failure to load a form through a URL is a common beginner's mistake.

9. Fill out **B**, and then submit the form **C**.

If you see a blank page, read the next section of the chapter for how to display the errors that presumably occurred.

If you see an error notice **D** or see that a variable does not have a value when printed, you likely misspelled either the form element's **name** value or the **$_POST** array's index (or you filled out the form incompletely).

TIP If you want to pass a preset value along to a PHP script, use the hidden type of input within your HTML form. For example, inserting

```
<input type="hidden"
name="form_page"
value="feedback.html">
```

between the form tags will create a variable in the handling script named `$_POST['form_page']` with the value feedback.html.

TIP Notice that the value of radio button and certain menu variables is based on the `value` attribute of the selected item (for example, excellent from the radio button). This is also true for checkboxes. For text boxes, the value of the variable is what the user typed.

TIP If the `handle_form.php` script displays extra slashes in submitted strings, see the "Magic Quotes" sidebar for an explanation and solution.

TIP As a brute-force way of seeing all the form data submitted to a PHP script, call `print_r($_POST)`, in the same way that Chapter 2 calls `print_r()` with `$_SERVER`.

TIP You can also access form data, regardless of the form's method, in the `$_REQUEST` predefined variable. `$_GET` and `$_POST` are more precise, however, and therefore preferable.

Magic Quotes

Earlier versions of PHP had a feature known as *Magic Quotes*, which has since been removed (as of PHP 5.4). Magic Quotes—when enabled—automatically escapes single and double quotation marks found in submitted form data. So the string *I'd like more information* would be turned into *I\'d like more information*.

The escaping of potentially problematic characters can be useful and even necessary in some situations. But if the Magic Quotes feature is enabled on your PHP installation, you'll see these backslashes when the PHP script prints out the form data. You can undo its effect using the **stripslashes()** function. To apply it to the **handle_form.php** script, you would do this, for example:

```
$comments = stripslashes
 ($_POST['comments']);
```

instead of just this:

```
$comments = $_POST['comments'];
```

That will have the effect of converting an escaped submitted string back to its original, non-escaped value.

If you're not seeing extraneous slashes added to submitted form data, you don't need to worry about Magic Quotes.

Displaying Errors

One of the very first issues that arise when it comes to debugging PHP scripts is that you may not even see the errors that occur. After you install PHP on a web server, it will run under a default configuration with respect to security, performance, how it handles data, and so forth. One of the default settings is to not display any errors. In other words, the `display_errors` setting will be off **Ⓐ**. When that's the case, what you might see when a script has an error is a blank page. (This is common on fresh installations of PHP; most hosting companies will enable `display_errors`.)

The reason that errors should not be displayed on a live site is that it's a security risk. Simply put, PHP's errors often give away too much information for the public at large to see (not to mention that showing PHP errors looks unprofessional). But you, the developer, *do need* to see these errors in order to fix them!

To have PHP display errors, you can do one of the following:

- Turn `display_errors` back on for PHP as a whole. (See the "Configuring PHP" section of Appendix A, "Installation and Configuration," for more information.)
- Turn `display_errors` back on for an individual script.

While developing a site, the first option is by far preferred. However, it's a possibility only for those with administrative control over the server. But anyone can use the second option by including this line in a script:

```
ini_set('display_errors', 1);
```

The `ini_set()` function allows a script to temporarily override a setting in PHP's configuration file (many, but not all, settings can be altered this way). The previous example changes the `display_errors` setting to *on*, which is represented by the number 1.

Although this second method can be implemented by anyone, the downside is that if your script contains certain kinds of errors (discussed next), the script cannot be executed. In that situation, this line of code won't be executed, and the particular error—or any that prevents a script from running at all—still results in a blank page.

display_errors	Off	Off
display_startup_errors	On	On
doc_root	*no value*	*no value*
docref_ext	*no value*	*no value*
docref_root	*no value*	*no value*
enable_dl	Off	Off

Ⓐ Run a `phpinfo()` script (for example, Script 1.2) to view your server's `display_errors` setting.

To display errors in a script:

1. Open **handle_form.php** in your text editor or IDE, if it is not already open.

2. As the first line of PHP code, enter the following (**Script 3.4**):

   ```
   ini_set('display_errors', 1);
   ```

   Again, this line tells PHP you'd like to see any errors that occur. You should call it first thing in your PHP section so the rest of the PHP code will abide by this new setting.

3. Save the file as **handle_form.php**.

4. Upload the file to your web server, and test it in your browser.

   If the resulting page has no errors in it, then the script will run as it did before. If you saw a blank page when you ran the form earlier, you should now see the actual error messages (like those in **D** in the previous section). Again, if you see such errors, you likely misspelled the name of a form element, misspelled the index in the **$_POST** array, or didn't fill out the form completely.

TIP Make sure **display_errors** is enabled anytime you're having difficulties debugging a script. If you installed PHP on your computer, I highly recommend enabling it in your PHP configuration while you learn (again, see Appendix A).

TIP If you see a blank page when running a PHP script, also check the HTML source code for errors or other problems.

TIP Remember that the **display_errors** directive only controls whether error messages are sent to the browser. It doesn't create errors or prevent them from occurring in any way.

TIP Failure to use an equals sign after name in a form element will also cause problems:
`<input name"something">`

Script 3.4 This addition to the PHP script turns on the **display_errors** directive so that errors will be shown.

```
1   <!doctype html>
2   <html lang="en">
3   <head>
4       <meta charset="utf-8">
5       <title>Your Feedback</title>
6   </head>
7   <body>
8   <?php // Script 3.4 - handle_form.php #2
9
10  ini_set('display_errors', 1); // Let
    me learn from my mistakes!
11
12  // This page receives the data from
    feedback.html.
13  // It will receive: title, name, email,
    response, comments, and submit in
    $_POST.
14
15  // Create shorthand versions of the
    variables:
16  $title = $_POST['title'];
17  $name = $_POST['name'];
18  $response = $_POST['response'];
19  $comments = $_POST['comments'];
20
21  // Print the received data:
22  print "<p>Thank you, $title $name, for
    your comments.</p>
23  <p>You stated that you found this
    example to be '$response' and
    added:<br>$comments</p>";
24
25  ?>
26  </body>
27  </html>
```

Error Reporting

Another PHP configuration issue you should be aware of, along with **display_errors**, is *error reporting*. PHP has more than a dozen different levels of errors, and you can define your own (a subject not covered in this book). **Table 3.1** lists the four most important general error levels, along with a description and example of each.

You can set what errors PHP reports on in two ways. First, you can adjust the **error_reporting** level in PHP's configuration file (again, see Appendix A). If you are running your own PHP server, you'll probably want to adjust that global setting while developing your scripts.

The second option is to use the **error_reporting()** function in a script. The function takes either a number or one or more *constants*—nonquoted strings with predetermined meanings—to adjust the levels. (Each constant is associated with a number.) The most important of these constants are listed in **Table 3.2**, in order from most forgiving to least.

TABLE 3.1 PHP Error Levels

Type	Description	Example
Notice	Nonfatal error that may or may not be indicative of a problem	Referring to a variable that has no value
Warning	Nonfatal error that is most likely problematic	Misusing a function
Parse error	Fatal error caused by a syntactical mistake	Omission of a semicolon or an imbalance of quotation marks, braces, or parentheses
Error	A general fatal error	Memory allocation problem

TABLE 3.2 Error Reporting Constants

Name
E_ERROR
E_WARNING
E_PARSE
E_NOTICE
E_STRICT
E_DEPRECATED

Using this information, you could add any of the following to a script:

```
error_reporting(E_WARNINGS);
error_reporting(E_ALL);
error_reporting(E_ALL & ~E_STRICT);
```

The first line says that only warnings and below should be reported. The second requests that all errors be reported. The last example states that you want to see all error messages except strict ones (the & ~ means *and not*). E_STRICT also notifies you of code that could be problematic in certain environments or future versions of PHP. Keep in mind that adjusting this setting doesn't prevent or create errors; it just affects whether or not errors are reported.

It's generally best to develop and test PHP scripts using the highest level of error reporting possible. To accomplish that, declare that you want *all errors* error reporting:

```
error_reporting(E_ALL);
```

Otherwise, the default level of error reporting (as of this writing) is **E_ALL & ~E_NOTICE & ~E_STRICT & ~E_DEPRECATED**. Unless you override this default setting, you will not be told about notices, strict errors, and deprecated code. As a developer, you want to be notified of any potential or actual problem with your code.

Let's apply this adjustment to the **handle_form.php** page.

To adjust error reporting in a script:

1. Open **handle_form.php** (Script 3.4) in your text editor or IDE, if it is not open already.

2. After the **ini_set()** line, add the following (**Script 3.5**):

   ```
   error_reporting(E_ALL);
   ```

Script 3.5 Adjust a script's level of error reporting to give you more or less feedback on potential and existing problems. In my opinion, more is always better.

```
1   <!doctype html>
2   <html lang="en">
3   <head>
4       <meta charset="utf-8">
5       <title>Your Feedback</title>
6   </head>
7   <body>
8   <?php // Script 3.5 - handle_form.php #3
9
10  ini_set('display_errors', 1); // Let me
    learn from my mistakes!
11  error_reporting(E_ALL); // Show all
    possible problems!
12
13  // This page receives the data from
    feedback.html.
14  // It will receive: title, name, email,
    response, comments, and submit in
    $_POST.
15
16  // Create shorthand versions of the
    variables:
17  $title = $_POST['title'];
18  $name = $_POST['name'];
19  $response = $_POST['response'];
20  $comments = $_POST['comments'];
21
22  // Print the received data:
23  print "<p>Thank you, $title $name, for
    your comments.</p>
24  <p>You stated that you found this
    example to be '$response' and
    added:<br>$comments</p>";
25
26  ?>
27  </body>
28  </html>
```

A Try the form one more time...

B ...and here's the result (if filled out completely and without any programmer errors).

3. Save the file as `handle_form.php`.

4. Place the file in the proper directory for your PHP-enabled server, and test it in your browser by submitting the form (**A** and **B**).

   At this point, if the form is filled out completely and the **$_POST** indexes exactly match the names of the form elements, you shouldn't see any errors (as in the figures). If any problems exist, including any potential problems (thanks to **E_STRICT**), they should be displayed and reported.

TIP The PHP manual lists all the error-reporting levels, but those listed here are the most important.

TIP The code in this book was tested using the highest level of error reporting: E_ALL.

TIP Prior to PHP 5.4.0, E_STRICT was not included in E_ALL, so the highest level of error reporting could be achieved using

`error_reporting(E_ALL | E_STRICT);`

The vertical bar, known as the pipe, is the equivalent of an "or" conditional.

Manually Sending Data to a Page

The last example for this chapter is a slight tangent to the other topics but plays off the idea of handling form data with PHP. As discussed in the earlier section "Choosing a Form Method," if a form uses the GET method, the resulting URL is something like

```
http://example.com/page.php?
→ var=value&age=20&...
```

The receiving page (here, **page.php**) is sent a series of *name=value* pairs, each of which is separated by an ampersand (**&**). The whole sequence is preceded by a question mark (immediately after the handling script's name).

To access the values passed to the page in this way, turn to the **$_GET** variable. Just as you would when using **$_POST**, refer to the specific name as an index in **$_GET**. In that example, **page.php** receives a **$_GET['var']** variable with a value of *value*, a **$_GET['age']** variable with a value of *20*, and so forth.

You can pass data to a PHP script in this way by creating an HTML form that uses the GET method. But you can also use this same idea to send data to a PHP page *without* the use of the form. Normally you'd do so by creating links:

```
<a href="page.php?id=22">
→ Some Link</a>
```

That link, which could be dynamically generated by PHP, will pass the value *22* to **page.php**, accessible in **$_GET['id']**.

To try this for yourself, the next pair of scripts will easily demonstrate this concept, using a hard-coded HTML page.

Script 3.6 This HTML page uses links to pass values to a PHP script in the URL (thereby emulating a form that uses the GET method).

```
1   <!doctype html>
2   <html lang="en">
3   <head>
4       <meta charset="utf-8">
5       <title>Greetings!</title>
6   </head>
7   <body>
8   <!-- Script 3.6 - hello.html -->
9   <div><p>Click a link to say hello:</p>
10
11  <ul>
12      <li><a href="hello.
        php?name=Michael">Michael</a></li>
13      <li><a href="hello.
        php?name=Celia">Celia</a></li>
14      <li><a href="hello.
        php?name=Jude">Jude</a></li>
15      <li><a href="hello.
        php?name=Sophie">Sophie</a></li>
16  </ul>
17
18  </div>
19  </body>
20  </html>
```

A The simple HTML page, with four links to the PHP script.

To create the HTML page:

1. Begin a new document in your text editor or IDE, to be named **hello.html** (**Script 3.6**):

```
<!doctype html>
<html lang="en">
<head>
  <meta charset="utf-8">
  <title>Greetings!</title>
</head>
<body>
<!-- Script 3.6 - hello.html -->
```

2. Create links to a PHP script, passing values along in the URL:

```
<ul>
   <li><a href="hello.php?name=
   → Michael">Michael</a></li>
   <li><a href="hello.php?name=
   → Celia">Celia</a></li>
   <li><a href="hello.php?name=
   → Jude">Jude</a></li>
   <li><a href="hello.php?name=
   → Sophie">Sophie</a></li>
</ul>
```

The premise here is that the user will see a list of links, each associated with a specific name **A**. When the user clicks a link, that name is passed to **hello.php** in the URL **B**.

continues on next page

```
8    <!-- Script 3.6 - hello.html -->
9    <div><p>Click a link to say hello:</p>
10
11   <ul>
12          <li><a href="hello.php?name=Michael">Michael</a></li>
13          <li><a href="hello.php?name=Celia">Celia</a></li>
14          <li><a href="hello.php?name=Jude">Jude</a></li>
15          <li><a href="hello.php?name=Sophie">Sophie</a></li>
16   </ul>
```

B The HTML source of the page shows how values are being passed along in the URL for the four links.

If you want to use different names, that's fine, but stick to one-word names without spaces or punctuation or else they won't be passed to the PHP script properly.

3. Complete the HTML page:

```
</div>
</body>
</html>
```

4. Save the script as **hello.html**, and place it within the proper directory on your PHP-enabled server.

5. Load the HTML page through a URL in your browser.

   Although you can view HTML pages without going through a URL, you'll click links in this page to access the PHP script, so you'll need to start off using a URL here. Don't click any of the links yet, because the PHP script doesn't exist!

To create the PHP script:

1. Begin a new document in your text editor or IDE, to be named **hello.php** (**Script 3.7**):

```
<!doctype html>
<html lang="en">
<head>
  <meta charset="utf-8">
  <title>Greetings!</title>
  <style type="text/css">
  .bold {
    font-weight: bolder;
  }
  </style>
</head>
<body>
```

Script 3.7 This PHP page refers to the **name** value passed in the URL in order to print a greeting.

```
1   <!doctype html>
2   <html lang="en">
3   <head>
4      <meta charset="utf-8">
5      <title>Greetings!</title>
6      <style type="text/css">
7      .bold {
8         font-weight: bolder;
9      }
10     </style>
11  </head>
12  <body>
13  <?php // Script 3.7 - hello.php
14
15  ini_set('display_errors', 1); // Let me
    learn from my mistakes!
16  error_reporting(E_ALL); // Show all
    possible problems!
17
18  // This page should receive a name value
    in the URL.
19
20  // Say "Hello":
21  $name = $_GET['name'];
22  print "<p>Hello, <span
    class=\"bold\">$name</span>!</p>";
23
24  ?>
25  </body>
26  </html>
```

C By clicking the first link, *Michael* is passed along in the URL and is greeted by name.

D By clicking the second link, *Celia* is sent along in the URL and is also greeted by name.

2. Begin the PHP code:

```
<?php // Script 3.7 - hello.php
```

3. Address the error management, if desired:

```
ini_set('display_errors', 1);
error_reporting(E_ALL);
```

These two lines, which configure how PHP responds to errors, are explained in the pages leading up to this section. They may or may not be necessary for your situation but can be helpful.

4. Use the **name** value passed in the URL to create a greeting:

```
$name = $_GET['name'];
print "<p>Hello, <span class=
→ \"bold\">$name</span>!</p>";
```

The **name** variable is sent to the page through the URL (see Script 3.6). To access that value, refer to **$_GET['name']**. Again, you would use **$_GET** (as opposed to **$_POST**) because the value is coming from a GET request.

As with earlier PHP scripts, the value in the predefined variable (**$_GET**) is first assigned to another variable, to simplify the syntax in the **print** statement.

5. Complete the PHP code and the HTML page:

```
?>
</body>
</html>
```

6. Save the script as **hello.php**, and place it within the proper directory on your PHP-enabled server.

It should be saved in the same directory as **hello.html** (Script 3.6).

7. Click the links in **hello.html** to view the result **C** and **D**.

continues on next page

TIP If you run `hello.php` directly (that is, without clicking any links), you'll get an error notice because no name value would be passed along in the URL **E**.

TIP Because `hello.php` reads a value from the URL, it actually works independently of `hello.html`. For example, you can directly edit the `hello.php` URL to greet anyone, even if `hello.html` does not have a link for that name **F**.

TIP If you want to use a link to send multiple values to a script, separate the name=value pairs (for example, `first_name=Larry`) with the ampersand (&). So, another link may be `hello.php?first_name=Larry&last_name=Ullman`. You should continue to use only single words, without punctuation or spaces, however (until you later learn about the `urlencode()` function).

TIP Although the example here—setting the value of a person's name—may not be very practical, this basic technique is useful on many occasions. For example, a PHP script might constitute a template, and the content of the resulting web page would differ based on the values the page received in the URL.

E If the `$_GET['name']` variable isn't assigned a value, the browser prints out this awkward message, along with the error notice.

F Any value assigned to **name** (lowercase) in the URL is used by the PHP script.

Review and Pursue

If you have any problems with the review questions or the pursue prompts, turn to the book's supporting forum (www.LarryUllman.com/forums/).

Review

- What is the significance of a form's **action** attribute?

- What is the significance of a form's **method** attribute? Is it more secure to use GET or POST? Which method type can be bookmarked in the browser?

- What predefined variable will contain the data from a form submission? Note: There are multiple answers.

- Why must an HTML page that contains a form that's being submitted to a PHP script be loaded through a URL?

- Under what circumstances will attempts to enable **display_errors** in a script not succeed? Why is it less secure to enable **display_errors** on live sites?

Pursue

- Load **feedback.html** in your browser without going through a URL (that is, the address bar would likely start with *file://*). Fill out and submit the form. Observe the result so that you can recognize this problem, and understand its cause, in case you see similar results in the future.

- If you have not already, and if you can, make sure that **display_errors** is enabled on your development environment.

- If you have not already, and if you can, make sure that **error_reporting** is set to **E_ALL** on your development environment (or **E_ALL | E_STRICT** in earlier versions of PHP).

- Try introducing different errors in a PHP script—by improperly balancing quotation marks, failing to use semicolons, referring to variables improperly, and so on—to see the result.

- Experiment with the **hello.html** and **hello.php** pages to send different values, including numbers, to the PHP script through the URL.

- Create a variation on **hello.html** that sends multiple *name=value* pairs to a PHP script. Have the PHP script then print all the received values.

- If you are the inquisitive type and don't mind waiting for answers, try passing more complicated values to a page through the URL. Try using spaces and punctuation to see what happens.

- Create a new HTML form that performs a task you envision yourself needing (or a lighter-weight version of that functionality). Then create the PHP script that handles the form, printing just the received data.

Using Numbers

Chapter 2, "Variables," briefly discussed the various types of variables, how to assign values to them, and how they're generally used. In this chapter, you'll work specifically with number variables—both integers (whole numbers) and floating-point numbers (aka floats or decimals).

You'll begin by creating an HTML form that will be used to generate number variables. Then you'll learn how to perform basic arithmetic, how to format numbers, and how to cope with operator precedence. The last two sections of this chapter cover incrementing and decrementing numbers, plus generating random numbers. Throughout the chapter, you'll also learn about other useful number-related PHP functions.

Creating the Form

Most of the PHP examples in this chapter will perform various calculations based on an e-commerce premise. A form will take price, quantity, discount amount, tax rate, and shipping cost 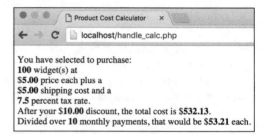, and the PHP script that handles the form will return a total cost. That cost will also be broken down by the number of payments the user wants to make in order to generate a monthly cost value **B**.

To start, let's create an HTML page that allows the user to enter the values.

To create the HTML form:

1. Begin a new HTML document in your text editor or IDE, to be named **calculator.html** (Script 4.1):

   ```
   <!doctype html>
   <html lang="en">
   <head>
     <meta charset="utf-8">
     <title>Product Cost Calculator
     → </title>
   </head>
   <body><!-- Script 4.1 -
   → calculator.html -->
   <div><p>Fill out this form to
   → calculate the total cost:</p>
   ```

2. Create the initial form tag:

   ```
   <form action="handle_calc.php"
   method="post">
   ```

   This form tag begins the HTML form. Its **action** attribute indicates that the form data will be submitted to a page named **handle_calc.php**. The tag's **method** attribute tells the page to use POST to send the data. See Chapter 3, "HTML Forms and PHP," for more details on choosing a method.

A This form takes numbers from the user and sends them to a PHP page.

B The PHP script performs a series of calculations on the submitted data and outputs the results. The results will look like this by the end of the chapter.

Script 4.1 This basic HTML form will provide the numbers for various mathematical calculations over multiple PHP scripts.

```
1    <!doctype html>
2    <html lang="en">
3    <head>
4        <meta charset="utf-8">
5        <title>Product Cost Calculator</title>
6    </head>
7    <body><!-- Script 4.1 - calculator.html
     -->
8    <div><p>Fill out this form to calculate
     the total cost:</p>
9
10   <form action="handle_calc.php"
     method="post">
11
12   <p>Price: <input type="text"
     name="price" size="5"></p>
13
14   <p>Quantity: <input type="number"
     name="quantity" size="5" min="1"
     value="1"></p>
15
16   <p>Discount: <input type="text"
     name="discount" size="5"></p>
17
18   <p>Tax: <input type="text" name="tax"
     size="5"> (%)</p>
19
20   <p>Shipping method: <select
     name="shipping">
21   <option value="5.00">Slow and steady</
     option>
22   <option value="8.95">Put a move on it.</
     option>
23   <option value="19.36">I need it
     yesterday!</option>
24   </select></p>
25
26   <p>Number of payments to make: <input
     type="number" name="payments" size="5"
     min="1" value="1"></p>
27
28   <input type="submit" name="submit"
     value="Calculate!">
29
30   </form>
31
32   </div>
33   </body>
34   </html>
```

3. Create the inputs for the price, quantity, discount, and tax:

```
<p>Price: <input type="text"
→ name="price" size="5"></p>
<p>Quantity: <input type=
→ "number" name="quantity"
size="5" min="1" value="1"></p>
<p>Discount: <input type="text"
→ name="discount" size="5"></p>
<p>Tax: <input type="text"
→ name="tax" size="5"> (%)</p>
```

Although HTML5 does have a number input type, it's not always the right solution because it's more naturally suited to taking integer values. For that reason, the quantity input will be a number type, whereas the others will be text.

To guide the user, a parenthetical indicates that the tax should be entered as a percent.

Remember that the names used for the inputs should correspond to valid PHP variable names: Use letters, numbers, and the underscore only; don't start with a number; and so forth.

continues on next page

4. Add a field in which the user can select a shipping method:

```
<p>Shipping method: <select
→ name="shipping">
<option value="5.00">Slow and
→ steady</option>
<option value="8.95">Put a move
→ on it.</option>
<option value="19.36">I need it
→ yesterday!</option>
</select></p>
```

The shipping selection is made using a drop-down menu. The value of the selected option is the cost for that option. If the user selects, for example, the *Put a move on it.* option, the value of **$_POST['shipping']** in **handle_calc.php** will be *8.95*.

5. Complete the HTML form:

```
<p>Number of payments to make:
→ <input type="number"
→ name="payments" size="5"
→ min="1" value="1"></p>
<input type="submit" name=
→ "submit" value="Calculate!">
</form>
```

The final two input types take a number for how many payments are required and then create a submit button (labeled *Calculate!*). The closing form tag marks the end of the form section of the page.

6. Complete the HTML page:

```
</div>
</body>
</html>
```

7. Save the script as **calculator.html**, and view it in your browser.

Because this is an HTML page, you can view it directly in a browser.

```
1   <!doctype html>
2   <html lang="en">
3   <head>
4     <meta charset="utf-8">
5     <title>Product Cost Calculator</
    title>
6     <style type="text/css">
7       .number { font-weight: bold; }
8     </style>
9   </head>
10  <body>
11  <?php // Script 4.2 - handle_calc.php
12  /* This script takes values from
    calculator.html and performs
13  total cost and monthly payment
    calculations. */
14
15  // Address error handling, if you want.
16
17  // Get the values from the $_POST array:
18  $price = $_POST['price'];
19  $quantity = $_POST['quantity'];
20  $discount = $_POST['discount'];
21  $tax = $_POST['tax'];
22  $shipping = $_POST['shipping'];
23  $payments = $_POST['payments'];
24
25  // Calculate the total:
26  $total = $price * $quantity;
27  $total = $total + $shipping;
28  $total = $total - $discount;
29
30  // Determine the tax rate:
31  $taxrate = $tax / 100;
32  $taxrate = $taxrate + 1;
33
34  // Factor in the tax rate:
35  $total = $total * $taxrate;
36
37  // Calculate the monthly payments:
38  $monthly = $total / $payments;
39
```

code continues on next page

Performing Arithmetic

Just as you learned in grade school, basic mathematics involves the principles of addition, subtraction, multiplication, and division. These are performed in PHP using the most obvious operators:

- Addition (**+**)
- Subtraction (**-**)
- Multiplication (*****)
- Division (**/**)

To use these operators, you'll create a PHP script that calculates the total cost for the sale of some widgets. This handling script could be the basis of a shopping cart application—a very practical web page feature (although in this case the relevant number values will come from **calculator.html**).

When you're writing this script, be sure to note the comments (**Script 4.2**) used to illuminate the different lines of code and the reasoning behind them.

To create your sales cost calculator:

1. Create a new document in your text editor or IDE, to be named **handle_calc.php** (Script 4.2):

```
<!doctype html>
<html lang="en">
<head>
  <meta charset="utf-8">
  <title>Product Cost Calculator
  </title>
  <style type="text/css">
    .number {font-weight:bold;}
  </style>
</head>
<body>
```

continues on next page

The head of the document defines one CSS class, named *number*. Any element within the page that has that class value will be given extra font weight. In other words, when the numbers from the form, and the results of the various calculations, are printed in the script's output, they'll be made more obvious.

2. Insert the PHP tag and address error handling, if desired:

```
<?php // Script 4.2 -
→ handle_calc.php
```

Depending on your PHP configuration, you may or may not want to add a couple of lines that turn on **display_errors** and adjust the level of error reporting. See Chapter 3 for specifics.

(However, as also mentioned in that chapter, it's best to make these adjustments in PHP's primary configuration file.)

3. Assign the **$_POST** elements to local variables:

```
$price = $_POST['price'];
$quantity = $_POST['quantity'];
$discount = $_POST['discount'];
$tax = $_POST['tax'];
$shipping = $_POST['shipping'];
$payments = $_POST['payments'];
```

The script will receive all the form data in the predefined **$_POST** variable. To access individual form values, refer to **$_POST['index']**, replacing *index* with the corresponding form element's **name** value. These values are assigned to individual local variables here, to make it easier to use them throughout the rest of the script.

Note that each variable is given a descriptive name and is written entirely in lowercase letters.

Script 4.2 *continued*

```
40   // Print out the results:
41   print "<p>You have selected to
     purchase:<br>
42   <span class=\"number\">$quantity</
     span> widget(s) at <br>
43   $<span class=\"number\">$price</span>
     price each plus a <br>
44   $<span class=\"number\">$shipping</
     span> shipping cost and a <br>
45   <span class=\"number\">$tax</span>
     percent tax rate.<br>
46   After your $<span
     class=\"number\">$discount</span>
     discount, the total cost is
47   $<span class=\"number\">$total</
     span>.<br>
48   Divided over <span
     class=\"number\">$payments</span>
     monthly payments, that would be
     $<span class=\"number\">$monthly</
     span> each.</p>";
49
50   ?>
51   </body>
52   </html>
```

4. Begin calculating the total cost:

```php
$total = $price * $quantity;
$total = $total + $shipping;
$total = $total - $discount;
```

The asterisk (*) indicates multiplication in PHP, so the total is first calculated as the number of items purchased (**$quantity**) multiplied by the price. Then the shipping cost is added to the total value (remember that the shipping cost correlates to the **value** attribute of each shipping drop-down menu's **option** tags), and the discount is subtracted.

Note that it's perfectly acceptable to determine a variable's value in part by using that variable's existing value (as is done in the last two lines).

5. Calculate the tax rate and the new total:

```php
$taxrate = $tax / 100;
$taxrate = $taxrate + 1;
$total = $total * $taxrate;
```

The tax rate should be entered as a percent—for example, 8 or 5.75. This number is then divided by 100 to get the decimal equivalent of the percent (.08 or .0575). Finally, you calculate how much something costs with tax by adding 1 to the percent and then multiplying that new rate by the total. This is the mathematical equivalent of multiplying the decimal tax rate times the total and then adding this result to the total (for example, a 5 percent tax on $100 is $5, making the total $105, which is the same as multiplying $100 times 1.05).

6. Calculate the monthly payment:

```php
$monthly = $total / $payments;
```

As an example of division, assume that the widgets can be paid for over the course of many months. Hence, you divide the total by the number of payments to find the monthly payment.

7. Print the results:

```php
print "<p>You have selected to
  purchase:<br>
<span class=\"number\">$quantity
  </span> widget(s) at <br>
$<span class=\"number\">$price
  </span> price each plus a <br>
$<span class=\"number\">$shipping
  </span> shipping cost and a <br>
<span class=\"number\">$tax
  </span> percent tax rate.<br>
After your $<span class=
  \"number\">$discount</span>
  discount, the total cost is
$<span class=\"number\">$total
  </span>.<br>
Divided over <span class=
  \"number\">$payments</span>
  monthly payments, that would be
  $<span class=\"number\">
  $monthly</span> each.</p>";
```

The **print** statement sends every value to the browser along with some text. To make it easier to read, **
** tags are added to format the browser result; in addition, the **print** function operates over multiple lines to make the PHP code cleaner. Each variable's value will be highlighted in the browser by wrapping it within span tags that have a **class** attribute of *number* (see Step 1).

8. Close the PHP section, and complete the HTML page:

```php
?>
</body>
</html>
```

9. Save the script as **handle_calc.php**, and place it in the proper directory for your PHP-enabled server.

Make sure that **calculator.html** is in the same directory.

continues on next page

10. Test the script in your browser by filling out **Ⓐ** and submitting **Ⓑ** the form.

Not to belabor the point, but make sure you start by loading the HTML form through a URL (*http://something*) so that when it's submitted, the PHP script is also run through a URL.

You can experiment with these values to see how effectively your calculator works. If you omit any values, the resulting message will just be a little odd but the calculations should still work **Ⓒ**.

TIP As you'll certainly notice, the calculator comes up with numbers that don't correspond well to real dollar values (see **Ⓑ** and **Ⓒ**). In the next section, "Formatting Numbers," you'll learn how to address this issue.

TIP If you want to print the value of the total before tax or before the discount (or both), you can do so in two ways. You can insert the appropriate `print` statements immediately after the proper value has been determined but before the `$total` variable has been changed again. Or you can use new variables to represent the values of the subsequent calculations (for example, `$total_with_tax` and `$total_less_discount`).

TIP Attempting to print a dollar sign followed by the value of a variable, such as $10 (where 10 comes from a variable), has to be handled carefully. You can't use the syntax `$$variable`, because the combination of two dollar signs creates a type of variable that's too complex to discuss in this book. One solution is to put something—a space or an HTML tag, as in this example—between the dollar sign and the variable name. Another option is to escape the first dollar sign:

```
print "The total is \$$total";
```

A third option is to use concatenation, which is introduced in the next chapter.

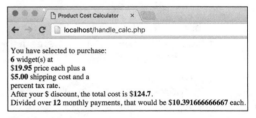

🅐 The HTML form...

You have selected to purchase:
6 widget(s) at
$19.95 price each plus a
$5.00 shipping cost and a
6 percent tax rate.
After your **$10.00** discount, the total cost is **$121.582**.
Divided over **12** monthly payments, that would be **$10.131833333333** each.

🅑 ...and the resulting calculations.

You have selected to purchase:
6 widget(s) at
$19.95 price each plus a
$5.00 shipping cost and a
percent tax rate.
After your $ discount, the total cost is **$124.7**.
Divided over **12** monthly payments, that would be **$10.391666666667** each.

🅒 You can omit or change any value and rerun the calculator. Here the tax and discount values have been omitted.

TIP This script performs differently, depending on whether the various fields are submitted. The only truly problematic field is the number of monthly payments: If this is omitted, you'll see a division-by-zero warning. Chapter 6, "Control Structures," will cover validating form data before it's used.

Formatting Numbers

Although the calculator is on its way to being practical, it still has one legitimate problem: You can't ask someone to make a monthly payment of $10.13183333! To create more usable numbers, you need to format them.

Two functions are appropriate for this purpose. The first, **round()**, rounds a value to a specified number of decimal places. The function's first argument is the number to be rounded. This can be either a number or a variable that has a numeric value. The second argument is optional; it represents the number of decimal places to which to round. If omitted, the number will be rounded to the nearest integer. For example:

```
round(4.30); // 4
round(4.289, 2); // 4.29
$num = 236.26985;
round($num); // 236
```

The other function you can use in this situation is **number_format()**. It works like **round()** in that it takes a number (or a variable with a numeric value) and an optional decimal specifier. This function has the added benefit of formatting the number with commas, the way it would commonly be written:

```
number_format(428.4959, 2); // 428.50
number_format(428, 2); // 428.00
number_format(1234567); // 1,234,567
```

Let's rewrite the PHP script to format the numbers appropriately.

To format numbers:

1. Open **handle_calc.php** in your text editor or IDE, if it is not already open (Script 4.2).

2. After all the calculations but before the **print** statement, add the following (**Script 4.3**):

   ```
   $total = number_format($total, 2);
   $monthly = number_format
   → ($monthly, 2);
   ```

   To format these two numbers, apply this function after every calculation has been made but before they're sent to the browser. The second argument (the 2) indicates that the resulting number should have exactly two decimal places; this setting rounds the numbers and adds zeros at the end, as necessary.

Script 4.3 The `number_format()` function is applied to the values of two number variables, so they are more appropriate to the example.

```
1    <!doctype html>
2    <html lang="en">
3    <head>
4        <meta charset="utf-8">
5        <title>Product Cost Calculator</
     title>
6        <style type="text/css">
7            .number { font-weight: bold;}
8        </style>
9    </head>
10   <body>
11   <?php // Script 4.3 - handle_calc.php #2
12   /* This script takes values from
     calculator.html and performs
13   total cost and monthly payment
     calculations. */
14
15   // Address error handling, if you want.
16
17   // Get the values from the $_POST array:
18   $price = $_POST['price'];
19   $quantity = $_POST['quantity'];
20   $discount = $_POST['discount'];
21   $tax = $_POST['tax'];
22   $shipping = $_POST['shipping'];
23   $payments = $_POST['payments'];
24
25   // Calculate the total:
26   $total = $price * $quantity;
27   $total = $total + $shipping;
28   $total = $total - $discount;
29
30   // Determine the tax rate:
31   $taxrate = $tax/100;
32   $taxrate = $taxrate + 1;
33
34   // Factor in the tax rate:
35   $total = $total * $taxrate;
36
37   // Calculate the monthly payments:
38   $monthly = $total / $payments;
39
40   // Apply the proper formatting:
41   $total = number_format($total, 2);
42   $monthly = number_format($monthly, 2);
43
```

code continues on next page

Script 4.3 *continued*

```
44   // Print out the results:
45   print "<p>You have selected to
     purchase:<br>
46   <span class=\"number\">$quantity</span>
     widget(s) at <br>
47   $<span class=\"number\">$price</span>
     price each plus a <br>
48   $<span class=\"number\">$shipping</span>
     shipping cost and a <br>
49   <span class=\"number\">$tax</span>
     percent tax rate.<br>
50   After your $<span
     class=\"number\">$discount</span>
     discount, the total cost is
51   $<span class=\"number\">$total</
     span>.<br>
52   Divided over <span
     class=\"number\">$payments</span>
     monthly payments, that would be $<span
     class=\"number\">$monthly</span> each.</
     p>";
53
54   ?>
55   </body>
56   </html>
```

3. Save the file, place it in the same directory as `calculator.html`, and test it in your browser **A** and **B**.

TIP Another, much more complex way to format numbers is to use the `printf()` and `sprintf()` functions. Because of their tricky syntax, they're not discussed in this book; see the PHP manual for more information.

TIP Non-Windows versions of PHP also have a `money_format()` function, which can be used in lieu of `number_format()`.

TIP The `round()` function rounds exact halves (.5, .05, .005, and so on) up, although this behavior can be configured. See the PHP manual for details.

TIP In PHP, function calls can have spaces between the function name and its parentheses or not. Both of these are fine:

```
round ($num);
round($num);
```

TIP The `number_format()` function takes two other optional arguments that let you specify what characters to use to indicate a decimal point and break up thousands. This is useful, for example, for cultures that write 1,000.89 as 1.000,89. See the PHP manual for the correct syntax, if you want to use this option.

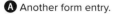

Fill out this form to calculate the total cost:

Price: 99.00

Quantity: 4

Discount: 25.00

Tax: 5.5 (%)

Shipping method: Put a move on it.

Number of payments to make: 24

[Calculate!]

A Another form entry.

Product Cost Calculator

localhost/handle_calc.php

You have selected to purchase:
4 widget(s) at
$99.00 price each plus a
$8.95 shipping cost and a
5.5 percent tax rate.
After your **$25.00** discount, the total cost is **$400.85**.
Divided over **24** monthly payments, that would be **$16.70** each.

B The updated version of the script returns more appropriate number values thanks to the `number_format()` function.

Understanding Precedence

Inevitably, after a discussion of the various sorts of mathematical operators comes the discussion of precedence. *Precedence* refers to the order in which a series of calculations are executed. For example, what is the value of the following variable?

```
$number = 10 - 4 / 2;
```

Is **$number** worth 3 (10 minus 4 equals 6, divided by 2 equals 3) or 8 (4 divided by 2 equals 2, subtracted from 10 equals 8)? The answer here is 8, because division takes precedence over subtraction.

Appendix B, "Resources and Next Steps," shows the complete list of operator precedence for PHP (including operators that haven't been covered yet). However, instead of attempting to memorize a large table of peculiar characters, you forgo any deliberation by using parentheses. Parentheses always take precedence over any other operator. Thus:

```
$number = (10 - 4) / 2; // 3
$number = 10 - (4 / 2); // 8
```

Using parentheses in your calculations ensures that you never see peculiar results due to precedence issues. Parentheses can also be used to rewrite complex calculations in fewer lines of code. Let's rewrite the **handle_calc.php** script, combining multiple lines into one by using parentheses, while maintaining accuracy.

To manage precedence:

1. Open **handle_calc.php** in your text editor or IDE, if it is not already open (Script 4.3).

Script 4.4 By using parentheses, calculations made over multiple lines (compare with Script 4.3) can be condensed without affecting the script's mathematical accuracy.

```
1   <!doctype html>
2   <html lang="en">
3   <head>
4      <meta charset="utf-8">
5      <title>Product Cost Calculator</
    title>
6      <style type="text/css">
7         .number { font-weight: bold;}
8      </style>
9   </head>
10  <body>
11  <?php // Script 4.4 - handle_calc.php #3
12  /* This script takes values from
       calculator.html and performs
13  total cost and monthly payment
       calculations. */
14
15  // Address error handling, if you want.
16
17  // Get the values from the $_POST array:
18  $price = $_POST['price'];
19  $quantity = $_POST['quantity'];
20  $discount = $_POST['discount'];
21  $tax = $_POST['tax'];
22  $shipping = $_POST['shipping'];
23  $payments = $_POST['payments'];
24
25  // Calculate the total:
26  $total = (($price * $quantity) +
       $shipping) - $discount;
27
28  // Determine the tax rate:
29  $taxrate = ($tax / 100) + 1;
30
31  // Factor in the tax rate:
32  $total = $total * $taxrate;
33
34  // Calculate the monthly payments:
35  $monthly = $total / $payments;
36
37  // Apply the proper formatting:
38  $total = number_format ($total, 2);
39  $monthly = number_format ($monthly, 2);
40
```

code continues on next page

Script 4.4 *continued*

```
41    // Print out the results:
42    print "<p>You have selected to
      purchase:<br>
43    <span class=\"number\">$quantity</span>
      widget(s) at <br>
44    $<span class=\"number\">$price</span>
      price each plus a <br>
45    $<span class=\"number\">$shipping</span>
      shipping cost and a <br>
46    <span class=\"number\">$tax</span>
      percent tax rate.<br>
47    After your $<span
      class=\"number\">$discount</span>
      discount, the total cost is
48    $<span class=\"number\">$total</
      span>.<br>
49    Divided over <span
      class=\"number\">$payments</span>
      monthly payments, that would be $<span
      class=\"number\">$monthly</span> each.</
      p>";
50
51    ?>
52    </body>
53    </html>
```

Ⓐ Testing the form one more time.

2. Replace the three lines that initially cal-culate the order total with the following (**Script 4.4**):

$total = (($price * $quantity) +
→ $shipping) - $discount;

In this script, it's fine to make all the calculations in one step, as long as you use parentheses to ensure that the math works properly. The other option is to memorize PHP's rules of prece-dence for multiple operators, but using parentheses is a lot easier.

3. Change the two lines that calculate and add in the tax to this:

$taxrate = ($tax / 100) + 1;

Again, the tax calculations can be made in one line instead of two separate ones.

4. Save the script, place it in the same directory as **calculator.html**, and test it in your browser **Ⓐ** **Ⓑ**.

TIP Be sure that you match your parentheses consistently as you create your formulas (every opening parenthesis requires a closing paren-thesis). Failure to do so will cause parse errors.

TIP Granted, using the methods applied here, you could combine all the total calculations into just one line of code (instead of three)—but there is such a thing as oversimplifying.

Ⓑ Even though the calculations have been condensed, the math works out the same. If you see different results or get an error message, double-check your parentheses for balance (an equal number of opening and closing parentheses).

Incrementing and Decrementing a Number

PHP, like most programming languages, includes shortcuts that let you avoid ugly constructs such as

`$tax = $tax + 1;`

When you need to increase the value of a variable by 1 (known as an *incremental* adjustment) or decrease the value of a variable by 1 (a *decremental* adjustment), you can use **++** and **--**, respectively:

```
$var = 20; // 20
$var++; // 21
$var++; // 22
$var--; // 21
```

Solely for the sake of testing this concept, you'll rewrite the `handle_calc.php` script one last time.

To increment the value of a variable:

1. Open `handle_calc.php` in your text editor or IDE, if it is not already open (Script 4.4).

2. Change the tax rate calculation from Script 4.3 to read as follows (**Script 4.5**):

   ```
   $taxrate = $tax / 100;
   $taxrate++;
   ```

   The first line calculates the tax rate as the **$tax** value divided by 100. The second line increments this value by 1 so that it can be multiplied by the total to determine the total with tax.

3. Save the script, place it in the same directory as **calculator.html**, and test it in your browser ❶ ❷.

Script 4.5 Incrementing or decrementing a number is a common operation using **++** or **--**, respectively.

```
1   <!doctype html>
2   <html lang="en">
3   <head>
4       <meta charset="utf-8">
5       <title>Product Cost Calculator</
    title>
6       <style type="text/css">
7           .number { font-weight: bold;}
8       </style>
9   </head>
10  <body>
11  <?php // Script 4.3 - handle_calc.php #4
12  /* This script takes values from
    calculator.html and performs
13  total cost and monthly payment
    calculations. */
14
15  // Address error handling, if you want.
16
17  // Get the values from the $_POST array:
18  $price = $_POST['price'];
19  $quantity = $_POST['quantity'];
20  $discount = $_POST['discount'];
21  $tax = $_POST['tax'];
22  $shipping = $_POST['shipping'];
23  $payments = $_POST['payments'];
24
25  // Calculate the total:
26  $total = (($price * $quantity) +
    $shipping) - $discount;
27
28  // Determine the tax rate:
29  $taxrate = $tax / 100;
30  $taxrate++;
31
32  // Factor in the tax rate:
33  $total = $total * $taxrate;
34
35  // Calculate the monthly payments:
36  $monthly = $total / $payments;
37
38  // Apply the proper formatting:
39  $total = number_format ($total, 2);
40  $monthly = number_format ($monthly, 2);
41
```

code continues on next page

Script 4.5 *continued*

```
42    // Print out the results:
43    print "<p>You have selected to
      purchase:<br>
44    <span class=\"number\">$quantity</span>
      widget(s) at <br>
45    $<span class=\"number\">$price</span>
      price each plus a <br>
46    $<span class=\"number\">$shipping</span>
      shipping cost and a <br>
47    <span class=\"number\">$tax</span>
      percent tax rate.<br>
48    After your $<span
      class=\"number\">$discount</span>
      discount, the total cost is
49    $<span class=\"number\">$total</
      span>.<br>
50    Divided over <span
      class=\"number\">$payments</span>
      monthly payments, that would be $<span
      class=\"number\">$monthly</span> each.</
      p>";
51
52    ?>
53    </body>
54    </html>
```

TIP Although functionally it doesn't matter whether you code $taxrate = $taxrate + 1; or the abbreviated $taxrate++, the latter method (using the increment operator) is more professional and common.

TIP In Chapter 6, you'll see how the increment operator is commonly used in conjunction with loops.

Arithmetic Assignment Operators

PHP also supports a combination of mathematical and assignment operators. These are +=, -=, *=, and /=. Each will assign a value to a variable by performing a calculation on it. For example, these next two lines both add 5 to a variable:

```
$num = $num + 5;
$num += 5;
```

This means the **handle_calc.php** script could determine the tax rate using this:

```
$tax = $_POST['tax']; // Say, 5
$tax /= 100; // Now $tax is .05
$tax += 1; // 1.05
```

You'll frequently see these shorthand ways of performing arithmetic.

Product Cost Calculator ×

← → C localhost/calculator.html

Fill out this form to calculate the total cost:

Price: 5.00

Quantity: 100

Discount: 10.00

Tax: 7.5 (%)

Shipping method: Slow and steady ◇

Number of payments to make: 10

[Calculate!]

A The last execution of the form.

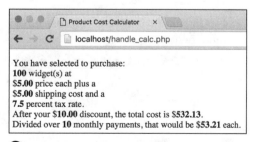

Product Cost Calculator ×

← → C localhost/handle_calc.php

You have selected to purchase:
100 widget(s) at
$5.00 price each plus a
$5.00 shipping cost and a
7.5 percent tax rate.
After your **$10.00** discount, the total cost is **$532.13**.
Divided over **10** monthly payments, that would be **$53.21** each.

B It won't affect your calculations if you use the long or short version of incrementing a variable (compare Scripts 4.4 and 4.5).

Creating Random Numbers

The last function you'll learn about in this chapter is `mt_rand()`, a random-number generator. All it does is output a random number:

```php
$n = mt_rand(); // 31
$n = mt_rand(); // 87
```

The `mt_rand()` function can also take minimum and maximum parameters, if you prefer to limit the generated number to a specific range:

```php
$n = mt_rand(0, 10);
```

These values are *inclusive*, so in this case 0 and 10 are feasible returned values.

As an example of generating random numbers, let's create a simple "Lucky Numbers" script.

To generate random numbers:

1. Begin a new document in your text editor or IDE, to be named **random.php** (**Script 4.6**):

   ```php
   <!doctype html>
   <html lang="en">
   <head>
     <meta charset="utf-8">
     <title>Lucky Numbers</title>
   </head>
   <body>
   ```

2. Include the PHP tag and address error management, if you need to:

   ```php
   <?php // Script 4.6 - random.php
   ```

Script 4.6 The `rand()` function generates a random number.

```php
1   <!doctype html>
2   <html lang="en">
3   <head>
4       <meta charset="utf-8">
5       <title>Lucky Numbers</title>
6   </head>
7   <body>
8   <?php // Script 4.6 - random.php
9   /* This script generates 3 random
    numbers. */
10
11  // Address error handling, if you want.
12
13  // Create three random numbers:
14  $n1 = mt_and(1, 99);
15  $n2 = mt_rand(1, 99);
16  $n3 = mt_rand(1, 99);
17
18  // Print out the numbers:
19  print "<p>Your lucky numbers are:<br>
20  $n1<br>
21  $n2<br>
22  $n3</p>";
23
24  ?>
25  </body>
26  </html>
```

A The three random numbers created by invoking the **mt_rand()** function.

B Running the script again produces different results.

3. Create three random numbers:

```
$n1 = mt_rand(1, 99);
$n2 = mt_rand(1, 99);
$n3 = mt_rand(1, 99);
```

This script prints out a person's lucky numbers, like those found on the back of a fortune cookie. These numbers are generated by calling the **mt_rand()** function three separate times and assigning each result to a different variable.

4. Print out the numbers:

```
print "<p>Your lucky numbers
are:<br>
$n1<br>
$n2<br>
$n3</p>";
```

The **print** statement is fairly simple. The numbers are printed, each on its own line, by using the HTML break tag.

5. Close the PHP code and the HTML page:

```
?>
</body>
</html>
```

6. Save the file as **random.php**, place it in the proper directory for your PHP-enabled server, and test it in your browser **A**. Refresh the page to see different numbers **B**.

TIP The getrandmax() function returns the largest possible random number that can be created using mt_rand(). This value differs by operating system.

TIP PHP has other functions for generating random numbers, such as random_int(). Unlike mt_rand(), random_init() creates cryptographically secure random numbers.

Review and Pursue

If you have any problems with the review questions or the pursue prompts, turn to the book's supporting forum (www.LarryUllman.com/forums/).

Review

- What are the four primary arithmetic operators?
- Why will the following code not work:

  ```
  print "The total is $$total";
  ```

  What must be done instead?
- Why must an HTML page that contains a form that's being submitted to a PHP script be loaded through a URL?
- What functions can be used to format numerical values? How do you format numbers to a specific number of decimals?
- What is the importance of operator precedence?
- What are the incremental and decremental operators?
- What are the arithmetic assignment operators?

Pursue

- Look up the PHP manual page for one of the new functions mentioned in this chapter. Use the links on that page to investigate a couple of other number-related functions that PHP has.
- Create another HTML form for taking numeric values. Then create the PHP script that receives the form data, performs some calculations, formats the values, and prints the results.

Other Mathematical Functions

PHP has a number of built-in functions for manipulating mathematical data. This chapter introduced **round()**, **number_format()**, and **mt_rand()**.

PHP has broken **round()** into two other functions. The first, **ceil()**, rounds every number to the next highest integer. The second, **floor()**, rounds every number to the next lowest integer.

Another function the calculator page could make good use of is **abs()**, which returns the absolute value of a number. In case you don't remember your absolute values, the function works like this:

```
$number = abs(-23); // 23
$number = abs(23); // 23
```

In layman's terms, the absolute value of a number is always a positive number.

Beyond these functions, PHP supports all the trigonometry, exponent, base conversion, and logarithm functions you'll ever need. See the PHP manual for more information.

Using Strings

As introduced in Chapter 2, "Variables," a second category of variables used by PHP is strings—a collection of characters enclosed within either single or double quotation marks. The value of a string variable may be a single letter, a word, a sentence, a paragraph, HTML code, or even a jumble of nonsensical letters, numbers, and symbols (which might represent a password). Strings may be the most common variable type used in PHP.

This chapter covers PHP's most basic built-in functions and operators for manipulating string data, regardless of whether the string originates from a form or is first declared within the script. Some common techniques will be introduced: joining strings together, trimming strings, and encoding strings. Other uses for strings are illustrated in subsequent chapters.

In This Chapter

Creating the HTML Form

As in Chapter 3, "HTML Forms and PHP," let's begin by creating an HTML form that sends different values—in the form of string variables—to a PHP script. The theoretical example being used is an online bulletin board or forum where users can post a message, their email address, and their first and last names **A**.

To create the HTML form:

1. Begin a new HTML document in your text editor or IDE, to be named **posting.html** (Script 5.1):

```
<!doctype html>
<html lang="en">
<head>
  <meta charset="utf-8">
  <title>Forum Posting</title>
</head>
<body>
<!-- Script 5.1 - posting.html -->
<div><p>Please complete this form
→ to submit your posting:</p>
```

2. Create the initial form tag:

```
<form action="handle_post.php"
→ method="post">
```

This form will send its data to the **handle_post.php** script and will use the POST method.

3. Add inputs for the first name, last name, and email address:

```
<p>First Name: <input type="text"
→ name="first_name" size="20"></p>
<p>Last Name: <input type="text"
→ name="last_name" size="20"></p>
<p>Email Address: <input type=
→ "email" name="email"
size="30"></p>
```

A This HTML form is the basis for most of the examples in this chapter.

Script 5.1 This form sends string data to a PHP script.

```
1   <!doctype html>
2   <html lang="en">
3   <head>
4       <meta charset="utf-8">
5       <title>Forum Posting</title>
6   </head>
7   <body>
8   <!-- Script 5.1 - posting.html -->
9   <div><p>Please complete this form to
    submit your posting:</p>
10
11  <form action="handle_post.php"
    method="post">
12
13      <p>First Name: <input type="text"
        name="first_name" size="20"></p>
14
15      <p>Last Name: <input type="text"
        name="last_name" size="20"></p>
16
17      <p>Email Address: <input type="email"
        name="email" size="30"></p>
18
19      <p>Posting: <textarea name="posting"
        rows="9" cols="30"></textarea></p>
20
21      <input type="submit" name="submit"
        value="Send My Posting">
22
23  </form>
24  </div>
25  </body>
26  </html>
```

The form uses two basic text input types and one email type. Remember that the various inputs' name values should adhere to the rules of PHP variable names (no spaces; must not begin with a number; must consist only of letters, numbers, and the underscore).

4. Add an input for the posting:

```
<p>Posting: <textarea name=
→ "posting" rows="9" cols="30">
→ </textarea></p>
```

The posting field is a **textarea**, which is a larger type of text input box.

5. Create a submit button, and close the form:

```
<input type="submit"
→ name="submit"
→ value="Send My Posting">
</form>
```

Every form must have a submit button (or a submit image).

6. Complete the HTML page:

```
</div>
</body>
</html>
```

continues on next page

7. Save the file as **posting.html**, place it in the appropriate directory on your PHP-enabled server, and view it in your browser Ⓐ.

This is an HTML page, so it doesn't have to be on a PHP-enabled server in order for you to view it. But because it will eventually send data to a PHP script, it's best to place the file on your server.

TIP Technically speaking, all form data, aside from uploaded files, is sent to the handling script as strings. This includes numeric data entered into text boxes, options selected from drop-down menus, checkbox or radio button values, and so forth. Even the form in Chapter 4, "Using Numbers," sent strings with numeric values to the handling script.

TIP Many forum systems written in PHP are freely available for your use. This book doesn't discuss how to fully develop one, but a multilingual forum is developed in my *PHP and MySQL for Dynamic Web Sites (Fourth Edition): Visual QuickPro Guide* (Peachpit Press, 2012).

TIP This book's website has a forum where readers can post questions and other readers (and the author) answer questions. You can find it at www.LarryUllman.com/forums/.

Concatenating Strings

Concatenation is an unwieldy term but a useful concept. It refers to the appending of one item onto another. Specifically, in programming, you concatenate *strings*. The period (**.**) is the operator for performing this action, and it's used like so:

```
$s1 = 'Hello, ';
$s2 = 'world!';
$greeting = $s1 . $s2;
```

The result of this concatenation is that the **$greeting** variable has a value of *Hello, world!*

Because of the way PHP deals with variables, the same effect could be accomplished using

```
$greeting = "$s1$s2";
```

This code works because PHP replaces variables within double quotation marks with their value. However, the formal method of using the period to concatenate strings is more commonly used and is recommended (it will be more obvious what's occurring in your code).

Another way of performing concatenation involves the *concatenation assignment operator*:

```
$greeting = 'Hello, ';
$greeting .= 'world!';
```

This second line roughly means "assign to **$greeting** its current value plus the concatenation of *world!*" The end result is **$greeting** having the value *Hello, world!* once again.

The **posting.html** script sends several string variables to the **handle_post.php** page. Of those variables, the first and last names could logically be concatenated. You'll write the PHP script with this in mind.

To use concatenation:

1. Begin a new document in your text editor or IDE, to be named **handle_post.php** (Script 5.2):

```
<!doctype html>
<html lang="en">
<head>
    <meta charset="utf-8">
    <title>Forum Posting</title>
</head>
<body>
```

2. Create the initial PHP tag, and address error management, if necessary:

```
<?php // Script 5.2 -
→ handle_post.php
```

If you don't have **display_errors** enabled, or if **error_reporting** is set to the wrong level, see Chapter 3 for the lines to include here to alter those settings.

3. Assign the form data to local variables:

```
$first_name =
→ $_POST['first_name'];
$last_name =
→ $_POST['last_name'];
$posting = $_POST['posting'];
```

The form uses the POST method, so all the form data will be available in **$_POST**.

This example doesn't have a line for the email address because you won't be using it yet, but you can replicate this code to reference that value as well.

Script 5.2 This PHP script demonstrates concatenation, one of the most common manipulations of a string variable. Think of it as addition for strings.

```
1    <!doctype html>
2    <html lang="en">
3    <head>
4        <meta charset="utf-8">
5        <title>Forum Posting</title>
6    </head>
7    <body>
8    <?php // Script 5.2 - handle_post.php
9    /* This script receives five values from
     posting.html:
10   first_name, last_name, email, posting,
     submit */
11
12   // Address error management, if you
     want.
13
14   // Get the values from the $_POST array:
15   $first_name = $_POST['first_name'];
16   $last_name = $_POST['last_name'];
17   $posting = $_POST['posting'];
18
19   // Create a full name variable:
20   $name = $first_name . ' ' .
     $last_name;
21
22   // Print a message:
23   print "<div>Thank you, $name, for your
     posting:
24   <p>$posting</p></div>";
25
26   ?>
27   </body>
28   </html>
```

A The HTML form in use...

B ...and the resulting PHP page.

4. Create a new **$name** variable using concatenation:

```
$name = $first_name . ' ' .
$last_name;
```

This act of concatenation takes two variables plus a space and joins them all together to create a new variable, named **$name**. Assuming that you entered *Elliott* and *Smith* as the names, **$name** would be equal to *Elliott Smith*.

5. Print out the message to the user:

```
print "<div>Thank you, $name,
→ for your posting:
<p>$posting</p></div>";
```

This message reports back to the user what was entered in the form.

6. Close the PHP section and complete the HTML page:

```
?>
</body>
</html>
```

7. Save your script as **handle_post.php**, place it in the same directory as **posting.html** (on your PHP-enabled server), and test both the form and the script in your browser **A** **B**.

As a reminder, you must load the form through a URL (*http://something*) so that, when the form is submitted, the handling PHP script is also run through a URL.

TIP You can link as many strings as you want using concatenation. You can even join numbers to strings:

```php
$new_string = $s1 . $s2 . $number;
```

This works because PHP is weakly typed, meaning that its variables aren't locked in to one particular format. Here, the `$number` variable will be turned into a string and appended to the value of the `$new_string` variable.

TIP Concatenation can be used in many ways, even when feeding arguments to a function. An uncommon but functional example would be

```php
$text = nl2br($heading . $body);
```

The `nl2br()` function, first mentioned in Chapter 1, "Getting Started with PHP," will be discussed in detail next.

TIP If you used quotation marks of any kind in your form and saw extraneous slashes in the printed result, see the sidebar "Magic Quotes" in Chapter 3 for an explanation of the cause and for the fix. This is uncommon in current versions of PHP.

TIP As a reminder, it's important to understand the difference between single and double quotation marks in PHP. Characters within single quotation marks are treated literally; characters within double quotation marks are interpreted (for example, a variable's name will be replaced by its value). See Chapter 3 for a refresher.

TIP Taking the first and last names as separate inputs makes for a good concatenation example. However, not everyone has just two names, and it's best not to make such assumptions in your own registration forms. A more inclusive example would have a single input for the user's name.

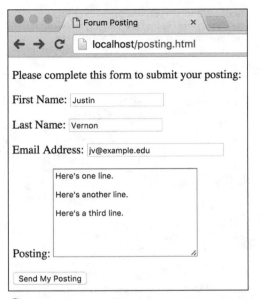

Please complete this form to submit your posting:

First Name: Justin

Last Name: Vernon

Email Address: jv@example.edu

Here's one line.

Here's another line.

Here's a third line.

Posting:

Send My Posting

A Newlines in form data like textareas...

Thank you, Justin Vernon, for your posting:

Here's one line. Here's another line. Here's a third line.

B ...are not rendered by the browser.

Handling Newlines

A common question beginning PHP developers have involves handling newlines in strings. The **textarea** form element allows a user to enter text over multiple lines by pressing Return/Enter. Each use of Return/Enter equates to a newline in the resulting string. These newlines work within a **textarea** but have no effect on a rendered PHP page **A** **B**.

To create the equivalent of newlines in a rendered web page, you use the break tag: **
. Fortunately, PHP has the **nl2br() function, which automatically converts newlines into break tags:

$var = nl2br($var);

Let's apply this function to **handle_post.php** so that the user's posting retains its formatting.

To convert newlines to breaks:

1. Open **handle_post.php** (Script 5.2) in your text editor or IDE, if it is not already open.

continues on next page

2. Apply the **nl2br()** function when assigning a value to the **$posting** variable (**Script 5.3**):

```
$posting = nl2br($_POST
→['posting'], false);
```

Now **$posting** will be assigned the value of **$_POST['posting']**, with any newlines converted to HTML break tags.

The second argument to the function— the Boolean **false**—says that you *do not want* XHTML-compliant break tags created. In other words, the default behavior is for this function to replace newlines with **
**. In HTML5, **
** is more commonly used.

Script 5.3 When you use the **nl2br()** function, newlines entered into the posting **textarea** are honored when displayed in the browser.

```
1   <!doctype html>
2   <html lang="en">
3   <head>
4       <meta charset="utf-8">
5       <title>Forum Posting</title>
6   </head>
7   <body>
8   <?php // Script 5.3 - handle_post.php #2
9   /* This script receives five values from
    posting.html:
10  first_name, last_name, email, posting,
    submit */
11
12  // Address error management, if you
    want.
13
14  // Get the values from the $_POST array:
15  $first_name = $_POST['first_name'];
16  $last_name = $_POST['last_name'];
17  $posting = nl2br($_POST['posting'],
    false);
18
19  // Create a full name variable:
20  $name = $first_name . ' ' . $last_name;
21
22  // Print a message:
23  print "<div>Thank you, $name, for your
    posting:
24  <p>$posting</p></div>";
25
26  ?>
27  </body>
28  </html>
```

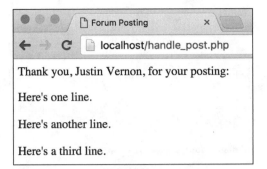

C Now the same submitted data **A** is properly displayed over multiple lines in the browser.

```
1  <!doctype html>
2  <html lang="en">
3  <head>
4        <meta charset="utf-8">
5        <title>Forum Posting</title>
6  </head>
7  <body>
8  <div>Thank you, Justin Vernon, for your posting:
9  <p>Here's one line.<br>
10 <br>
11 Here's another line.<br>
12 <br>
13 Here's a third line.</p></div></body>
14 </html>
```

D The HTML source, corresponding to **B**, shows the effect that newlines have in the browser (i.e., they add spacing within the HTML source code).

3. Save the file, place it in the same directory as **posting.html** (on your PHP-enabled server), and test again in your browser **C**.

TIP Newlines can also be inserted into strings by placing the newline character—\n— between double quotation marks.

TIP Other HTML tags, such as paragraph tags, also affect spacing in the rendered web page. You can turn newlines (or any character) into paragraph tags using a replacing function, but the code for doing so is far more involved than just invoking **nl2br( )**.

TIP Newlines present in strings sent to the browser will have an effect, but only in the HTML source of the page **D**.

HTML and PHP

As stated several times over by now, PHP is a server-side technology that's frequently used to send data to the browser. This data can be in the form of plain text, HTML code, or, more commonly, both.

In this chapter's primary example, data is entered in an HTML form and then printed back to the browser using PHP. A potential problem is that the user can enter HTML characters in the form, which can affect the resulting page's formatting **A** **B**—or, worse, cause security problems.

You can use a few PHP functions to manipulate HTML tags within PHP string variables:

- `htmlspecialchars()` converts certain HTML tags into their entity versions.

- `htmlentities()` turns all HTML tags into their entity versions.

- `strip_tags()` removes all HTML and PHP tags.

The first two functions turn an HTML tag (for example, `<span>`) into an entity version like `&lt;span&gt;`. The entity version appears in the output but isn't rendered. You might use either of these if you wanted to display code without enacting it. The third function, `strip_tags()`, removes HTML and PHP tags entirely.

A If the user enters HTML code in the posting...

B ...it's rendered by the browser when reprinted.

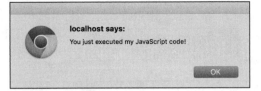

C Displaying HTML submitted by a user in a browser can have terrible consequences, such as the execution of JavaScript.

You ought to watch for special tags in user-provided data for two reasons. First, as already mentioned, submitted HTML would likely affect the rendered page (for example, mess up a table, tweak the CSS, or just add formatting where there shouldn't be any). The second concern is more important. Because JavaScript is placed within HTML **script** tags, a malicious user could submit JavaScript that would be executed when it's redisplayed on the page **C**. This is how *cross-site scripting* (XSS) attacks are performed.

To see the impact these functions have, this next rewrite of **handle_post.php** will use each of them and display the respective results.

To address HTML in PHP:

1. Open **handle_post.php** (Script 5.3) in your text editor or IDE, if it is not already open.

2. Before the **print** line, add the following (**Script 5.4**):

   ```php
   $html_post = htmlentities
   ➝ ($_POST['posting']);
   $strip_post = strip_tags
   ➝ ($_POST['posting']);
   ```

   To clarify the difference between how these two functions work, apply them both to the posting text, creating two new variables in the process. Refer to **$_POST['posting']** here and not **$posting** because **$posting** already reflects the application of the **nl2br()** function, which means that break tags may have been introduced that were not explicitly entered by the user.

3. Alter the **print** statement to read as follows:

   ```php
   print "<div>Thank you, $name,
   ➝ for your posting:
   <p>Original: $posting</p>
   <p>Entity: $html_post</p>
   <p>Stripped: $strip_post</p>
   ➝ </div>";
   ```

   To highlight the different results, print out the three different versions of the posting text. First is the original posting as it was entered, after being run through **nl2br()**. Next is the **htmlentities()** version of the posting, which will show the HTML tags without rendering them. Finally, the **strip_tags()** version will be printed; it doesn't include any HTML (or PHP) tags.

Script 5.4 This version of the PHP script addresses HTML tags in two different ways.

```
1    <!doctype html>
2    <html lang="en">
3    <head>
4        <meta charset="utf-8">
5        <title>Forum Posting</title>
6    </head>
7    <body>
8    <?php // Script 5.4 - handle_post.php #3
9    /* This script receives five values from
     posting.html:
10   first_name, last_name, email, posting,
     submit */
11
12   // Address error management, if you
     want.
13
14   // Get the values from the $_POST array:
15   $first_name = $_POST['first_name'];
16   $last_name = $_POST['last_name'];
17   $posting = nl2br($_POST['posting']);
18
19   // Create a full name variable:
20   $name = $first_name . ' ' . $last_name;
21
22   // Adjust for HTML tags:
23   $html_post =
     htmlentities($_POST['posting']);
24   $strip_post =
     strip_tags($_POST['posting']);
25
26   // Print a message:
27   print "<div>Thank you, $name, for
     your posting:
28   <p>Original: $posting</p>
29   <p>Entity: $html_post</p>
30   <p>Stripped: $strip_post</p></div>";
31
32   ?>
33   </body>
34   </html>
```

D The HTML characters entered as part of a posting will now be addressed by PHP.

E The resulting PHP page shows the original post as it would look if printed without modification, the effect of `htmlentities()`, and the effect of `strip_tags()`.

4. Save the file, place it in the same directory as **posting.html** (on your PHP-enabled server), and test it again in your browser **D** **E**.

   If you view the HTML source code of the resulting PHP page **F**, you'll also see the effect that applying these functions has.

TIP For security purposes, it's almost always a good idea to use `htmlentities()`, `htmlspecialchars()`, or `strip_tags()` to any user-provided data that's being printed to the browser. The only reason I don't do so in this book is to minimize clutter.

TIP Today's browsers can identify and block execution of potentially malicious JavaScript, although you should not rely on that behavior.

TIP The `html_entity_decode()` function does just the opposite of `htmlentities()`, turning HTML entities into their respective HTML code.

TIP Another useful function for outputting strings in the browser is `wordwrap()`. This function wraps a string to a certain number of characters.

TIP To turn newlines into breaks while still removing any HTML or PHP tags, apply `nl2br()` after `strip_tags()`:

`$posting = nl2br(strip_tags`
`↝ ($_POST['posting']));`

In that line, the `strip_tags()` function will be called first, and its result will be sent to the `nl2br()` function.

```
<p>Original: I don't understand why it says <em>something</em>.</p>
<p>Entity: I don't understand why it says &lt;em&gt;something&lt;/em&gt;.</p>
<p>Stripped: I don't understand why it says something.</p></div></body>
```

F The HTML source for the content displayed in **E**.

Encoding and Decoding Strings

At the end of Chapter 3, the section "Manually Sending Data to a Page" demonstrated how to use the thinking behind the GET form method to send data to a page. In that example, instead of using an actual form, data was appended to the URL, making it available to the receiving script. I was careful to say that only single words could be passed this way, without spaces or punctuation. But what if you want to pass several words as one variable value or use special characters?

To safely pass any value to a PHP script through the URL, apply the **urlencode()** function. As its name implies, this function takes a string and *encodes* it (changes its format) so that it can properly be passed as part of a URL. Among other things, the function replaces spaces with plus signs (**+**) and translates special characters (for example, the apostrophe) into less problematic versions. You can use the function like so:

```
$string = urlencode($string);
```

To demonstrate one application of **urlencode()**, let's update the **handle_post.php** page so that it also creates a link that passes the user's name and email address to a third page.

Script 5.5 This script encodes two variables before adding them to a link. Then the values can be successfully passed to another page.

```
1   <!doctype html>
1   <html lang="en">
2   <head>
3       <meta charset="utf-8">
4       <title>Forum Posting</title>
5   </head>
6   <body>
7   <?php // Script 5.5 - handle_post.php #4
8   /* This script receives five values from
    posting.html:
9   first_name, last_name, email, posting,
    submit */
10
11  // Address error management, if you
    want.
12
13  // Get the values from the $_POST array:
14  $first_name = $_POST['first_name'];
15  $last_name = $_POST['last_name'];
16  $posting = nl2br($_POST['posting']);
17
18  // Create a full name variable:
19  $name = $first_name . ' ' . $last_name;
20
21  // Print a message:
22  print "<div>Thank you, $name, for your
    posting:
23  <p>$posting</p></div>";
24
25  // Make a link to another page:
26  $name = urlencode($name);
27  $email = urlencode($_POST['email']);
28  print "<p>Click <a href=\"thanks.php?
    name=$name&email=$email\">here</a> to
    continue.</p>";
29
30  ?>
31  </body>
32  </html>
```

To use urlencode():

1. Open **handle_post.php** (Script 5.4) in your text editor or IDE, if it is not already open.

2. Delete the **htmlentities()** and **strip_tags()** lines added in the previous set of steps (**Script 5.5**).

3. Revert to the older version of the print invocation:

   print "<div>Thank you, $name,
   → for your posting:
   <p>$posting</p></div>";

4. After the **print** statement, add the following:

   $name = urlencode($name);
   $email = urlencode($_POST
   → ['email']);

   This script will pass these two variables to a second page. In order for it to do so, they must both be encoded.

   Because the script has not previously referred to or used the **$email** variable, the second line both retrieves the email value from the **$_POST** array and encodes it in one step. This is the same as having these two separate lines:

   $email = $_POST['email'];
   $email = urlencode($email);

continues on next page

5. Add another **print** statement that creates the link:

```
print "<p>Click <a href=\
→ "thanks.php?name=$name&email=
→ $email\">here</a> to continue.
→ </p>";
```

The primary purpose of this **print** statement is to create an HTML link in the web page, the source code of which would be something like

```
<a href="thanks.php?name=
→ Larry+Ullman&email=
→ larry%40example.com">here</a>
```

To accomplish this, begin by hard-coding most of the HTML and then include the appropriate variable names. Because the HTML code requires that the URL for the link be in double quotation marks —and the **print** statement already uses double quotation marks—you must escape them (by preceding them with backslashes) in order for them to be printed.

6. Save the file, place it in the proper directory of your PHP-enabled server, and test it again in your browser **A** **B**.

Note that clicking the link will result in a server error, because the **thanks.php** script hasn't yet been written.

A Another use of the form.

B The handling script now displays a link to another page.

7. View the HTML source code of the handling page to see the resulting link in the HTML code **C**.

TIP Values sent directly from a form are automatically URL-encoded prior to being sent and decoded upon arrival at the receiving script. You only need the `urlencode()` function to manually encode data (as in the example).

TIP The `urldecode()` function does just the opposite of `urlencode()`—it takes an encoded URL and turns it back into a standard form. You'll use it less frequently, though, because PHP will automatically decode most values it receives.

TIP Since you can use concatenation with functions, the new `print` statement could be written as follows:

```
print 'Click <a href="thanks.php?
→ name=' . $name . '&email=' .
→ $email . '">here</a> to continue.';
```

This method has two added benefits over the original approach. First, it uses single quotation marks to start and stop the statement, meaning you don't need to escape the double quotation marks. Second, the variables used are more obvious—they aren't buried in a lot of other code.

```
<p>Click <a href="thanks.php?name=Christopher+O%27Reilly&email=chris.oreilly%40example.com">here</a> to continue.</p>
```

C The HTML source code of the page **B** shows the dynamically generated link.

TIP You do not need to encode numeric PHP values in order to use them in a URL, because they do not contain problematic characters. That being said, it won't hurt to encode them either.

TIP At the end of the chapter you'll be prompted to create thanks.php, which greets the user by name and email address **D**.

Thank you, Christopher O'Reilly. We will contact you at chris.oreilly@example.com.

D The third page in this process—to be created by you at the end of the chapter—prints a message based on values it receives in the URL.

Encrypting and Decrypting Strings

Frequently, in order to protect data, programmers *encrypt* it—alter its state by transforming it to a form that's more difficult, if not impossible, to discern. Passwords are an example of a value you might want to encrypt. Depending on the level of security you want to establish, usernames, email addresses, and phone numbers are likely candidates for encryption too.

You can use the **password_hash()** function to encrypt data, but be aware that no decryption option is available (it's known as *one-way* encryption). So a password may be encrypted using it and then stored, but the decrypted value of the password can never be determined. Using this function in a web application, you might encrypt a user's password upon registration; then, when the user logged in, the password the user entered at that time would also be encrypted, and the two protected versions of the password would be compared. The syntax for using **password_hash()** is

```
$data = password_hash($data, PASSWORD_DEFAULT);
```

The second argument says to use the default encryption algorithm (the algorithm determining how quickly and securely the encryption is performed).

If the data is being stored in a database, you can also use functions built into the database application (for example, MySQL, PostgreSQL, Oracle, or SQL Server) to perform encryption and decryption. Depending on the technology you're using, it most likely provides both one- and two-way encryption tools.

Comparing Strings

To compare two strings, you can always use the equality operator, which you'll learn about in the next chapter. Otherwise, you can use the **strcmp()** function. It indicates how two strings compare by returning a whole number: 0 if they are the same, and a positive or negative number if one is "greater" than the other. PHP also has a case-insensitive companion, **strcasecmp()**.

To see if a substring is contained within another string (that is, to find a needle in a haystack), you'll use these functions:

- **strstr()** returns the haystack from the first occurrence of a needle to the end.

- **strpos()** searches through a haystack and returns the numeric location of a particular needle.

Both of these functions also have a case-insensitive alternative: **stristr()** and **stripos()**, respectively. Each of these functions is normally used in a conditional to test whether the substring was found.

Finding Substrings

PHP has a few functions you can use to pull apart strings, search through them, and perform comparisons. Although these functions are normally used with conditionals, discussed in Chapter 6, "Control Structures," they are important enough that they'll be introduced here; later chapters will use them more formally.

Earlier in this chapter, you learned how to join strings using concatenation. Along with making larger strings out of smaller pieces, PHP easily lets you extract subsections from a string. The trick to using any method to pull out a subsection of a string is that you must know something about the string itself in order to know how to break it up.

The **strtok()** function creates a substring, referred to as a *token*, from a larger string by using a predetermined separator (such as a comma or a space). For example, if you have users enter their full name in one field (presumably with their first and last names separated by a space), you can pull out their first name with this code:

```
$first = strtok($_POST['name'], ' ');
```

That line tells PHP to extract everything from the beginning of **$_POST['name']** until it finds a blank space.

If you have users enter their full name in the format *Surname, First*, you can find their surname by writing

```
$last = strtok($_POST['name'], ', ');
```

A second way to pull out sections of a string is by referring to the *indexed position* of the characters within the string. The indexed position of a string is the numerical location of a character, counting from the beginning. However, PHP—like most programming languages—begins all indexes with the number 0. For example, to index the string *Larry*, you begin with the L at position 0, followed by *a* at 1, *r* at 2, the second *r* at 3, and *y* at 4. Even though the string length of *Larry* is 5, its index goes from 0 to 4. In short, indexes always go from 0 to the length minus 1.

With this in mind, you can call on the **substr()** function to create a substring based on the index position of the substring's characters:

```
$sub = substr($string, 0, 10);
```

The first argument is the master string from which the substring will be derived. Second, indicate where the substring begins, as its indexed position (0 means that you want to start with the first character). Third, from that starting point, state how many characters the substring should contain (10). If the master string does not have that many characters in it, the resulting substring will end with the end of the master string. This argument is optional; if omitted, the substring will also go until the end of the master string.

You can also use negative numbers to count backward from the end of the string:

```
$string = 'aardvark';
$sub = substr($string, -3, 3); // ark
```

Script 5.6 This version of `handle_post.php` counts the number of words in the posting and trims the displayed posting down to just the first 50 characters.

```
1   <!doctype html>
2   <html lang="en">
3   <head>
4       <meta charset="utf-8">
5       <title>Forum Posting</title>
6   </head>
7   <body>
8   <?php // Script 5.6 - handle_post.php #5
9   /* This script receives five values from
    posting.html:
10  first_name, last_name, email, posting,
    submit */
11
12  // Address error management, if you
    want.
13
14  // Get the values from the $_POST array:
15  $first_name = $_POST['first_name'];
16  $last_name = $_POST['last_name'];
17  $posting = nl2br($_POST['posting']);
18
19  // Create a full name variable:
20  $name = $first_name . ' ' . $last_name;
21
22  // Get a word count:
23  $words = str_word_count($posting);
24
25  // Get a snippet of the posting:
26  $posting = substr($posting, 0, 50);
27
28  // Print a message:
29  print "<div>Thank you, $name, for
    your posting:
30  <p>$posting...</p>
31  <p>($words words)</p></div>";
32
33  ?>
34  </body>
35  </html>
```

The second line says that three characters should be returned starting at the third character from the end. With that particular example, you can again omit the third argument and have the same result:

$sub = substr($string, -3); // ark

To see how many characters are in a string, use **strlen()**:

print strlen('Hello, world!'); // 13

The count will include spaces and punctuation. To see how many *words* are in a string, use **str_word_count()**. This function, along with **substr()**, will be used in this next revision of the **handle_post.php** script.

To create substrings:

1. Open **handle_post.php** (Script 5.5) in your text editor or IDE, if it is not already open.

2. Before the **print** statement, add the following (**Script 5.6**):

   $words = str_word_count
   → ($posting);

   This version of the script will do two new things with the user's posting. One will be to display the number of words it contains. That information is gathered here and assigned to the **$words** variable.

   continues on next page

3. On the next line (also before the `print` statement), add

```
$posting = substr($posting, 0,
→ 50);
```

The second new thing this script will do is limit the displayed posting to its first 50 characters. You might use this, for example, if one page shows the beginning of a post, then a link takes the user to the full posting. To implement this limit, the `substr()` function is called.

4. Update the `print` statement to read

```
print "<div>Thank you, $name,
→ for your posting:
<p>$posting...</p>
<p>($words words)</p></div>";
```

There are two changes here. First, ellipses are added after the posting to indicate that this is just part of the whole posting. Then, within another paragraph, the number of words is printed.

5. Delete the two `urlencode()` lines and the corresponding `print` line.

I'm referring specifically to the code added in the previous incarnation of the script, linking to `thanks.php`.

6. Save the file, place it in the proper directory of your PHP-enabled server, and test it again in your browser Ⓐ Ⓑ.

Ⓐ Postings longer than 50 characters...

Ⓑ ...will be cut short. The word count is also displayed.

TIP If you want to check whether a string matches a certain format—for example, to see if it's a syntactically valid postal code—you need to use regular expressions. Regular expressions are an advanced concept in which you define patterns and then see if a value fits the mold. See the PHP manual or my book *PHP and MySQL for Dynamic Web Sites (Fourth Edition): Visual QuickPro Guide* (Peachpit Press, 2012).

Adjusting String Case

A handful of PHP functions are used to change the case of a string's letters:

- **ucfirst()** capitalizes the first letter of the string.
- **ucwords()** capitalizes the first letter of words in a string.
- **strtoupper()** makes an entire string uppercase.
- **strtolower()** makes an entire string lowercase.

Due to the variance in people's names around the globe, there's no flawless way to automatically format names with PHP (or any programming language). In fact, I would be hesitant to alter the case of user-supplied data unless you have good cause to do so.

Replacing Parts of a String

Instead of just finding substrings within a string, as the previous section discusses, you might find that you need to *replace substrings* with new values. You can do so using the **str_ireplace()** function:

```
$string = str_ireplace($needle,
→ $replacement, $haystack);
```

This function replaces every occurrence of **$needle** found in **$haystack** with **$replacement**. For example:

```
$me = 'Larry E. Ullman';
$me = str_ireplace('E.', 'Edward',
→ $me);
```

The **$me** variable now has a value of *Larry Edward Ullman*.

That function performs a *case-insensitive* search. To be more restrictive, you can perform a *case-sensitive* search using **str_replace()**. In this next script, **str_ireplace()** will be used to eliminate "bad words" in submitted text.

There's one last string-related function I want to discuss: **trim()**. This function removes any white space—spaces, new-lines, and tabs—from the beginning and end of a string. It's quite common for extra spaces to be added to a string variable, either because a user enters information carelessly or due to sloppy HTML code. For purposes of clarity, data integrity, and web design, it's worth your while to delete those spaces from the strings before you use them. Extra spaces sent to the browser could make the page appear odd, and those sent to a database or cookie could have unfortunate consequences at a later date (for example, if a password has a superfluous space, it might not match when it's entered without the space).

The **trim()** function automatically strips away any extra spaces from both the beginning and the end of a string (but not the middle). The format for using **trim()** is as follows:

```
$string = ' extra space before and
→ after text ';
$string = trim($string);
// $string is now equal to 'extra
→ space before and after text'
```

To use str_ireplace () and trim():

1. Open **handle_post.php** (Script 5.6) in your text editor or IDE, if it is not already open.

2. Apply **trim()** to the form data (**Script 5.7**):

```
$first_name = trim($_POST
→ ['first_name']);
$last_name = trim($_POST
→ ['last_name']);
$posting = trim($_POST
→ ['posting']);
```

Just in case the incoming data has extraneous white space at its beginning or end, the **trim()** function is applied.

3. Remove the use of **substr()**:

```
$posting = substr($posting,
→ 0, 50);
```

You'll want to see the entire posting for this example, so remove this invocation of **substr()**.

4. Before the **print** statement, add

```
$posting = str_ireplace
→ ('badword', 'XXXXX', $posting);
```

This specific example flags the use of a bad word in a posting by crossing it out. Rather than an actual curse word, the code uses *badword*. (You can use whatever you want, of course.)

Script 5.7 This final version of the handling script applies the **trim()** function and then replaces uses of **badword** with a bunch of Xs.

```
1   <!doctype html>
2   <html lang="en">
3   <head>
4       <meta charset="utf-8">
5       <title>Forum Posting</title>
6   </head>
7   <body>
8   <?php // Script 5.7 - handle_post.php #6
9   /* This script receives five values from
    posting.html:
10  first_name, last_name, email, posting,
    submit */
11
12  // Address error management, if you
    want.
13
14  // Get the values from the $_POST array.
15  // Strip away extra spaces using trim():
16  $first_name =
    trim($_POST['first_name']);
17  $last_name =
    trim($_POST['last_name']);
18  $posting = trim($_POST['posting']);
19
20  // Create a full name variable:
21  $name = $first_name . ' ' . $last_name;
22
23  // Get a word count:
24  $words = str_word_count($posting);
25
26  // Take out the bad words:
27  $posting = str_ireplace('badword',
    'XXXXX', $posting);
28
29  // Print a message:
30  print "<div>Thank you, $name, for your
    posting:
31  <p>$posting</p>
32  <p>($words words)</p></div>";
33
34  ?>
35  </body>
36  </html>
```

Please complete this form to submit your posting:

First Name: Bad

Last Name: Poster

Email Address: faker@bad.example.com

Posting: I feel like using a BADWORD in my post!

Send My Posting

Ⓐ If users enter a word you'd prefer they not use...

Thank you, Bad Poster, for your posting:

I feel like using a XXXXX in my post!

(9 words)

Ⓑ ...you can have PHP replace it.

If you'd like to catch many bad words, you can use multiple lines, like so:

```
$posting = str_ireplace
→ ('badword1', 'XXXXX', $posting);
$posting = str_ireplace
→ ('badword2', 'XXXXX', $posting);
$posting = str_ireplace
→ ('badword3', 'XXXXX', $posting);
```

5. Update the **print** statement so that it no longer uses the ellipses:

```
print "<div>Thank you, $name,
→ for your posting:
<p>$posting</p>
<p>($words words)</p></div>";
```

6. Save the file, place it in the proper directory of your PHP-enabled server, and test again in your browser Ⓐ Ⓑ.

TIP The str_ireplace() function will even catch bad words in context. For example, if you entered I feel like using badwords, the result would be I feel like using XXXXXs.

TIP The str_ireplace() function can also take an array of needle terms, an array of replacement terms, and even an array as the haystack. Because you may not know what an array is yet, this technique isn't demonstrated here.

TIP If you need to trim excess spaces from the beginning or the end of a string but not both, PHP breaks the trim() function into two more specific functions: rtrim() removes spaces found at the end of a string variable (on its right side), and ltrim() handles those at the beginning (its left). They're both used just like trim():

```
$string = rtrim($string);
$string = ltrim($string);
```

Review and Pursue

If you have any problems with the review questions or the pursue prompts, turn to the book's supporting forum (www.LarryUllman.com/forums/).

Review

- How do you create a string?

- What are the differences between using single and double quotation marks?

- What is the concatenation operator? What is the concatenation assignment operator?

- What is the impact of having a newline in a string printed to the browser? How do you convert a newline character to a break tag?

- What problems can occur when HTML is entered into form elements whose values will later be printed back to the browser? What steps can be taken to sanctify submitted form data?

- What function makes data safe to pass in a URL?

- How do you escape problematic characters within a string? What happens if you do not escape them?

- The characters in a string are indexed beginning at what number?

- What does the `trim()` function do?

Pursue

- Look up the PHP manual page for one of the new functions mentioned in this chapter. Use the links on that page to examine a couple of other string-related functions that PHP has.

- Check out the PHP manual page specifically for the `substr()` function. Read the other examples found on that page to get a better sense of how `substr()` can be used.

- Write the `thanks.php` script that goes along with Script 5.5. If you need help, revisit the `hello.php` script from Chapter 3 (Script 3.7).

- Rewrite the `print` statement in the final version of `handle_post.php` (Script 5.7) so that it uses single quotation marks and concatenation instead of double quotation marks.

- Create another HTML form for taking string values. Then create the PHP script that receives the form data, addresses any HTML or PHP code, manipulates the data in some way, and prints out the results.

Control
Structures

Control structures—conditionals and loops—are a staple of programming languages. PHP has two conditionals—**if** and **switch**—both of which you'll master in this chapter. Conditionals allow you to establish a test and then perform actions based on the results. This functionality provides the ability to make websites even more dynamic.

The discussion of **if** conditionals requires introduction of two last categories of operators: comparison and logical (you've already seen the arithmetic and assignment operators in the previous chapters). You'll commonly use these operators in your conditionals, along with the Boolean concepts of TRUE and FALSE.

Finally, this chapter introduces loops, which allow you to repeat an action for a specified number of iterations. Loops can save you programming time and help you get the most functionality out of arrays, as you'll see in the next chapter.

In This Chapter

Creating the HTML Form

As with the previous chapters, the examples in this chapter are based on an HTML form that sends data to a PHP page. In this case, the form is a simple registration page that requests the following information **A**:

- Email address
- Password
- Confirmation of the password
- Year of birth (to verify age)
- Favorite color (for customization purposes)
- Agreement to the site's terms (a common requirement)

The following steps walk through the creation of this form before getting into the PHP code.

To create the HTML form:

1. Begin a new HTML document in your text editor or IDE, to be named **register.html** (Script 6.1):

   ```
   <!doctype html>
   <html lang="en">
   <head>
     <meta charset="utf-8">
     <title>Registration Form</title>
   </head>
   <body>
   <!-- Script 6.1 - register.html -->
   <div><p>Please complete this
   → form to register:</p>
   ```

2. Create the initial form tag:

   ```
   <form action="handle_reg.php"
   → method="post">
   ```

A The HTML form used in this chapter.

Script 6.1 This pseudo-registration form is the basis for the examples in this chapter.

```
1   <!doctype html>
2   <html lang="en">
3   <head>
4       <meta charset="utf-8">
5       <title>Registration Form</title>
6   </head>
7   <body>
8   <!-- Script 6.1 - register.html -->
9   <div><p>Please complete this form to
    register:</p>
10
11  <form action="handle_reg.php"
    method="post">
12
13      <p>Email Address: <input type="text"
        name="email" size="30"></p>
14
15      <p>Password: <input type="password"
        name="password" size="20"></p>
16
17      <p>Confirm Password: <input
        type="password" name="confirm"
        size="20"></p>
18
```

code continues on next page

```
19      <p>Year You Were Born: <input
        type="text" name="year" value="YYYY"
        size="4"></p>
20
21      <p>Favorite Color:
22      <select name="color">
23      <option value="">Pick One</option>
24      <option value="red">Red</option>
25      <option value="yellow">Yellow</
        option>
26      <option value="green">Green</option>
27      <option value="blue">Blue</option>
28      </select></p>
29
30      <p><input type="checkbox"
        name="terms" value="Yes"> I agree to
        the terms (whatever they may be).</p>
31
32      <input type="submit" name="submit"
        value="Register">
33
34   </form>
35
36   </div>
37   </body>
38   </html>
```

Password: •••••••

B A password input type as it's being filled out.

As with many of the previous examples, this page uses the POST method. The handling script, identified by the **action** attribute, will be **handle_reg.php**, found in the same directory as the HTML form.

3. Create inputs for the email address and passwords:

```
<p>Email Address: <input
→ type="email" name="email"
→ size="30"></p>
<p>Password: <input
→ type="password"
→ name="password" size="20"></p>
<p>Confirm Password: <input
→ type="password" name="confirm"
→ size="20"></p>
```

These lines should be self-evident by now. Each line is wrapped in HTML **<p></p>** tags to improve the spacing in the browser. Also, note that two password inputs are created—the second is used to confirm the text entered in the first. Password input types don't reveal what the user enters **B**, so the standard is to require the user to enter passwords twice (theoretically ensuring that users know exactly what password they provided).

4. Create an input for the user's birth year:

```
<p>Year You Were Born: <input
→ type="text" name="year"
→ placeholder="YYYY" size="4"></p>
```

Rather than use a drop-down menu that displays 50 or 100 years, have users enter their birth year in a text box. By presetting the **placeholder** attribute of the input, you make the text box indicate the proper format for the year **A**.

continues on next page

5. Create a drop-down menu for the user's favorite color:

```
<p>Favorite Color:
<select name="color">
<option value="">Pick One</option>
<option value="red">Red</option>
<option value="yellow">Yellow
→ </option>
<option value="green">Green
→ </option>
<option value="blue">Blue
→ </option>
</select></p>
```

The truth is that I'm adding this input so that it can be used for a specific example later in the chapter, but it might be used to customize the look of the site after the user logs in. Naturally, you can add as many colors as you want here.

6. Create a checkbox for the user to agree to the site's terms:

```
<p><input type="checkbox"
→ name="terms" value="Yes">
→ I agree to the terms (whatever
→ they may be).</p>
```

Many sites have some sort of terms or licensing that the user must indicate acceptance of, normally by selecting a checkbox. This particular form doesn't have a link to where the user can read the terms, but it probably doesn't matter because no one reads them (and this is just a hypothetical example anyway). In any case, using this element, you'll be able to see how checkboxes are treated by the handling PHP script.

7. Add a submit button and close the form:

```
<input type="submit" name=
→ "submit" value="Register">
</form>
```

8. Complete the HTML page:

```
</div>
</body>
</html>
```

9. Save the file as **register.html**, place it in the proper directory for your PHP-enabled server, and load the page in your browser.

TIP It's becoming more common to not require a password confirmation, relying instead on password reset functionality should users make a mistake or forget what they entered. I definitely prefer not having to confirm the password (and I used a password management application regardless), but you will see both approaches online.

TIP Most registration pages use either a nickname or an email address for the username. If you use the email address as a username, it's easier for your users to remember their registration information (a user may have only a couple of email addresses but a gazillion usernames for different sites around the web). Furthermore, email addresses are, by their nature, unique to an individual, whereas usernames are not.

The if Conditional

The basic programming conditional is the standard **if** (what used to be called an **if-then** conditional—the **then** is now implied). The syntax for this kind of conditional is simple:

```
if (condition) {
   statement(s);
}
```

The *condition* must go within parentheses; then the *statement(s)* are placed within braces (you'll also see these referred to as "curly braces" or "curly brackets"). The statements are commands to be executed—for example, printing a string or adding two numbers together. Each separate statement must have its own semicolon indicating the end of the line, but there's no limit on the number of statements that can be associated with a conditional.

The statements are normally indented from the initial **if** line to indicate that they're the result of a conditional, but that format isn't syntactically required. You'll also see people use this syntax:

```
if (condition)
{
   statement(s);
}
```

How you arrange your braces is a matter of personal preference—and the source of minor online skirmishes. Just pick a style you like and stick to it.

Failure to use a semicolon after each statement, forgetting an opening or closing parenthesis or brace, or using a semicolon after either of the braces will cause errors to occur. Be mindful of your syntax as you code with conditionals!

PHP uses the Boolean concepts of TRUE and FALSE when determining whether to execute the statements. If the condition is TRUE, the statements are executed; if it's FALSE, they are not executed 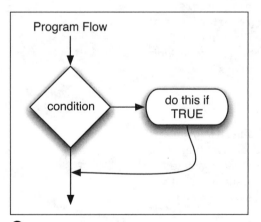.

Ⓐ How an **if** conditional affects the program flow of a script.

Over the course of this chapter, a PHP script will be developed until it fully validates the `register.html` form data. To start, this first version of the script will just create the basic shell of the validation process, defining and using a variable with a Boolean value that will track the success of the validation process.

To create an if conditional:

1. Begin a new document in your text editor or IDE, to be named `handle_reg.php` (Script 6.2):

   ```
   <!doctype html>
   <html lang="en">
   <head>
     <meta charset="utf-8">
     <title>Registration</title>
   </head>
   <body>
   <h1>Registration Results</h1>
   ```

2. Begin the PHP section and address error management, if necessary:

   ```
   <?php // Script 6.2 -
   → handle_reg.php
   ```

   If you don't have `display_errors` enabled, or if `error_reporting` is set to the wrong level, see Chapter 3, "HTML Forms and PHP," for the lines to include here to alter those settings.

3. Create a flag variable:

   ```
   $okay = true;
   ```

   To validate the form data, a *flag* variable will be used to represent whether or not the form was properly completed. It's known as a "flag" variable because the variable stores a simple value that indicates a status. For example: yes, the form was filled out entirely or no, it was not.

Script 6.2 This shell of a PHP script will be expanded to completely validate the form data.

```
1   <!doctype html>
2   <html lang="en">
3   <head>
4       <meta charset="utf-8">
5       <title>Registration</title>
6   </head>
7   <body>
8   <h1>Registration Results</h1>
9   <?php // Script 6.2 - handle_reg.php
10  /* This script receives seven values
    from register.html:
11  email, password, confirm, year, terms,
    color, submit */
12
13  // Address error management, if you
    want.
14
15  // Flag variable to track success:
16  $okay = true;
17
18  // If there were no errors, print a
    success message:
19  if ($okay) {
20      print '<p>You have been
        successfully registered (but not
        really).</p>';
21  }
22  ?>
23  </body>
24  </html>
```

The variable is initialized with a Boolean value of *TRUE*, meaning that the assumption is that the form was completed properly. Booleans are *case-insensitive* in PHP, so you could also write *True* or *TRUE*.

4. Print a message if everything is all right:

```
if ($okay) {
    print '<p>You have been
→ successfully registered (but
→ not really).</p>';
}
```

Over the course of this chapter, validation routines will be added to this script, checking the submitted form data. If any data fails a routine, then **$okay** will be set to FALSE. In that case, this conditional will also be FALSE, so the message won't be printed. However, if the data passes every validation routine, then **$okay** will still be TRUE, in which case this message will be printed.

5. Complete the PHP section and the HTML page:

```
?>
</body>
</html>
```

6. Save the file as **handle_reg.php**, place it in the proper directory for your PHP-enabled server (in the same directory as **register.html**), and test both in your browser **B** and **C**.

Of course, the fact is that this particular script will always print the success message, because no code will set **$okay** to **FALSE**. You can even run the script directly and see the same result.

> **TIP** If the statement area of your conditional is only one line long, you technically don't need the braces. In that case, you can write the conditional using either of these formats:
>
> if (*condition*) *statement*;
>
> or
>
> if (*condition*)
>   *statement*;
>
> You may run across code in these formats. However, I think it's best to always use the multiline format, with the braces (as demonstrated in the syntax introduction) to improve consistency and minimize errors.

B Filling out the HTML form to any degree...

Registration Results

You have been successfully registered (but not really).

C ...results in just this.

Validation Functions

PHP has dozens of functions commonly used to validate form data. Of these functions, three of the most important ones are used in this chapter's examples.

First up is the `empty()` function, which checks to see if a given variable has an "empty" value. A variable is considered to have an empty value if the variable has no value, has a value of 0, or has a value of FALSE. In any of these cases, the function returns TRUE; otherwise, it returns FALSE:

```
$var1 = 0;
$var2 = 'something';
$var3 = ' '; // An empty string
empty($var); // TRUE, no defined
→ value
empty($var1); // TRUE, empty value
empty($var2); // FALSE, non-empty
→ value
empty($var3); // TRUE, empty value
```

This function is perfect for making sure that text boxes in forms have been filled out. For example, if you have a text input named *email* and the user doesn't enter anything in it before submitting the form, then the `$_POST['email']` variable will exist but will have an empty value.

Next is the `isset()` function, which is almost the opposite of `empty()`, albeit with a slight difference. The `isset()` function returns TRUE if a variable has any value (including 0, FALSE, or an empty string). If the variable does not have a value, `isset()` returns FALSE:

```
$var1 = 0;
$var2 = 'something';
$var3 = ' '; // An empty string
isset($var); // FALSE, no defined
→ value
isset($var1); // TRUE
isset($var2); // TRUE
isset($var3); // TRUE
```

The `isset()` function is commonly used to validate nontext form elements like checkboxes, radio buttons, and select menus. It's also regularly used to confirm that a variable exists, regardless of its value.

Finally, the `is_numeric()` function returns TRUE if the submitted variable has a valid numerical value and FALSE otherwise. Integers, decimals, and even strings (if they're a valid number) can all pass the `is_numeric()` test:

```
$var1 = 2309;
$var2 = '80.23';
$var3 = 'Bears';
is_numeric($var1); // TRUE
is_numeric($var2); // TRUE
is_numeric($var3); // FALSE
```

An interesting thing to note is that using `is_numeric()` on a variable that doesn't exist not only returns FALSE, but also generates a warning. For this reason, you'll often see `isset()` used along with other validation functions like `is_numeric()`.

Let's start applying these functions to the PHP script to perform data validation.

Script 6.3 Using `if` conditionals and the `empty()` function, this PHP script checks if email address and password values were provided.

```
1   <!doctype html>
2   <html lang="en">
3   <head>
4       <meta charset="utf-8">
5       <title>Registration</title>
6       <style type="text/css"
        media="screen">
7           .error { color: red; }
8       </style>
9   </head>
10  <body>
11  <h1>Registration Results</h1>
12  <?php // Script 6.3 - handle_reg.php #2
13  /* This script receives seven values
    from register.html:
14  email, password, confirm, year, terms,
    color, submit */
15
16  // Address error management, if you
    want.
17
18  // Flag variable to track success:
19  $okay = true;
20
21  // Validate the email address:
22  if (empty($_POST['email'])) {
23      print '<p class="error">Please
        enter your email address.</p>';
24      $okay = false;
25  }
26
27  // Validate the password:
28  if (empty($_POST['password'])) {
29      print '<p class="error">Please
        enter your password.</p>';
30      $okay = false;
31  }
32
33  // If there were no errors, print a
    success message:
34  if ($okay) {
35      print '<p>You have been successfully
        registered (but not really).</p>';
36  }
37  ?>
38  </body>
39  </html>
```

To validate form data:

1. Open **handle_reg.php** (Script 6.2) in your text editor or IDE, if it is not already open.

2. Within the document's head, define a CSS class (**Script 6.3**):

   ```
   <style type="text/css"
   → media="screen">
     .error { color: red; }
   </style>
   ```

   This CSS class will be used to format any printed registration errors.

3. Validate the email address:

   ```
   if (empty($_POST['email'])) {
     print '<p class="error">
     → Please enter your email
     → address.</p>';
     $okay = false;
   }
   ```

   This `if` conditional uses the code `empty($_POST['email'])` as its condition. If that variable is empty, meaning it has no value, a value of 0, or a value of an empty string, the conditional is TRUE. In that case, the **print** statement will be executed and the **$okay** variable will be assigned a value of FALSE (indicating that everything is not okay).

   If the variable isn't empty, then the conditional is FALSE, the **print** function is never called, and **$okay** will retain its original value.

   continues on next page

4. Repeat the validation for the password:

```
if (empty($_POST['password'])) {
    print '<p class="error">Please
    → enter your password.</p>';
    $okay = false;
}
```

This is a repeat of the email validation, but with the variable name and **print** statement changed accordingly. The other form inputs will be validated in time.

All the printed error messages are placed within HTML paragraph tags that have a **class** value of *error*. By doing so, the CSS formatting will be applied (i.e., the errors will be printed in red).

5. Save the file as **handle_reg.php**, place it in the same directory as **register.html** (on your PHP-enabled server), and test both the form and the script in your browser **A** and **B**.

6. Resubmit the form in different states of completeness to test the results more.

If you do provide both email address and password values, the result will be exactly like that in **C** in the section "The if Conditional," because the **$okay** variable will still have a value of TRUE.

A If you omit the email address or password form input...

Registration Results

Please enter your email address.

Please enter your password.

B ...you'll see messages like these.

TIP When you use functions within conditionals, as with `empty()` here, it's easy to forget a closing parenthesis and see a parse error. Be extra careful with your syntax when you're coding any control structure.

TIP One use of the `isset()` function is to avoid referring to a variable unless it exists. If PHP is set to report notices (see "Error Reporting" in Chapter 3), then, for example, using `$var` if it has not been defined will cause an error. You can avoid this by coding

```php
if (isset($var)) {
    // Do whatever with $var.
}
```

TIP Even though almost all form data is sent to a PHP script as strings, the `is_numeric()` function can still be used for values coming from a form because it can handle strings that contain only numbers.

TIP The `isset()` function can take any number of variables as arguments:

```php
if (isset($var1, $var2)) {
    print 'Both variables exist.';
}
```

If all the named variables are set, the function returns TRUE; if any variable is not set, the function returns FALSE.

TIP Once you're more comfortable with PHP, you'll start using the `filter()` function for validation, too. It's a wonderful tool, but a bit too complicated for beginners.

Using else

The next control structure to discuss is the **if-else** conditional. This control structure allows you to execute one or more statements when a condition is TRUE and execute one or more other statements when the condition is FALSE:

```
if (condition) {
   statement(s);
} else {
   other_statement(s);
}
```

The important thing to remember when using this construct is that unless the condition is explicitly met, the **else** statement will be executed. In other words, the statements after the **else** constitute the *default action*, whereas the statements after the **if** condition are the exception to the rule 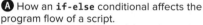.

Let's rewrite the **handle_reg.php** page, incorporating an **if-else** conditional to validate the birth year. In the process, a new variable will be created, representing the user's age.

To use else:

1. Open **handle_reg.php** (Script 6.3) in your text editor or IDE, if it is not already open.

2. After the password validation but before the **$okay** conditional, begin a new conditional (**Script 6.4**):

   ```
   if (is_numeric($_POST['year'])) {
   ```

   Because the **year** variable should be a number, you can use the **is_numeric()** function, rather than **empty()**, to check its value. This is a basic start to this particular form element's validation; later scripts will expand on this.

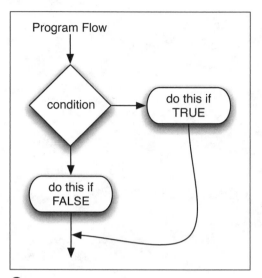

A How an **if-else** conditional affects the program flow of a script.

Script 6.4 By adding an **if-else** conditional, this script validates the birth year and creates a new variable in the process.

```
1    <!doctype html>
2    <html lang="en">
3    <head>
4       <meta charset="utf-8">
5       <title>Registration</title>
6       <style type="text/css"
         media="screen">
7          .error { color: red; }
8       </style>
9    </head>
10   <body>
11   <h1>Registration Results</h1>
12   <?php // Script 6.4 - handle_reg.php #3
13   /* This script receives seven values
        from register.html:
14   email, password, confirm, year, terms,
        color, submit */
15
16   // Address error management, if you
        want.
17
18   // Flag variable to track success:
19   $okay = true;
20
```

code continues on next page

```
21  // Validate the email address:
22  if (empty($_POST['email'])) {
23      print '<p class="error">Please enter
        your email address.</p>';
24      $okay = false;
25  }
26
27  // Validate the password:
28  if (empty($_POST['password'])) {
29      print '<p class="error">Please enter
        your password.</p>';
30      $okay = false;
31  }
32
33  // Validate the birth year:
34  if (is_numeric($_POST['year'])) {
35      $age = 2016 - $_POST['year']; //
        Calculate age this year.
36  } else {
37      print '<p class="error">Please
        enter the year you were born as
        four digits.</p>';
38      $okay = false;
39  }
40
41  // If there were no errors, print a
    success message:
42  if ($okay) {
43      print '<p>You have been successfully
        registered (but not really).</p>';
44      print "<p>You will turn $age this
        year.</p>";
45  }
46  ?>
47  </body>
48  </html>
```

3. Create a new variable:

   $age = 2016 - $_POST['year'];

   If the **$_POST['year']** variable has a numeric value (meaning that the conditional is TRUE), then the **$age** variable is assigned the value of the current year minus the provided year. For now, without knowledge of PHP's date functions, just hard-code the current year into the equation.

4. Add an **else** clause:

   ```
   } else {
       print '<p class="error">Please
       → enter the year you were born
       → as four digits.</p>';
       $okay = false;
   }
   ```

   If the year does not have a numeric value, an error message is printed and the **$okay** variable is set to FALSE (as is the case if any validation routine fails).

5. After the final **print** statement but within the same **$okay** conditional, also print out the value of **$age**:

   **print "<p>You will turn $age this
   → year.</p>";**

   If the **$okay** variable still has a value of TRUE, then the submitted data passed every validation routine. This means that the user's age has been calculated (in the sense of how old that user will be at some point this year), and it can be printed, too.

continues on next page

6. Save your script, place it in the same directory as `register.html` (on your PHP-enabled server), and test it in your browser again  **B**, **C**, and **D**.

> **TIP** Another good validation function is `checkdate()`, which you can use to confirm that a date exists (or existed in the past). You'd use it like so:
>
> ```
> if (checkdate($month, $day, $year))
> ⇢ {...
> ```

Registration Form ✕

← → C 🔲 localhost/register.html

Please complete this form to register:

Email Address: `me@example.com`

Password: `••••••••`

Confirm Password: `••••••••`

Year You Were Born: `YYYY`

Favorite Color: `Green ◊`

☑ I agree to the terms (whatever they may be).

`Register`

B Test the form again, without providing a year value, and...

Registration ✕

← → C 🔲 localhost/handle_reg.php

Registration Results

Please enter the year you were born as four digits.

C ...you'll see this.

Registration ✕

← → C 🔲 localhost/handle_reg.php

Registration Results

You have been successfully registered (but not really).

You will turn 52 this year.

D If the user provides a numeric value for their birth year, the user's age will now be calculated and printed (assuming that an email address and password was also provided).

More Operators

Previous chapters discussed most of PHP's operators along with the variable types that use them. These operators include *arithmetic* for numbers: addition (+), subtraction (-), multiplication (*), and division (/), along with the increment (++) and decrement (--) shortcuts for increasing or decreasing the value of a number by 1. Then there is the *assignment* operator (=), which is used to set the value of a variable, regardless of type. You've also learned about *concatenation* (.), which appends one string to another.

When it comes to creating conditionals, the *comparison* and *logical* operators are the most important. **Table 6.1** lists the operators to be discussed, along with those you've already seen.

Comparison

When the assignment operator (the equals sign) was introduced in Chapter 2, "Variables," you learned that its meaning isn't exactly what you'd conventionally think it to be. The line

`$var = 5;`

doesn't state that **$var** *is equal to* 5 but that it *is assigned the value of* 5. This is an important distinction.

When you're writing conditionals, you'll often want to see if a variable is equal to a specific value—to match usernames or passwords, perhaps, which you can't do with the equals sign alone (because that operator is used for assigning a value, not equating values). Instead, for comparisons, use the equality operator (==):

```
$var = 5;
if ($var == 5) { ...
```

continues on next page

TABLE 6.1 PHP's Operators

Operator	Usage	Type
+	Addition	Arithmetic
-	Subtraction	Arithmetic
*	Multiplication	Arithmetic
/	Division	Arithmetic
%	Modulus (remainder of a division)	Arithmetic
++	Incrementation	Arithmetic
-	Decrementation	Arithmetic
*	Assigns a value to a variable	Assignment
/	Equality	Comparison
%	Inequality	Comparison
<	Less than	Comparison
>	Greater than	Comparison
<=	Less than or equal to	Comparison
>=	Greater than or equal to	Comparison
<=>	Returns an integer reflecting comparison	Comparison
!	Negation	Logical
AND	And	Logical
&&	And	Logical
OR	Or	Logical
||	Or	Logical
XOR	Exclusive or	Logical
??	Null coalescing	Logical
.	Concatenation	String

These two lines of code together first establish the value of **$var** as 5 and then make a TRUE conditional that checks if **$var** is equal to 5. This example demonstrates the significant difference that one more equals sign makes in your PHP code and why *you must distinguish carefully between the assignment and comparison operators*.

The next comparison operator—*not equal to*—is represented by an exclamation mark coupled with an equals sign (!=). The remaining comparison operators are identical to their mathematical counterparts: less than (<), greater than (>), less than or equal to (<=), and greater than or equal to (>=).

As a demonstration of comparison operators, you'll check that the user's birth year is before 2016 and that the confirmed password matches the original password.

To use comparison operators:

1. Open **handle_reg.php** (Script 6.4) in your text editor or IDE, if it is not already open.

2. After the password validation, check that the two passwords match (**Script 6.5**):

```
if ($_POST['password']
→ != $_POST['confirm']) {
  print '<p class="error">
  → Your confirmed password
  → does not match the original
  → password.</p>';
  $okay = false;
}
```

To compare these two string values, use the inequality operator. Alternatively, you could use one of the string comparison functions (see Chapter 5, "Using Strings"), but != is just fine.

Script 6.5 This version of the form-handling script uses comparison operators to validate the password and year values.

```
1   <!doctype html>
2   <html lang="en">
3   <head>
4       <meta charset="utf-8">
5       <title>Registration</title>
6       <style type="text/css"
        media="screen">
7           .error { color: red; }
8       </style>
9   </head>
10  <body>
11  <h1>Registration Results</h1>
12  <?php // Script 6.5 - handle_reg.php #4
13  /* This script receives seven values
    from register.html:
14  email, password, confirm, year, terms,
    color, submit */
15
16  // Address error management, if you
    want.
17
18  // Flag variable to track success:
19  $okay = true;
20
21  // Validate the email address:
22  if (empty($_POST['email'])) {
23      print '<p class="error">Please enter
        your email address.</p>';
24      $okay = false;
25  }
26
27  // Validate the password:
28  if (empty($_POST['password'])) {
29      print '<p class="error">Please enter
        your password.</p>';
30      $okay = false;
31  }
32
33  // Check the two passwords for equality:
34  if ($_POST['password'] != $_
    POST['confirm']) {
35      print '<p class="error">Your
        confirmed password does not match
        the original password.</p>';
36      $okay = false;
37  }
38
```

code continues on next page

```
39   // Validate the birth year:
40   if (is_numeric($_POST['year'])) {
41       $age = 2016 - $_POST['year']; //
         Calculate age this year.
42   } else {
43       print '<p class="error">Please enter
         the year you were born as four
         digits.</p>';
44       $okay = false;
45   }
46
47   // Check that they were born before this
     year:
48   if ($_POST['year'] >= 2016) {
49       print '<p class="error">Either you
         entered your birth year wrong or
         you come from the future!</p>';
50       $okay = false;
51   }
52
53   // If there were no errors, print a
     success message:
54   if ($okay) {
55       print '<p>You have been successfully
         registered (but not really).</p>';
56       print "<p>You will turn $age this
         year.</p>";
57   }
58
59   ?>
60   </body>
61   </html>
```

3. After the year validation, report an error if the year is greater than or equal to 2016:

```
if ($_POST['year'] >= 2016) {
    print '<p class="error">Either
    → you entered your birth year
    → wrong or you come from the
    → future!</p>';
    $okay = false;
}
```

If the user entered the year of birth as 2016 or later, it's presumably a mistake. (If you're reading this book after 2016, change the year accordingly).

continues on next page

4. Save your script, place it in the same directory as `register.html` (on your PHP-enabled server), and test it in your browser again Ⓐ and Ⓑ.

> **TIP** Before you compare two string values that come from a form (like the password and confirmed password), it's a good idea to apply the `trim()` function to both, to get rid of any errant spaces. I didn't do so here, so as not to overcomplicate matters, but this habit is recommended. It's also prudent to apply `trim()` to values used for logging in, such as usernames or email addresses.

> **TIP** Another method of checking that a text input type has been filled out (as opposed to using the `empty()` function) is this:

```php
if (strlen($var) > 0 ) {
    // $var is okay.
}
```

> **TIP** New in PHP 7 is the "spaceship" operator: `<=>`. This operator returns: –1 if the left operand is less than the right operand; 1 if the left operand is greater than the right; and 0 if the two are equal. The password confirmation conditional could be written this way:

```php
if ( ($_POST['password'] <=>
→ $_POST['confirm']) == 0) {
```

Except that is unnecessarily complex!

Logical

Writing conditions in PHP comes down to identifying TRUE or FALSE situations. You can do this by using functions and comparative operators, as you've already seen. *Logical* operators—the final operator type discussed in this chapter—help you create more elaborate or obvious constructs.

Ⓐ Run the form once again...

Ⓑ ...with two new validation checks in place.

Nesting Conditionals

Besides using logical operators to create more complex conditionals, you can use *nesting* for this purpose (the process of placing one control structure inside another). The key to doing so is to place the interior conditional as the *statement(s)* section of the exterior conditional. For example:

```
if (condition1) {
  if (condition2) {
    statement(s)2;
  } else { // condition2 else
    other_statement(s)2;
  } // End of 2
} else { // condition1 else
  other_statement(s)1;
} // End of 1
```

As you can see from this example, you can cut down on the complexity of these structures by using extensive indentations and comments. As long as every conditional is syntactically correct, there are no rules as to how many levels of nesting you can have, whether you use an **else** clause or even whether a sub-conditional is part of the **if** or the **else** section of the main conditional.

In PHP, one example of a TRUE condition is simply a variable name that has a value that isn't zero, an empty string, or FALSE, such as

```
$var = 5;
if ($var) { ...
```

You've already seen this with the **$okay** variable being used in the handling PHP script.

A condition is also TRUE if it makes logical sense:

```
if (5 >= 3) { ...
```

A condition will be FALSE if it refers to a variable and that variable has no value (or a value of 0 or an empty string), or if you've created an illogical construct. The following condition is always FALSE:

```
if (5 <= 3) { ...
```

In PHP, the exclamation mark (!) is the *not* operator. You can use it to invert the TRUE/FALSE status of a statement. For example:

```
$var = 'value';
if ($var) {... // TRUE
if (!$var) {... // FALSE
if (isset($var)) {... // TRUE
if (!isset($var)) {... // FALSE
if (!empty($var)) {... // TRUE
```

To go beyond simple one-part conditions, PHP supports five more types of logical operators: two versions of *and* (**AND** and **&&**), two versions of *or* (**OR** and **||**—a character called the *pipe*, put together twice), and *or not* (**XOR**). When you have two options for one operator (as with *and* and *or*), they differ only in precedence. For almost every situation, you can use either version of *and* or either version of *or* interchangeably.

Using parentheses and logical operators, you can create even more complex **if** conditionals. For an **AND** conditional, every conjoined part must be TRUE in order for the whole conditional to be TRUE. With **OR**, at least one subsection must be TRUE to render the whole condition TRUE. These conditionals are TRUE:

```
if ( (5 <= 3) OR (5 >= 3) ) { ...
if ( (5 > 3) AND (5 < 10) ) { ...
```

These conditionals are FALSE:

```
if ( (5 != 5) AND (5 > 3) ) { ...
if ( (5 != 5) OR (5 < 3) ) { ...
```

As you construct your conditionals, remember two important things: First, in order for the statements that are the result of a conditional to be executed, the entire conditional must have a TRUE value; second, by using parentheses, you can ignore rules of precedence and ensure that your operators are addressed in the order of your choosing.

To demonstrate logical operators, let's add more conditionals to the **handle_reg.php** page. You'll also nest one of the year conditionals inside another conditional (see the sidebar "Nesting Conditionals" for more).

To use logical operators:

1. Open **handle_reg.php** (Script 6.5) in your text editor or IDE, if it is not already open.

2. Delete the existing year validations (**Script 6.6**).

   You'll entirely rewrite these conditionals as one nested conditional, so it's best to get rid of the old versions entirely.

Script 6.6 Here the handling PHP script is changed so that the year validation routine uses both multiple and nested conditions. Also, the terms of agreement checkbox is now validated.

```
1   <!doctype html>
2   <!doctype html>
3   <html lang="en">
4   <head>
5       <meta charset="utf-8">
6       <title>Registration</title>
7       <style type="text/css"
        media="screen">
8          .error { color: red; }
9       </style>
10  </head>
11  <body>
12  <h1>Registration Results</h1>
13  <?php // Script 6.6 - handle_reg.php #5
14  /* This script receives seven values
    from register.html:
15  email, password, confirm, year, terms,
    color, submit */
16
17  // Address error management, if you
    want.
18
19  // Flag variable to track success:
20  $okay = true;
21
22  // Validate the email address:
23  if (empty($_POST['email'])) {
24      print '<p class="error">Please enter
        your email address.</p>';
25      $okay = false;
26  }
27
28  // Validate the password:
29  if (empty($_POST['password'])) {
30      print '<p class="error">Please enter
        your password.</p>';
31      $okay = false;
32  }
33
34  // Check the two passwords for equality:
35  if ($_POST['password'] != $_
    POST['confirm']) {
36      print '<p class="error">Your
        confirmed password does not match the
        original password.</p>';
37      $okay = false;
38  }
```

code continues on next page

```
39
40    // Validate the year:
41    if ( is_numeric($_POST['year']) AND
      (strlen($_POST['year']) == 4) ) {
42
43        // Check that they were born before
          2016.
44        if ($_POST['year'] < 2016) {
45            $age = 2016 - $_POST['year'];
              // Calculate age this year.
46        } else {
47            print '<p class="error">Either
              you entered your birth year
              wrong or you come from the
              future!</p>';
48            $okay = false;
49        } // End of 2nd conditional.
50
51    } else { // Else for 1st conditional.
52
53        print '<p class="error">Please
          enter the year you were born as
          four digits.</p>';
54        $okay = false;
55
56    } // End of 1st conditional.
57
58    // Validate the terms:
59    if ( !isset($_POST['terms'])) {
60        print '<p class="error">You must
          accept the terms.</p>';
61        $okay = false;
62    }
63
64    // If there were no errors, print a
      success message:
65    if ($okay) {
66        print '<p>You have been successfully
          registered (but not really).</p>';
67        print "<p>You will turn $age this
          year.</p>";
68    }
69    ?>
70    </body>
71    </html>
```

3. Check that the year variable is a four-digit number:

```
if ( is_numeric($_POST['year'])
→ AND (strlen($_POST['year'])
→ == 4) ) {
```

This conditional has two parts. The first you've already seen—it tests for a valid numeric value. The second part gets the length of the year variable (using the **strlen()** function) and checks if the length value is equal to 4. Because of the **AND**, this conditional is TRUE only if both conditions are met.

4. Create a subconditional to check if the year value is before 2016:

```
if ($_POST['year'] < 2016) {
    $age = 2016 - $_POST['year'];
} else {
    print '<p class="error">
→ Either you entered your birth
→ year wrong or you come from
→ the future!</p>';
    $okay = FALSE;
} // End of 2nd conditional
```

This **if-else** conditional acts as the *statements* part of the main conditional, and is thus executed only if that condition is TRUE. This **if-else** checks whether the year variable is less than 2016 (i.e., the user must have been born before the current year). If that condition is TRUE, the user's age is calculated as before. Otherwise, an error message is printed and the **$okay** variable is set to FALSE (indicating that a problem occurred).

Note that this conditional is just the opposite of the previous version: verifying that a value is less than some number instead of greater than or equal to that number.

continues on next page

5. Complete the main year conditional:

```
} else { // Else for 1st
conditional.
    print '<p class="error">Please
→ enter the year you were born
→ as four digits.</p>';
      $okay = FALSE;
} // End of 1st conditional.
```

This **else** section completes the conditional begun in Step 3. If at least one of the conditions set forth there is FALSE, this message is printed, and **$okay** is set to FALSE.

6. Confirm that the terms checkbox wasn't ignored:

```
if (!isset($_POST['terms'])) {
    print '<p class="error">You
→ must accept the terms.</p>';
    $okay = FALSE;
}
```

If the **$_POST['terms']** variable is not set, then the user failed to select that box, and an error should be reported. To be more exact, this conditional could be

```
if ( !isset($_POST['terms']) AND
→ ($_POST['terms'] != 'Yes') ) {
```

7. Those are the only changes to the script, so you can now save it again, place it in the same directory as **register.html** (on your PHP-enabled server), and test it in your browser again **C** and **D**.

C The PHP script now catches if the year isn't a four-digit number, as will be the case with this form submission.

D Error messages are printed if fields are incorrectly filled out or if the terms checkbox is not selected.

8. If desired, change your **year** value to be in the future, and submit the form again **E**.

> **TIP** It's very easy in long, complicated conditionals to forget an opening or closing parenthesis or brace, which will produce either error messages or unexpected results. Find a system (like spacing out your conditionals and using comments) to help clarify your code. Another good technique is to create the conditional's entire structure first, and then go back to add the details.

> **TIP** If you have problems getting your `if-else` statements to execute, print out the values of your variables to help debug the problem. A conditional may not be TRUE or FALSE because a variable doesn't have the value you think it does.

The Null Coalescing Operator

New in PHP 7 is the null coalescing operator, which is a fancy name for a useful shortcut. Often you'll want to check if a variable has a value and, if not, assign a default value to it. Before PHP 7, this would be done using code like

```php
if (isset($_POST['var'])) {
    $var = $_POST['var'];
} else {
    $var = 'default value';
}
```

Thanks to the null coalescing operator, `??`, that code can be abbreviated to

```php
$var = $_POST['var'] ?? 'default
▸ value';
```

The result is semantically the same, but the latter requires one-fourth as many lines of code.

E The year validation still checks that the date is before 2016.

Using elseif

Similar to the **if-else** conditional is **if-elseif** (or **if-elseif-else**). This conditional acts like a running **if** statement and can be expanded to whatever complexity you require:

```
if (condition1) {
   statement(s);
} elseif (condition2) {
   other_statement(s);
}
```

Here's another example **A**:

```
if (condition1) {
   statement(s);
} elseif (condition2) {
   other_statement(s);
} else {
   other_other_statement(s);
}
```

Understand that this structure means, for example, that *other_statement(s)* are only executed if *condition1* is FALSE but *condition2* is TRUE. If both conditions are FALSE, the *other_other_statement(s)* are executed.

If the **else** is present, you must always make it the last part of a conditional because it's executed unless one of the conditions to that point has been met (again, **else** represents the *default* behavior). You can, however, continue to use **elseif**s as many times as you want as part of one **if** conditional. You may also forgo an **else** clause if you don't need a default result.

As an example of this, let's create a conditional that prints a message based on the selected color value.

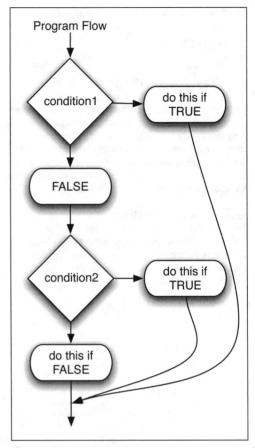

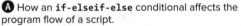 **A** How an **if-elseif-else** conditional affects the program flow of a script.

```
1   <!doctype html>
2   <html lang="en">
3   <head>
4       <meta charset="utf-8">
5       <title>Registration</title>
6       <style type="text/css"
        media="screen">
7           .error { color: red; }
8       </style>
9   </head>
10  <body>
11  <h1>Registration Results</h1>
12  <?php // Script 6.7 - handle_reg.php #6
13  /* This script receives seven values
    from register.html:
14  email, password, confirm, year, terms,
    color, submit */
15
16  // Address error management, if you
    want.
17
18  // Flag variable to track success:
19  $okay = true;
20
21  // Validate the email address:
22  if (empty($_POST['email'])) {
23      print '<p class="error">Please enter
        your email address.</p>';
24      $okay = false;
25  }
26
27  // Validate the password:
28  if (empty($_POST['password'])) {
29      print '<p class="error">Please enter
        your password.</p>';
30      $okay = false;
31  }
32
33  // Check the two passwords for equality:
34  if ($_POST['password'] != $_
    POST['confirm']) {
35      print '<p class="error">Your
        confirmed password does not match the
        original password.</p>';
36      $okay = false;
37  }
38
```

code continues on next page

To use elseif:

1. Open **handle_reg.php** (Script 6.6) in your text editor or IDE, if it is not already open.

2. Before the **$okay** conditional, begin a new conditional (**Script 6.7**):

   ```
   if ($_POST['color'] == 'red') {
     $color_type = 'primary';
   ```

   The color value comes from a select menu with four possible options: *red*, *yellow*, *green*, and *blue*. This conditional will determine whether the user has selected a primary—red, yellow, or blue—or secondary (all others) color. The first condition checks if the value of **$_POST['color']** is equal to the string *red*.

   Be certain to use the *equality* operator —two equals signs—and not the *assignment* operator—one—in the conditional.

3. Add an **elseif** clause for the second color:

   ```
   } elseif ($_POST['color'] ==
   → 'yellow') {
     $color_type = 'primary';
   ```

   The **elseif** continues the main conditional begun in Step 2. The condition itself is a replication of the condition in Step 2, using a new color comparison.

continues on next page

4. Add **elseif** clauses for the other two colors:

```
} elseif ($_POST['color'] ==
→ 'green') {
  $color_type = 'secondary';
} elseif ($_POST['color'] ==
→ 'blue') {
  $color_type = 'primary';
```

Once you understand the main concept, it's just a matter of repeating the **elseif**s for every possible color value.

5. Add an **else** clause:

```
} else {
  print '<p class="error">
→ Please select your favorite
→ color.</p>';
  $okay = FALSE;
}
```

If the user didn't select a color, or if the user manipulated the form to submit a different color value (other than *red*, *yellow*, *green*, or *blue*), none of the conditions will be TRUE, meaning this **else** clause will take effect. That clause prints an error and assigns a value of FALSE to **$okay**, indicating a problem.

It doesn't matter in what order the colors are checked, so long as the **else** clause comes last.

Script 6.7 *continued*

```
39    // Check the two passwords for equality:
40    if ($_POST['password'] != $_
      POST['confirm']) {
41        print '<p class="error">Your
          confirmed password does not match the
          original password.</p>';
42        $okay = false;
43    }
44
45    // Validate the year:
46    if ( is_numeric($_POST['year']) AND
      (strlen($_POST['year']) == 4) ) {
47
48        // Check that they were born before
          2016.
49        if ($_POST['year'] < 2016) {
50            $age = 2016 - $_POST['year']; //
              Calculate age this year.
51        } else {
52            print '<p class="error">Either you
              entered your birth year wrong or
              you come from the future!</p>';
53            $okay = false;
54        } // End of 2nd conditional.
55
56    } else { // Else for 1st conditional.
57
58        print '<p class="error">Please enter
          the year you were born as four
          digits.</p>';
59        $okay = false;
60
61    } // End of 1st conditional.
62
63    // Validate the terms:
64    if ( !isset($_POST['terms'])) {
65        print '<p class="error">You must
          accept the terms.</p>';
66        $okay = false;
67    }
68
69    // Validate the color:
70    if ($_POST['color'] == 'red') {
71        $color_type = 'primary';
72    } elseif ($_POST['color'] ==
      'yellow') {
73        $color_type = 'primary';
74    } elseif ($_POST['color'] == 'green')
      {
```

code continues on next page

Script 6.7 *continued*

```
75        $color_type = 'secondary';
76    } elseif ($_POST['color'] == 'blue')
      {
77        $color_type = 'primary';
78    } else { // Problem!
79        print '<p class="error">Please
          select your favorite color.</p>';
80        $okay = false;
81    }
82
83    // If there were no errors, print a
      success message:
84    if ($okay) {
85        print '<p>You have been successfully
          registered (but not really).</p>';
86        print "<p>You will turn $age this
          year.</p>";
87        print "<p>Your favorite color is a
          $color_type color.</p>";
88    }
89    ?>
90    </body>
91    </html>
```

Registration Results

You have been successfully registered (but not really).

You will turn 11 this year.

Your favorite color is a secondary color.

B The script now prints a message acknowledging the user's color choice.

Registration Results

Please select your favorite color.

C Failure to select a color results in this error message.

6. Within the **$okay** conditional, print the user's favorite color type:

   ```
   print "<p>Your favorite color is
   → a $color_type color.</p>";
   ```

7. Save the script, place it in the same directory as **register.html** (on your PHP-enabled server), and test it in your browser again, using different color options **B** and **C**.

TIP One thing most beginner developers don't realize is that it's possible—in fact, quite easy—for a hacker to submit data to your PHP script without using your HTML form. It's also easy with modern browsers to manipulate forms. For these reasons, it's important that you validate the existence of expected variables (i.e., that they are set), their type, and their values.

TIP PHP also allows you to write elseif as two words, if you prefer:

```
if (condition1) {
    statement(s);
} else if (condition2) {
    statement(s)2;
}
```

The Switch Conditional

Once you get to the point where you have longer **if-elseif-else** conditionals, you may find that you can save programming time and clarify your code by using a **switch** conditional instead. The **switch** conditional takes only one possible condition, normally just a variable:

```
switch ($var) {
   case value1:
      statement(s)1;
      break;
   case value2:
      statement(s)2;
      break;
   default:
      statement(s)3;
      break;
}
```

You must understand how a **switch** conditional works in order to use it properly. After the keyword **switch**, a variable is identified within parentheses. PHP will then look at each case in order, trying to identify a matching value. Note that, as with any other use of strings and numbers in PHP, numeric values would not be quoted; string values should be. After the **case value** section, a *colon* (not a semicolon) prefaces the associated statements, which are normally indented beginning on the following line.

Once PHP finds a case that matches the value of the conditional variable, it executes the subsequent statements. Here's the tricky part: Once PHP has found a matching case, it will continue going through the **switch** until it either comes to the end of the **switch** conditional (the closing brace) or hits a **break** statement, at which point it exits the **switch** construct. Thus, it's imperative that you close every case—even the

Script 6.8 Switch conditionals can simplify complicated **if-elseif** conditionals.

```
1    <!doctype html>
2    <html lang="en">
3    <head>
4       <meta charset="utf-8">
5       <title>Registration</title>
6       <style type="text/css"
         media="screen">
7          .error { color: red; }
8       </style>
9    </head>
10   <body>
11   <h1>Registration Results</h1>
12   <?php // Script 6.8 - handle_reg.php #7
13   /* This script receives seven values
        from register.html:
14   email, password, confirm, year, terms,
        color, submit */
15
16   // Address error management, if you
        want.
17
18   // Flag variable to track success:
19   $okay = true;
20
21   // Validate the email address:
22   if (empty($_POST['email'])) {
23      print '<p class="error">Please enter
           your email address.</p>';
24      $okay = false;
25   }
26
27   // Validate the password:
28   if (empty($_POST['password'])) {
29      print '<p class="error">Please enter
           your password.</p>';
30      $okay = false;
31   }
32
33   // Check the two passwords for equality:
34   if ($_POST['password'] != $_
        POST['confirm']) {
35      print '<p class="error">Your
           confirmed password does not match the
           original password.</p>';
36      $okay = false;
37   }
38
```

code continues on next page

```
39    // Validate the year:
40    if ( is_numeric($_POST['year']) AND
      (strlen($_POST['year']) == 4) ) {
41
42        // Check that they were born before
          2016.
43        if ($_POST['year'] < 2016) {
44            $age = 2016 - $_POST['year']; //
              Calculate age this year.
45        } else {
46            print '<p class="error">Either you
              entered your birth year wrong or
              you come from the future!</p>';
47            $okay = false;
48        } // End of 2nd conditional.
49
50    } else { // Else for 1st conditional.
51
52        print '<p class="error">Please enter
          the year you were born as four
          digits.</p>';
53        $okay = false;
54
55    } // End of 1st conditional.
56
57    // Validate the terms:
58    if ( !isset($_POST['terms'])) {
59        print '<p class="error">You must
          accept the terms.</p>';
60        $okay = false;
61    }
62
63    // Validate the color:
64    switch ($_POST['color']) {
65        case 'red':
66            $color_type = 'primary';
67            break;
68        case 'yellow':
69            $color_type = 'primary';
70            break;
71        case 'green':
72            $color_type = 'secondary';
73            break;
74        case 'blue':
75            $color_type = 'primary';
76            break;
77        default:
```

code continues on next page

default case, for consistency's sake—with a **break** (the sidebar "Break, Exit, Die, and Continue" discusses this keyword in more detail).

This previous **switch** conditional is like a rewrite of

```
if ($var == value1) {
    statement(s)1;
} elseif ($variable == value2) {
    statement(s)2;
} else {
    statement(s)3;
}
```

Because the **switch** conditional uses the value of **$var** as its condition, it first checks to see if **$var** is equal to *value1*, and if so, it executes *statement(s)1*. If not, it checks to see if **$var** is equal to *value2*, and if so, it executes *statement(s)2*. If neither condition is met, the default action of the **switch** conditional is to execute *statement(s)3*.

With this in mind, let's rewrite the colors conditional as a **switch**.

To use a switch conditional:

1. Open **handle_reg.php** (Script 6.7) in your text editor or IDE, if it is not already open.

2. Delete the extended colors conditional (**Script 6.8**).

3. Begin the **switch**:

   ```
   switch ($_POST['color']) {
   ```

   As mentioned earlier, a **switch** conditional takes only one condition: a variable's name. In this example, it's **$_POST['color']**.

continues on next page

4. Create the first case:

```
case 'red':
  $color_type = 'primary';
  break;
```

The first case checks to see if `$_POST['color']` has a value of *red*. If so, then the same statement is executed as before. Next you include a **break** statement to exit the **switch**.

5. Add a case for the second color:

```
case 'yellow':
  $color_type = 'primary';
  break;
```

6. Add cases for the remaining colors:

```
case 'green':
  $color_type = 'secondary';
  break;
case 'blue':
  $color_type = 'primary';
  break;
```

Script 6.8 *continued*

```
78      print '<p class="error">Please
        select your favorite color.</
        p>';
79      $okay = false;
80      break;
81  } // End of switch.
82
83  // If there were no errors, print a
    success message:
84  if ($okay) {
85      print '<p>You have been successfully
        registered (but not really).</p>';
86      print "<p>You will turn $age this
        year.</p>";
87      print "<p>Your favorite color is a
        $color_type color.</p>";
88  }
89  ?>
90  </body>
91  </html>
```

Break, Exit, Die, and Continue

PHP includes many *language constructs*—tools that aren't functions but still do something in your scripts. For example, **print** is a language construct. Another example is **break**, which is demonstrated in the **switch**. A **break** exits the current structure, be it a **switch**, an **if-else** conditional, or a loop.

Similar to this is **continue**, which terminates the current iteration of a loop. Any remaining statements within the loop aren't executed, but the loop's condition is checked again to see if the loop should be entered.

exit and **die** are more potent versions of **break** (and they're synonymous). Instead of exiting the current structure, these two language constructs terminate the execution of the PHP script. Therefore, all PHP code after a use of **exit** or **die** is never executed. For that matter, any HTML after these constructs is never sent to the browser. You'll see **die** used most frequently as a heavy-handed error handling tool. **exit** is often used in conjunction with the **header()** function. You'll see an example of this in Chapter 8, "Creating Web Applications."

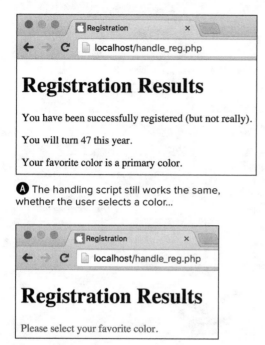

Registration Results

You have been successfully registered (but not really).

You will turn 47 this year.

Your favorite color is a primary color.

A The handling script still works the same, whether the user selects a color...

Registration Results

Please select your favorite color.

B ...or fails to.

7. Add a **default** case and complete the switch:

```
default:
    print '<p class="error">
    → Please select your favorite
    → color.</p>';
    $okay = FALSE;
    break;
} // End of switch.
```

This **default** case is the equivalent of the **else** clause used in the original conditional.

8. Save your script, place it in the same directory as **register.html** (on your PHP-enabled server), and test it in your browser again **A** and **B**.

TIP A **default** case isn't required in your **switch** conditional, but if it's used, it should be the last case. You could set up a **switch** so that if the value isn't explicitly met by one of the cases, nothing happens.

TIP If you're using a string in your **switch** conditional as the case value, keep in mind that it's case sensitive, meaning that Value won't match value.

TIP You can structure switch conditionals such that more than one case has the same result. However, that kind of programming, which requires sound knowledge of PHP's behavior, is unnecessarily clever for the beginning programmer.

The for Loop

Loops are the final type of control structure discussed in this chapter. As suggested earlier, loops are used to execute a section of code repeatedly. You may want to print something a certain number of times, or you may want to do something with each value in an array (an array is a list of values). For either of these cases, and many more, you can use a loop. (The latter example is demonstrated in the next chapter.)

PHP supports three kinds of loops: **for**, **while**, and **foreach**. The **while** loop is similar to **for**, but it's used most frequently when retrieving values from a database or reading from a text file (it's introduced in the sidebar "The while Loop" and covered in more detail in the next chapter). The **foreach** loop is related to using arrays and is introduced in the next chapter.

The **for** loop is designed to perform one or more statements for a determined number of iterations (unlike **while**, which runs until a condition is FALSE—similar, but significantly different, concepts). You normally use a dummy variable in the loop for this purpose:

```
for (initial expression; condition;
→ closing expression) {
   statement(s);
}
```

The initial expression is executed once: the first time the loop is called. Then the condition is used to determine whether to execute the statements. The closing expression is executed each time the condition is found to be TRUE, but only after the statements are executed **A**.

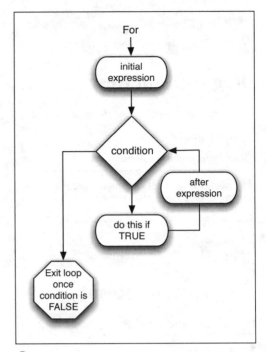

A This flowchart represents how a **for** loop is executed in PHP.

```
1    <!doctype html>
2    <html lang="en">
3    <head>
4        <meta charset="utf-8">
5        <title>Registration Form</title>
6    </head>
7    <body>
8    <!-- Script 6.9 - register.php -->
9    <div><p>Please complete this form to
     register:</p>
10
11   <form action="handle_reg.php"
     method="post">
12
13       <p>Email Address: <input type="text"
         name="email" size="30"></p>
14
15       <p>Password: <input type="password"
         name="password" size="20"></p>
16
17       <p>Confirm Password: <input
         type="password" name="confirm"
         size="20"></p>
18
19       <p>Date Of Birth:
20       <select name="month">
21       <option value="">Month</option>
22       <option value="1">January</option>
23       <option value="2">February</
         option>
24       <option value="3">March</option>
25       <option value="4">April</option>
26       <option value="5">May</option>
27       <option value="6">June</option>
28       <option value="7">July</option>
29       <option value="8">August</option>
30       <option value="9">September</
         option>
31       <option value="10">October</
         option>
32       <option value="11">November</
         option>
33       <option value="12">December</
         option>
34       </select>
35       <select name="day">
36       <option value="">Day</option>
```

code continues on next page

Here's a simple loop that prints out the numbers 1 through 10:

```
for ($i = 1; $i <= 10; $i++) {
    print $i;
}
```

To practice with the **for** loop, let's expand the registration form so that it asks users for their complete birthday. A **for** loop can be used to easily create a day drop-down menu in the HTML form.

To write a for loop:

1. Open **register.html** (Script 6.1) in your text editor or IDE, if it is not already open.

2. Remove the existing birth year prompt and input (**Script 6.9**).

   You'll replace this one prompt with three separate elements to represent the entire birthday: month, day, and year.

3. Where the birth year prompt was, after the password confirmation and before the color option, add a prompt and a list of months:

```
<p>Date Of Birth:
<select name="month">
<option value="">Month</option>
<option value="1">January</
→ option>
<option value="2">February</
→ option>
<option value="3">March</option>
<option value="4">April</option>
<option value="5">May</option>
<option value="6">June</option>
<option value="7">July</option>
<option value="8">August</option>
<option value="9">September</
→ option>
```

continues on next page

```
<option value="10">October</
→ option>
<option value="11">November</
→ option>
<option value="12">December</
→ option>
</select>
```

First is a textual prompt, telling users to supply their entire date of birth. Next comes a select menu in which users can pick their birth month. The value for each option is numeric; the viewed text is a string (the month's name).

4. Begin a select menu for the day of the month the user was born:

```
<select name="day">
<option value="">Day</option>
```

This code starts the **select** form element. The list of possible values will be generated using PHP.

5. Create a new PHP section:

```
<?php
```

Because PHP can be embedded within HTML, you'll use it to populate the drop-down menu. Begin with the standard PHP tag.

Script 6.9 *continued*

```
37    <?php // Print out 31 days:
38    for ($i = 1; $i <= 31; $i++) {
39        print "<option
          value=\"$i\">$i</option>\n";
40    }
41    ?>
42    </select>
43    <input type="text" name="year"
      value="YYYY" size="4"></p>
44
45    <p>Favorite Color:
46    <select name="color">
47    <option value="">Pick One</option>
48    <option value="red">Red</option>
49    <option value="yellow">Yellow</
      option>
50    <option value="green">Green</option>
51    <option value="blue">Blue</option>
52    </select></p>
53
54    <p><input type="checkbox"
      name="terms" value="Yes"> I agree to
      the terms (whatever they may be).</p>
55
56    <input type="submit" name="submit"
      value="Register">
57
58    </form>
59
60    </div>
61    </body>
62    </html>
```

B The new version of the HTML form, with some dynamically generated content.

C If you view the HTML source code for the form, you'll see the data generated by the **for** loop.

6. Create a **for** loop to print out 31 days as select menu options:

```
for ($i = 1; $i <= 31; $i++) {
    print "<option
    value=\"$i\">$i</option>\n";
}
```

The loop begins by creating a dummy variable named **$i**. On the first use of the loop, this variable is set to 1. Then, as long as **$i** is less than or equal to 31, the contents of the loop are executed. These contents are the **print** line, which creates code like

```
<option value="1">1</option>
```

followed by a return (created with **\n**). After this statement is executed, the **$i** variable is incremented by 1. Then the condition (**$i <= 31**) is checked again, and the process is repeated.

7. Close the PHP section, and the select element:

```
?>
</select>
```

8. Save the file as **register.php**.

You must save the file with the **.php** extension now in order for the PHP code to be executed.

9. Place the file in the proper directory for your PHP-enabled server, and test it in your browser **B**.

As long as this script is in the same directory as **handle_reg.php**, you can even fill out and submit the form as you would with the plain HTML version.

10. If desired, view the HTML source code to see the PHP-generated options **C**.

TIP It's conventional to use simple variables as the counters within `for` loops: `$i`, `$j`, `$k`, and so on.

TIP Just as you can write the `if` conditional on one line if you have only one statement, you can do the same with the `while` and `for` loops. Again, though, this isn't recommended.

TIP Loops can be nested inside each other. You can also place conditionals within loops, loops within conditionals, and so forth.

TIP Pay close attention to your loop's condition so that the loop ends at some point. Otherwise, you'll create an infinite loop, and the script will run and run and run.

The while Loop

The second of the three types of loops that exist in PHP—the `while` loop—is designed to continue working as long as the condition you establish is TRUE. Like the `for` loop, it checks the value of the condition before each iteration. Once the condition becomes FALSE, the `while` loop is exited:

```
while (condition) {
    statement(s);
}
```

The main difference between `for` and `while` is that `while` doesn't include a system for setting initial conditions or for executing closing expressions.

You also have the option of using the `do...while` loop, which guarantees that the statements are executed at least once (this isn't necessarily true of the `while` loop):

```
do {
    statement(s);
} while (condition);
```

Although there is a fair amount of overlap regarding when you can use the two major loop constructs (`while` and `for`), you'll discover as you program that sometimes one is more logical than the other. The `while` loop is frequently used in the retrieval of data from a database (see Chapter 12, "Intro to Databases").

Review and Pursue

If you have any problems with the review questions or the pursue prompts, turn to the book's supporting forum (www.LarryUllman.com/forums/).

Review

- What is the basic structure of an **if** conditional in PHP? An **if-else** conditional? An **if-elseif**? An **if-elseif-else**?

- What are the differences between the **empty()** and **isset()** functions?

- What is the **assignment** operator? What is the equality operator?

- Without knowing anything about **$var**, will the following conditional be TRUE or FALSE? Why?

  ```
  if ($var = 'donut') {
  ```

- What do these operators mean?
  - **&&**
  - **||**
  - **!**

- What is the syntax of a **switch** conditional? When is a **switch** most commonly used?

- What is the syntax of a **for** loop?

Pursue

- Check out the PHP manual's pages for the various operators.

- Rewrite **handle_reg.php** so that it uses a variable for the current year, instead of hard-coding that value.

- For debugging purposes, add code to the beginning of the **handle_reg.php** script that prints out the values of the received variables. Hint: There's a short and a long way to do this.

- Rewrite one of the versions of **handle_reg.php** so that it prints the user's favorite color selection in the user's favorite color. Hint: You'll want to use CSS and concatenation.

- Update **handle_reg.php** so that it validates the user's birthday by looking at the three individual form elements: month, day, and year. Create a variable that represents the user's birthday in the format *XX/DD/YYYY* (again, you'll use concatenation for this).

7

Using Arrays

The next—and last—variable type you'll learn about in this book is the array. Arrays are significantly different from numbers or strings, and you can't make the most of programming in PHP without understanding them.

Because of their unique nature, this chapter will cover arrays more deliberately and slowly than the other variable types. The chapter begins with an introduction to the concept, along with the basics of creating and using arrays. Then it covers multidimensional arrays and some of the array-related functions. The chapter concludes with array-string conversions and a demonstration on how to create an array from an HTML form.

In This Chapter

What Is an Array?

Arrays constitute a complicated but very useful notion. Whereas numbers and strings are *scalar* variables—meaning they always have only a single value—an array is a collection of multiple values assembled into one overriding variable. An array can consist of numbers and/or strings and/or other arrays, which allows this one variable to hold exponentially more information than a simple string or number can. For example, if you wanted to create a grocery list using strings, your code would look something like this:

```
$item1 = 'apples';
$item2 = 'bananas';
$item3 = 'oranges';
```

For each added item, you'd need to create a new string. This approach is cumbersome, and it makes it difficult to refer back to the entire list or any specific value later in your code. You can greatly simplify matters by placing your entire list into one array (say, **$items**), which contains everything you need (**Table 7.1**).

As an array, your list can be added to, sorted, searched, and so forth. With this context in mind, let's look into the syntax of arrays.

TABLE 7.1 Grocery List Array

Item Number	Item
1	apples
2	bananas
3	oranges

Syntactical rules for arrays

The other variable types you've dealt with—numbers and strings—have a variable name and a corresponding value (for example, **$first_name** could be equal to *Larry*). Arrays also have a name, derived using the same conventions:

- They begin with a dollar sign.
- They continue with a letter or underscore.
- They finish with any combination of letters, numbers, or the underscore.

But arrays differ in that they contain multiple *elements*. Think of each row in Table 7.1 as an element. An element consists of an *index* or *key*—the two words can be used interchangeably—and a value. In Table 7.1, the Item Number is the key, and the Item is the value.

An array's index is used as a reference point to the values. An array can use either numbers or strings as its keys, or both, depending on how you set it up.

Generally, when you use an array it looks the same as any other variable, except that you include a key in brackets (**[]**, sometimes referred to as *square brackets*) to reference particular values. Whereas **$items** refers to the array as a whole, **$items[1]** points to a specific element in the array (in this example, *apples*).

Creating an Array

The formal method of creating an array is to use the **array()** function. Its syntax is

```
$list = array('apples', 'bananas',
→ 'oranges');
```

Arrays automatically begin their indexing at 0, unless otherwise specified. In that example—which doesn't specify an index for the elements—the first item, *apples*, is automatically indexed at 0, the second item at 1, and the third at 2.

If you desire, you can assign the index when using **array()**:

```
$list = array(1 => 'apples', 2 =>
→ 'bananas', 3 => 'oranges');
```

Because PHP is very liberal when it comes to blank space in your code, you can make this structure easier to read by writing it over multiple lines:

```
$list = array(
   1 => 'apples',
   2 => 'bananas',
   3 => 'oranges'
);
```

(For better legibility, it's common to indent the array elements as shown here, although this is not required.)

As of PHP 5.4, you can also create arrays using the *short array syntax*. Simply use brackets instead of a call to **array()**:

```
$list = ['apples', 'bananas',
→ 'oranges'];
```

Naturally, you can set the indexes with this syntax as well:

```
$list = [
   1 => 'apples',
   2 => 'bananas',
   3 => 'oranges'
];
```

Finally, the index value you specify doesn't have to be a number—you can use strings instead. As an example, you could create an array that records the soup of the day for each day of the week, as in the following script. This example will also demonstrate how you can, and cannot, print out an array (which has already been demonstrated but is worth rehashing).

```
1   <!doctype html>
2   <html lang="en">
3   <head>
4       <meta charset="utf-8">
5       <title>No Soup for You!</title>
6   </head>
7   <body>
8   <h1>Mmm...soups</h1>
9   <?php // Script 7.1 - soups1.php
10  /* This script creates and prints out an
    array. */
11  // Address error management, if you
    want.
12
13  // Create the array:
14  $soups = [
15      'Monday' => 'Clam Chowder',
16      'Tuesday' => 'White Chicken
        Chili',
17      'Wednesday' => 'Vegetarian'
18  ];
19
20  // Try to print the array:
21  print "<p>$soups</p>";
22
23  // Print the contents of the array:
24  print_r($soups);
25
26  ?>
27  </body>
28  </html>
```

To create an array:

1. Begin a new document in your text editor or IDE, to be named **soups1.php** (Script 7.1):

   ```
   <!doctype html>
   <html lang="en">
   <head>
       <meta charset="utf-8">
       <title>No Soup for You!</title>
   </head>
   <body>
   <h1>Mmm...soups</h1>
   ```

2. Begin the PHP section of the script, and address error handling, if necessary:

   ```
   <?php // Script 7.1 - soups1.php
   ```

   If you don't have **display_errors** enabled, or if **error_reporting** is set to the wrong level, see Chapter 3, "HTML Forms and PHP," for the lines to include here to alter those settings.

3. Create an array:

   ```
   $soups = [
       'Monday' => 'Clam Chowder',
       'Tuesday' => 'White Chicken
       → Chili',
       'Wednesday' => 'Vegetarian'

   ];
   ```

   This is the proper short array syntax format for initializing—creating and assigning a value to—an array in PHP, using strings as the indices. Because both the keys and values are strings, you surround them with quotation marks. As with all strings, you can use either single or double quotation marks, as long as you're mindful of other quotation marks that might be found within the string.

   If you are not using at least PHP version 5.4, or if you prefer to be more explicit, use the **array()** function instead.

continues on next page

4. Attempt to print the array:

```
print "<p>$soups</p>";
```

As you've already seen, arrays are also different from scalar variables in that they can't be printed using this syntax.

5. Use the `print_r()` function to print out the array differently:

```
print_r($soups);
```

In Chapter 2, "Variables," you learned how to use `print_r()` to show the contents and structure of any variable. Use it here so you can see the difference between the way this function and `print` work with arrays.

6. Close the PHP and the HTML sections:

```
?>
</body>
</html>
```

7. Save your document as **soups1.php**, place it in the proper directory for your PHP-enabled server, and test it in your browser **A**.

Remember to run the PHP script through a URL.

No Soup for You! ×

← → C localhost/soups1.php

Mmm...soups

(!) Notice: Array to string conversion in /Users/larry/Sites/soups1.php on line *21*

Call Stack

#	Time	Memory	Function	Location
1	0.0018	366680	{main}( )	.../soups1.php:0

Array

Array ([Monday] => Clam Chowder [Tuesday] => White Chicken Chili [Wednesday] => Vegetarian)

A Because an array is structured differently than other variable types, a request to print out an array results in the word *Array*. On the other hand, the `print_r()` function prints the array's contents and structure.

TIP The practice of beginning any index at 0 is standard in PHP and most other programming languages. As unnatural as this counting system may seem, it's here to stay, so you have two possible coping techniques. First, manually start all your arrays indexed at position 1. Second, unlearn a lifetime of counting from 1. You can decide which is easier, but most programmers just get used to this odd construct.

TIP You must refer to an array's elements via the same index used to create the array. In the `$soups` example, `$soups[0]` has no value even though the array obviously has a first element (the first element normally being indexed at 0 numerically).

TIP With numeric indexes, you can set the first index and the others will follow sequentially. For example:

```
$list = [1 => 'apples', 'bananas',
→ 'oranges'];
```

Now bananas is indexed at 2 and oranges at 3.

TIP The `range()` function can also be used to create an array of items based on a range of values. Here are two examples:

```
$ten = range(1, 10);
$alphabet = range('a', 'z');
```

The `range()` function includes a step parameter that lets you specify increments:

```
$evens = range (0, 100, 2);
```

TIP If you use the `var_dump()` function in your script in lieu of `print_r()`, it shows not only the contents of the array but also its structure in a more detailed format **B**.

TIP An array whose keys are numbers is known as an indexed array. If the keys are strings, it's referred to as an associative array. Other languages refer to associative arrays as hashes.

```
array (size=3)
  'Monday' => string 'Clam Chowder' (length=12)
  'Tuesday' => string 'White Chicken Chili' (length=19)
  'Wednesday' => string 'Vegetarian' (length=10)
```

B The `var_dump()` function (used with Script 7.1 instead of the `print_r()` function) shows how many elements are in an array and how long each string value is.

Adding Items to an Array

In PHP, once an array exists, you can add extra elements to the array with the assignment operator (the equals sign), in a way similar to how you assign a value to a string or a number. When doing so, you can specify the key of the added element or not specify it, but in either case, you must refer to the array with brackets.

Here's a definition of the **$list** array:

```
$list = [
    1 => 'apples',
    2 => 'bananas',
    3 => 'oranges'
];
```

To add two items to that, you'd write

```
$list[] = 'pears';
$list[] = 'tomatoes';
```

If you don't specify the key, each element is appended to the existing array, indexed with the next sequential number. Now *pears* is located at 4 and *tomatoes* at 5.

If you do specify the index, the value is assigned at that location. Any existing value already indexed at that point is overwritten, like so:

```
$list[3] = 'pears';
$list[4] = 'tomatoes';
```

Now, the value of the element in the fourth position of the array is *tomatoes*, and no element of **$list** is equal to *oranges* (that value was overwritten by *pears*). With this in mind, unless you intend to overwrite any existing data, you'll be better off not naming a specific key when adding values to your arrays. However, if the array uses strings for indices, you'll probably want to specify keys so that you don't end up with an unusual combination of string keys and numeric keys.

Deleting Arrays and Array Elements

You won't frequently need to delete an individual item from an array, but it's possible to do using the **unset()** function. This function eliminates a variable and frees up the memory it used. When applied to an array element, that element is deleted:

```
unset($array[4]);
unset($array['key']);
```

Removing a single element will not re-index the array, however. The code removes one element, no element is now indexed at 4, and every other element continues to be indexed where they were.

If you apply **unset()** to an entire array or any other variable type, the whole variable is deleted:

```
unset($array);
unset($string);
```

You can also *reset* an array (empty it without deleting the variable altogether) using the **array()** function or short array syntax:

```
$array = array();
$array = [];
```

This has the effect of initializing the variable: making it exist and defining its type without assigning a value.

Script 7.2 You can directly add elements to an array one at a time by assigning each element a value with the assignment operator. The `count()` function will help you keep track of how many elements the array contains.

```
1    <!doctype html>
2    <html lang="en">
3    <head>
4        <meta charset="utf-8">
5        <title>No Soup for You!</title>
6    </head>
7    <body>
8    <h1>Mmm...soups</h1>
9    <?php // Script 7.2 - soups2.php
10   /* This script creates and prints out an
     array. */
11   // Address error management, if you
     want.
12
13   // Create the array:
14   $soups = [
15       'Monday' => 'Clam Chowder',
16       'Tuesday' => 'White Chicken Chili',
17       'Wednesday' => 'Vegetarian'
18   ];
19
20   // Count and print the current number of
     elements:
21   $count1 = count($soups);
22   print "<p>The soups array originally
     had $count1 elements.</p>";
23
24   // Add three items to the array:
25   $soups['Thursday'] = 'Chicken
     Noodle';
26   $soups['Friday'] = 'Tomato';
27   $soups['Saturday'] = 'Cream of
     Broccoli';
28
29   // Count and print the number of
     elements again:
30   $count2 = count($soups);
31   print "<p>After adding 3 more soups,
     the array now has $count2 elements.
     </p>";
32
33   // Print the contents of the array:
34   print_r($soups);
35
36   ?>
37   </body>
38   </html>
```

To test this process, in the following task you'll rewrite **soups1.php** to add more elements to the array. To see the difference adding more elements makes, you'll print out the number of elements in the array before and after the new additions. Just as you can find the length of a string—how many characters it contains—by using **strlen()**, you can determine the number of elements in an array by using **count()**:

`$how_many = count($array);`

To add elements to an array:

1. Open **soups1.php** in your text editor or IDE, if it is not already open.

2. After the array is initialized on lines 14 through 18, add the following (**Script 7.2**, to be named **soups2.php**):

   ```
   $count1 = count($soups);
   print "<p>The soups array
   → originally had $count1
   → elements.</p>";
   ```

   The **count()** function determines how many elements are in **$soups**. By assigning that value to a variable, you can easily print out the number.

3. Add three more elements to the array:

   ```
   $soups['Thursday'] = 'Chicken
   → Noodle';
   $soups['Friday'] = 'Tomato';
   $soups['Saturday'] = 'Cream of
   → Broccoli';
   ```

   This code adds three more soups—indexed at *Thursday*, *Friday*, and *Saturday*—to the existing array.

   continues on next page

4. Recount how many elements are in the array, and print out this value:

```
$count2 = count ($soups);
print "<p>After adding 3 more
→ soups, the array now has
→ $count2 elements.</p>";
```

This second **print** call is a repetition of the first, showing how many elements the array now contains.

5. Delete this line:

```
print "<p>$soups</p>";
```

This line isn't needed anymore, so you can get rid of it (you now know that you can't print out an array that easily).

6. Save your script as **soups2.php**, place it in the proper directory for your PHP-enabled server, and test it in your browser **A**.

TIP Be very careful when you directly add elements to an array. There's a correct way to do it—

```
$array[] = 'Add This';
```

or

```
$array[1] = 'Add This';
```

—and an incorrect way:

```
$array = 'Add This';
```

If you forget to use the brackets, the new value will replace the entire existing array, leaving you with a simple string or number.

TIP The code

```
$array[] = 'Value';
```

creates the $array variable if it doesn't yet exist.

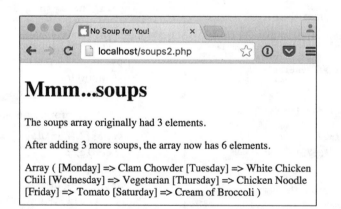

A A direct way to ensure that the new elements were successfully added to the array is to count the number of elements before and after you make the additions.

TIP While working with these arrays, I'm using single quotation marks to enclose both the keys and the values. Nothing needs to be interpolated (like a variable), so double quotation marks aren't required. It's perfectly acceptable to use double quotation marks, though, if you want to.

TIP You don't (and, in fact, shouldn't) quote your keys if they're numbers, variables, or constants (you'll learn about constants in Chapter 8, "Creating Web Applications"). For example:

```
$day = 'Sunday';
$soups[$day] = 'Mushroom';
```

TIP The sizeof() function is an alias to count(). It also returns the number of elements in an array.

Merging Arrays

PHP has a function that allows you to append one array onto another. Think of it as concatenation for arrays. The function, **array_merge()**, works like so:

```
$new_array = array_merge($array1, $array2);
```

You could also write the **soups2.php** page using this function:

```
$soups2 = [
    'Thursday' => 'Chicken Noodle',
    'Friday' => 'Tomato',
    'Saturday' => 'Cream of Broccoli'
];
$soups = array_merge($soups, $soups2);
```

You could even accomplish this result with the plus sign (thus adding two arrays together):

```
$soups = $soups + $soups2;
```

or

```
$soups += $soups2;
```

A difference between using **array_merge()** and the plus sign is that **array_merge()** will re-index the arrays in the new array, whereas the plus sign maintains the existing indexes. Also, with array addition, only elements in the second array indexed at new positions are added in. Any element in the second array indexed at the same position as an element in the first array will be ignored.

Accessing Array Elements

Regardless of how you establish an array, there's only one way to retrieve a specific element (or value) from it, and that is to refer to its index:

```
print "The first item is $array[0]";
```

If the array uses strings for indexes, you must quote the index, which results in a problematic syntax when you're trying to print an individual array element **Ⓐ**:

```
print "<p>Monday's soup is
→ $soups['Monday'].</p>";
```

To combat this issue, wrap the whole array construct within braces (aka curly brackets) **Ⓑ**:

```
print "<p>Monday's soup is
→ {$soups['Monday']}.</p>";
```

Ironically, the feature that makes arrays so useful—being able to store multiple values in one variable—also gives it a limitation

that the other variable types don't have: You must know the keys of the array in order to access its elements. If the array was set using strings, like the **$soups** array, then referring to **$soups[1]** points to nothing **Ⓒ**. For that matter, because *indexes are case-sensitive*, **$soups['monday']** is meaningless because **Clam Chowder** was indexed at **$soups['Monday']**.

The fastest and easiest way to access all the values of an array is to use a **foreach** loop. This construct loops through every element of an array:

```
foreach ($array as $key => $value) {
    print "<p>Key is $key. Value is
    → $value</p>";
}
```

With each iteration of the loop, the current array element's key will be assigned to the **$key** variable and the value to **$value**. Note that you can use any variable name here: **$k** and **$v** are likely choices, too.

You can now write a new soups script to use this knowledge.

(!) Parse error: syntax error, unexpected '' (T_ENCAPSED_AND_WHITESPACE), expecting identifier (T_STRING) or variable (T_VARIABLE) or number (T_NUM_STRING) in /Users/larry/Sites/temp.php on line *20*

Ⓐ Referencing within double quotation marks a specific element in an associative array will cause parse errors.

Mmm...soups

Monday's soup is Clam Chowder.

Ⓑ Wrapping an array element reference in braces is one way to avoid parse errors.

(!) Notice: Undefined offset: 0 in /Users/larry/Sites/temp.php on line *20*

Call Stack				
#	Time	Memory	Function	Location
1	0.0001	369280	{main}( )	.../temp.php:0

Ⓒ Referring to an array index that does not exist will create an *Undefined offset* or *Undefined Index* notice.

```
1    <!doctype html>
2    <html lang="en">
3    <head>
4        <meta charset="utf-8">
5        <title>No Soup for You!</title>
6    </head>
7    <body>
8    <h1>Mmm...soups</h1>
9    <?php // Script 7.3 - soups3.php
10   /* This script creates and prints out an
     array. */
11
12   // Address error management, if you
     want.
13
14   // Create the array:
15   $soups = [
16       'Monday' => 'Clam Chowder',
17       'Tuesday' => 'White Chicken Chili',
18       'Wednesday' => 'Vegetarian',
19       'Thursday' => 'Chicken Noodle',
20       'Friday' => 'Tomato',
21       'Saturday' => 'Cream of Broccoli'
22   ];
23
24   // Print each key and value:
25   foreach ($soups as $day => $soup) {
26       print "<p>$day: $soup</p>\n";
27   }
28
29   ?>
30   </body>
31   </html>
```

To print out the values of any array:

1. Begin a new document in your text editor or IDE (**Script 7.3**, to be named **soups3.php**):

   ```
   <!doctype html>
   <html lang="en">
   <head>
       <meta charset="utf-8">
       <title>No Soup for You!</title>
   </head>
   <body>
   <h1>Mmm...soups</h1>
   ```

2. Start the PHP section of the page, and address error management, if needed:

   ```
   <?php // Script 7.3 - soups3.php
   ```

3. Create the **$soups** array:

   ```
   $soups = [
       'Monday' => 'Clam Chowder',
       'Tuesday' => 'White Chicken
       → Chili',
       'Wednesday' => 'Vegetarian',
       'Thursday' => 'Chicken
       → Noodle',
       'Friday' => 'Tomato',
       'Saturday' => 'Cream of
       → Broccoli'
   ];
   ```

   Here the entire array is created at once, although you could create the array in steps, as in the preceding script, if you'd rather.

   continues on next page

4. Create a **foreach** loop to print out each day's soup:

```
foreach ($soups as $day =>
→ $soup) {
   print "<p>$day: $soup</p>\n";
}
```

The **foreach** loop iterates through every element of the **$soups** array, assigning each index to **$day** and each value to **$soup**. These values are then printed out within HTML paragraph tags. The **print** statement concludes with a newline character (created by **\n**), which will make the HTML source code of the page more legible.

5. Close the PHP section and the HTML page:

```
?>
</body>
</html>
```

6. Save the page as **soups3.php**, place it in the proper directory for your PHP-enabled server, and test it in your browser **D**.

TIP One option for working with arrays is to assign a specific element's value to a separate variable using the assignment operator:

```
$total = $array[1];
```

By doing this, you can preserve the original value in the array and still manipulate the value separately as a variable.

TIP If you need to access only an array's values (and not its keys), you can use this **foreach** structure:

```
foreach ($array as $value) {
   // Do whatever.
}
```

TIP Another way to access all of a numerically indexed array's elements is to use a **for** loop:

```
for ($n = 0; $n < count($array);
→ $n++) {
   print "The value is $array[$n]";
}
```

TIP The braces are used to avoid errors when printing array values that have strings for keys. Here are two examples where using quotation marks is not problematic, so the braces aren't required:

```
$name = trim($array['name']);
$total = $_POST['qty'] *
→ $_POST['price'];
```

TIP Braces can also be used to separate a variable reference from a dollar sign or other characters:

```
print "The total is ${$total}.";
```

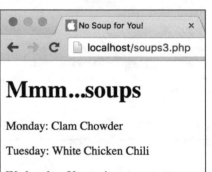

● ● ● No Soup for You!   ✕

← → C   localhost/soups3.php

Mmm...soups

Monday: Clam Chowder

Tuesday: White Chicken Chili

Wednesday: Vegetarian

Thursday: Chicken Noodle

Friday: Tomato

Saturday: Cream of Broccoli

D The execution of the loop for every element in the array generates this page. The **foreach** construct allows the script to access each key and value without prior knowledge of what they are.

Creating Multidimensional Arrays

Multidimensional arrays are both simple and complicated at the same time. The structure and concept may be somewhat difficult to grasp, but creating and accessing multidimensional arrays in PHP is surprisingly easy.

You use a multidimensional array to create an array containing more information than a standard array. You accomplish this by using other arrays for values instead of just strings and numbers. For example:

```
$fruits = ['apples', 'bananas',
→'oranges'];
$meats = ['steaks', 'hamburgers',
→'pork chops'];
$groceries = [
   'fruits' => $fruits,
   'meats' => $meats,
   'other' => 'peanuts',
   'cash' => 30.00
];
```

This array, **$groceries**, now consists of one string (*peanuts*), one floating-point number (*30.00*), and two arrays (**$fruits** and **$meats**).

Pointing to an element in an array within an array can seem tricky. The key (pardon the pun) is to continue adding indexes in brackets as necessary, working from the outer array inward. With that example, *bananas* is at **$groceries['fruits'][1]**. First, you point to the element (in this case, an array) in the **$groceries** array by using **['fruits']**. Then, you point to the element in that array based on its position—it's the second item, so you use the index **[1]**.

In this next task, you'll write a script that creates another multidimensional array example.

To use multidimensional arrays:

1. Begin a new document in your text editor or IDE, to be named **books.php** (Script 7.4):

   ```
   <!doctype html>
   <html lang="en">
   <head>
     <meta charset="utf-8">
     <title>Larry Ullman's Books and
     → Chapters</title>
   </head>
   <body>
   <h1>Some of Larry Ullman's
   → Books</h1>
   ```

2. Create the initial PHP tags, and address error management, if necessary:

   ```
   <?php // Script 7.4 - books.php
   ```

3. Create the first array:

   ```
   $phpvqs = [1 => 'Getting
   → Started with PHP', 'Variables',
   → 'HTML Forms and PHP', 'Using
   → Numbers'];
   ```

   To build up the multidimensional array, you'll create three standard arrays and then use them as the values for the larger array. This array (named **$phpvqs**, which is short for *PHP for the Web: Visual QuickStart Guide*) uses numbers for the keys and strings for the values. The numbers begin with 1 and correspond to the chapter numbers. The values are the chapter titles.

Script 7.4 The multidimensional **$books** array stores a lot of information in one big variable.

```
1   <!doctype html>
2   <html lang="en">
3   <head>
4       <meta charset="utf-8">
5       <title>Larry Ullman's Books and
        Chapters</title>
6   </head>
7   <body>
8   <h1>Some of Larry Ullman's Books</h1>
9   <?php // Script 7.4 - books.php
10  /* This script creates and prints out a
    multidimensional array. */
11  // Address error management, if you
    want.
12
13  // Create the first array:
14  $phpvqs = [1 => 'Getting Started with
    PHP', 'Variables', 'HTML Forms and PHP',
    'Using Numbers'];
15
16  // Create the second array:
17  $phpadv = [1 => 'Advanced PHP
    Techniques', 'Developing Web
    Applications', 'Advanced Database
    Concepts', 'Basic Object-Oriented
    Programming'];
18
19  // Create the third array:
20  $phpmysql = [1 => 'Introduction to
    PHP', 'Programming with PHP', 'Creating
    Dynamic Web Sites', 'Introduction to
    MySQL'];
21
22  // Create the multidimensional array:
23  $books = [
24      'PHP VQS' => $phpvqs,
25      'PHP Advanced VQP' => $phpadv,
26      'PHP and MySQL VQP' => $phpmysql
27  ];
28
29  // Print out some values:
30  print "<p>The third chapter of my
    first book is <i>{$books['PHP VQS']
    [3]}</i>.</p>";
```

code continues on next page

```
31    print "<p>The first chapter of my
      second book is <i>{$books['PHP
      Advanced VQP'][1]}</i>.</p>";
32    print "<p>The fourth chapter of my
      fourth book is <i>{$books['PHP and
      MySQL VQP'][4]}</i>.</p>";
33
34    // See what happens with foreach:
35    foreach ($books as $key => $value) {
36        print "<p>$key: $value</p>\n";
37    }
38
39    ?>
40    </body>
41    </html>
```

4. Create the next two arrays:

```
$phpadv = [1 => 'Advanced PHP
→ Techniques', 'Developing Web
→ Applications', 'Advanced
⋯ Database Concepts', 'Basic
→ Object-Oriented Programming'];
$phpmysql = [1 => 'Introduction
→ to PHP', 'Programming with PHP',
→ 'Creating Dynamic Web Sites',
→ 'Introduction to MySQL'];
```

For each array, add only the book's first four chapters for simplicity's sake. These other two arrays represent my *PHP Advanced and Object-Oriented Programming: Visual QuickPro Guide (3rd Edition)* (ISBN: 078-5342832181) and *PHP and MySQL for Dynamic Web Sites: Visual QuickPro Guide (4th Edition)* (ISBN: 978-0321784070) books.

5. Create the main, multidimensional array:

```
$books = [
  'PHP VQS' => $phpvqs,
  'PHP Advanced VQP' => $phpadv,
  'PHP and MySQL VQP' =>
  → $phpmysql
];
```

The **$books** array is the master array for this script. It uses strings for keys, which are shortened versions of the book titles, and arrays for values. Use the short array syntax or the **array()** function to create it, as you would any other array.

continues on next page

6. Print out the name of the third chapter of the *PHP Visual QuickStart Guide* book:

```
print "<p>The third chapter of
→ my first book is <i>{$books
→ ['PHP VQS'][3]}</i>.</p>";
```

Following the rules stated earlier, all you need to do to access any individual chapter name is to begin with **$books**, follow that with the first index (**['PHP VQS']**), and follow that with the next index (**[3]**). Because you're placing this in a **print** call, you enclose the whole construct in braces to avoid parse errors.

7. Print out two more examples:

```
print "<p>The first chapter of my
→ second book is <i>{$books['PHP
→ Advanced VQP'][1]}</i>.</p>";
print "<p>The fourth chapter of
→ my fourth book is <i>{$books
→ ['PHP and MySQL VQP'][4]}
→ </i>.</p>";
```

8. Run the **$books** array through a **foreach** loop to see the results:

```
foreach ($books as $key =>
→ $value) {
    print "<p>$key: $value</p>\n";
}
```

The **$key** variable will be assigned each abbreviated book title, and the **$value** variable ends up containing each chapter array.

9. Close the PHP section and complete the HTML page:

```
?>
</body>
</html>
```

10. Save the file as **books.php**, place it in the proper directory for your PHP-enabled server, and test it in your browser **A**.

A The second through fourth lines are generated by **print** statements. The error message and the last line show the results of the **foreach** loop (and the notices come from attempting to print an array).

```
PHP VQS
Chapter 1 is Getting Started with PHP
Chapter 2 is Variables
Chapter 3 is HTML Forms and PHP
Chapter 4 is Using Numbers

PHP Advanced VQP
Chapter 1 is Advanced PHP Techniques
Chapter 2 is Developing Web Applications
Chapter 3 is Advanced Database Concepts
Chapter 4 is Basic Object-Oriented Programming

PHP and MySQL VQP
Chapter 1 is Introduction to PHP
Chapter 2 is Programming with PHP
Chapter 3 is Creating Dynamic Web Sites
Chapter 4 is Introduction to MySQL
```

B One **foreach** loop within another can access every element of a two-dimensional array.

```
Array
(
    [PHP VQS] => Array
        (
            [1] => Getting Started with PHP
            [2] => Variables
            [3] => HTML Forms and PHP
            [4] => Using Numbers
        )

    [PHP Advanced VQP] => Array
        (
            [1] => Advanced PHP Techniques
            [2] => Developing Web Applications
            [3] => Advanced Database Concepts
            [4] => Basic Object-Oriented Programming
        )

    [PHP and MySQL VQP] => Array
        (
            [1] => Introduction to PHP
            [2] => Programming with PHP
            [3] => Creating Dynamic Web Sites
            [4] => Introduction to MySQL
        )

)
```

C The **print_r()** function shows the structure and contents of the **$books** array.

TIP To access every element of every array, you can nest two **foreach** loops like this **B**:

```
foreach ($books as $title =>
→ $chapters) {
  print "<p>$title";
  foreach ($chapters as $number =>
  → $chapter) {
    print "<br />Chapter $number is
    → $chapter";
  }
  print '</p>';
}
```

TIP Using the **print_r()** or **var_dump()** function (preferably enclosed in HTML <pre> tags for better formatting), you can view an entire multidimensional array **C**.

TIP You can create a multidimensional array in one statement instead of using several steps as in this example. However, doing so isn't recommended for beginners, because it's all too easy to make syntactical errors as a statement becomes more and more nested.

TIP Although all the subarrays in this example have the same structure (numbers for indexes and four elements), that isn't required with multidimensional arrays.

TIP To learn about the greater "Larry Ullman collection," including the three books referenced here, head to www.LarryUllman.com.

Sorting Arrays

PHP supports a variety of ways to sort an array. *Sort* refers to an alphabetical sort if the values being sorted are strings, or a numerical sort if the values being sorted are numbers. When sorting an array, you must keep in mind that an array consists of pairs of *keys and values*. Thus, an array can be sorted based on the keys or the values. This is further complicated by the fact that you can sort the values and keep the corresponding keys aligned, or you can sort the values and have them be assigned new keys.

To sort the values without regard to the keys, use **sort()**. To sort these values (again, without regard to the keys) in reverse order, use **rsort()**. The syntax for every sorting function is

function_name(**$array**);

So, **sort()** and **rsort()** are used as follows:

```
sort($array);
rsort($array);
```

To sort the values while maintaining the correlation between each value and its key, use **asort()**. To sort the values in reverse while maintaining the key correlation, use **arsort()**.

To sort by the keys while maintaining the correlation between the key and its value, use **ksort()**. Conversely, **krsort()** sorts the keys in reverse. **Table 7.2** lists all these functions.

Finally, **shuffle()** randomly reorganizes the order of an array. Like **sort()** and **rsort()**, **shuffle()** drops the existing keys in the process.

As an example of sorting arrays, you'll create a list of students and the grades they received on a test, and then sort this list first by grade and then by name.

TABLE 7.2 Array Sorting Functions

Function	Sorts By	Maintains Key-Values?
sort()	Values	No
rsort()	Values (inverse)	No
asort()	Values	Yes
arsort()	Values (inverse)	Yes
ksort()	Keys	Yes
krsort()	Keys (inverse)	Yes

Script 7.5 PHP provides a number of different functions for sorting arrays, including `arsort()` and `ksort()`.

```
1    <!doctype html>
2    <html lang="en">
3    <head>
4        <meta charset="utf-8">
5        <title>My Little Gradebook</title>
6    </head>
7    <body>
8    <?php // Script 7.5 - sort.php
9    /* This script creates, sorts, and
     prints out an array. */
10
11   // Address error management, if you
     want.
12
13   // Create the array:
14   $grades = [
15       'Richard' => 95,
16       'Sherwood' => 82,
17       'Toni' => 98,
18       'Franz' => 87,
19       'Melissa' => 75,
20       'Roddy' => 85
21   ];
22
23   // Print the original array:
24   print '<p>Originally the array looks
     like this: <br>';
25   foreach ($grades as $student => $grade)
     {
26       print "$student: $grade<br>\n";
27   }
28   print '</p>';
29
30   // Sort by value in reverse order, then
     print again:
31   arsort($grades);
32   print '<p>After sorting the array by
     value using arsort(), the array looks
     like this: <br>';
33   foreach ($grades as $student => $grade)
     {
34       print "$student: $grade<br>\n";
35   }
36   print '</p>';
37
```

code continues on next page

To sort an array:

1. Begin a new document in your text editor or IDE, to be named **sort.php** (Script 7.5):

   ```
   <!doctype html>
   <html lang="en">
   <head>
       <meta charset="utf-8">
       <title>My Little Gradebook
       → </title>
   </head>
   <body>
   ```

2. Begin the PHP section, and address error handling, if desired:

   ```
   <?php // Script 7.5 - sort.php
   ```

3. Create the array:

   ```
   $grades = [
       'Richard' => 95,
       'Sherwood' => 82,
       'Toni' => 98,
       'Franz' => 87,
       'Melissa' => 75,
       'Roddy' => 85
   ];
   ```

   The **$grades** array consists of six students' names along with their corresponding grades. Because the grades are numbers, they don't need to be quoted when assigning them.

4. Print a caption, and then print each element of the array using a **foreach** loop:

   ```
   print '<p>Originally the array
   → looks like this: <br>';
   foreach ($grades as $student =>
   → $grade) {
   print "$student: $grade<br>\n";
   }
   print '</p>';
   ```

   continues on next page

Because the **$grades** array will be printed three times, captions indicating each state of the array will be useful. At first, the script prints the array in the original order. To do that, use a **foreach** loop, where each index—the student's name—is assigned to **$student**, and each value—the student's grade—is assigned to **$grade**. The final **print** call closes the HTML paragraph.

5. Sort the array in reverse order by value to determine who has the highest grade:

arsort($grades);

To determine who has the highest grade, you need to use **arsort()** instead of **asort()**. The latter, which sorts the array in numeric order, would order the grades 75, 82, 85, and so on, rather than the desired 98, 95, 87.

You also must use **arsort()** and not **rsort()** in order to maintain the key-value relationship (**rsort()** would eliminate the student's name associated with each grade).

6. Print the array again (with a caption), using another loop:

print '<p>After sorting the array
→ by value using arsort(), the
**→ array looks like this:
';**
foreach ($grades as $student =>
→ $grade) {
**   print "$student: $grade
\n";**
}
print '</p>';

7. Sort the array by key to put the array in alphabetical order by student name:

ksort ($grades);

The **ksort()** function organizes the array by key (in this case, alphabetically) while maintaining the key-value correlation.

Script 7.5 *continued*

```
38   // Sort by key, then print again:
39   ksort($grades);
40   print '<p>After sorting the array by
     key using ksort(), the array looks like
     this: <br>';
41   foreach ($grades as $student => $grade)
     {
42       print "$student: $grade<br>\n";
43   }
44   print '</p>';
45
46   ?>
47   </body>
48   </html>
```

Originally the array looks like this:
Richard: 95
Sherwood: 82
Toni: 98
Franz: 87
Melissa: 75
Roddy: 85

After sorting the array by value using arsort(), the array looks like this:
Toni: 98
Richard: 95
Franz: 87
Roddy: 85
Sherwood: 82
Melissa: 75

After sorting the array by key using ksort(), the array looks like this:
Franz: 87
Melissa: 75
Richard: 95
Roddy: 85
Sherwood: 82
Toni: 98

A You can sort an array in a number of ways with varied results. Pay close attention to whether you want to maintain your key-value association when choosing a sort function.

8. Print a caption and the array one last time:

```
print '<p>After sorting the array
→ by key using ksort(), the array
→ looks like this: <br>';
foreach ($grades as $student =>
→ $grade) {
    print "$student: $grade<br>\n";
}
print '</p>';
```

9. Complete the script with the standard PHP and HTML tags:

```
?>
</body>
</html>
```

10. Save your script as **sort.php**, place it in the proper directory for your PHP-enabled server, and test it in your browser **A**.

TIP Because each element in an array must have its own unique key, the `$grades` array will only work using unique student names.

TIP The `natsort()` and `natcasesort()` functions sort a string (while maintaining key-value associations) using natural order. The most obvious example of natural order sorting is that it places name2 before name12, whereas `sort()` orders them name12 and then name2.

TIP The `usort()`, `uasort()`, and `ursort()` functions let you sort an array using a user-defined comparison function. These functions are most often used with multidimensional arrays.

Transforming Between Strings and Arrays

Now that you have an understanding of both strings and arrays, this next section introduces two functions for switching between the formats. The first, **implode()**, turns an array into a string. The second, **explode()**, does just the opposite. Here are some reasons to use these functions:

- To turn an array into a string in order to pass that value appended to a URL (which you can't do as easily with an array)

- To turn an array into a string in order to store that information in a database

- To turn a string into an array to convert a comma-delimited text field (say, a keyword search area of a form) into its separate parts

The syntax for using **explode()** is as follows:

```
$array = explode(separator, $string);
```

The *separator* refers to whatever character(s) define where one value ends and another begins. Commonly this is a comma, a tab, or a blank space. Thus your code might be

```
$array = explode(',', $string);
```

or

```
$array = explode(' ', $string);
```

To go from an array to a string, you need to define what the separator (aka the *glue*) should be, and PHP does the rest:

```
$string = implode(glue, $array);
$string = implode(',', $array);
```

or

```
$string = implode(' ', $array);
```

To demonstrate how to use **explode()** and **implode()**, you'll create an HTML form that takes a space-delimited string of names from the user **A**. The PHP script will then turn the string into an array so that it can sort the list. Finally, the code will create and return the alphabetized string **B**.

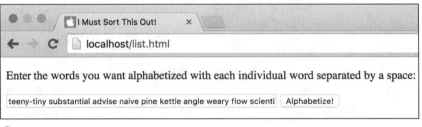

A This HTML form takes a list of words, which is then alphabetized by the **list.php** script **B**.

B Here's the same list, alphabetized for the user. This process is quick and easy to code, but doing so would be impossible without arrays.

Script 7.6 This is a simple HTML form where a user can submit a list of words. Including detailed instructions for how the form should be used is a prudent web design policy.

```
1    <!doctype html>
2    <html lang="en">
3    <head>
4        <meta charset="utf-8">
5        <title>I Must Sort This Out!</title>
6    </head>
7    <body>
8    <!-- Script 7.6 - list.html -->
9    <div><p>Enter the words you want
     alphabetized with each individual word
     separated by a space:</p>
10
11   <form action="list.php" method="post">
12
13       <input type="text" name="words"
         size="60">
14       <input type="submit" name="submit"
         value="Alphabetize!">
15
16   </form>
17   </div>
18   </body>
19   </html>
```

To create the HTML form:

1. Begin a new document in your text editor or IDE, to be named **list.html** (Script 7.6):

```
<!doctype html>
<html lang="en">
<head>
    <meta charset="utf-8">
    <title>I Must Sort This Out!
    → </title>
</head>
<body>
<!-- Script 7.6 - list.html -->
```

2. Create an HTML form with a text input:

```
<div><p>Enter the words you
→ want alphabetized with each
→ individual word separated by
→ a pace:</p>
    <form action="list.php"
    → method="post">
        <input type="text"
        → name="words" size="60">
```

It's important in cases like this to instruct the user. For example, if the user enters a comma-delimited list, the PHP script won't be able to handle the string properly (after completing both scripts, try using commas in lieu of spaces and see what happens).

3. Create a submit button, and then close the form and the HTML page:

```
<input type="submit" name=
"submit" value="Alphabetize!">
</form>
</div>
</body>
</html>
```

4. Save your script as **list.html**, and place it in the proper directory for your PHP-enabled server.

Now you'll write the **list.php** page to process the data generated by **list.html**.

To convert between strings and arrays:

1. Begin a new document in your text editor or IDE, to be named **list.php** (Script 7.7):

```
<!doctype html>
<html lang="en">
<head>
  <meta charset="utf-8">
  <title>I Have This Sorted
→ Out</title>
</head>
<body>
<?php // Script 7.7 - list.php
```

2. Turn the incoming string, **$_POST['words']**, into an array:

```
$words_array = explode(' ' ,
→ $_POST['words']);
```

This line of code creates a new array, **$words_array**, out of the string **$_POST['words']**. Each space between the words in **$_POST['words']** indicates that the next word should be a new array element. Hence the first word becomes **$words_array[0]**, then there is a space in **$_POST['words']**, then the second word becomes **$words_array[1]**, and so forth, until the end of **$_POST['words']**.

3. Sort the array alphabetically:

```
sort($words_array);
```

Because you don't need to maintain key-value associations in the **$words_array**, you can use **sort()** instead of **asort()**.

Script 7.7 Because the **explode()** and **implode()** functions are so simple and powerful, you can quickly and easily sort a submitted list of words (of practically any length) in just a couple of lines.

```
1   <!doctype html>
2   <html lang="en">
3   <head>
4       <meta charset="utf-8">
5       <title>I Have This Sorted Out</title>
6   </head>
7   <body>
8   <?php // Script 7.7 - list.php
9   /* This script receives a string in
    $_POST['words']. It then turns it into
    an array,
10  sorts the array alphabetically, and
    reprints it. */
11
12  // Address error management, if you
    want.
13
14  // Turn the incoming string into an
    array:
15  $words_array = explode(' ' ,
    $_POST['words']);
16
17  // Sort the array:
18  sort($words_array);
19
20  // Turn the array back into a string:
21  $string_words = implode('<br>',
    $words_array);
22
23  // Print the results:
24  print "<p>An alphabetized version of
    your list is: <br>$string_words</p>";
25
26  ?>
27  </body>
28  </html>
```

4. Create a new string out of the sorted array:

```
$string_words = implode('<br>',
→ $words_array);
```

Arrays don't print as easily as strings, so turn **$words_array** into a string named **$string_words**. The resulting string starts with the value of **$words_array[0]**, followed by the HTML **
** tag, the value of **$words_array[1]**, and so on. Using **
** instead of a space or comma gives the list a more readable format when it's printed to the browser.

5. Print the new string to the browser:

```
print "<p>An alphabetized
→ version of your list is:
→ <br>$string_words</p>";
```

6. Close the PHP section and the HTML page:

```
?>
</body>
</html>
```

7. Save your page as **list.php**, place it in the same directory as **list.html**, and test both scripts in your browser **Ⓐ** and **Ⓑ**.

TIP You'll also run across code written using the join() function, which is synonymous with implode().

TIP As an extra precaution, use the techniques covered in Chapter 6, "Control Structures," to verify that $_POST['words'] is not empty before attempting to explode it. Better yet, check that at least one comma is present first!

Creating an Array from a Form

Throughout this chapter, you've established arrays entirely from within a PHP page. You can, however, send an array of data to a PHP script via an HTML form. In fact, every time you use **$_POST**, this is the case. But you can take this one step further by creating arrays using an HTML form. Such arrays will then be a part of the greater **$_POST** array (thereby making **$_POST** a multidimensional array).

A logical use of this capability is in dealing with checkboxes, where users might need to select multiple options from a group **Ⓐ**. The HTML source code for a checkbox is as follows:

```
<input type="checkbox"
→ name="topping" value="Ham">
```

The problem in this particular case is that each form element must have a unique name. If you created several checkboxes, each with a name of *topping*, only the value of the last selected checkbox would be received in the PHP script. If you were to create unique names for each checkbox—*ham*, *tomato*, *black_olives*, and so on—working with the selected values would be tedious.

The workaround is to use array syntax, as demonstrated in the next example.

To create an array with an HTML form:

1. Begin a new document in your text editor or IDE, to be named **event.html** (Script 7.8):

    ```
    <!doctype html>
    <html lang="en">
    <head>
      <meta charset="utf-8">
      <title>Add an Event</title>
    </head>
    <body>
    <!-- Script 7.8 - event.html -->
    <div><p>Use this form to add an
    → event:</p>
    ```

2. Begin the HTML form:

    ```
    <form action="event.php"
    → method="post">
    ```

    This form will be submitted to **event.php**, found in the same directory as this HTML page.

3. Create a text input for an event name:

    ```
    <p>Event Name: <input type="text"
    → name="name" size="30"></p>
    ```

    This example allows the user to enter an event name and the days of the week when it takes place.

Pizza Toppings: ☐ Extra Tomato ☐ Ham ☐ Sausage ☐ Pepperoni
☐ Black Olives ☐ Turnips ☐ Kumquats

Ⓐ Checkboxes in an HTML form, presenting several possible options.

Script 7.8 This HTML form has an array for the checkbox input names.

```
1    <!doctype html>
2    <html lang="en">
3    <head>
4        <meta charset="utf-8">
5            <title>Add an Event</title>
6    </head>
7    <body>
8    <!-- Script 7.8 - event.html -->
9    <div><p>Use this form to add an event:</
     p>
10
11   <form action="event.php" method="post">
12
13       <p>Event Name: <input type="text"
         name="name" size="30"></p>
14       <p>Event Days:
15       <input type="checkbox"
         name="days[]" value="Sunday"> Sun
16       <input type="checkbox"
         name="days[]" value="Monday"> Mon
17       <input type="checkbox"
         name="days[]" value="Tuesday"> Tue
18       <input type="checkbox"
         name="days[]" value="Wednesday">
         Wed
19       <input type="checkbox"
         name="days[]" value="Thursday">
         Thu
20       <input type="checkbox"
         name="days[]" value="Friday"> Fri
21       <input type="checkbox"
         name="days[]" value="Saturday">
         Sat
22       </p>
23       <input type="submit" name="submit"
         value="Add the Event!">
24
25   </form>
26   </div>
27   </body>
28   </html>
```

4. Create the days checkboxes:

```
<p>Event Days:
<input type="checkbox" name=
→ "days[]" value="Sunday"> Sun
<input type="checkbox" name=
→ "days[]" value="Monday"> Mon
<input type="checkbox" name=
→ "days[]" value="Tuesday"> Tue
<input type="checkbox" name=
→ "days[]" value="Wednesday"> Wed
<input type="checkbox" name=
→ "days[]" value="Thursday"> Thu
<input type="checkbox" name=
→ "days[]" value="Friday"> Fri
<input type="checkbox" name=
→ "days[]" value="Saturday"> Sat
</p>
```

All of these checkboxes use *days[ ]* as the **name** value, which creates a **$_POST['days']** array in the PHP script. The **value** attributes differ for each checkbox, corresponding to the day of the week.

5. Complete the HTML form:

```
<input type="submit"
→ name="submit" value="Add the
→ Event!">
</form>
```

6. Complete the HTML page:

```
</div>
</body>
</html>
```

7. Save your page as **event.html**, and place it in the proper directory for your PHP-enabled server.

You also need to write the **event.php** page to handle this HTML form.

To handle the HTML form:

1. Begin a new document in your text editor or IDE, to be named **event.php** (**Script 7.9**):

```
<!doctype html>
<html lang="en">
<head>
  <meta charset="utf-8">
  <title>Add an Event</title>
</head>
<body>
```

2. Create the initial PHP tag, address error management (if need be), and print an introductory message:

```
<?php // Script 7.9 - event.php
print "<p>You want to add an
→ event called <b>{$_POST['name']}
→ </b> which takes place on:
→ <br>";
```

The **print** line prints out the value of the event's name. In a real-world version of this script, you would add a conditional to check that a name value was entered first (see Chapter 6).

3. Begin a conditional to check that at least one weekday was selected:

```
if (isset($_POST['days']) AND
→ is_array($_POST['days'])) {
```

If no checkbox was selected, then **$_POST['days']** won't be an existing variable. To avoid an error caused by referring to a variable that does not exist, the first part of the conditional checks that **$_POST['days']** is set.

Script 7.9 This PHP script receives an array of values in **$_POST['days']**.

```
1    <!doctype html>
2    <html lang="en">
3    <head>
4        <meta charset="utf-8">
5        <title>Add an Event</title>
6    </head>
7    <body>
8    <?php // Script 7.9 - event.php
9    /* This script handle the event form. */
10
11   // Address error management, if you
     want.
12
13   // Print the text:
14   print "<p>You want to add an event
     called <b>{$_POST['name']}</b> which
     takes place on: <br>";
15
16   // Print each weekday:
17   if (isset($_POST['days']) AND
     is_array($_POST['days'])) {
18
19       foreach ($_POST['days'] as $day) {
20           print "$day<br>\n";
21       }
22
23   } else {
24       print 'Please select at least one
         weekday for this event!';
25   }
26
27   // Complete the paragraph:
28   print '</p>';
29   ?>
30   </body>
31   </html>
```

The List Function

The `list()` function is used to assign array element values to individual variables. Start with an example:

```
$date = ['Thursday', 23,
→ 'October'];
list($weekday, $day, $month) =
→ $date;
```

Now there is a **$weekday** variable with a value of *Thursday*, a **$day** variable with a value of *23*, and a **$month** variable with a value of *October*.

Using `list()` has two caveats. First, `list()` works only on arrays numerically indexed starting at 0. Second, when you're using the `list()` function, you must acknowledge each array element. You could not do this:

```
list($weekday, $month) = $date;
```

But you can use empty values to ignore elements:

```
list ($weekday, , $month) =
$date;
```

or

```
list (, , $month) = $date;
```

The `list()` function is often used when retrieving values from a database.

The second part of the condition—and both must be TRUE for the entire condition to be TRUE—confirms that **$_POST['days']** is an array. This is a good step to take because a **foreach** loop will create an error if it receives a variable that isn't an array ❸.

4. Print each selected weekday:

```
foreach ($_POST['days'] as $day)
{
    print "$day<br>\n";
}
```

To print out each selected weekday, run the **$_POST['days']** array through a **foreach** loop. The array contains the values (from the HTML form inputs; for example, *Monday*, *Tuesday*, and so on) for every checkbox that was selected.

5. Complete the **is_array()** conditional:

```
} else {
    print 'Please select at least
    → one weekday for this event!';
}
```

If no weekday was selected, then the **isset()** AND **is_array()** condition is **FALSE**, and this message is printed.

continues on next page

⚠	Warning: Invalid argument supplied for foreach() in /Users/larry/Sites/event.php on line *16*			
Call Stack				
#	Time	Memory	Function	Location
1	0.0003	370880	{main}( )	.../event.php:0

❸ Attempting to use **foreach** on a variable that is not an array is a common cause of errors.

6. Complete the main paragraph, the PHP section, and the HTML page:

```
print '</p>';
?>
</body>
</html>
```

7. Save the page as **event.php**, place it in the same directory as **event.html**, and test both pages in your browser **C**, **D**, and **E**.

TIP The same technique demonstrated here can be used to allow a user to select multiple options in a drop-down menu. Just give the menu a name with a syntax like *something[]*, and the PHP script will receive every selection in *$_POST['something']*.

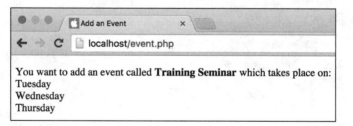

C The HTML form with its checkboxes.

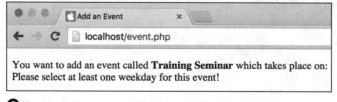

D The results of the HTML form.

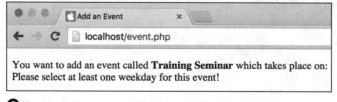

E If users don't select any of the day checkboxes, they'll see this message.

Review and Pursue

If you have any problems with the review questions or the pursue prompts, turn to the book's supporting forum (www.LarryUllman.com/forums/).

Review

- What's the difference between an *indexed* array and an *associative* array?

- What is the *short array syntax* and when was it added to PHP?

- When should you use quotation marks for an array's key or value? When shouldn't you?

- How do you print a specific array element? How do you print out every element in an array?

- What happens if you don't use the brackets when adding an element to an array?

- What function returns the number of elements in an array?

- When must you use braces for printing array elements?

- What is the difference between the **sort()** and **asort()** functions? Between **sort()** and **rsort()**?

- What is the syntax for **explode()**? For **implode()**? If you don't remember, check out the PHP manual page for either function.

Pursue

- Check out the PHP manual's pages for the array-related functions. Look into some of the other available array functions. I recommend familiarizing yourself with **array_key_exists()**, **array_search()**, and **in_array()**.

- Rewrite **soups2.php** so that it displays the number of elements in the array without using a separate variable. Hint: You'll need to concatenate the **count()** function call into the **print** statement.

- Create another script that creates and displays a multidimensional array (or some of it, anyway).

- Rewrite **list.php** so that it uses **foreach** instead of **implode()** but still prints out each sorted word on its own line in the browser. Also add some form validation so that it attempts to parse and sort the string only if it has a value.

- Modify **event.php** so that it prints the selected days as an unordered list.

- Add validation conditionals to both **list.php** and **event.php** that check for submitted form values before using them.

Creating Web Applications

The book to this point has covered the fundamentals of programming with PHP; now it's time to begin tying it all together into actual web applications. In this chapter, you'll learn a number of functions and techniques for making your websites more professional, more feature-rich, and easier to maintain.

First, you'll learn how to use external files to break pages into individual pieces, allowing you to separate the logic from the presentation. Then you'll tinker with constants, a special data type in PHP. After that, you'll be introduced to some of the date- and time-related functions built into PHP.

Two of the chapter's topics discuss techniques rather than functions: having the same page both display and handle an HTML form, and having a form remember user-submitted values. After that, you'll see how easy it can be to send email from PHP. The chapter concludes with the slightly more advanced topics of output buffering and HTTP headers.

In This Chapter

Creating Templates

Every example thus far has been a one-page script that handles an HTML form, sorts arrays, performs calculations, and so on. As you begin to develop multiple-page websites (which is to say, *web applications*), it quickly becomes impractical to repeat common elements on multiple pages.

On more sophisticated websites, many features, such as the HTML design, will be used by every, or almost every, page within the site. You can put these elements into each page, but when you need to make a change, you'll be required to make that change over and over again. You can save time by creating *templates* that separate out the repeating content from the page-specific materials. For example, a website may have navigation, copyright, and other features that repeat across multiple pages  and .

When you first start doing dynamic web development, creating and using templates can be daunting. The key is to start with a basic prototype, as if you were creating a static web page, and then divide that prototype into reusable parts. By using the PHP functions introduced in the next section of this chapter, you can easily include the repeating parts in each page while the new content is generated on a page-by-page basis.

To create the template in use by this chapter's examples, let's start with the prototype. This example's layout **C** was created using the Concise CSS Framework (http://concisecss.com). Concise CSS is one of many frameworks available that make developing stylish and responsive web pages a breeze, even for nondesigners.

A The home page for the fifth edition of this book has its page-specific content in the left column and common elements in the right.

B The table of contents page uses some of the same common elements as the home page **A**, thanks to the templates.

C The design for this chapter's examples, as a single, static HTML page.

Script 8.1 This script represents the basic look each page in the site should have.

```
1    <!doctype html>
2    <html>
3    <head>
4        <meta charset="utf-8">
5        <meta http-equiv="X-UA-Compatible"
         content="IE=edge,chrome=1">
6        <meta name="viewport"
         content="width=device-width,
         initial-scale=1.0">
7        <meta name="HandheldFriendly"
         content="True">
8        <title>Raise High the Roof Beam!</
         title>
9        <link rel="stylesheet" type="text/
         css" media="screen" href="css/
         concise.min.css" />
10       <link rel="stylesheet" type="text/
         css" media="screen" href="css/
         masthead.css" />
11   </head>
12   <body>
13
14   <header container class="siteHeader">
15       <div row>
16           <h1 column=4 class="logo"><a
             href="index.php">Raise High the
             Roof Beam!</a></h1>
17           <nav column="8" class="nav">
18               <ul>
19                   <li><a href="books.
                     php">Books</a></li>
20                   <li><a href="#">Stories</
                     a></li>
21                   <li><a href="#">Quotes</
                     a></li>
22                   <li><a href="login.
                     php">Login</a></li>
23                   <li><a href="register.
                     php">Register</a></li>
24               </ul>
25           </nav>
26       </div>
27   </header>
28
29       <main container class="siteContent">
30       <!-- BEGIN CHANGEABLE CONTENT. -->
31           <h2>Welcome to a J.D. Salinger
             Fan Club</h2>
32
```

code continues on next page

To create the layout model:

1. Begin a new HTML document in your text editor or IDE, to be named **template.html** (Script 8.1):

```
<!doctype html>
<html>
<head>
    <meta charset="utf-8">
    <meta http-equiv="X-UA-
 → Compatible" content=
 → "IE=edge,chrome=1">
    <meta name="viewport"
 → content="width=device-width,
 → initial-scale=1.0">
    <meta name="HandheldFriendly"
 → content="True">
    <title>Raise High the Roof
 → Beam!</title>
```

The first step in developing any template system is to create a model document—an example of what a basic page should look like. Once you've created this, you can break it down into its parts.

This template begins with the meta tags recommended by the Concise CSS Framework.

2. Add the CSS code:

```
<link rel="stylesheet" type=
 → "text/css" media="screen"
 → href="css/concise.min.css" />
<link rel="stylesheet" type=
 → "text/css" media="screen"
 → href="css/masthead.css" />
```

This example uses CSS for the formatting and layout controls. The CSS itself is stored in two external files that become part of this page through the link tag. The files are **concise.min.css** and **masthead.css**, stored in a folder named **css**.

continues on next page

Note that you'll need to download the CSS files from the book's corresponding website (www.LarryUllman.com). You'll find it as part of the book's downloadable code.

3. Close the HTML head, and begin the body:

```
</head>
<body>
```

4. Create the page's header:

```
<header container
class="siteHeader">
  <div row>
    <h1 column=4
    → class="logo"><a
    → href="index.php">Raise
    → High the Roof Beam!</a>
    → </h1>
    <nav column="8" class="nav">
      <ul>
        <li><a href=
        → "books.php">Books
        → </a></li>
        <li><a href="#">Stories
        → </a></li>
        <li><a href="#">Quotes
        → </a></li>
        <li><a href=
        → "login.php">Login
        → </a></li>
        <li><a href=
        → "register.php">
        → Register</a></li>
      </ul>
    </nav>
  </div>
</header>
```

Script 8.1 *continued*

```
33        <p>Lorem ipsum dolor sit
          amet, consectetur adipisicing
          elit, sed do eiusmod tempor
          incididunt ut labore et
          dolore magna aliqua. Ut
          enim ad minim veniam, quis
          nostrud exercitation ullamco
          laboris nisi ut aliquip ex ea
          commodo consequat. Duis aute
          irure dolor in reprehenderit
          in voluptate velit esse
          cillum dolore eu fugiat
          nulla pariatur. Excepteur
          sint occaecat cupidatat non
          proident, sunt in culpa qui
          officia deserunt mollit anim
          id est laborum.</p>
34        <!-- END CHANGEABLE CONTENT. -->
35        </main>
36
37        <footer container class="siteFooter">
38          <p>Design uses <a href="http://
          concisecss.com/">Concise CSS
          Framework</a></p>
39        </footer>
40
41    </body>
42    </html>
```

The *header* area (also defined in the CSS code) creates the banner and the primary navigation links to the other pages in the web application. The specific links reference four PHP scripts, all of which will be developed in this chapter.

5. Begin, and mark, the start of the page-specific content:

```
<main container class=
→ "siteContent">

<!-- BEGIN CHANGEABLE CONTENT. -->
```

Everything up until this comment will remain the same for every page in the web application. To indicate where the page-specific content begins (for your own benefit), include an HTML comment. When making a choice, err on the side of overcommenting your HTML and PHP code!

Just before the comment, the *siteContent* area is begun. This area is defined in the CSS code and properly formats the main content part of the page. In other words, on every page, that page's content will go within the one **main** that has a **class** of *siteContent*.

6. Create the page's content:

```
<h2>Welcome to a J.D. Salinger
→ Fan Club</h2>
<p>Lorem ipsum dolor sit
→ amet...</p>
```

For the prototype, the content is just a header and a whole lot of text (there's more in the actual script than I've included in this step).

7. Mark the end of the changeable content:

```
<!-- END CHANGEABLE CONTENT. -->
</div>
```

The code in Step 6 is the only text that will change on a page-by-page basis. Just as an HTML comment indicates where that section starts, one here indicates where it ends.

8. Add the footer:

```
<footer container
class="siteFooter">
    <p>Design uses <a href="http://
    → concisecss.com/">Concise CSS
    → Framework</a></p>
</footer>
```

The footer includes a credit.

9. Finish the HTML page:

```
</body>
</html>
```

10. Save the file as **template.html**, and test it in your browser Ⓒ.

Once you've completed a prototype that you like, you can break it into its various parts to generate the template system.

To create the header file:

1. Open **template.html** (Script 8.1) in your text editor or IDE, if it isn't already open.

2. Select everything from the initial HTML code to the **<!-- BEGIN CHANGEABLE CONTENT -->** HTML comment .

   Part of the benefit of identifying the start of the page-specific content with an HTML comment is that it simplifies breaking the model into its parts.

```
template.html                    ✕
1    <!doctype html>
2    <html>
3  ▼ <head>
4      <meta charset="utf-8">
5      <meta http-equiv="X-UA-Compatible" content="IE=edge,chrome=1">
6      <meta name="viewport" content="width=device-width, initial-scale=1.0">
7      <meta name="HandheldFriendly" content="True">
8      <title>Raise High the Roof Beam!</title>
9      <link rel="stylesheet" type="text/css" media="screen" href="css/concise.min.css" />
10     <link rel="stylesheet" type="text/css" media="screen" href="css/masthead.css" />
11   </head>
12   <body>
13
14 ▼ <header container class="siteHeader">
15 ▼   <div row>
16       <h1 column=4 class="logo"><a href="index.php">Raise High the Roof Beam!</a></h1>
17 ▼     <nav column="8" class="nav">
18 ▼       <ul>
19           <li><a href="books.php">Books</a></li>
20           <li><a href="#">Stories</a></li>
21           <li><a href="#">Quotes</a></li>
22           <li><a href="login.php">Login</a></li>
23           <li><a href="register.php">Register</a></li>
24         </ul>
25       </nav>
26     </div>
27 ▼ </header>
28
29   <main container class="siteContent">
30 ▼   <!-- BEGIN CHANGEABLE CONTENT. -->
31       <h2>Welcome to a J.D. Salinger Fan Club</h2>
32         <p>Lorem ipsum dolor sit amet, consectetur adipisicing elit, sed do eiusmod tempor incididunt
          ut labore et dolore magna aliqua. Ut enim ad minim veniam, quis nostrud exercitation ullamco
          laboris nisi ut aliquip ex ea commodo consequat. Duis aute irure dolor in reprehenderit in
          voluptate velit esse cillum dolore eu fugiat nulla pariatur. Excepteur sint occaecat
          cupidatat non proident, sunt in culpa qui officia deserunt mollit anim id est laborum.</p>
33     <!-- END CHANGEABLE CONTENT. -->
34   </main>
35
36   <footer container class="siteFooter">
37     <p>Design uses <a href="http://concisecss.com/">Concise CSS Framework</a></p>
38   </footer>
39
40 </body>
41 </html>
```

D Using the prototype file, select and copy the initial lines of code to create the header.

Script 8.2 This is a basic header file that creates the HTML head information, includes the CSS file, and begins the body.

```
1   <!doctype html>
2   <html>
3   <head>
4       <meta charset="utf-8">
5       <meta http-equiv="X-UA-Compatible"
        content="IE=edge,chrome=1">
6       <meta name="viewport"
        content="width=device-width,
        initial-scale=1.0">
7       <meta name="HandheldFriendly"
        content="True">
8       <title>Raise High the Roof Beam!
        </title>
9       <link rel="stylesheet" type="text/
        css" media="screen" href="css/
        concise.min.css" />
10      <link rel="stylesheet" type="text/
        css" media="screen" href="css/
        masthead.css" />
11  </head>
12  <body>
13
14  <header container class="siteHeader">
15      <div row>
16          <h1 column=4 class="logo"><a
            href="index.php">Raise High the
            Roof Beam!</a></h1>
17          <nav column="8" class="nav">
18              <ul>
19                  <li><a href="books.
                    php">Books</a></li>
20                  <li><a href="#">Stories
                    </a></li>
21                  <li><a href="#">Quotes
                    </a></li>
22                  <li><a href="login.
                    php">Login</a></li>
23                  <li><a href="register.
                    php">Register</a></li>
24              </ul>
25          </nav>
26      </div>
27  </header>
28
29      <main container class="siteContent">
30      <!-- BEGIN CHANGEABLE CONTENT. -->
31          <!-- Script 8.2 - header.html -->
```

3. Copy this code.

   Using your Edit menu or keyboard shortcut (Ctrl+C on Windows, Command+C on the Macintosh), copy all the highlighted code to your computer's clipboard.

4. Create a new, blank document in your text editor or IDE, to be named **header.html**.

5. Paste the copied text into the document (**Script 8.2**).

   Using your Edit menu or keyboard shortcut (Ctrl+V on Windows, Command+V on the Macintosh), paste all the highlighted code into this new document.

6. Save the file as **header.html**.

Now that the header file has been created, you'll make the footer file using the same process.

To create the footer file:

1. Open **template.html** (Script 8.1) in your text editor or IDE, if it isn't already open.

2. Select everything from the **<!-- END CHANGEABLE CONTENT -->** HTML comment to the end of the script **Ⓔ**.

3. Copy this code.

4. Create a new, blank document in your text editor, to be named **footer.html**.

5. Paste the copied text into the document (Script 8.3).

6. Save the file as **footer.html**.

> **TIP** There are many far more complex template systems you can use in PHP to separate the design from the logic. The best known of these is probably Smarty (www.smarty.net).

Script 8.3 This is a basic footer file that concludes the HTML page.

```
1              <!-- Script 8.3 - footer.html -->
2      <!-- END CHANGEABLE CONTENT. -->
3      </main>
4
5      <footer container class="siteFooter">
6          <p>Design uses <a href="http://
           concisecss.com/">Concise CSS
           Framework</a></p>
7      </footer>
8
9  </body>
10  </html>
```

```
29      <main container class="siteContent">
30      <!-- BEGIN CHANGEABLE CONTENT. -->
31          <h2>Welcome to a J.D. Salinger Fan Club</h2>
32              <p>Lorem ipsum dolor sit amet, consectetur adipisicing elit, sed do eiusmod tempor incididunt
                ut labore et dolore magna aliqua. Ut enim ad minim veniam, quis nostrud exercitation ullamco
                laboris nisi ut aliquip ex ea commodo consequat. Duis aute irure dolor in reprehenderit in
                voluptate velit esse cillum dolore eu fugiat nulla pariatur. Excepteur sint occaecat
                cupidatat non proident, sunt in culpa qui officia deserunt mollit anim id est laborum.</p>
33      <!-- END CHANGEABLE CONTENT. -->
34      </main>
35
36      <footer container class="siteFooter">
37          <p>Design uses <a href="http://concisecss.com/">Concise CSS Framework</a></p>
38      </footer>
39
40  </body>
41  </html>
```

Ⓔ Again using the prototype file, select and copy the concluding lines of code for the footer.

CSS Templates

Cascading Style Sheets (CSS) have been an increasingly important part of the web for some time. Their initial usage was focused on cosmetics (font sizes, colors, and so on), but now CSS is commonly used, as in this chapter, to control the layout of pages.

This example defines three areas of the page—*header, main* (i.e., content), and *footer*. The *main* area will change for each page. The other areas contain standard items, such as navigation links, that appear on each page of the site.

Just to be clear: The relationship between PHP and CSS is the same as that between PHP and HTML—PHP runs on the server and HTML and CSS are significant to the browser. As with HTML, you *can* use PHP to generate CSS, but in this example, the CSS is hard-coded into a separate file.

Using External Files

As the preceding section stated, you can save development time by creating separate pages for particular elements and then incorporating them into the main PHP pages using specific functions. Two of these functions are `include()` and `require()`:

```
include('file.php');
require('file.html');
```

Both functions work the same way, with one relatively key difference: If an `include()` function fails, the PHP script generates a warning **A** but continues to run. Conversely, if `require()` fails, it terminates the execution of the script **B**.

Both `include()` and `require()` incorporate the referenced file into the main file (for clarity's sake, the file that has the `include()` or `require()` line is the *including* or *parent* file). The result is the same as if the included code were part of the parent file in the first place.

Understanding this basic idea is key to making the most of external files: Including a file makes it as if that file's contents were in the parent script to begin with. This means that any code within the included file not within PHP tags is treated as HTML. And this is true regardless of what extension the included file has, because it's the extension of the *including* file that counts.

(!) Warning: include(templates/header.html): failed to open stream: No such file or directory in /Users/larry/Sites/index.php on line 6				
Call Stack				
#	Time	Memory	Function	Location
1	0.0011	365880	{main}( )	.../index.php:0

(!) Warning: include(): Failed opening 'templates/header.html' for inclusion (include_path='.:/usr/local/php5/lib/php') in /Users/larry/Sites/index.php on line 6				
Call Stack				
#	Time	Memory	Function	Location
1	0.0011	365880	{main}( )	.../index.php:0

Welcome to a J.D. Salinger Fan Club!

Lorem ipsum dolor sit amet, consectetur adipisicing elit, sed do eiusmod tempor incididunt ut labore et dolore magna aliqua. Ut enim ad minim veniam, quis nostrud exercitat reprehenderit in voluptate velit esse cillum dolore eu fugiat nulla pariatur. Excepteur sint occaecat cupidatat non proident, sunt in culpa qui officia deserunt mollit anim id est l

A When an `include()` fails, warnings are issued, but the script continues to execute.

(!) Warning: require(templates/header.html): failed to open stream: No such file or directory in /Users/larry/Sites/index.php on line 6				
Call Stack				
#	Time	Memory	Function	Location
1	0.0001	365872	{main}( )	.../index.php:0

(!) Fatal error: require(): Failed opening required 'templates/header.html' (include_path='.:/usr/local/php5/lib/php') in /Users/larry/Sites/index.php on line 6				
Call Stack				
#	Time	Memory	Function	Location
1	0.0001	365872	{main}( )	.../index.php:0

B When a `require()` function call fails, warnings and errors are issued and the script stops running.

There are many reasons to use included files. You could put your own defined functions into a common file (see Chapter 10, "Creating Functions," for information on writing your own functions). You might also want to place your database access information into a configuration file. First, however, let's include the template files created in the preceding section of the chapter in order to make pages abide by a consistent design.

To use external files:

1. Create a new document in your text editor or IDE, to be named **index.php**.

2. Start with the initial PHP tags, and add any comments (**Script 8.4**):

   ```
   <?php // Script 8.4 - index.php
   /* This is the home page for this
   → site.
   It uses templates to create the
   → layout. */
   ```

   Notice that, with the template system, the very first line of the script is the PHP tag. There's no need to begin with the initial HTML, because that is now stored in the **header.html** file.

3. Address error management, if necessary.

   This topic is discussed in Chapter 3, "HTML Forms and PHP," and may or may not need to be addressed in your scripts. See that chapter for more; this will be the last time I specifically mention it in this chapter.

Script 8.4 Once the two included files have been created, the **include()** function incorporates them into the parent file to create the complete HTML page on the fly.

```
1   <?php // Script 8.4 - index.php
2   /* This is the home page for this site.
3   It uses templates to create the layout.
    */
4
5   // Include the header:
6   include('templates/header.html');
7   // Leave the PHP section to display lots
    of HTML:
8   ?>
9
10  <h2>Welcome to a J.D. Salinger Fan
    Club!</h2>
11  <p>Lorem ipsum dolor sit amet,
    consectetur adipisicing elit, sed do
    eiusmod tempor incididunt ut labore et
    dolore magna aliqua. Ut enim ad minim
    veniam, quis nostrud exercitation
    ullamco laboris nisi ut aliquip ex ea
    commodo consequat. Duis aute irure dolor
    in reprehenderit in voluptate velit esse
    cillum dolore eu fugiat nulla pariatur.
    Excepteur sint occaecat cupidatat non
    proident, sunt in culpa qui officia
    deserunt mollit anim id est laborum.</p>
12
13  <?php // Return to PHP.
14  include('templates/footer.html');
    // Include the footer.
15  ?>
```

File Navigation and Site Structure

To be able to use external files, you need to understand file navigation on your computer or server. Just as you must correctly refer to other pages in HTML links or images in websites, you must properly point a parent file to the included scripts. You can do this by using *absolute* or *relative* paths. An absolute path is a complete, specific address, like the following:

```
include('C:\inetpub\wwwfiles\
 file.php');
include('/Users/larry/Sites/
 file.php');
```

As long as the included file isn't moved, an absolute path will always work.

A relative path indicates where the included file is in relation to the parent file. These examples assume both are within the same directory:

```
include('file.php');
include('./file.php');
```

The included file can also be in a directory below the parent one, as in this chapter's example (also see Ⓒ):

```
include('templates/header.html');
```

Or, the included file could be in the directory above the parent:

```
include('../file.php');
```

Finally, a note on site structure: Once you divvy up your web application into multiple pieces, you should begin thinking about arranging the files in appropriate folders. Complex sites might have the main folder, another for images, one for administration files, and a special directory for templates and included files. As long as you properly reference the files in your **include()** or **require()** statement, structuring your applications will work fine and give the added benefit of making them easier to maintain.

4. Include the header file:

```
include('templates/header.html');
```

To use the template system, you include the header file here by invoking the **include()** function. Because the header file contains only HTML, all of its contents will be immediately sent to the browser as if they were part of this file. This line uses a *relative path* to refer to the included file (see the "File Navigation and Site Structure" sidebar) and assumes that the file is stored in the **templates** directory.

5. Close the PHP section, and create the page-specific content:

```
?>
<h2>Welcome to a J.D. Salinger
 Fan Club</h2>
<p>Lorem ipsum dolor sit
 amet...</p>
```

Because the bulk of this page is standard HTML, it's easier to just exit out of the PHP section and then add the HTML rather than using **print** to send it to the browser. Again, there's more blather in the actual script than I've included here.

6. Create another PHP section, and include the footer file:

```
<?php
include('templates/footer.html');
?>
```

To finish the page, you need to include the footer file, which displays the footer and closes the HTML code. To do this, you create a new section of PHP—you can have multiple sections of PHP code within a script—and call the **include()** function again.

continues on next page

7. Save the file as **index.php**.

8. Create a folder named **templates** within the main web document directory on your PHP-enabled computer or server.

   To further separate the design elements from the main content, the header and footer files go within their own directory.

9. Place **header.html** and **footer.html** in the **templates** directory you just created.

10. Place **index.php** in the same directory as the **templates** folder.

    The relative locations on the computer between the index page and the two HTML pages must be correct in order for the code to work. The two HTML pages go within the **templates** folder, and the **templates** folder and **index.php** are in the same folder (such as the web root directory).

11. Create a folder named **css** within the main web document directory on your PHP-enabled computer or server.

    The CSS scripts will need to go in this directory.

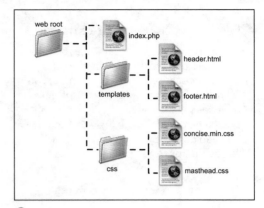

C How the files and folders should be organized on your PHP-enabled server.

12. Place the `concise.min.css` and `masthead.css` scripts, available as part of the book's downloadable code, in the `css` directory **C**.

Even though the header file includes the CSS scripts, the reference to that script must be relative to `index.php`. It's that page, after all, that will include `header.html`.

13. Run `index.php` in your browser **D**.

The resulting page should look exactly like the original layout (**C** in the previous section of the chapter).

14. View the page's source code in your browser.

The source code should be exactly like the source code of the `template.html` script (Script 8.1), aside from the added comments for the script names and numbers.

Raise High the Roof Beam!   Books   Stories   Quotes   Login   Register

Welcome to a J.D. Salinger Fan Club!

Lorem ipsum dolor sit amet, consectetur adipisicing elit, sed do eiusmod tempor incididunt ut labore et dolore magna aliqua. Ut enim ad minim veniam, quis nostrud exercitation ullamco laboris nisi ut aliquip ex ea commodo consequat. Duis aute irure dolor in reprehenderit in voluptate velit esse cillum dolore eu fugiat nulla pariatur. Excepteur sint occaecat cupidatat non proident, sunt in culpa qui officia deserunt mollit anim id est laborum.

Design uses Concise CSS Framework

D This page has been dynamically generated using included files.

TIP All three files in this template system—header.html, footer.html, and index.php—must use the same *encoding* in order to avoid problems (see Chapter 1, "Getting Started with PHP," for more on encoding). Each file's encoding must also match the encoding established in the HTML code.

TIP The require() and include() functions can be used with or without parentheses:

```
require 'filename.html';
```

TIP You might sometimes use a variable that stores the name of the file to be included:

```
require $filename;
```

TIP Both include() and require() have variations: include_once() and require_once(). Each is identical to its counterpart except that it ensures that the same file can be included only one time (in a parent script). You should generally avoid using these, because they'll adversely affect the script's performance.

TIP If a section of PHP executes only a single command, it's common to place both it and the PHP tags on a single line:

```
<?php include('filename.html'); ?>
```

TIP If you see error messages like those in Ⓐ and Ⓑ, the parent script can't locate an included file. This problem is most likely caused by a misspelled included filename or an error in the path (for example, using header.html instead of templates/header.html).

TIP If the rendered page does not seem to be reflecting the CSS styling, the HTML page can't find the corresponding file. Make sure you've stored the file in the proper folder, with the correct name, and that the reference is correct relative to index.php.

TIP A file's extension is less important for included files because they aren't intended to be run directly. As a general rule of thumb, you'll be safe using .html for an included file containing only or mostly HTML (in which case the extension indicates it's an HTML-related file) and .php for included files containing only or mostly PHP. Some programmers use an .inc extension (for include), but security risks can arise with this practice. For that reason, use the .php extension for any file containing sensitive information (like database access parameters). And, of course, always use the .php extension for any PHP script that will be executed directly.

TIP Another good use of an external file is to place your error settings code there so that those changes are applied to every page in the website.

TIP The final closing PHP tag is not required, and many developers advocate omitting it because it's unnecessary and the script may run faster without it.

Using Constants

Many of PHP's data types have already been discussed in this book, primarily: numbers, strings, and arrays. *Constants* are another data type, but unlike variables, their values cannot change.

Whereas variables are assigned values via the assignment operator (=), constants are assigned values using the **define()** function:

```
define('CONSTANT_NAME', value);
```

Notice that—as a rule of thumb—constants are named using all capital letters, although doing so isn't required. Most important, constants don't use the initial dollar sign as variables do, because constants are not variables. Here are two constants:

```
define('PI', 3.14);
define('CURRENCY', 'euros');
```

As with any value, quote those that are strings, not those that are numbers.

Referring to constants is generally straightforward:

```
print CURRENCY;
number_format(PI, 1);
```

But using constants within quotation marks is more complicated. You can't print constants within single or double quotation marks, like this **A**:

```
print "The cost is 468 CURRENCY";
print 'The cost is 468 CURRENCY';
```

Instead, concatenation or multiple **print** statements are required:

```
print 'The cost is 468 ' . CURRENCY;
```

or

```
print 'The cost is 468 ';
print CURRENCY;
```

Along with the **define()** function for creating constants is the **defined()** function (note the final "d"). This function returns TRUE if the submitted constant has been defined. It's often used as the basis for a conditional:

```
if (defined('CONSTANT_NAME')) { ...
```

As an example of working with constants, you'll give the sample application the ability to display a different title (which appears at the top of the browser window) for each page. To accomplish this, you'll define a constant in the parent script that will then be printed by the header file. This technique works because any variables or constants that exist in the parent document before the **include()** or **require()** call are available to the included file (it's as if the included file were part of the parent file).

The cost is 468 CURRENCY

A The value of a constant cannot be printed using the constant's name within quotation marks.

To use constants:

1. Create a new PHP document in your text editor or IDE, to be named **books.php** (Script 8.5):

```
<?php // Script 8.5 - books.php
```

2. Define the page title as a constant:

```
define('TITLE', 'Books by J.D.
→ Salinger');
```

Here one constant is defined, named **TITLE**, and given the value *Books by J.D. Salinger*.

3. Include the header file:

```
include('templates/header.html');
```

This script uses the same header file as all the others, although you'll modify that file shortly to take the constant into account.

4. Close the PHP section, and create the HTML:

```
?>
<h2>J.D. Salinger's Books</h2>
<ul>
  <li>The Catcher in the Rye</li>
  <li>Nine Stories</li>
  <li>Franny and Zooey</li>
  <li>Raise High the Roof Beam,
  → Carpenters and Seymour: An
  → Introduction</li>
</ul>
```

The content here is simple but serves the page's purpose nicely.

5. Create a new PHP section that includes the footer file:

```
<?php include('templates/
→ footer.html'); ?>
```

Script 8.5 This script uses the same template system as **index.php** (Script 8.4) but also uses a constant to identify the page's title.

```
1   <?php // Script 8.5 - books.php
2   /* This page lists J.D. Salinger's
    bibliography. */
3
4   // Set the page title and include the
    header file:
5   define('TITLE', 'Books by J.D.
    Salinger');
6   include('templates/header.html');
7
8   // Leave the PHP section to display lots
    of HTML:
9   ?>
10
11  <h2>J.D. Salinger's Books</h2>
12  <ul>
13      <li>The Catcher in the Rye</li>
14      <li>Nine Stories</li>
15      <li>Franny and Zooey</li>
16      <li>Raise High the Roof Beam,
        Carpenters and Seymour: An
        Introduction</li>
17  </ul>
18
19  <?php include('templates/footer.html');
    ?>
```

Script 8.6 The `header.html` file is modified so that it can set the page title value based on the existence and value of a constant.

```
1    <!doctype html>
2    <html>
3    <head>
4        <meta charset="utf-8">
5        <meta http-equiv="X-UA-Compatible"
         content="IE=edge,chrome=1">
6        <meta name="viewport"
         content="width=device-width,
         initial-scale=1.0">
7        <meta name="HandheldFriendly"
         content="True">
8        <title><?php // Print the page
         title.
9        if (defined('TITLE')) { // Is the
         title defined?
10           print TITLE;
11       } else { // The title is not
         defined.
12           print 'Raise High the Roof
             Beam! A J.D. Salinger Fan
             Club';
13       }
14       ?></title>
15       <link rel="stylesheet" type="text/
         css" media="screen" href="css/
         concise.min.css" />
16       <link rel="stylesheet" type="text/
         css" media="screen" href="css/
         masthead.css" />
17   </head>
18   <body>
19
20   <header container class="siteHeader">
21       <div row>
22           <h1 column=4 class="logo"><a
             href="index.php">Raise High the
             Roof Beam!</a></h1>
23           <nav column="8" class="nav">
24               <ul>
25                   <li><a href="books.
                     php">Books</a></li>
26                   <li><a href="#">Stories
                     </a></li>
27                   <li><a href="#">Quotes
                     </a></li>
28                   <li><a href="login.
                     php">Login</a></li>
```

code continues on next page

As mentioned earlier in a tip, since the remaining PHP code consists of just one line it can all be written on a single line, including the opening and closing PHP tags. Just be certain to leave a space between the executed code—the `include()`—and the tags.

6. Save the file as `books.php`.

To take advantage of the constant, you now need to modify the `header.html` file.

To print out a constant:

1. Open `header.html` (Script 8.2) in your text editor or IDE.

2. Delete the *Raise High the Roof Beam!* text that appears between the title tags (line 6).

   Now that the page title will be determined on a page-by-page basis, you don't need it to be hard-coded into the page.

3. In the place of the deleted text (between the title tags), add the following (**Script 8.6**):

```php
<?php
if (defined('TITLE')) {
    print TITLE;
} else {
    print 'Raise High the Roof
    → Beam!';
}
?>
```

To have PHP create the page title, you need to begin by starting a section of PHP code between the title tags. Then you use a conditional to see if the **TITLE** constant has been defined. If it has, print its value as the page title. If **TITLE** hasn't been defined, print a default title.

4. Save the file as `header.html`.

continues on next page

5. Upload **books.php** and **header.html** to your PHP-enabled server. The new PHP script, **books.php**, should go in the same directory as **index.php**; **header.html** should replace the previous version, in the same directory—**templates**—as **footer.html**.

6. Run **books.php** in your browser **B**.

7. View **index.php** (the home page) in your browser **C**.

8. If you want, add the constant definition line to **index.php** to change its title.

TIP The formal rules for naming constants are exactly like those for variables except for the omission of a dollar sign. Constant names must begin with a letter or an underscore; can contain any combination of letters, numbers, and the underscore; and are case-sensitive.

TIP PHP runs with several predefined constants. These include PHP_VERSION (the version of PHP running) and PHP_OS (the operating system of the server).

TIP In Chapter 9, "Cookies and Sessions," you'll learn about another constant, SID (which stands for session ID).

TIP An added benefit of using constants is that they're global in scope. This concept will mean more to you after you read the section "Understanding Variable Scope" in Chapter 10.

TIP Not only can the value of a constant never be changed, a constant can't be deleted (*unset*, technically).

TIP As of PHP 5.6, a constant can contain an array of values. In earlier versions of the language, a constant was scalar: it could store only a single value.

Script 8.6 *continued*

```
29              <li><a href="register.
                php">Register</a></li>
30          </ul>
31        </nav>
32      </div>
33    </header>
34
35      <main container class="siteContent">
36      <!-- BEGIN CHANGEABLE CONTENT. -->
37        <!-- Script 8.6 - header.html -->
```

B The books page uses a PHP constant to create its title.

C Because the index page didn't have a TITLE constant defined in it, the default page title is used (thanks to the conditional in Script 8.6).

Working with the Date and Time

PHP has a few functions for working with the date and time, the most important of which is **date()**. The only thing the **date()** function does is return date and time information in a format based on the arguments it's fed, but you'd be surprised how useful

that can be. The basic usage of the **date()** function is just

date('*formatting*');

A long list of possible options is available for formatting, as indicated in Table 8.1 (the PHP manual lists a few more). These parameters can also be combined—for example, **date('l F j, Y')** returns *Thursday January 26, 2017*.

TABLE 8.1 Date() Function Formatting

Character	Meaning	Example
Y	Year as 4 digits	2017
y	Year as 2 digits	17
L	Is it a leap year?	1 (for yes)
n	Month as 1 or 2 digits	2
m	Month as 2 digits	02
F	Month	February
M	Month as 3 letters	Feb
j	Day of the month as 1 or 2 digits	8
d	Day of the month as 2 digits	08
l (lowercase L)	Day of the week	Monday
D	Day of the week as 3 letters	Mon
w	Day of the week as a single digit	0 (Sunday)
z	Day of the year: 0 to 365	189
t	Number of days in the month	31
S	English ordinal suffix for a day, as 2 characters	rd
g	Hour; 12-hour format as 1 or 2 digits	6
G	Hour; 24-hour format as 1 or 2 digits	18
h	Hour; 12-hour format as 2 digits	06
H	Hour; 24-hour format as 2 digits	18
i	Minutes	45
s	Seconds	18
u	Microseconds	1234
a	am or pm	am
A	AM or PM	PM
U	Seconds since the epoch	1048623008
e	Time zone	UTC
I (capital i)	Is it daylight savings?	1 (for yes)
O	Difference from GMT	+0600

The `date()` function can take a second argument, named a *timestamp*. A timestamp is a number representing how many seconds have passed since midnight on January 1, 1970—a moment known as the *epoch*.

The `time()` function returns the timestamp for the current moment. The `mktime()` function can return a timestamp for a particular time and date:

```
mktime(hour, minute, second, month,
→ day, year);
```

So the code

```
$ts = mktime(12, 30, 0, 11, 5,
→ 2016);
```

assigns to `$ts` the number of seconds from the epoch to 12:30 on November 5, 2016. That number can then be fed into the `date()` function like so:

```
date('D', $ts);
```

This returns *Sat*, which is the three-letter format for that day of the week.

An important thing to understand is that timestamps and the epoch use Universal Coordinated Time (curiously abbreviated UTC), which is equivalent to Greenwich Mean Time (GMT).

As of PHP 5.1, you should establish the server's time zone prior to calling any date- or time-related function. To do so, use

```
date_default_timezone_set(timezone);
```

The *timezone* value is a string like *America/New_York* or *Pacific/Auckland*. There are too many to list here (Africa alone has over 50), but see the PHP manual for them all. If you don't take this step, you might see errors about a date or time function used without the time zone being set.

Finally, realize that at least three time zones are involved, then:

- UTC
- The server's time zone
- The time zone of the user

Because PHP is a server-side technology, these functions reflect either UTC or the date and time on the server. To get the time on the client (in other words, on the computer where the browser viewing the page is located), you must use JavaScript.

To demonstrate the `date()` function, let's update the footer file so that it shows the current date and time in the sidebar Ⓐ. It's a trivial use of the function but will get you started sufficiently.

To use date():

1. Open **footer.html** (Script 8.3) in your text editor or IDE.

2. After the Concise CSS Framework mention, add the following (**Script 8.7**):

   ```
   <p><?php
   ```

   The initial HTML paragraph tag will wrap the date and time. Then open a PHP section so that you can call the `date()` function.

3. Establish the time zone:

   ```
   date_default_timezone_set
   → ('America/New_York');
   ```

   Before calling `date()`, you must set the time zone. To find yours, see www.php.net/timezones.

Welcome to a J.D. Salinger

Lorem ipsum dolor sit amet, consectetur adipisicing elit, sed do eiu
exercitation ullamco laboris nisi ut aliquip ex ea commodo conseq
Excepteur sint occaecat cupidatat non proident, sunt in culpa qui d

Design uses Concise CSS Framework

1:10 am Tuesday March 29

A The site now displays the date and time in the footer, thanks to the `date()` function.

Script 8.7 The altered `footer.html` file uses the `date()` function to print the current date and time.

```
1          <!-- Script 8.7 - footer.html -->
2      <!-- END CHANGEABLE CONTENT. -->
3      </main>
4
5      <footer container class="siteFooter">
6          <p>Design uses <a href="http://
           concisecss.com/">Concise CSS
           Framework</a></p>
7      <p class="float-right"><?php // Print
       the current date and time...
8      // Set the timezone:
9      date_default_timezone_
       set('America/
       New_York');
10
11     // Now print the date and time:
12     print date('g:i a l F j');
13     ?></p>
14     </footer>
15
16  </body>
17  </html>
```

4. Use the `date()` function to print out the current date and time:

   `print date('g:i a l F j');`

   Using the formatting parameters from Table 8.1, the `date()` function will return a value like *4:15 pm Tuesday February 22*. This value will immediately be printed.

5. Close the PHP section, and finish the HTML code:

   `?></p>`

6. Save the file as `footer.html`, place it in the `templates` directory of your PHP-enabled server, and test it in your browser **A**.

TIP The server's time zone can also be set in the PHP configuration file (see Appendix A, "Installation and Configuration"). Establishing the time zone there is generally a better idea than doing so on a script-by-script basis.

TIP Added to PHP 5.3 are new ways to create and manipulate dates and times using the `DateTime` class. While useful, this new tool requires familiarity with object-oriented programming, therefore making it beyond the scope of this beginner's book.

Handling HTML Forms with PHP, Revisited

All the examples in this book so far have used two separate scripts for handling HTML forms: one that displayed the form and another that received and processed the form's data. There's certainly nothing wrong with this method, but coding the entire process in one script has its advantages. To make a page both display and handle a form, use a conditional **Ⓐ**.

```
if (/* form has been submitted */) {
   // Handle the form.
} else {
   // Display the form.
}
```

There are many ways to determine if a form has been submitted. One option is to check whether any of the form's variables are set:

```
if (isset($_POST['something'])) { ...
```

However, if the user submitted the form without completing it, that variable may not be set (depending on the corresponding form element type). A more reliable solution is to add a hidden input to a form so that it can be checked:

```
<input type="hidden" name=
→ "submitted" value="true">
```

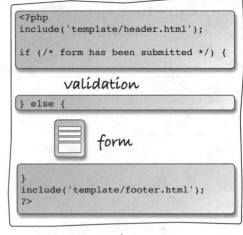

Ⓐ This flowchart represents how the same PHP script can both display and handle an HTML form.

Again, the only purpose of this hidden input is to reliably indicate that the form has been submitted, even if the user did nothing to complete the form. To check for that, the handling PHP code would use this conditional:

```
if (isset($_POST['submitted'])) {
...
```

Another way of checking for a form's submission is to examine *how the page was accessed*. When you have a form that will be submitted back to the same page, two different types of requests will be made of that script **B**. The first request, which loads the form, will be a GET request. This is the standard request made of most web pages. When the form is submitted, and its **action** attribute points to the same page, a second request of the script will be made, this time a POST request (assuming the form uses the POST method). With this in mind, you can test for a form's submission by checking the request type, found in the **$_SERVER** array:

```
if ($_SERVER['REQUEST_METHOD'] ==
→ 'POST') { ...
```

As an example of this, you'll create the basics of a login form.

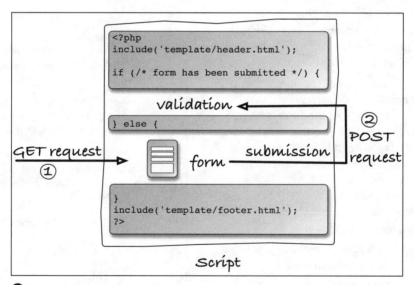

B When the same PHP script both displays and handles an HTML form, the script will be requested using two different methods.

To use one page to display and handle a form:

1. Begin a new PHP document in your text editor or IDE, to be named **login.php** (**Script 8.8**):

   <?php // Script 8.8 - login.php

2. Define the page title as a constant and include the header file:

   define('TITLE', 'Login');
   include('templates/header.html');

   Using the constant system developed earlier in the chapter, give this page its own unique page title.

3. Add some introductory text:

   print '<h2>Login Form</h2>
     <p>Users who are logged in
     → **can take advantage of certain**
     → **features like this, that, and**
     → **the other thing.</p>';**

   This text, which appears outside the main conditional, will always show in the browser, whether the form is being displayed or has been submitted. Because the core of this script revolves around a PHP conditional, it's arguably clearer to print out HTML from PHP rather than exit out of the PHP code as you did in the previous two examples (**index.php** and **books.php**).

4. Begin the conditional to check whether the form has been submitted:

   if ($_SERVER['REQUEST_METHOD'] ==
     → **'POST') {**

   To test whether the form has been submitted, check whether **$_SERVER['REQUEST_METHOD']** equals *POST* (case-sensitive).

Script 8.8 The login page serves two purposes: It displays the login form and handles its submission.

```
1   <?php // Script 8.8 - login.php
2   /* This page lets people log into the
    site (in theory). */
3
4   // Set the page title and include the
    header file:
5   define('TITLE', 'Login');
6   include('templates/header.html');
7
8   // Print some introductory text:
9   print '<h2>Login Form</h2>
10      <p>Users who are logged in can take
        advantage of certain features like
        this, that, and the other thing.
        </p>';
11
12  // Check if the form has been submitted:
13  if ($_SERVER['REQUEST_METHOD'] ==
    'POST') {
14
15      // Handle the form:
16      if ( (!empty($_POST['email'])) &&
        (!empty($_POST['password'])) ) {
17
18          if ( (strtolower($_
            POST['email']) == 'me@example.
            com') && ($_POST['password'] ==
            'testpass') ) { // Correct!
19
20              print '<p class="text--
                success">You are logged
                in!<br>Now you can blah,
                blah, blah...</p>';
21
22          } else { // Incorrect!
23
24              print '<p class="text--
                error">The submitted email
                address and password do not
                match those on file!<br>Go
                back and try again.</p>';
25
26          }
27
28      } else { // Forgot a field.
29
```

code continues on next page

```
30              print '<p class="text--
                error">Please make sure you
                enter both an email address and
                a password!<br>Go back and try
                again.</p>';
31
32      }
33
34  } else { // Display the form.
35
36          print '<form action="login.
            php" method="post"
            class="form--inline">
37          <p><label for="email">Email
            Address:</label><input
            type="email" name="email"
            size="20"></p>
38          <p><label for="password">Password:
            </label><input type="password"
            name="password" size="20"></p>
39          <p><input type="submit"
            name="submit" value="Log In!"
            class="button--pill"></p>
40          </form>';
41
42  }
43
44  include('templates/footer.html'); //
    Need the footer.
45  ?>
```

5. Create a nested pair of conditionals to process the form data:

```php
if ( (!empty($_POST['email'])) &&
(!empty($_POST['password'])) ) {
  if ( (strtolower
  → ($_POST['email']) ==
  → 'me@example.com') &&
  → ($_POST['password'] ==
  → 'testpass') ) { // Correct!
    print '<p class="text--
    → success">You are logged
    → in!<br>Now you can blah,
    → blah, blah...</p>';
  } else { // Incorrect!
    print '<p class="text--
    → error">The submitted email
    → address and password do not
    → match those on file!<br>Go
    → back and try again.</p>';
  }
} else { // Forgot a field.
  print '<p class="text--
  → error">Please make sure you
  → enter both an email address
  → and a password!<br>Go back
  → and try again.</p>';
}
```

These conditionals handle the form data. The first conditional checks that both the email address and password variables have values. If they don't, a message is displayed (*Please make sure...*). Within that first conditional, another conditional checks whether the email address is equal to *me@example.com* and the password is equal to *testpass*. If so, let's say the user is logged in (it would be too advanced at this juncture to store and retrieve user information to create a real login system). Otherwise, a message indicates that the wrong values were entered.

Be certain to use the equals operator (==) here and not the assignment operator (=) in this conditional, which is a common mistake. Also, in case users enter their address as *Me@example.com*, or any other capitalized permutation, the **strtolower()** function is first applied to the email address, prior to checking for equality.

Finally, some Concise CSS Framework classes are used to add styling—green and red coloring—to the printed text.

6. Complete the main conditional:

```
} else { // Display the form.
  print '<form action=
→ "login.php" method="post"
→ class="form--inline">
  <p><label for="email">
→ Email Address:</label>
→ <input type="email"
→ name="email" size="20"></p>
  <p><label for="password">
→ Password:</label><input type=
→ "password" name="password"
→ size="20"></p>
  <p><input type="submit" name=
→ "submit" value="Log In!"
→ class="button--pill"></p>
  </form>';
}
```

This concludes the main conditional, which checks whether the form has been submitted. If the form hasn't been submitted, then the form is displayed. The form itself is very simple **C**.

To clarify a point of possible confusion, even though the form's **method** attribute has a value of *post* (all lowercase), to check for the form's submission the request method value is still *POST* (all uppercase).

Login Form

Users who are logged in can take advantage of certain

Email Address: [   ]

Password: [   ]

[Log In!]

C This simple login page takes an email address and a password.

Login Form

Users who are logged in can take advantage of certain features like this,

You are logged in!
Now you can blah, blah, blah...

D Upon successfully logging in, the user sees this message.

Login Form

Users who are logged in can take advantage of certain features like this,

Please make sure you enter both an email address and a password!
Go back and try again.

E Failure to submit either an email address or a password results in this message.

Login Form

Users who are logged in can take advantage of certain features like this,

The submitted email address and password do not match those on file!
Go back and try again.

F If either the email address or the password doesn't match that in the script, the user sees this error message.

7. Require the footer file, and complete the PHP page:

```
include('templates/footer.html');
?>
```

8. Save the file as **login.php**, place it in the same directory as **index.php**, and test it in your browser **D**, **E**, and **F**.

TIP This trick of checking for the presence of a hidden input can be confusing. It works because the same script—login.php—will be accessed twice by the user. The first time the form will not have been submitted, so a conditional checking if $_POST['submitted'] is set will be FALSE and the form will be displayed. Then the page will be accessed again after the user clicks submit, at which point the conditional becomes TRUE.

TIP If you want a page to handle a form and then immediately display the form again, use this:

```
if ($_SERVER['REQUEST_METHOD'] ==
→ 'POST') {
    // Handle the form.
}
// Display the form.
```

Making Forms Sticky

A *sticky* form remembers values entered into it. A common example is a search engine, which often displays your terms in the search box, even when showing the results of the search. You might also want to use sticky forms on occasions where the user failed to complete a form accurately and therefore must resubmit it **A**.

From a technological standpoint, sticky forms work by having their form element values predetermined. You can make this happen by setting the **value** attribute of text inputs:

```
<input type="text" name="first_name"
→ value="Stephanie">
```

To have PHP preset that value, print the appropriate variable between the quotation marks:

```
<input type="text" name="first_name"
→ value="<?php print $_POST['first_
→ name']; ?>">
```

The first time the form is run, the PHP code prints nothing (because the variable has no value). If the form is displayed again after submission, a value that the user originally entered in the form input will be displayed there automatically. That's the basic idea, but a more professional implementation would address two things.

Registration Form

Register so that you can take advantage of certain features

Please enter your last name!

Your password did not match your confirmed password!

Please try again!

First Name: `Larry`

Last Name:

Email Address: `me@example.com`

Password: `••••••••`

A Creating sticky forms makes it easier for users to correct omissions in incomplete form submissions.

```
        <p><label for="first_name">First Name:</label><input type="text" name="first_name" size="20" value="<br />
<font size='1'><table class='xdebug-error xe-notice' dir='ltr' border='1' cellspacing='0' cellpadding='1'>
<tr><th align='left' bgcolor='#f57900' colspan='5'><span style='background-color: #cc0000; color: #fce94f; font-size: x-large;'>( ! )</span> Notice: Undefined
index: first_name in /Users/larry/Sites/register.php on line <i>68</i></th></tr>
<tr><th align='left' bgcolor='#e9b96e' colspan='5'>Call Stack</th></tr>
<tr><th align='center' bgcolor='#eeeeec'>#</th><th align='left' bgcolor='#eeeeec'>Time</th><th align='left' bgcolor='#eeeeec'>Memory</th><th align='left'
bgcolor='#eeeeec'>Function</th><th align='left' bgcolor='#eeeeec'>Location</th></tr>
<tr><td bgcolor='#eeeeec' align='center'>1</td><td bgcolor='#eeeeec' align='center'>0.0001</td><td bgcolor='#eeeeec' align='right'>377024</td><td
bgcolor='#eeeeec'>{main}(  )</td><td title='/Users/larry/Sites/register.php' bgcolor='#eeeeec'>.../register.php<b>1</b>0</td></tr>
</table></font>
"></p>
```

B The HTML source of the page shows the PHP error caused by referring to a variable that does not exist.

Registration Form

Register so that you can take advantage of certain features

First Name:

Last Name:

Email Address:

Password:

Confirm Password:

Register!

The registration form as the user first sees it.

First, it's best not to refer to variables that don't exist. Doing so creates PHP warnings, and with the PHP code buried in a form element's attribute, the warning itself will only be fully visible in the HTML source code . To avoid that, check that the variable is set before printing it:

```
<input type="text" name="first_name"
→ value="<?php if (isset($_POST
→ ['first_name']) { print $_POST
→ ['first_name']; } ?>">
```

Second, certain characters that could be in a submitted value will cause problems if printed as a form element's value. To prevent such problems, apply the **htmlspecialchars()** function (discussed in Chapter 5, "Using Strings"). With this in mind, a longer but better version of this code is as follows:

```
<input type="text" name="first_name"
→ value="<?php if (isset($_POST
→ ['first_name']) { print
→ htmlspecialchars($_POST
→ ['first_name']); } ?>">
```

To demonstrate this concept, you'll create the shell of a registration form .

To make a sticky form:

1. Create a new PHP script in your text editor or IDE, to be named **register.php** (Script 8.9):

```
<?php // Script 8.9 -
→ register.php
```

2. Set the page title, and include the HTML header:

```
define('TITLE', 'Register');
include('templates/header.html');
```

3. Add some introductory text:

```
print '<h2>Registration Form</h2>
    <p>Register so that you can
    → take advantage of certain
    → features like this, that, and
    → the other thing.</p>';
```

4. Check whether the form has been submitted:

```
if ($_SERVER['REQUEST_METHOD'] ==
→ 'POST') {
```

Like the login page, this one script both displays and handles the registration form. To check whether the form has been submitted, the same code previously explained is used here.

5. Create a flag variable:

```
$problem = false;
```

The **$problem** variable will be used to indicate whether a problem occurred. Specifically, you want to make sure that every form input has been filled out before you formally register the user. Initially, this variable is set to FALSE, because no problems have occurred.

This is the same approach used in Chapter 6, "Control Structures."

Script 8.9 The registration form uses a sticky feature so that it recalls the values previously entered into it.

```
1   <?php // Script 8.9 - register.php
2   /* This page lets people register for
    the site (in theory). */
3
4   // Set the page title and include the
    header file:
5   define('TITLE', 'Register');
6   include('templates/header.html');
7
8   // Print some introductory text:
9   print '<h2>Registration Form</h2>
10      <p>Register so that you can take
        advantage of certain features like
        this, that, and the other thing.</
        p>';
11
12  // Check if the form has been submitted:
13  if ($_SERVER['REQUEST_METHOD'] ==
    'POST') {
14
15      $problem = false; // No problems so
        far.
16
17      // Check for each value...
18      if (empty($_POST['first_name'])) {
19          $problem = true;
20          print '<p class="text--
            error">Please enter your first
            name!</p>';
21      }
22
23      if (empty($_POST['last_name'])) {
24          $problem = true;
25          print '<p class="text--
            error">Please enter your last
            name!</p>';
26      }
27
28      if (empty($_POST['email'])) {
29          $problem = true;
30          print '<p class="text--
            error">Please enter your email
            address!</p>';
31      }
32
```

code continues on next page

```
33      if (empty($_POST['password1'])) {
34          $problem = true;
35          print '<p class="text--
            error">Please enter a password!
            </p>';
36      }
37
38      if ($_POST['password1'] != $_
        POST['password2']) {
39          $problem = true;
40          print '<p class="text--error">Your
            password did not match your
            confirmed password!</p>';
41      }
42
43      if (!$problem) { // If there weren't
        any problems...
44
45          // Print a message:
46          print '<p class="text-
            -success">You are now
            registered!<br>Okay, you are not
            really registered but...</p>';
47
48          // Clear the posted values:
49          $_POST = [];
50
51      } else { // Forgot a field.
52
53          print '<p class="text--
            error">Please try again!</p>';
54
55      }
56
57  } // End of handle form IF.
58
59  // Create the form:
60  ?>
61  <form action="register.php"
    method="post" class="form--inline">
62
63      <p><label for="first_name">First
        Name:</label><input type="text"
        name="first_name" size="20"
        value="<?php if (isset($_POST['first_
        name'])) { print htmlspecialchars($_
        POST['first_name']); } ?>"></p>
64
```

code continues on next page

6. Check that a first name was entered:

```
if (empty($_POST['first_name']))
{
    $problem = true;
    print '<p class="text--
→ error">Please enter your
→ first name!</p>';
}
```

As a simple test to determine whether the user has entered a first name value, check that the variable isn't empty. (This technique was first discussed in Chapter 6.) If the variable is empty, then indicate a problem by setting that variable to TRUE and print an error message. The error message has a class type of *text--error*, so that the CSS formatting is applied. (That class is defined within the Concise CSS Framework.)

7. Repeat the validation for the last name and email address:

```
if (empty($_POST['last_name'])) {
    $problem = true;
    print '<p class="text--
→ error">Please enter your last
→ name!</p>';
}
if (empty($_POST['email'])) {
    $problem = true;
    print '<p class="text--
→ error">Please enter your
→ email address!</p>';
}
```

Both of these checks are variations on the username validation routine.

continues on next page

8. Validate the passwords:

```php
if (empty($_POST['password1'])) {
  $problem = true;
  print '<p class="text--
  ➞error">Please enter a
  ➞password!</p>';
}
if ($_POST['password1'] != $_
POST['password2']) {
  $problem = true;
  print '<p class="text--
  ➞error">Your password did
  ➞not match your confirmed
  ➞password!</p>';
}
```

The password validation requires two conditionals. The first checks whether the **$_POST['password1']** variable is empty. The second checks whether the **$_POST['password1']** variable isn't equal to the **$_POST['password2']** variable. You don't need to see if **$_POST['password2']** is empty because if it is and **$_POST['password1']** isn't, the second conditional will catch that problem. If **$_POST['password1']** and **$_POST['password2']** are both empty, the first conditional will catch the mistake.

9. Check whether a problem occurred:

```php
if (!$problem) {
  print '<p class="text--
  ➞success">You are now
  ➞registered!<br>Okay, you
  ➞are not really registered
  ➞but...</p>';
  $_POST = [];
```

If there were no problems, the **$problem** variable is still FALSE, and the initial condition here is TRUE (the condition is that **$problem** has a value of FALSE). In that case, the registration

Script 8.9 *continued*

```
65   <p><label for="last_name">Last
     Name:</label><input type="text"
     name="last_name" size="20"
     value="<?php if (isset($_
     POST['last_name'])) { print
     htmlspecialchars($_POST['last_
     name']); } ?>"></p>
66
67   <p><label for="email">Email
     Address:</label><input
     type="email" name="email"
     size="20" value="<?php if
     (isset($_POST['email'])) { print
     htmlspecialchars($_POST['email']);
     } ?>"></p>
68
69   <p><label
     for="password1">Password:
     </label><input type="password"
     name="password1" size="20"
     value="<?php if (isset($_
     POST['password1'])) {
     print htmlspecialchars($_
     POST['password1']); } ?>"></p>
70   <p><label for="password2">Confirm
     Password:</label><input
     type="password" name="password2"
     size="20" value="<?php if
     (isset($_POST['password2']))
     { print htmlspecialchars($_
     POST['password2']); } ?>"></p>
71
72   <p><input type="submit"
     name="submit" value="Register!"
     class="button--pill"></p>
73
74   </form>
75
76   <?php include('templates/footer.html');
     // Need the footer. ?>
```

process would take place. The formal registration process, where the data is stored in a file or database, has not yet been developed, so a simple message appears in its stead here.

Next, the **$_POST** variable is assigned the value of an empty array using the short array syntax. This line has the effect of wiping out the contents of the **$_POST** variable (i.e., resetting it as an empty array). This step is taken only upon a successful (theoretical) registration so that the values are not redisplayed in the registration form (e.g., see Step 12).

10. Complete the conditionals:

```
} else { // Forgot a field.
  print '<p class="text--
    error">Please try again!
    </p>';
}
} // End of handle form IF.
```

The **else** clause applies if a problem occurred, in which case the user is asked to complete the form again.

11. Begin the HTML form:

```
?>
  <form action="register.php"
    method="post"  class=
    "form--inline">
```

Unlike the login example, this page always displays the form. Therefore, the form isn't part of any conditional. Also, because there's a lot of HTML to be generated, it'll be easier to leave the PHP section of the page and just output the HTML directly.

12. Create the sticky first name input:

```
<p><label for="first_name">
  First Name:</label><input
  type="text" name="first_name"
  size="20" value="<?php if
  (isset($_POST['first_name']))
  { print htmlspecialchars($_
  POST['first_name']); } ?>"></p>
```

To make the first name input sticky, preset its **value** attribute by printing out the **$_POST['first_name']** variable, but only if it's set. The conditional is therefore put within PHP tags within the HTML's **value** section of the form element. As already mentioned, the **htmlspecialchars()** function is used to handle any potentially problematic characters.

Note that if the user filled out the form properly, the entire **$_POST** array will have been reset, making this PHP conditional FALSE.

If it helps your comprehension, write out the PHP code:

```
<p><label for="first_name">
  First Name:</label><input
  type="text" name="first_name"
  size="20" value="<?php
if (isset($_POST['first_name']))
{
  print htmlspecialchars
    ($_POST['first_name']);
} ?>"></p>
```

continues on next page

13. Repeat the process for the last name and email address:

```
<p><label for="last_name">
→ Last Name:</label><input
→ type="text" name="last_name"
→ size="20" value="<?php if
→ (isset($_POST['last_name']))
→ { print htmlspecialchars
→ ($_POST['last_name']); } ?>">
→ </p>
<p><label for="email">Email
→ Address:</label><input type=
→ "email" name="email"
→ size="20" value="<?php if
→ (isset($_POST['email'])) {
→ print htmlspecialchars($_POST
→ ['email']); } ?>"></p>
```

These are variations on Step 12, switching the variable names as appropriate.

14. Add the rest of the form:

```
<p><label for="password1">
→ Password:</label><input
→ type="password"
→ name="password1" size="20"
→ value="<?php if (isset
→ ($_POST['password1'])) {
→ print htmlspecialchars
→ ($_POST['password1']); } ?>">
→ </p>
<p><label for="password2">
→ Confirm Password:</label>
→ <input type="password"
→ name="password2" size="20"
→ value="<?php if (isset
→ ($_POST['password2'])) {
→ print htmlspecialchars
→ ($_POST['password2']); } ?>">
→ </p>
<p><input type="submit"
→ name="submit"
→ value="Register!"
→ class="button--pill"></p>
</form>
```

Registration Form

Register so that you can take advantage of certain features

Please enter your last name!

Please enter a password!

Your password did not match your confirmed password!

Please try again!

First Name: Larry

Last Name:

Email Address: me@example.com

Password:

Confirm Password: ·········

D The registration form indicates any problems and retains the form values.

Registration Form

Register so that you can take advantage of certain features

You are now registered!
Okay, you are not really registered but...

First Name:

E The registration form after the user successfully fills it out.

It used to be the case that you couldn't preset a value for a password input, but most browsers now support this feature. Then there is the submit button and the closing **form** tag.

15. Complete the PHP page:

```
<?php include('templates/
→ footer.html'); ?>
```

The last step is to include the HTML footer.

16. Save the file as **register.php**, place it in the proper directory on your PHP-enabled server, and test it in your browser **D** and **E**.

TIP You should quote all attribute values in form inputs. If you don't quote your values, any spaces in them mark the end of the value (for example, *Larry Ullman* will display as just *Larry* in the form input).

TIP To preset the status of radio buttons or checkboxes as selected, add the code **checked="checked"** to the **input** tag:

```
<input type="checkbox" name=
→ "interests[]" value="Skiing"
→ checked="checked">
```

Of course, you'd need to use a PHP conditional to see if that text should be added to the element's definition.

TIP To preselect a pull-down menu, use **selected="selected"**:

```
<select name="year">
<option value="2017">2017</option>
<option value="2018" selected=
→ "selected">2018</option>
</select>
```

Again, you'd need to use a PHP conditional to see if that text should be added to the element's definition.

TIP To preset the value of a text area, place the value between the **textarea** tags:

```
<textarea name="comments" rows="10"
→ cols="50">preset value</textarea>
```

Sending Email

Sending email using PHP is *theoretically* simple, merely requiring only PHP's `mail()` function. This function uses the server's email application (such as **sendmail** on Unix or Mac OS X) or an SMTP (Simple Mail Transfer Protocol) server to send out the messages. The basic usage of this function is as follows:

`mail(to, subject, body);`

The first argument is the email address (or *addresses*, separated by commas) to which the email should be sent. The second argument establishes the message's subject line, and the third argument creates the message's content.

This function can take another argument through which you can add more details (*additional headers*) to the email, including a *From* address, email priority, and carbon-copy (CC) addresses:

```
mail('someone@example.com', 'Test
→ Email', 'This is a test email',
→ 'From: 'email@example.com');
```

Although doing so is easy in theory, using this function in real-world code can be far more complex. For starters, setting up your own computer to send out email can be a challenge (see the sidebar "Configuring Your Server to Send Email").

Second, you should take steps to prevent malicious people from using your forms to send out spam. In our next example, an email will be sent to the provided email address. If a conniving user supplies multiple addresses **Ⓐ**, an email will be sent to each one. You can safeguard against this in many ways. For the level of this book, one simple option is to confirm that there's only a single @ present in the provided address (i.e., it's only one email address).

Email Address:	me@example.com,you@example.edu,whomever@example.ne

Ⓐ A user could easily attempt to send emails to multiple recipients through a form like this.

Script 8.10 In PHP, you can send email by calling the `mail()` function.

```
1   <?php // Script 8.9 - register.php
2   /* This page lets people register for
    the site (in theory). */
3
4   // Set the page title and include the
    header file:
5   define('TITLE', 'Register');
6   include('templates/header.html');
7
8   // Print some introductory text:
9   print '<h2>Registration Form</h2>
10      <p>Register so that you can take
        advantage of certain features like
        this, that, and the other thing.
        </p>';
11
12  // Check if the form has been submitted:
13  if ($_SERVER['REQUEST_METHOD'] ==
    'POST') {
14
15      $problem = false; // No problems so
        far.
16
17      // Check for each value...
18      if (empty($_POST['first_name'])) {
19          $problem = true;
20          print '<p class="text--
            error">Please enter your first
            name!</p>';
21      }
22
23      if (empty($_POST['last_name'])) {
24          $problem = true;
25          print '<p class="text--
            error">Please enter your last
            name!</p>';
26      }
27
```

code continues on next page

```
28    if (empty($_POST['email']) ||
      (substr_count($_POST['email'],
      '@') != 1) ) {
29        $problem = true;
30        print '<p class="text--
          error">Please enter your email
          address!</p>';
31    }
32
33    if (empty($_POST['password1'])) {
34        $problem = true;
35        print '<p class="text--
          error">Please enter a password!
          </p>';
36    }
37
38    if ($_POST['password1'] != $_
      POST['password2']) {
39        $problem = true;
40        print '<p class="text--error">Your
          password did not match your
          confirmed password!</p>';
41    }
42
43    if (!$problem) { // If there weren't
      any problems...
44
45        // Print a message:
46        print '<p class="text-
          -success">You are now
          registered!<br>Okay, you are not
          really registered but...</p>';
47
48        // Send the email:
49        $body = "Thank you, {$_
          POST['first_name']}, for
          registering with the J.D.
          Salinger fan club!'.";
50        mail($_POST['email'],
          'Registration Confirmation',
          $body, 'From: admin@example.
          com');
51
52        // Clear the posted values:
53        $_POST = [];
54
55    } else { // Forgot a field.
56
```

code continues on next page

You can count how many times a substring is present in a string using the aptly named **substr_count()** function:

```
if (substr_count($_POST
→['email'],'@') == 1) {...
```

With those caveats, let's add a **mail()** function call to the registration page so that you get a sense of how the function might be used.

To send email with PHP:

1. Open **register.php** (Script 8.9) in your text editor or IDE.

2. Change the email validation so that it also checks for a single "at" symbol (**Script 8.10**):

```
if (empty($_POST['email']) ||
→(substr_count($_POST['email'],
→'@') != 1) ) {
```

Now the email address validation fails if the value is empty or if it doesn't contain exactly one @. This doesn't constitute thorough validation—far from it—but the email address becomes less of a security risk to use. See the tips for ways to improve upon this.

3. After the registration message (line 46), add the following:

```
$body = "Thank you, {$_POST
→['first_name']}, for
→registering with the J.D.
→Salinger fan club!";
mail($_POST['email'],
→'Registration Confirmation',
→$body, 'From: admin@example.
→com');
```

continues on next page

```
57          print '<p class="text--error">Please try again!</p>';
58
59      }
60
61  } // End of handle form IF.
62
63  // Create the form:
64  ?>
65  <form action="register.php" method="post" class="form--inline">
66
67      <p><label for="first_name">First Name:</label><input type="text" name="first_name"
          size="20" value="<?php if (isset($_POST['first_name'])) { print htmlspecialchars(
          $_POST['first_name']); } ?>"></p>
68
69      <p><label for="last_name">Last Name:</label><input type="text" name="last_name"
          size="20" value="<?php if (isset($_POST['last_name'])) { print htmlspecialchars(
          $_POST['last_name']); } ?>"></p>
70
71      <p><label for="email">Email Address:</label><input type="email" name="email"
          size="20" value="<?php if (isset($_POST['email'])) { print htmlspecialchars(
          $_POST['email']); } ?>"></p>
72
73      <p><label for="password1">Password:</label><input type="password" name="password1"
          size="20" value="<?php if (isset($_POST['password1'])) { print htmlspecialchars(
          $_POST['password1']); } ?>"></p>
74
75      <p><label for="password2">Confirm Password:</label><input type="password"
          name="password2" size="20" value="<?php if (isset($_POST['password2'])) { print
          htmlspecialchars($_POST['password2']); } ?>"></p>
76
77      <p><input type="submit" name="submit" value="Register!" class="button--pill"></p>
78
79  </form>
80
81  <?php include('templates/footer.html'); // Need the footer. ?>
```

Registration Form

Register so that you can take advantage of certain features like this,

Please enter your email address!

Please try again!

First Name: Larry

Last Name: Ullman

Email Address: me@example.com,you@

B If users provide multiple email addresses **A**, they'll see an error message.

To: Larry Ullman
Registration Confirmation

Thank you, Larry, for registering with the J.D. Salinger fan club!

C This email was sent by the PHP script upon successful pseudo-registration.

Sometimes the easiest way to use this function is to establish the body as a variable and then feed it into the `mail()` function (as opposed to writing the email's body within the function call). The message itself is sent to the address with which the user registered, with the subject *Registration Confirmation*, from the address *admin@example.com*. If you'll be running this script on a live server, you should use an actual email address for that site as the *from* value.

4. Save the file, place it in the proper directory of your PHP- and email-enabled server, and test it in your browser **B**.

5. Upon successfully completing the form, check your email for the message **C**.

TIP The "Review and Pursue" section at the end of this chapter points you in the direction of an excellent tool for validating email addresses, provided you're using PHP version 5.2 or later.

TIP The HTML5 email input type limits the user to only entering a single email address, but that can easily be circumvented.

TIP In my *PHP and MySQL for Dynamic Web Sites: Visual QuickPro Guide* (Peachpit Press) and online in my forums (www.LarryUllman.com/forums/), I discuss other ways to secure the emails that get sent by a PHP script.

TIP If you have problems receiving the PHP-sent email, start by confirming that the mail server works on its own without involving PHP. Then make sure you're using a valid *from* address. Finally, try using different recipient addresses, and keep an eye on your spam folder to see that the message isn't getting put there (if applicable).

continues on next page

TIP It's possible to send email with attachments or HTML email, although doing so requires far more sophisticated coding (normally involving classes and objects). Fortunately, a number of programmers have already developed workable solutions that are available for use. See Appendix B, "Resources and Next Steps," for websites that may be of assistance.

TIP The `mail()` function returns a value (1 or 0) indicating its successful use. This value indicates only whether PHP was able to attempt to send the email (by using whatever email system is in place). There's no easy way to use PHP to see whether an email address is valid or whether the end user received the message.

TIP To send an email to multiple addresses, either use the *CC* parameter or separate each *TO* address with a comma.

TIP To create new lines within the email body, either create the message over multiple lines or use the newline character (\n) within double quotation marks.

TIP If you want to send multiple headers in addition to the *From* address, separate them with a combination of \r\n:

```
mail ('email@example.com',
→ 'Testing', $body, "From:
→ email@example.org\r\nBcc:
→ hidden@example.net,
→ third@example.com");
```

Configuring Your Server to Send Email

Sending email with PHP is easy, as long as your web server (or computer) is set up to send email. If you're using a web hosting service or your own Unix computer (such as Linux), this shouldn't be a problem at all. If you do have a problem, contact the hosting company for support.

If you're running your own server (for example, if you're developing locally), the ability to send email could be a sticking point. If you're using an all-in-one installer, such as MAMP or XAMPP (see Appendix A), it should also have an email server as part of the package. If you don't receive the email after registering, check the associated software's documentation for what you may need to do to enable email.

If you're using a web server built into the operating system, such as Apache on Mac OS X, you may already be set up to send email. To start, go ahead and try this example using a valid email address. If you don't receive the email, see Appendix A for information about getting `mail()` to work.

I'll also add that I almost never worry about getting PHP on my own computer to send out emails because I'll never be running live websites from my computer. In other words, why waste time getting something to work that you'll never end up using (whereas getting PHP to send out email on a live server does matter)?

Output Buffering

A handful of functions that you'll use in this chapter and the next can be called only if nothing has been sent to the browser. These functions include **header()**, **setcookie()**, and **session_start()**. If you use them after the browser has already received some text, HTML, or even a blank space, you'll get the dreaded "*headers already sent*" error message **A**.

One solution that I recommend for beginning PHP developers is to make use of *output buffering* (also named *output control*). In a normal PHP script, any HTML outside the PHP tags is immediately sent to the browser. This is also true when any **print** statement is executed. With output buffering, the HTML and printed data—the output—will instead be placed into a buffer (that is, memory). At the end of the script, the buffer will then be sent to the browser, or if more appropriate, the buffer can be cleared without being sent to the browser. There are many reasons to use output buffering, but for beginners, one benefit is that you can use certain functions without worrying about *headers already sent* errors. Although you haven't dealt with any of the named functions yet, this chapter introduces output buffering now. Using this feature will greatly reduce errors when you begin using headers (in the next section of this chapter), cookies (in the next chapter), and sessions (also in the next chapter).

To begin output buffering, invoke the **ob_start()** function at the very top of your page. Once you call it, every **print** and similar function will send data to a memory buffer rather than to the browser. Conversely, HTTP calls, such as **header()** and **setcookie()**, won't be buffered and will operate as usual. To be more explicit, it must be invoked before any **print** statements or any HTML gets sent to the browser.

> (!) Warning: Cannot modify header information - headers already sent by (output started at /Users/larry/Sites/templates/header.html:8) in /Users/larry/Sites/login.php on line 22

A If the browser receives any HTML prior to a **header()** call, you'll see this error message.

At the conclusion of the script, call the `ob_end_flush()` function to send the accumulated buffer to the browser. Or use the `ob_end_clean()` function to delete the buffered data without passing it along. Both functions also turn off output buffering for that script. PHP automatically runs `ob_end_flush()` at the conclusion of a script if it isn't otherwise done. But it's still a good idea to call it yourself.

From a programmer's perspective, output buffering allows you to structure a script in a more linear form, without concern for HTTP headers. Let's remake `header.html` and `footer.html` so that every page uses output buffering. You won't appreciate the benefits yet, but the number of errors you *won't see* over the rest of this book will go a long way toward preserving your programming sanity.

To use output buffering:

1. Open `header.html` (Script 8.7) in your text editor or IDE.

2. At the very top of the page, before any HTML code, add the following (**Script 8.11**):

```php
<?php
ob_start();
?>
```

Script 8.11 Add output buffering to the web application by calling the `ob_start()` function at the top of the `header.html` script.

```
1    <?php // Script 8.11 - header.html #3
2
3    // Turn on output buffering:
4    ob_start();
5
6    ?><!doctype html>
7    <html>
8    <head>
9        <meta charset="utf-8">
10       <meta http-equiv="X-UA-Compatible"
         content="IE=edge,chrome=1">
11       <meta name="viewport"
         content="width=device-width,
         initial-scale=1.0">
12       <meta name="HandheldFriendly"
         content="True">
13       <title><?php // Print the page title.
14       if (defined('TITLE')) { // Is the
         title defined?
15           print TITLE;
16       } else { // The title is not defined.
17           print 'Raise High the Roof Beam!
             A J.D. Salinger Fan Club';
18       }
19       ?></title>
20       <link rel="stylesheet" type="text/
         css" media="screen" href="css/
         concise.min.css" />
21       <link rel="stylesheet" type="text/
         css" media="screen" href="css/
         masthead.css" />
22   </head>
23   <body>
24   <header container class="siteHeader">
25       <div row>
26           <h1 column=4 class="logo">
             <a href="index.php">Raise High
             the Roof Beam!</a></h1>
27           <nav column="8" class="nav">
```

code continues on next page

Script 8.11 *continued*

```
28              <ul>
29                  <li><a href="books.
                    php">Books</a></li>
30                  <li><a href="#">Stories
                    </a></li>
31                  <li><a href="#">Quotes
                    </a></li>
32                  <li><a href="login.
                    php">Login</a></li>
33                  <li><a href="register.
                    php">Register</a></li>
34              </ul>
35          </nav>
36      </div>
37  </header>
38
39      <main container class="siteContent">
40      <!-- BEGIN CHANGEABLE CONTENT. -->
41          <!-- BEGIN CHANGEABLE CONTENT.
                -->
```

Script 8.12 Output buffering is completed at the end of the footer file using **ob_end_flush()**, which sends the accumulated buffer to the browser.

```
1       <!-- END CHANGEABLE CONTENT. -->
2       </main>
3
4       <footer container class="siteFooter">
5           <p>Design uses <a href="http://
            concisecss.com/">Concise CSS
            Framework</a></p>
6       <p class="float-right"><?php // Print
        the current date and time...
7       // Set the timezone:
8       date_default_timezone_set('America/
        New_York');
9
10      // Now print the date and time:
11      print date('g:i a l F j');
12      ?></p>
13      </footer>
14
15  </body>
16  </html><?php // Script 8.12 - footer.
    html #3
17
18  // Send the buffer to the browser and
    turn off buffering:
19  ob_end_flush();
20  ?>
```

The key to using output buffering is to call the **ob_start()** function as early as possible in a script. In this example, you create a special section of PHP prior to any HTML and call **ob_start()** there. By turning on output buffering in your header file and turning it off in your footer file, you buffer every page in the application.

3. Open **footer.html** (Script 8.7) in your text editor or IDE.

4. At the end of the script, after all the HTML, add the following (**Script 8.12**):

```
<?php
ob_end_flush();
?>
```

This code turns off output buffering and sends the accumulated buffer to the browser. In other words, all the HTML is sent at this point.

continues on next page

5. Save both files, and place them in the **templates** directory of your PHP-enabled server.

6. Test any page in your browser **B**.

TIP As a reminder, PHP code can be placed in a file with an .html extension—as in these two examples here—if that file is being included by a PHP script (such as index.php).

TIP For some time now, output buffering has been automatically enabled in PHP's default configuration. The code added in this section of the chapter will work regardless of that setting.

TIP You can set the maximum buffer size in php.ini (PHP's configuration file). The default is 4,096 bytes.

TIP The ob_get_length() function returns the length (in number of characters) of the current buffer contents.

TIP The ob_get_contents() function returns the current buffer so that it can be assigned to a variable, should the need arise. For example, you could take the accumulated content and process it to add dynamic highlighting or text manipulation.

TIP The ob_flush() function sends the current contents of the buffer to the browser and then discards them, allowing a new buffer to be started. This function lets your scripts maintain more moderate buffer sizes.

TIP The ob_clean() function deletes the current contents of the buffer without stopping the buffer process.

TIP PHP automatically runs ob_end_flush() at the conclusion of a script if it isn't otherwise done. But it's still a good idea to call it yourself.

Raise High the Roof Beam!

J.D. Salinger's Books

- The Catcher in the Rye
- Nine Stories
- Franny and Zooey
- Raise High the Roof Beam, Carpenters and Seymour: An Introduction

Design uses Concise CSS Framework

9:58 am Sunday April 3

B The site works the same as it did previously, but it will be easier to work with when you use HTTP headers in the next section of this chapter.

Manipulating HTTP Headers

Most interactions between a server and a browser (the client) take place over HTTP (Hypertext Transfer Protocol). This is why the addresses for pages begin with *http://*. But HTTP communications between browsers and servers go beyond just sending HTML, images, and the like. These additional communications can be accomplished using HTTP *headers*. There are dozens of uses for HTTP headers, all of which you can do using PHP's **header()** function.

Perhaps the most common use of the **header()** function is to redirect the user from one page to another. To redirect the user's browser with PHP, you send a *location* header:

```
header('Location: page.php');
```

When using the **header()** function to redirect the browser, follow that line by calling **exit()** to cancel the execution of the script (because the browser has been redirected to another page):

```
header('Location: page.php');
exit();
```

If you don't invoke **exit()**, the rest of the script's code will be executed, despite the fact that the browser has moved on.

The most important thing to understand about using **header()** is that the function must be called before anything else is sent to the browser—otherwise, you'll see the all-too-common *headers already sent* error message (see Ⓐ in the section "Output Buffering"). If your page receives *any* HTML or even blank space, the **header()** function won't work.

Fortunately, you learned about output buffering in the previous section. Because output buffering is turned on in the application, nothing is sent to the browser until the very last line of the footer script (when **ob_end_flush()** is called). By using this method, you can avoid the dreaded *headers already sent* error message.

To practice redirection, you'll update the login page to take the user to a welcome page upon successful login.

To use the header() function:

1. Open **login.php** in your text editor or IDE (Script 8.8).

2. Delete the *You are logged in...* **print** statement (**Script 8.13**).

   Because the user is redirected to another page, there's no need to include this message.

3. Where the **print** statement was, add the following:

   ```
   ob_end_clean();
   header('Location: welcome.php');
   exit();
   ```

   The first line destroys the page buffer (because the accumulated buffer won't be used). This isn't strictly required but is a good idea. The next line redirects the user to **welcome.php**. The third line terminates the execution of the rest of the script.

4. Save the file, and place it in the proper directory for your PHP-enabled server (along with the other scripts from this chapter).

Now you need to create the **welcome.php** page to which the user will be redirected.

Script 8.13 The new version of the login page redirects the user to another page using the **header()** function.

```
1    <?php // Script 8.13 - login.php #2
2    /* This page lets people log into the
     site (in theory). */
3
4    // Set the page title and include the
     header file:
5    define('TITLE', 'Login');
6    include('templates/header.html');
7
8    // Print some introductory text:
9    print '<h2>Login Form</h2>
10       <p>Users who are logged in can take
         advantage of certain features like
         this, that, and the other thing.
         </p>';
11
12   // Check if the form has been submitted:
13   if ($_SERVER['REQUEST_METHOD'] ==
     'POST') {
14
15       // Handle the form:
16       if ( (!empty($_POST['email'])) &&
         (!empty($_POST['password'])) ) {
17
18           if ( (strtolower($_POST['email'])
             == 'me@example.com') && ($_
             POST['password'] == 'testpass') )
             { // Correct!
19
20               // Redirect the user to the
                 welcome page!
21               ob_end_clean(); // Destroy
                 the buffer!
22               header('Location: welcome.
                 php');
23               exit();
24
25           } else { // Incorrect!
26
27               print '<p class="text--
                 error">The submitted email
                 address and password do not
                 match those on file!<br>Go
                 back and try again.</p>';
28
29           }
30
```

code continues on next page

Script 8.13 *continued*

```
31      } else { // Forgot a field.
32
33          print '<p class="text--error">
            Please make sure you enter both
            an email address and a password!
            <br>Go back and try again.</p>';
34
35      }
36
37  } else { // Display the form.
38
39      print '<form action="login.php"
        method="post" class="form--inline">
40      <p><label for="email">Email
        Address:</label><input type="email"
        name="email" size="20"></p>
41      <p><label for="password">Password:</
        label><input type="password"
        name="password" size="20"></p>
42      <p><input type="submit"
        name="submit" value="Log In!"
        class="button--pill"></p>
43      </form>';
44
45  }
46
47  include('templates/footer.html'); //
    Need the footer.
48  ?>
```

Script 8.14 The welcome page greets users after they've logged in.

```
1   <?php // Script 8.14 - welcome.php
2   /* This is the welcome page. The user is
    redirected here
3   after they successfully log in. */
4
5   // Set the page title and include the
    header file:
6   define('TITLE', 'Welcome to the J.D.
    Salinger Fan Club!');
7   include('templates/header.html');
8
9   // Leave the PHP section to display lots
    of HTML:
10  ?>
11
```

code continues on next page

To write welcome.php:

1. Begin a new PHP document in your text editor or IDE, to be named `welcome.php` (Script 8.14):

```
<?php // Script 8.14 - welcome.php
```

2. Define the page title, and include the header:

```
define('TITLE', 'Welcome to the
→ J.D. Salinger Fan Club!');
include('templates/header.html');
```

3. Create the page content:

```
?>
<h2>Welcome to the J.D. Salinger
→ Fan Club!</h2>
<p>You've successfully logged
→ in and can now take advantage
→ of everything the site has to
→ offer.</p>
```

4. Return to PHP, and include the footer:

```
<?php include('templates/
→ footer.html'); ?>
```

continues on next page

5. Save the script as **welcome.php**, place it in the same directory as the new version of **login.php**, and test it in your browser **Ⓐ**, **Ⓑ**, and **Ⓒ**.

> **TIP** The headers_sent() function returns TRUE if the page has already received HTTP headers and the header() function can't be used.

> **TIP** Using the GET method trick, you can pass values from one page to another using header():

```
$var = urlencode('Pass this text');
header("Location: page.php?
→ message=$var");
```

> **TIP** The header() function should technically use a full path to the target page when redirecting. For example, it should be

```
header('Location: http://
→ www.example.com/welcome.php');
```

or

```
header('Location: http://localhost/
→ welcome.php');
```

> **TIP** In my book *PHP and MySQL for Dynamic Web Sites: Visual QuickPro Guide*, I show some code for dynamically generating an absolute URL based on the location of the current script.

Script 8.14 *continued*

```
12    <h2>Welcome to the J.D. Salinger Fan
      Club!</h2>
13    <p>You've successfully logged in and
      can now take advantage of everything the
      site has to offer.</p>
14    <p>Lorem ipsum dolor sit amet,
      consectetur adipisicing elit, sed do
      eiusmod tempor incididunt ut labore et
      dolore magna aliqua. Ut enim ad minim
      veniam, quis nostrud exercitation
      ullamco laboris nisi ut aliquip ex ea
      commodo consequat. Duis aute irure dolor
      in reprehenderit in voluptate velit esse
      cillum dolore eu fugiat nulla pariatur.
      Excepteur sint occaecat cupidatat non
      proident, sunt in culpa qui officia
      deserunt mollit anim id est laborum.</p>
15
16    <?php include('templates/footer.html');
      // Need the footer. ?>
```

Login Form

Users who are logged in can take advantage of certain

Email Address: me@example.com

Password: ••••••••

Log In!

Ⓐ The login form...

Raise High the Roof Beam!

Welcome to the J.D. Salinger Fan Club!

You've successfully logged in and can now take advantage of everything the site has to offer.

Lorem ipsum dolor sit amet, consectetur adipisicing elit, sed do eiusmod tempor incididunt ut labo exercitation ullamco laboris nisi ut aliquip ex ea commodo consequat. Duis aute irure dolor in rep Excepteur sint occaecat cupidatat non proident, sunt in culpa qui officia deserunt mollit anim id e

Ⓑ ...and the redirection if the user properly logged in.

Login Form

Users who are logged in can take advantage of certain features like this,

Please make sure you enter both an email address and a password! Go back and try again.

Ⓒ If users don't properly log in, they remain on the login page.

Review and Pursue

If you have any problems with the review questions or the pursue prompts, turn to the book's supporting forum (www.LarryUllman.com/forums/).

Review

- What is the difference between `include()` and `require()`?

- Why can you put PHP code into an included file even when it uses an `.html` extension?

- What are the differences between *relative* and *absolute* references to a file?

- How do you define a constant? Are constant names case-sensitive or case-insensitive? How do you check if a constant has been defined?

- What is the *epoch*? What is a *timestamp*?

- What is the significance of `$_SERVER['REQUEST_METHOD']`?

- How do you have a form element "remember" previously submitted values?

- How can you see a PHP error that occurs within a form element (for example, when presetting a form's element's value)?

- What does the *headers already sent* error mean? How can it be prevented?

Pursue

- Create a new prototype design for this chapter's examples, and then create new header and footer files. View any of the site's pages again (you should not need to change any of the PHP scripts).

- Change the parameters to the **date()** function in **footer.html** to display the date and/or time in a different manner.

- Rewrite the password conditionals found in **register.php** as a nested pair of conditionals. Hint: See Chapter 6 for examples.

- If you're using PHP 5.2 or later, check out the PHP manual pages for the *Filter* extension. Then incorporate the **filter_var()** function to validate the email address in **register.php**.

- Change the subject and body of the email sent upon (pseudo-) registration to something more interesting and informative.

- Update **login.php** so that it also shows the form upon a failed login attempt.

Cookies and Sessions

Chapter 8, "Creating Web Applications," covered a number of techniques for developing more fully realized websites. One missing piece—the focus of this chapter —is how to maintain "state" as the user traverses a multipage site. The Hypertext Transfer Protocol (HTTP) is a stateless technology, meaning that it has no built-in method for tracking a user or remembering data from one page of an application to the next. This is a serious problem, because e-commerce applications, user registration and login systems, and other common online services rely on being able to follow the same user from page to page. Fortunately, maintaining state is quite simple with PHP.

This chapter discusses the two primary methods for tracking data: cookies and sessions. You'll start by learning how to create, read, modify, and delete cookies. Then you'll see how easy it is to master sessions, a more potent option for maintaining state.

In This Chapter

What Are Cookies?

Prior to the existence of cookies, traversing a website was a trip without a history. Although the browser tracks the pages you visit, allowing you to use the Back button to return to previously visited pages and indicating visited links in a different color, the server does not follow what individual users see and do. This is still true for sites that don't use cookies, as well as for users who have disabled cookies in their web browsers 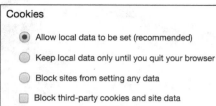.

A Most browsers let users set the cookie-handling preferences. In Internet Explorer 11, you will find this in the Advanced Privacy Settings area.

Debugging Cookies

When you begin working with cookies in PHP, you'll need to know how to debug your cookie-related scripts when difficulties arise. Three areas might cause you problems:

- Sending the cookie with PHP
- Receiving the cookie in your browser
- Accessing a cookie in a PHP script

The first and last issues can be debugged by printing out the variable values in your PHP scripts, as you'll soon learn. The second issue requires that you know how to work with cookies in your browser. For debugging purposes, you'll want your browser to notify you when a cookie is being sent. This is an easy option in Internet Explorer and not readily available in the other browsers.

With Internet Explorer on Windows, you can do this by choosing Internet Options under the Tools menu. Then click the Privacy tab, followed by the Advanced button under Settings. Click "Override automatic cookie handling," and then choose Prompt for both First-party and Third-party Cookies (you can actually block the third-party cookies, if you'd rather). Other versions of Internet Explorer may use different variations on this process. Internet Explorer also has a Developer Tools window (linked under the Tools menu) that can be useful.

The current versions of Chrome, Opera, Firefox, and Safari no longer offer the ability to be prompted when cookies are created, which is unfortunate. But you can view existing cookies in any browser, normally by finding the cookies area (often under Privacy) within the browser's preferences or options.

A browser's developer tools, or third-party extensions such as Firebug, will normally show existing cookies for the site being viewed without you having to navigate through the browser settings. If you're not using Internet Explorer, you'll want to find what developer tools or extensions are available for your browser of choice.

Why is that a problem? If the server can't track a user, there can be no shopping carts for making purchases online. If cookies didn't exist (or if they're disabled in the browser), people wouldn't be able to use popular sites that require user registration. In short, without cookies, there would be no Amazon or Facebook or any of the other most popular or useful sites (not in their current incarnations, at least).

Cookies are simply a way for a server to store information on the user's computer. By doing so, the server can remember the user over the course of a visit or through several visits. Think of a cookie as a name tag: You tell the server your name, and it gives you a name tag. Then it can know who you are by referring back to the name tag.

This brings up another point about the security issues involved with cookies. Cookies have gotten a bad rap because users believe cookies allow a server to know too much about them. However, a cookie can only be used to store information that you give it, so it's as secure as you want it to be (although to be fair, your "giving" of information is normally not a conscious choice).

PHP has solid support for cookies. In this chapter, you'll learn how to set a cookie, retrieve information from a cookie, and then delete the cookie. You'll also see some of the optional parameters you can use to apply limits to a cookie's existence.

Before moving on, you ought to know two more things about cookies. The first is how to debug cookie-related problems. You'll inevitably need to know how to do that, so the topic is discussed in the sidebar "Debugging Cookies." The second is how a cookie is transmitted and received ⓑ. Cookies are stored in the browser, but only the site that originally sent a cookie can read it. Also, the cookies are read by the site when the page on that site is requested by the browser. In other words, when the user enters a URL in the address bar and clicks Go (or whatever), the site reads any cookies it has access to and then serves up the requested page. This order is important because it dictates when and how cookies can be accessed.

TIP The ability to send, read, and delete cookies is one of the few overlaps between server-side PHP and browser-side JavaScript.

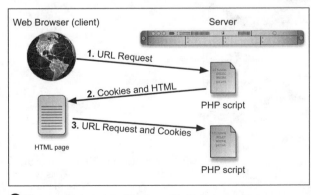

ⓑ How cookies are sent back and forth between the server and the client.

Creating Cookies

An important thing to understand about cookies is that *they must be sent from the server to the client prior to any other information*. This means a script should send cookies before any `print` statement, before including an external file that contains HTML, and so forth.

Should the server attempt to send a cookie after the web browser has already received HTML—even an extraneous white space—an error message will result and the cookie won't be sent **A**. This is by far the most common cookie-related error.

Cookies are sent using the `setcookie()` function:

```
setcookie(name, value);
setcookie('CookieName', 'This is the
→ cookie value.');
```

That line of code sends to the browser a cookie with the name *CookieName* and the value *This is the cookie value*. **B**.

You can continue to send more cookies to the browser with subsequent uses of the `setcookie()` function, although you're limited by the browser as to how many cookies can be sent from the same site:

```
setcookie('name2', 'some value');
setcookie('name3', 'another value');
```

There's no universal, hard limit as to how many cookies a browser will accept from one site, but you should keep the number to a minimum.

Finally, when creating cookies, you can—as you'll see in this example—use a variable for the name or value attribute of your cookies:

```
setcookie($cookie_name,
→ $cookie_value);
```

#	Time	Memory	Function	Location
			Warning: Cannot modify header information - headers already sent by (output started at /Users/larry/Sites/customize.php:8) in /Users/larry/Sites/customize.php on line *10*	
	Call Stack			
1	0.0001	361288	{main}( )	.../customize.php:0
2	0.0002	361496	setcookie ( )	.../customize.php:10

A A message like this is what you'll see if the `setcookie()` function is called after anything, even a blank line or space, has already been sent to the browser.

B If the browser is set to prompt the user for cookies, a message like this will appear for each cookie sent. (Note that the window, from Internet Explorer 11, shows the value in a URL-encoded format.)

C This form is used to select the font size and color for use on another PHP page.

D After submitting the form, the page shows a message and a link to another page (where the user's preferences will be used). You will create that page next.

Script 9.1 Two cookies will be used to store the user's choices for the font size and color. This page both displays and handles the form.

```
1    <?php // Script 9.1 - customize.php
2
3    // Handle the form if it has been
     submitted:
4    if (isset($_POST['font_size'],
     $_POST['font_color'])) {
5
6        // Send the cookies:
7        setcookie('font_size',
         $_POST['font_size']);
8        setcookie('font_color',
         $_POST['font_color']);
9
10       // Message to be printed later:
11       $msg = '<p>Your settings have been
         entered! Now see them <a href="view_
         settings.php">in action</a>.</p>';
12
```

code continues on next page

For an example of setting cookies, you'll create a script that allows the user to specify the default font size and color for a page. The page displays a form for choosing these values **C** and then handles the form submission **D**. A separate page, created in the next section of this chapter, will use these settings.

To send cookies:

1. Create a new PHP document in your text editor or IDE, to be named **customize.php** (Script 9.1):

   **<?php // Script 9.1 -
   → customize.php**

   The most critical issue with cookies is that they're created before anything is sent to the browser. To accomplish this, the script begins with a PHP section that handles the sending of cookies.

   Also be certain not to have any extraneous spaces or lines before the initial PHP tag.

2. Check whether the form has been submitted:

   **if (isset($_POST['font_size'],
   → $_POST['font_color'])) {**

   This page will both display and handle the form. It could use the same method explained in the previous chapter—checking if the **$_SERVER['REQUEST_ METHOD']** variable has a value of POST, but as an alternative approach, the script will perform basic, minimal validation as the test for a form submission. The conditional checks for the existence of two variables: **$_POST['font_ size']** and **$_POST['font_color']**. If both are set, the form submission will be addressed.

   continues on next page

3. Create the cookies:

```
setcookie('font_size',
→ $_POST['font_size']);
setcookie('font_color',
→ $_POST['font_color']);
```

These two lines create two separate cookies. One is named ***font_size*** and the other ***font_color***. Their values will be based on the selected values from the HTML form, which are stored in the **$_POST['font_size']** and **$_POST['font_color']** variables.

In a more fully developed application, you should first confirm that the variables have acceptable values.

4. Create a message and complete the conditional and the PHP section:

```
$msg = '<p>Your settings have
→ been entered! Now see them
→ <a href="view_settings.php">
→ in action</a>.</p>';
} // End of submitted IF.
?>
```

When the form has been submitted, the cookies will be sent and the **$msg** variable will be assigned a string value. This variable will be used later in the script to print a message. This approach is necessary; you can't print the message at this juncture because not even the HTML head has been created.

5. Create the HTML head and opening body tag:

```
<!doctype html>
<html lang="en">
<head>
  <meta charset="utf-8">
  <title>Customize Your Settings
  → </title>
</head>
<body>
```

Script 9.1 *continued*

```
13   } // End of submitted IF.
14   ?><!doctype html>
15   <html lang="en">
16   <head>
17       <meta charset="utf-8">
18       <title>Customize Your Settings
         </title>
19   </head>
20   <body>
21   <?php // If the cookies were sent, print
     a message.
22   if (isset($msg)) {
23       print $msg;
24   }
25   ?>
26
27   <p>Use this form to set your
     preferences:</p>
28
29   <form action="customize.php"
     method="post">
30       <select name="font_size">
31       <option value="">Font Size</option>
32       <option value="xx-small">xx-small
         </option>
33       <option value="x-small">x-small
         </option>
34       <option value="small">small</option>
35       <option value="medium">medium
         </option>
36       <option value="large">large</option>
37       <option value="x-large">x-large
         </option>
38       <option value="xx-large">xx-large
         </option>
39       </select>
40       <select name="font_color">
41       <option value="">Font Color</option>
42       <option value="999">Gray</option>
43       <option value="0c0">Green</option>
44       <option value="00f">Blue</option>
45       <option value="c00">Red</option>
46       <option value="000">Black</option>
47       </select>
48       <input type="submit" name="submit"
         value="Set My Preferences">
49   </form>
50
51   </body>
52   </html>
```

All this code must come after the **setcookie()** lines. Not to overstate this, but no text, HTML, or blank spaces can be sent to the browser prior to the **setcookie()** calls.

6. Create another PHP section to report on the cookies being sent:

```php
<?php
if (isset($msg)) {
   print $msg;
}
?>
```

This code prints out a message if the cookies have been sent. The first time the user comes to the page, the cookies haven't been sent, so **$msg** is not set, making this conditional FALSE, and this **print** invocation never runs. Once the form has been submitted, **$msg** has been set by this point, so this conditional is TRUE **D**.

7. Begin the HTML form:

```html
<p>Use this form to set your
→ preferences:</p>
<form action="customize.php"
→ method="post">
   <select name="font_size">
   <option value="">Font Size
→ </option>
   <option value="xx-small">
→ x-small</option>
   <option value="x-small">
→ x-small</option>
   <option value="small">
→ small</option>
   <option value="medium">
→ medium</option>
   <option value="large">
→ large</option>
   <option value="x-large">
→ x-large</option>
```

```html
<option value="xx-large">
→ xx-large</option>
   </select>
```

The HTML form itself is very simple **C**.

The user is given one drop-down menu to select the font size. The value for each corresponds to the CSS code used to set the document's font size: from *xx-small* to *xx-large*.

Because this script both displays and handles the form, the form's **action** attribute points to the same file.

8. Complete the HTML form:

```html
<select name="font_color">
<option value="">Font Color
→ </option>
<option value="999">Gray
→ </option>
<option value="0c0">Green
→ </option>
<option value="00f">Blue
→ </option>
<option value="c00">Red
→ </option>
<option value="000">Black
→ </option>
</select>
<input type="submit" name=
→ "submit" value="Set My
→ Preferences">
</form>
```

The second drop-down menu is used to select the font color. The menu displays the colors in text form, but the values are HTML color values. Normally such values are written using six characters plus a pound sign (for example, *#00cc00*), but CSS allows you to use just a three-character version, and the pound sign will be added on the page that uses these values.

continues on next page

9. Complete the HTML page:

```
</body>
</html>
```

10. Save the file as **customize.php**, and place it in the proper directory for your PHP-enabled server.

11. Make sure you've set your browser to prompt for each cookie, if possible.

   To guarantee that the script is working, you want the browser to prompt you for each cookie, if you can. See the "Debugging Cookies" sidebar.

12. Run the script in your browser **E** and **F**.

TIP Cookies are one of the few areas in PHP that can behave differently from browser to browser or operating system to operating system. You should test your cookie-based applications on as many browsers and operating systems as you can.

TIP If you use the output buffering technique taught in Chapter 8, then you can place your `setcookie()` calls anywhere within the script (because the browser won't receive the data until the `ob_end_flush()` function is called).

TIP Cookies are limited to approximately 4 KB of total data. This is more than sufficient for most applications.

TIP To test whether it's safe to send a cookie, use the `headers_sent()` function. It reports on whether HTTP headers have already been sent to the web browser.

E The user sees this message when the first `setcookie()` call is made, if they've opted to be prompted before accepting a cookie. This cookie is storing the value of *x-large* in a cookie named *font_size*.

F The Chrome Developer Tools shows the cookies received by the browser. The second cookie that's sent by the PHP script is named *font_color* and has a value of *c00*, representing the color gray.

```
1    <!doctype html>
2    <html lang="en">
3    <head>
4        <meta charset="utf-8">
5        <title>View Your Settings</title>
6        <style type="text/css">
7        body {
8    <?php // Script 9.2 - view_settings.php
9
10   // Check for a font_size value:
11   if (isset($_COOKIE['font_size'])) {
12       print "\t\tfont-size: " .
         htmlentities($_COOKIE['font_
         size']) . ";\n";
13   } else {
14       print "\t\tfont-size: medium;";
15   }
16
17   // Check for a font_color value:
18   if (isset($_COOKIE['font_color'])) {
19       print "\t\tcolor: #" .
         htmlentities($_COOKIE['font_
         color']) . ";\n";
20   } else {
21       print "\t\tcolor: #000;";
22   }
23
24   ?>
25       }
26       </style>
27   </head>
28   <body>
29   <p><a href="customize.php">Customize
     Your Settings</a></p>
30   <p><a href="reset.php">Reset Your
     Settings</a></p>
31
32   <p>yadda yadda yadda yadda yadda
33   yadda yadda yadda yadda yadda
34   yadda yadda yadda yadda yadda
35   yadda yadda yadda yadda yadda
36   yadda yadda yadda yadda yadda</p>
37
38   </body>
39   </html>
```

Reading from Cookies

Just as form data is stored in the **$_POST** array (assuming it used the POST method) and values passed to a script in the URL are stored in the **$_GET array**, the **setcookie()** function places cookie data in the **$_COOKIE** array. To retrieve a value from a cookie, you only need to refer to the cookie name as the index of this array. For example, to retrieve the value of the cookie established with the line

setcookie('user', 'trout');

you would use the variable

$_COOKIE['user'].

Unless you change the cookie's parameters (as you'll see later in this chapter), the cookie will automatically be accessible to every other page in your web application. You should understand, however, that a cookie is never accessible to a script immediately after it's been sent. You can't do this:

setcookie('user', 'trout');
print $_COOKIE['user']; // No value.

The reason for this is the order in which cookies are read and sent (see Ⓑ in the first section of this chapter).

To see how simple it is to access cookie values, let's write a script that uses the preferences set in **customize.php** to specify the page's text size and color. The script relies on CSS to achieve this effect.

To retrieve cookie data with PHP:

1. Begin a new PHP document in your text editor or IDE, to be named **view_settings.php** (Script 9.2):

```
<!doctype html>
<html lang="en">
<head>
```

continues on next page

```
<meta charset="utf-8">
<title>View Your Settings
→ </title>
```

2. Start the CSS section:

```
<style type="text/css">
body {
```

The page will use CSS to enact the user's preferences. The aim is to create code like

```
body {
  font-size: x-large;
  color: #999;
}
```

The two values will differ based on what the user selected in the **customize.php** page. In this step, you create the initial CSS tag.

3. Open a section of PHP code:

```
<?php // Script 9.2 -
→ view_settings.php
```

The script will now use PHP to print out the remaining CSS, based on the cookies.

4. Use the font size cookie value, if it exists:

```
if (isset($_COOKIE
→ ['font_size'])) {
  print "\t\tfont-size:
  → " . htmlentities($_COOKIE
  → ['font_size']) . ";\n";
} else {
  print "\t\tfont-size: medium;";
}
```

If the script can access a cookie with a name of *font_size*, it will print out that cookie's value as the CSS **font-size** value. The **isset()** function is sufficient to see if the cookie exists. If no such cookie exists, PHP will print out a default size, *medium*.

For security purposes, the cookie's value is not directly printed. Instead, it's run through the **htmlentities()** function, discussed in Chapter 5, "Using Strings." This function will prevent bad things from happening should the user manipulate the value of the cookie (which is easy to do).

Also note that two tabs (**\t**) and a newline (**\n**) are added to the **print** statements so that the resulting CSS code is formatted properly. Not that this affects the functionality of the page, but...

5. Repeat this process for the font color cookie:

```
if (isset($_COOKIE
→ ['font_color'])) {
  print "\t\tcolor:
  → #" . htmlentities($_COOKIE
  → ['font_color']) . ";\n";
} else {
  print "\t\tcolor: #000;";
}
```

Here the CSS's **color** attribute is being assigned a value. The cookie itself is used the same as in Step 4.

6. Close the PHP section, complete the CSS code, and finish the HTML head:

```
?>
  }
  </style>
</head>
```

7. Start the HTML body, and create links to two other pages:

```
<body>
<p><a href="customize.php">
→ Customize Your Settings</a></p>
<p><a href="reset.php">Reset Your
→ Settings</a></p>
```

A This page reflects the customized font choices made using the other PHP script.

B By viewing the source code of the page, you can also track how the CSS values change.

These two links take the user to two other PHP pages. The first, `customize.php`, has already been written and lets users define their settings. The second, `reset.php`, will be written later in the chapter and lets users delete their customized settings.

8. Add some text:

   ```
   <p>yadda yadda yadda yadda yadda
   yadda yadda yadda yadda yadda
   yadda yadda yadda yadda yadda
   yadda yadda yadda yadda yadda
   yadda yadda yadda yadda yadda</p>
   ```

   This text exists simply to show the effects of the cookie changes.

9. Complete the HTML page:

   ```
   </body>
   </html>
   ```

10. Save the file as `view_settings.php`, place it in the same directory as `customize.php`, and test it in your browser **A** by clicking the link on `customize.php`.

11. View the source of the page to see the resulting CSS code **B**.

12. Use the customize page to change your settings and return to this script.

    Each submission of the form will create two new cookies storing the form values, thereby replacing the existing cookies.

> **TIP** The value of a cookie is automatically encoded when it's sent and decoded on being received by the PHP page. The same is true of values sent by HTML forms.

Adding Parameters to a Cookie

Although passing just the **name** and **value** arguments to the **setcookie()** function will suffice for most of your cookie uses, you ought to be aware of the other arguments available. The function can take up to five more parameters, each of which limits the operation of the cookie:

```
setcookie(name, value, expiration,
→ path, domain, secure, httponly);
```

The *expiration* argument is used to set a specific length of time for a cookie to exist. If it isn't specified, the cookie will continue to be functional until the user closes the browser. Normally, you set the expiration time by adding a particular number of minutes or hours to the current time. You can find the current time in PHP by using the **time()** function (it returns a timestamp; see Chapter 8). Therefore, this line of code sets the expiration time of the cookie to be one hour (60 seconds times 60 minutes) from the current moment:

```
setcookie(name, value, time()+3600);
```

Because the expiration time will be calculated as the value of **time()** plus 3600, that argument isn't put in quotes (you don't want to literally pass *time() + 3600* as the expiration but rather the result of that calculation).

The *path* and *domain* arguments are used to limit a cookie to a specific folder in a website—the path—or to a specific domain. Using the **path** option, you could limit a cookie to exist only while a user is in a specific subfolder of the domain:

```
setcookie(name, value, time()+3600,
→ '/subfolder/');
```

Cookies are already specific to a domain, so the *domain* argument might be used to limit a cookie to a subdomain, such as **forum.example.com**:

```
setcookie(name, value, time()+3600, '',
→ 'forum.example.com');
```

Script 9.3 When you add the expiration arguments to the two cookies, the cookies will persist even after users have closed out of and later returned to their browser.

```
1    <?php // Script 9.1 - customize.php
2
3    // Handle the form if it has been submitted:
4    if (isset($_POST['font_size'], $_POST['font_color'])) {
5
6        // Send the cookies:
7        setcookie('font_size', $_POST['font_size'], time()+10000000, '/');
8        setcookie('font_color', $_POST['font_color'], time()+10000000, '/');
9
10       // Message to be printed later:
11       $msg = '<p>Your settings have been entered! Now see them <a href="view_settings.php">in
         action</a>.</p>';
12
13   } // End of submitted IF.
14   ?><!doctype html>
15   <html lang="en">
```

code continues on next page

```
16   <head>
17
18      <meta charset="utf-8">
19      <title>Customize Your Settings
        </title>
20   </head>
21   <body>
22   <?php // If the cookies were sent, print
     a message.
23   if (isset($msg)) {
24      print $msg;
25   }
26   ?>
27
28   <p>Use this form to set your
     preferences:</p>
29
30   <form action="customize.php"
     method="post">
31      <select name="font_size">
32      <option value="">Font Size</option>
33      <option value="xx-small">xx-small
        </option>
34      <option value="x-small">x-small
        </option>
35      <option value="small">small</option>
36      <option value="medium">medium
        </option>
37      <option value="large">large</option>
38      <option value="x-large">x-large
        </option>
39      <option value="xx-large">xx-large
        </option>
40      </select>
41      <select name="font_color">
42      <option value="">Font Color</option>
43      <option value="999">Gray</option>
44      <option value="0c0">Green</option>
45      <option value="00f">Blue</option>
46      <option value="c00">Red</option>
47      <option value="000">Black</option>
48      </select>
49      <input type="submit" name="submit"
        value="Set My Preferences">
50   </form>
51
52   </body>
53   </html>
```

The ***secure*** value dictates that a cookie should only be sent over a secure HTTPS connection. A value of 1 indicates that a secure connection must be used, whereas 0 indicates that a secure connection isn't necessary. You could ensure a secure cookie transmission for e-commerce sites:

```
setcookie('cart', '82ABC3012',
→ time()+3600, '',
→ 'shop.example.com', 1);
```

As with all functions that take arguments, you must pass all the values in order. In the preceding example, if there's no need to specify (or limit) the path, you use empty quotes. With the ***path*** argument, you can also use a single slash (***/***) to indicate the root folder (i.e., no path restriction). By doing so, you maintain the proper number of arguments and can still indicate that an HTTPS connection is necessary.

The final argument—***httponly***—was added in PHP 5.2. It can be used to restrict access to the cookie (for example, preventing a cookie from being read using JavaScript) but isn't supported by all browsers.

Let's add an expiration date to the existing **customize.php** page so that users' preferences will remain even after they've closed their browser and then returned to the site later.

To set a cookie's expiration date:

1. Open **customize.php** (Script 9.1) in your text editor or IDE.

2. Change the two **setcookie()** lines to read as follows (**Script 9.3**):

   ```
   setcookie('font_size', $_POST
   → ['font_size'], time()+10000000,
   → '/', '', 0);
   ```

continues on next page

```
setcookie('font_color', $_POST
→ ['font_color'], time()
→ +10000000, '/', '', 0);
```

To make these cookies persist for a long time (specifically, for a couple of months), set the expiration time to be 10,000,000 seconds from now. While you're at it, set the *path* argument to the root of the site (*/*). Doing so may improve the consistency of sending these cookies across the various browsers.

Because the expiration date of the cookies is set months into the future, the user's preferences, which are stored in the cookies, will be valid even after the user has closed and reopened the browser. Without this expiration date, users would see the default font size and color and have to reassign their preferences with every new browser session.

3. Save the file, place it in the proper directory for your PHP-enabled server, and test it again in your browser **A** and **B**.

TIP Not all browsers acknowledge a cookie's adjusted expiration time when the cookie is being sent from your own computer (i.e., from localhost). More generally, browsers can be inconsistent in how they handle local cookies.

TIP Here are some general guidelines for what kind of expiration date to use with your cookies: If the cookie should last as long as the user browses through the site, don't set an expiration time. If the cookie should continue to exist after the user has closed and reopened the browser, set an expiration time that's weeks or months in the future. And if the cookie can constitute a security risk, set an expiration time of an hour or a fraction thereof so that the cookie doesn't continue to exist too long after a user has left the browser.

TIP For security purposes, you can set a 5- or 10-minute expiration time on a cookie and have the cookie re-sent with every new page the user visits. This way, the cookie will continue to persist as long as the user is active but will automatically expire 5 or 10 minutes after the user's last action.

	Elements	Console	Sources	Network	Timeline	Profiles	Resources	Security	Audits
▶ 🗀 Frames	Name	Value ▲	Domain	Path	Expires / Max-Age				
🗎 Web SQL	font_color	0c0	localhost	/	2016-07-28T17:45:53.684Z				
🗎 IndexedDB	font_size	large	localhost	/	2016-07-28T17:45:53.684Z				
▶ ▦ Local Storage									
▶ ▦ Session Storage									
▼ 🍪 Cookies									
🍪 localhost									

A The browser's cookie reporting tools (here, Chrome's Developer Tools) now reflect the cookie expiration dates.

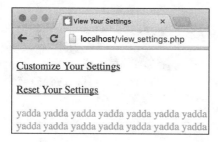

B The new cookie parameters don't adversely affect the functionality of the application.

Deleting a Cookie

The final thing to know about cookies is how to delete them. Although a cookie automatically expires when the user's browser is closed or when the expiration date/time is met, sometimes you'll want to manually delete the cookie as well. For example, websites that have registered users and login capabilities delete any created cookies when the user logs out.

The `setcookie()` function can take up to seven arguments, but only one is required— the name. If you send a cookie that consists of a name without a value, it will have the same effect as deleting the existing cookie of the same name. For example, to create the cookie `username`, you use this line:

```
setcookie('username', 'Larry');
```

To delete the `username` cookie, you code

```
setcookie('username', '');
```

or

```
setcookie('username', FALSE);
```

As an added precaution, you can also set an expiration date that's in the past Ⓐ:

```
setcookie('username', FALSE,
→ time() - 6000);
```

The only caveat when it comes to deleting a cookie is that you must use the same argument values that were used to set the cookie in the first place, aside from the value and expiration. For example, if you set a cookie while providing a domain value, you must also provide that value when deleting the cookie:

```
setcookie('user', 'larry',
→ time() + 3600, '',
→ 'forums.example.com');
setcookie('user', '', time() - 600,
→ '', 'forums.example.com');
```

continues on next page

To demonstrate this feature, let's add a reset page to the web application. This PHP script will destroy the sent cookies so that the user's preferences are forgotten.

1. Begin a new PHP script in your text editor or IDE, to be named **reset.php** (Script 9.4):

```php
<?php // Script 9.4 - reset.php
```

2. Delete the existing cookies by sending blank cookies. Then complete the PHP code:

```php
setcookie('font_size', '',
→ time() -  6000, '/');
setcookie('font_color', '',
→ time() - 6000, '/');
?>
```

These two lines send cookies named *font_size* and *font_color*, each with no value and an expiration time of more than an hour ago. As you did when creating cookies, you must call the **setcookie()** function before anything else is sent to the browser.

3. Create the HTML head:

```html
<!doctype html>
<html lang="en">
<head>
  <meta charset="utf-8">
  <title>Reset Your Settings
  → </title>
```

Script 9.4 To delete the existing cookies, send new cookies with the same names, empty values, and expirations in the past.

```php
1   <?php // Script 9.4 - reset.php
2
3   // Delete the cookies:
4   setcookie('font_size', '', time() -
    600, '/');
5   setcookie('font_color', '', time() -
    600, '/');
6
7   ?><!doctype html>
8   <html lang="en">
9   <head>
10     <meta charset="utf-8">
11     <title>Reset Your Settings</title>
12  </head>
13  <body>
14
15  <p>Your settings have been reset!
    Feel free to <a href="view_settings.
    php">customize</a> them again.</p>
16
17  </body>
18  </html>
```

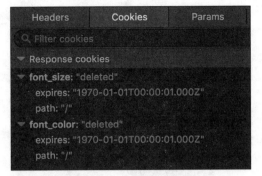

Ⓑ When the `setcookie()` function is used with a name but no value, the existing cookie of that name is deleted. The expiration date in the past also guarantees proper destruction of the existing cookie.

Reset Your Settings ✕
← → C ⬤ localhost/reset.php

Your settings have been reset! Feel free to customize them again.

Ⓒ The reset page sends two blank cookies and then displays this message.

View Your Settings ✕
← → C ⬤ localhost/view_settings.php

Customize Your Settings

Reset Your Settings

yadda yadda yadda yadda yadda yadda yadda yadda yadda yadda yadda yadda yadda yadda yadda yadda

Ⓓ After accessing the reset page, PHP destroys the cookies Ⓑ, which will have the effect of resetting the **view_settings.php** page to its default formatting.

4. Add the page's body:

```
<body>
<p>Your settings have been reset!
→ Feel free to <a href="view_
→ settings.php">customize</a>
→ them again.</p>
</body>
```

The body of this script merely tells users that their settings have been reset. A link is then provided to return to the main page.

5. Complete the HTML:

```
</html>
```

6. Save the page as **reset.php**, place it in the proper directory for your PHP-enabled server, and test it in your browser Ⓑ, Ⓒ, and Ⓓ.

To test this page, either click the appropriate link in **view_settings.php** (Script 9.2) or just go to this page directly.

TIP Just as creating a cookie doesn't take effect until another page is visited, deleting a cookie doesn't take effect until another page is visited. In other words, you can delete a cookie on a page but still access that cookie on it (because the cookie was received by the page before the delete cookie was sent).

TIP Just as creating cookies has mixed results using different browsers, the same applies to deleting them. Test your scripts on many browsers and play with the `setcookie()` settings to ensure the best all-around compatibility.

TIP Just as one example of how different browsers handle cookies, Firefox Developer Edition treats any cookie that expires in the past as having an expiration just after the epoch Ⓑ.

What Are Sessions?

A session, like a cookie, provides a way for you to track data for a user over a series of pages. The difference between the two—and this is significant—is that a cookie stores the data on the client (in the browser), whereas the session data is stored on the server. Because of this difference, sessions have numerous benefits over cookies:

- Sessions are generally more secure, because the data isn't transmitted back and forth between the client and server repeatedly.

- Sessions allow you to store more information than you can in a cookie.

- Sessions can be made to work even if the user doesn't accept cookies in their browser.

- You can more easily store other types of data in sessions, such as arrays and Booleans.

When you start a session, PHP generates a random session ID. Each user's session will have its own session ID, corresponding to the name of the text file on the server that stores the user's session data (Script 9.5).

So that every PHP script on a site can associate the same session data with a particular user, the session ID must be tracked as well. By default, this session ID is sent to the browser as a cookie **Ⓐ**. Subsequent PHP pages will use this cookie to retrieve the session ID and access the session information.

Over the next few pages, you'll see just how easy sessions are to work with in PHP.

Ⓐ A session cookie being sent to the browser.

Script 9.5 How session data is stored in a file on the server.

```
1   email|s:14:"me@example.
    com";loggedin|i:1292883103;
```

Choosing Between Sessions and Cookies

Sessions have many benefits over cookies, but there are still reasons why you would use the latter. Cookies have these advantages over sessions:

- Marginally easier to create and retrieve
- Require slightly less work from the server
- Normally persist over a longer period of time

As a rule of thumb, you should use cookies in situations where security is less of an issue and only a minimum of data is being stored. If security's a concern and there will be oodles of information to remember, you're best off with sessions. Understand, though, that using sessions may require a little more effort in writing your scripts.

Creating a Session

Creating, accessing, or deleting a session begins with the **session_start()** function. This function will attempt to send a cookie the first time a session is started, so it absolutely must be called prior to any HTML or white space being sent to the browser. Therefore, on pages that use sessions, you should call the **session_start()** function as one of the very first lines in your script:

```
<?php
session_start();
```

The first time a session is started, a random session ID is generated and a cookie is sent to the web browser with a name of *PHP-SESSID* (the session name) and a value like *mo7puk861tm60tbm4b8coh0og2*.

Once the session has been started, you can record data to it by assigning values to the **$_SESSION** array:

```
$_SESSION['first_name'] = 'Sam';
$_SESSION['age'] = 10;
```

Unlike with other arrays you might use in PHP, you should always treat this array as an associative array. In other words, you should explicitly use strings for the keys, such as *first_name* and *age*.

Each time a value is assigned to the **$_SESSION** array, PHP writes that data to a temporary file stored on the server (see Script 9.5).

To begin, you'll rewrite the login script from Chapter 8, this time storing the email address in a session.

To create a session:

1. Open **login.php** (Script 8.13) in your text editor or IDE.

2. Before the **ob_end_clean()** line, add the following (**Script 9.6**):

```
session_start();
$_SESSION['email'] =
→ $_POST['email'];
$_SESSION['loggedin'] = time();
```

To store values in a session, begin by calling the **session_start()** function. Although you normally have to call this function first thing in a script (because it may attempt to send a cookie), that's not required here because the header file for this script begins output buffering (see Chapter 8).

The session first stores the user's submitted email address in **$_SESSION['email']**. Then the time-stamp of when the user logged in is assigned to **$_SESSION['loggedin']**. This value is determined by calling the **time()** function, which returns the number of seconds that have elapsed since the *epoch* (midnight on January 1, 1970).

3. Save the file as **login.php**, and place it in the appropriate directory on your PHP-enabled computer.

This script should be placed in the same directory used in Chapter 8, because it requires some of those other files.

Script 9.6 This script stores two values in the session and then redirects the user to another page, where the session values can be accessed.

```
2   <?php // Script 9.6 - login.php #3
3   /* This page lets people log into the
    site (almost!). */
4
5   // Set the page title and include the
    header file:
6   define('TITLE', 'Login');
7   include('templates/header.html');
8
9   // Print some introductory text:
10  print '<h2>Login Form</h2>
11      <p>Users who are logged in can take
        advantage of certain features like
        this, that, and the other thing.
        </p>';
12
13  // Check if the form has been submitted:
14  if ($_SERVER['REQUEST_METHOD'] ==
    'POST') {
15
16      // Handle the form:
17      if ( (!empty($_POST['email'])) &&
        (!empty($_POST['password'])) ) {
18
19          if ( (strtolower($_POST['email'])
            == 'me@example.com') && ($_
            POST['password'] == 'testpass') )
            { // Correct!
20
21              // Do session stuff:
22              session_start();
23              $_SESSION['email'] =
                $_POST['email'];
24              $_SESSION['loggedin'] =
                time();
25
26              // Redirect the user to the
                welcome page!
27              ob_end_clean(); // Destroy the
                buffer!
28              header ('Location: welcome.
                php');
29              exit();
30
31          } else { // Incorrect!
32
```

code continues on next page

```
33                  print '<p class="text--
                    error">The submitted email
                    address and password do not
                    match those on file!<br>Go
                    back and try again.</p>';
34
35          }
36
37      } else { // Forgot a field.
38
39          print '<p class="text--
                    error">Please make sure you
                    enter both an email address and
                    a password!<br>Go back and try
                    again.</p>';
40
41      }
42
43  } else { // Display the form.
44
45      print '<form action="login.php"
                method="post" class="form--inline">
46      <p><label for="email">Email
                Address:</label><input type="email"
                name="email" size="20"></p>
47      <p><label for="password">Password:
                </label><input type="password"
                name="password" size="20"></p>
48      <p><input type="submit"
                name="submit" value="Log In!"
                class="button--pill"></p>
49      </form>';
50
51  }
52
53  include('templates/footer.html'); //
        Need the footer.
54  ?>
```

4. Load the form in your browser to ensure that it has no errors **A**.

   Don't complete and submit the login form yet, because the welcome page needs to be updated prior to logging in.

TIP The `php.ini` configuration file includes many session-related settings that you can tinker with if you have administrative-level control over your server. Open the `php.ini` file in a text editor and see the manual for more information.

TIP You can also alter some of the session settings using the `ini_set()` function.

TIP The `session_name()` function lets you change the name of the session (instead of using the default PHPSESSID). It must be used before every `session_start()` call, like so:
`session_name('YourVisit');`
`session_start();`

TIP The `session_set_cookie_params()` function alters the session cookie settings, such as the expiration time, the path, and the domain.

TIP The constant SID, short for Session ID, stores a string in the format name=ID. An example is PHPSESSID= mo7puk861tm60tbm4b8coh0og2.

TIP You can store any type of value—number, string, array, or object—or any combination thereof in your sessions.

Raise High the Roof Beam!

Login Form

Users who are logged in can take advantage of certain features like this, that, and the other thing.

Email Address:

Password:

Log In!

Design uses Concise CSS Framework

11:37 pm Sunday April 3

A The login form.

Accessing Session Variables

Now that you've stored values in a session, you need to know how to access them. The first step is to invoke the **session_start()** function. This is necessary on every page that will make use of sessions, whether it's creating a new session or accessing an existing one.

From there it's simply a matter of referencing the **$_SESSION** variable as you would any other array. With this in mind, you'll write another welcome page—similar to the one from Chapter 8—that accesses the stored **email** and **loggedin** values.

To access session variables:

1. Create a new PHP document in your text editor or IDE, to be named **welcome.php** (Script 9.7):

   ```php
   <?php // Script 9.7 - welcome.php
   ```

2. Begin the session:

   ```php
   session_start();
   ```

   When you're accessing session values, you should call the **session_start()** function before any data is sent to the browser.

3. Define a page title, and include the HTML header:

   ```php
   define('TITLE', 'Welcome to the
   → J.D. Salinger Fan Club!');
   include('templates/header.html');
   ```

   Because this page uses the same template system developed in Chapter 8, it also uses the same header system.

Script 9.7 You can access stored session values using the **$_SESSION** array, as long as your script uses **session_start()** first.

```php
1   <?php // Script 9.7 - welcome.php #2
2   /* This is the welcome page. The user is
    redirected here
3   after they successfully log in. */
4
5   // Need the session:
6   session_start();
7
8   // Set the page title and include the
    header file:
9   define('TITLE', 'Welcome to the J.D.
    Salinger Fan Club!');
10  include('templates/header.html');
11
12  // Print a greeting:
13  print '<h2>Welcome to the J.D. Salinger
    Fan Club!</h2>';
14  print '<p>Hello, ' . $_
    SESSION['email'] . '!</p>';
15
16  // Print how long they've been logged
    in:
17  date_default_timezone_set('America/
    New_York');
18  print '<p>You have been logged
    in since: ' . date('g:i a', $_
    SESSION['loggedin']) . '.</p>';
19
20  // Make a logout link:
21  print '<p><a href="logout.php">Logout
    </a></p>';
22
23  include('templates/footer.html'); //
    Need the footer.
24  ?>
```

4. Greet the user by email address:

```php
print '<h2>Welcome to the J.D.
Salinger Fan Club!</h2>';
print '<p>Hello, ' . $_SESSION
['email'] . '!</p>';
```

To access the stored user's address, refer to **$_SESSION['email']**. Here, that value is concatenated to the rest of the string that's being printed out.

5. Show how long the user has been logged in:

```php
date_default_timezone_set
('America/New_York');
print '<p>You have been logged
in since: ' . date('g:i a',
$_SESSION['loggedin']) .
'.</p>';
```

Show how long the user has been logged in, by referring to the **$_SESSION['loggedin']** variable. By using this as the second argument sent to the **date()** function, along with the appropriate formatting parameters, you make the PHP script create text like *11:22 pm*.

Before using the **date()** function, you need to set the default time zone (this is also discussed in Chapter 8). If you want, after setting the time zone here, you can remove the use of the same function from the footer file.

6. Complete the content:

```php
print '<p><a href="logout.php">
Logout</a></p>';
```

The next script will provide logout functionality, so a link to it is added here.

7. Include the HTML footer, and complete the HTML page:

```php
include('templates/footer.html');
?>
```

8. Save the file as **welcome.php**, place it in the proper directory for your PHP-enabled server, and test it (starting with **login.php**, Script 9.6) in your browser **A**.

TIP To see whether a particular session variable exists, use **isset($_SESSION['var'])** as you would to check if any other variable is set.

TIP A more secure version of this script would both check that the variables exist (in the session) before referring to them and run the values through an escaping function before printing them.

TIP Always remember that the data stored in a session is being stored as plain text in an openly readable text file. Don't be cavalier about what gets stored in a session, and never store sensitive information, such as credit card data, there.

TIP For added security, data can be encrypted prior to storing it in a session and decrypted upon retrieval. Doing so requires a cryptography library and more advanced PHP knowledge, however.

Welcome to the J.D. Salinger Fan Club!

Hello, me@example.com!

You have been logged in since: 11:57 pm.

Logout

A After successfully logging in (using *me@example.com* and *testpass* in the form), the user is redirected to this page, which greets them using the session values.

Deleting a Session

It's important to know how to delete a session, just as it's important to know how to delete a cookie: Eventually you'll want to get rid of the data you've stored. Session data exists in two places—in an array during the execution of the script and in a text file—so you'll need to delete both. But first you must begin with the **session_start()** function, as always:

```
session_start();
```

Then, you clear the session variables by resetting the **$_SESSION** array:

```
$_SESSION = []; // Or = array();
```

Finally, remove the session data from the server (where it's stored in temporary files). To do this, use

```
session_destroy();
```

With that in mind, let's write **logout.php**, which will delete the session, effectively logging out the user.

To delete a session:

1. Start a new PHP script in your text editor or IDE, to be named **logout.php** (**Script 9.8**).

   ```
   <?php // Script 9.8 - logout.php
   ```

2. Begin the session:

   ```
   session_start();
   ```

   Remember that you can't delete a session until you activate the session using this function.

3. Reset the session array:

   ```
   $_SESSION = [];
   ```

   As explained in Chapter 7, "Using Arrays," the short array syntax, equivalent to the **array()** function, creates a new, empty array. By assigning the result of

Script 9.8 Deleting a session is a three-step process: Start the session, reset the array, and destroy the session data.

```
25  <?php // Script 9.8 - logout.php
26  /* This is the logout page. It destroys
    the session information. */
27
28  // Need the session:
29  session_start();
30
31  // Reset the session array:
32  $_SESSION = [];
33
34  // Destroy the session data on the
    server:
35  session_destroy();
36
37  // Define a page title and include the
    header:
38  define('TITLE', 'Logout');
39  include('templates/header.html');
40
41  ?>
42
43  <h2>Welcome to the J.D. Salinger Fan
    Club!</h2>
44  <p>You are now logged out.</p>
45  <p>Thank you for using this site. We
    hope that you liked it.<br>
46  Blah, blah, blah...
47  Blah, blah, blah...</p>
48
49  <?php include('templates/footer.html');
    ?>
```

Welcome to the J.D. Salinger Fan Club!

You are now logged out.

Thank you for using this site. We hope that you liked it.
Blah, blah, blah... Blah, blah, blah...

Ⓐ The logout page destroys the session data.

this function call to **$_SESSION**, all the existing *key-value* pairs in **$_SESSION** will be erased.

4. Destroy the session data on the server:

   ```
   session_destroy();
   ```

   This step tells PHP to remove the actual session file on the server.

5. Include the HTML header, and complete this PHP section:

   ```
   define('TITLE', 'Logout');
   include('templates/header.html');
   ?>
   ```

6. Make the page content:

   ```
   <h2>Welcome to the J.D. Salinger
   → Fan Club!</h2>
   <p>You are now logged out.</p>
   <p>Thank you for using this site.
   → We hope that you liked it.<br />
   Blah, blah, blah...
   Blah, blah, blah...</p>
   ```

7. Include the HTML footer:

   ```
   <?php include('templates/
   → footer.html'); ?>
   ```

8. Save the file as **logout.php**, place it in the proper directory for your PHP-enabled server, and test it in your browser by clicking the link in **welcome.php** Ⓐ.

TIP To delete an individual session value, use unset(**$_SESSION['var']**);

An additional step would be to delete the session cookie too.

TIP The PHP module on the server will automatically perform garbage collection based on settings in its configuration. PHP uses garbage collection to manually delete session files from the server, with the assumption that they're no longer needed.

Review and Pursue

If you have any problems with the review questions or the pursue prompts, turn to the book's supporting forum (www.LarryUllman.com/forums/).

Review

- Where does a cookie store data? Where does a session store data? Which is generally more secure?

- Name two debugging techniques when trying to solve issues involving cookies.

- How do the path and domain arguments to the `setcookie()` function affect the accessibility of the cookie?

- How do you delete a cookie?

- What function must every page call if it needs to assign or access session data?

- Why do sessions also use cookies (by default)?

Pursue

- Make sure you know what developer tools exist for your browser of choice, and how to basically use them.

- Look up the PHP manual page for the `setcookie()` function. Review the information and user comments there for added instructions on cookies.

- Rewrite `customize.php` so that the script also applies the user's preferences. Hint: You need to take into account the fact that the cookies aren't available immediately after they've been set. Instead, you would write the CSS code using the `$_POST` values after the form has been submitted, the `$_COOKIE` values upon first arriving at the page (if the cookies exist), and the default values otherwise.

- Make the form in `customize.php` *sticky* so that it reflects the user's current choices.

- Rewrite `welcome.php` so that the `print` statement that greets the user by email address uses double quotation marks.

- For an added challenge, rewrite `welcome.php` so that the `print` statement that indicates how long the user has been logged in also uses double quotation marks. Hint: You'll need to use a variable.

- Update `welcome.php` so that it confirms a session variable exists before it attempts to use it. Also run the session values through an escaping function—see Chapter 5, "Using Strings"—to prevent XSS attacks.

- Rewrite the last three scripts so that the session uses a custom name.

Creating
Functions

Throughout this book, you've used dozens of functions that provide much-needed functionality, such as **date()**, **setcookie()**, and **number_format()**. Although those functions have already been defined by PHP, here you'll be creating your own. However, functions you've created and those built into PHP are used in the same manner.

Defining your own functions can save you oodles of time as a programmer. In fact, they constitute a big step in the process of creating web applications and building a solid library of PHP code to use in future projects.

In this chapter, you'll see how to write your own functions that perform specific tasks. After that, you'll learn how to pass information to a function, use default values in a function, and have a function return a value. You'll also learn how functions and variables work together.

In This Chapter

Creating and Using Simple Functions

As you program, you'll discover that you use certain sections of code frequently, either within a single script or over the course of several scripts. Placing these routines into a self-defined function can save you time and make your programming easier, especially as your websites become more complex. Once you create a function, the actions of that function take place each time the function is called, just as **print** sends text to the browser with each use.

The syntax for creating a user-defined function is

```
function function_name() {
    statement(s);
}
```

For example:

```
function whatever() {
    print 'whatever';
}
```

You can use roughly the same naming conventions for functions as you do for variables, just without the initial dollar sign. Second to that is the suggestion that you create *meaningful* function names, just as you ought to write representative variable names. For example, *create_header* would be a better function name than *function1*. Remember not to use spaces in the name, though—doing so constitutes two separate words for the function name, which will result in error messages. The underscore is a logical replacement for the space. Unlike variables, function names in PHP are *not case-sensitive*, but you should still stick with a consistent naming scheme.

A These pull-down menus are created by a user-defined PHP function.

Any valid PHP code can go within the statement(s) area of the function, including calls to other functions. Functions do not have a limit on the number of statements they can contain, but make sure you end each statement with a semicolon, just as you would within the rest of the PHP script. Functions can also contain any combination of control structures: conditionals and loops.

The exact formatting of a function isn't important as long as the requisite elements are there. These elements include the word *function*, the function's name, the opening and closing parentheses, the opening and closing braces, and the statement(s). It's conventional to indent a function's statement(s) from the **function** keyword line, for clarity's sake, as you would with a loop or conditional. In any case, select a format style that you like—which is both syntactically correct and logically sound—and stick to it.

You call (or invoke) the function by referring to it just as you do any built-in function. The line of code

```
whatever();
```

will cause the statement part of the previously defined function—the **print** command—to be executed.

Let's begin by creating a function that generates month, day, and year pull-down menus for a form **A**.

To create and call a basic function:

1. Start a new PHP document in your text editor or IDE, to be named `menus.php` (Script 10.1):

```
<!doctype html>
<html lang="en">
<head>
    <meta charset="utf-8">
    <title>Date Menus</title>
</head>
<body>
```

2. Begin the PHP section:

```
<?php // Script 10.1 - menus.php
```

3. Start defining a function:

```
function make_date_menus() {
```

The name of this function is *make_date_menus*, which is both descriptive of what the function does and easy to remember.

4. Create the month pull-down menu:

```
$months = [1 => 'January',
→ 'February', 'March', 'April',
→ 'May', 'June', 'July',
→ 'August', 'September',
→ 'October', 'November',
→ 'December'];
// Make the month pull-down menu:
print '<select name="month">';
foreach ($months as $key =>
→ $value) {
   print "\n<option value=\
   → "$key\">$value</option>";
}
print '</select>';
```

To generate a list of months, first create an array of the month names, indexed numerically, beginning at 1 for January. When you specify the index for the first array element, the others will follow sequentially without the need to be explicit in naming them.

After the array has been created, the initial select tag is printed out. Then, a **foreach** loop runs through the **$months** array. For each element in the array, the HTML option tag is printed, using each element's key (the numbers 1 through 12) as the option value and each element's value (January through December) as the displayed text. Each line is also preceded by a newline character (**\n**) so that each option starts on its own line within the HTML source.

5. Create the day pull-down menu:

```
print '<select name="day">';
for ($day = 1; $day <= 31;
→ $day++) {
   print "\n<option value=
   → \"$day\">$day</option>";
}
print '</select>';
```

The day menu is a lot easier to create. To do so, use a simple **for** loop, running through the numbers 1 through 31.

6. Create the year pull-down menu:

```
print '<select name="year">';
$start_year = date('Y');
for ($y = $start_year; $y <=
→ ($start_year + 10); $y++) {
   print "\n<option value=
   → \"$y\">$y</option>";
}
print '</select>';
```

To create the year pull-down menu, start by using the **date()** function to get the current year. Then create options for this year plus the next 10, using a **for** loop.

continues on page 274

Script 10.1 The function defined in this script creates three pull-down menus for a form.

```php
1    <!doctype html>
2    <html lang="en">
3    <head>
4       <meta charset="utf-8">
5       <title>Date Menus</title>
6    </head>
7    <body>
8    <?php // Script 10.1 - menus.php
9    /* This script defines and calls a function. */
10
11   // This function makes three pull-down menus for the months, days, and years.
12   function make_date_menus() {
13
14       // Array to store the months:
15       $months = [1 => 'January', 'February', 'March', 'April', 'May', 'June', 'July', 'August',
             'September', 'October', 'November', 'December'];
16
17       // Make the month pull-down menu:
18       print '<select name="month">';
19       foreach ($months as $key => $value) {
20          print "\n<option value=\"$key\">$value</option>";
21       }
22       print '</select>';
23
24       // Make the day pull-down menu:
25       print '<select name="day">';
26       for ($day = 1; $day <= 31; $day++) {
27          print "\n<option value=\"$day\">$day</option>";
28       }
29       print '</select>';
30
31       // Make the year pull-down menu:
32       print '<select name="year">';
33       $start_year = date('Y');
34       for ($y = $start_year; $y <= ($start_year + 10); $y++) {
35          print "\n<option value=\"$y\">$y</option>";
36       }
37       print '</select>';
38
39   } // End of make_date_menus() function.
40
41   // Make the form:
42   print '<form action="" method="post">';
43   make_date_menus();
44   print '</form>';
45
46   ?>
47   </body>
48   </html>
```

7. Close the function:

```
} // End of make_date_menus()
→ function.
```

When you're creating functions, it's easy to create parse errors by forgetting the closing brace. You may want to add comments to help you remember this final step.

8. Make the **form** tags, and call the function:

```
print '<form action="" method=
→ "post">';
make_date_menus();
print '</form>';
```

The **print** statements are used to create the HTML form tags. Without a form, the date pull-down menus won't appear properly in the script.

Once you've created your function, you simply have to call it by name—being careful to use the exact spelling—to make the function work. Be sure to include the parentheses as well.

9. Complete the PHP and HTML:

```
?>
</body>
</html>
```

10. Save the file as **menus.php**, place it in the proper directory for your PHP-enabled server, and run it in your browser Ⓐ.

11. If you want, check out the HTML source of the page to see what was dynamically generated Ⓑ.

Ⓑ The source of the page shows the HTML created by the **print** statements in the **make_date_menus()** function.

TIP If you see a *"Call to undefined function: some_function..."* error message, it means you're trying to call a function that doesn't exist **C**. If you're trying to call a PHP function, either you misspelled the name or it's not supported on your version of PHP. Check the PHP manual for more. If you're calling a user-defined function when you see this error, either it hasn't been defined or you've misspelled it. Recheck your spelling in both the definition of the function and its usage to see if you made a mistake.

TIP The `function_exists()` function returns **TRUE** or **FALSE** based on whether a function exists in PHP. This applies to both user-defined functions and those that can be built into PHP:

```
if (function_exists
→ ('some_function')){ ...
```

TIP Although you aren't required to, I recommend that you habitually define your functions at the beginning of a script (or in an included file), rather than at the end of the script.

TIP Some people prefer this syntax for laying out their functions:

```
function function_name()
{
    statement(s);
}
```

TIP User-defined functions add extra memory requirements to your PHP scripts, so you should be judicious in using them. If you find that your function merely calls another PHP function or has but one line of code, it's probably not the best use of this capability.

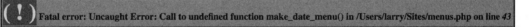

Fatal error: Uncaught Error: Call to undefined function make_date_menu() in /Users/larry/Sites/menus.php on line *43*

C This error means that the PHP script does not have access to a function defined under the given name. In this case, the problem is due to a missing "s" in the function call: `make_date_menus()` versus `make_date_menu()`.

Creating and Calling Functions That Take Arguments

Although being able to create a simple function is useful, writing one that takes input and does something with that input is even better. The input passed to a function is known as an *argument*. This is a concept you've seen before: The `sort()` function takes an array as an argument, which the function then sorts.

The syntax for writing functions that take arguments is as follows:

```
function function_name
→ ($arg1,$arg2, ...) {
   statement(s);
}
```

The function is defined with *parameters*: variables that are assigned the values sent to the function when you call it. The variables are defined using the same naming rules as any other variable in PHP:

```
function make_full_name($first,
→ $last) {
   print $first . ' ' . $last;
}
```

Functions that take input are called much like those that don't—you just need to remember to pass along the necessary values. You can do this either by passing variables:

```
make_full_name($fn, $ln);
```

or by sending literal values, as in

```
make_full_name('Larry', 'Ullman');
```

or some combination thereof:

```
make_full_name('Larry', $ln);
```

The important thing to note is that arguments are passed quite literally: The first variable in the function definition is assigned the first value in the call line, the second function variable is assigned the second call value, and so forth (A). Functions aren't smart enough to intuitively understand how you meant the values to be associated. This is also true if you fail to pass a value, in which case the function will assume that value is null (*null* isn't the mathematical 0, which is actually a value, but closer to the idea of the word *nothing*). The same thing applies if a function takes two arguments and you pass one—the second will be null, which might create an error (B).

(To clarify a minor point, the variables in the function definition are known as *parameters*; the values passed to the function when invoked are known as *arguments*. That being said, it's common enough to use the terms interchangeably.)

To demonstrate functions that take arguments, let's create a more interesting example. In Chapter 8, "Creating Web Applications," you learned how to make forms "sticky": having them remember their values from previous submissions. The code for a sticky text input might be

```
First Name: <input type="text"
→ name="first_name" size="20"
→ value="<?php if (isset
→ ($_POST ['first_name']))
→ { print htmlspecialchars
→ ($_POST ['first_name']); } ?>">
```

continues on next page

```
function make_full_name($first, $last) {
    print $first . ' ' . $last;
}

make_full_name($fn, $ln);

make_full_name('Larry', 'Ullman');

make_full_name('Larry', $ln);
```

(A) How values in function calls are assigned to function arguments.

Warning: Missing argument 2 for make_text_input(), called in /Users/larry/Sites/sticky1.php on line 35 and defined in /Users/larry/Sites/sticky1.php on line 13

(B) As with any function (user-defined or built into PHP), passing an incorrect number of arguments when calling it yields warnings.

Since many forms, such as `register.php` from Chapter 8, repeatedly use similar code, you have a good candidate for a user-defined function.

This next script will define and call a function that creates sticky text inputs. The function will take one argument for the input's name, and another for the input's label (its textual prompt). The function will be called multiple times by the script to generate multiple inputs **C**. Upon form submission, the previously entered values will be remembered **D**.

To create and call a function that takes an argument:

1. Start a new PHP document in your text editor or IDE, to be named `sticky1.php` (Script 10.2):

   ```
   <!doctype html>
   <html lang="en">
   <head>
     <meta charset="utf-8">
     <title>Sticky Text Inputs
     → </title>
   </head>
   <body>
   ```

2. Begin the PHP section:

   ```
   <?php // Script 10.2 -
   → sticky1.php
   ```

3. Start defining a function:

   ```
   function make_text_input
   → ($name, $label) {
   ```

   The `make_text_input()` function requires two arguments, which will be assigned to the `$name` and `$label` variables.

continues on page 280

C These three form inputs are created by a user-defined function.

D The form inputs reflect the values entered by the user.

```
1    <!doctype html>
2    <html lang="en">
3    <head>
4        <meta charset="utf-8">
5        <title>Sticky Text Inputs</title>
6    </head>
7    <body>
8    <?php // Script 10.2 - sticky1.php
9    /* This script defines and calls a function that creates a sticky text input. */
10
11   // This function makes a sticky text input.
12   // This function requires two arguments be passed to it.
13   function make_text_input($name, $label) {
14
15       // Begin a paragraph and a label:
16       print '<p><label>' . $label . ': ';
17
18       // Begin the input:
19       print '<input type="text" name="' . $name . '" size="20" ';
20
21       // Add the value:
22       if (isset($_POST[$name])) {
23           print ' value="' . htmlspecialchars($_POST[$name]) . '"';
24       }
25
26       // Complete the input, the label and the paragraph:
27       print '></label></p>';
28
29   } // End of make_text_input() function.
30
31   // Make the form:
32   print '<form action="" method="post">';
33
34   // Create some text inputs:
35   make_text_input('first_name', 'First Name');
36   make_text_input('last_name', 'Last Name');
37   make_text_input('email', 'Email Address');
38
39   print '<input type="submit" name="submit" value="Register!"></form>';
40
41   ?>
42   </body>
43   </html>
```

4. Print an opening paragraph and a label tag:

```
print '<p><label>' . $label .
→ ': ';
```

The code being generated by this function will be essentially like that just indicated (and in Chapter 8), but it will be wrapped in a paragraph tag and the input's label will be formally placed within label tags. The value of the label (for example, *First Name*) will be passed to the function when the function is called.

5. Begin the text input:

```
print '<input type="text"
→ name="' . $name . '"
→ size="20" ';
```

The PHP **print** statement just creates the HTML input tag, but the value of the tag's **name** attribute will come from the **$name** variable. This variable is assigned a value, such as *first_name*, when the function is called.

6. If applicable, add the input's preset value:

```
if (isset($_POST[$name])) {
  print ' value="' .
  htmlspecialchars
  → ($_POST [$name]) . '"';
}
```

The code in Step 5 didn't actually complete the text input (the closing **>** wasn't created), so another clause—specifically **value="whatever"**—can still be added. But that clause should only be added if **$_POST['*input_name*']** is set, so the conditional checks for that. As with the code in Chapter 8, the value is printed only after being run through **htmlspecialchars()**.

7. Complete the input, the label, the paragraph, and the function:

```
print '></label></p>';
} // End of make_text_input()
→ function.
```

8. Make the form tags, and call the function:

```
print '<form action=""
→ method="post">';
make_text_input('first_name',
→ 'First Name');
```

It's important that the form uses the POST method, because the function checks for existing values in **$_POST**. You can actually omit an **action** value, in which case the form will automatically be submitted back to the same page.

To create a "first name" input, call the **make_text_input()** function, passing it the name the input should have and an appropriate label.

9. Create two more inputs:

```
make_text_input('last_name',
→ 'Last Name');
make_text_input('email', 'Email
→ Address');
```

Now the script has used the same function three times, in three different ways. The result will be three distinct text inputs.

Note that although HTML5 has an email input type, for the sake of simplicity, only plain text inputs are being created.

10. Complete the form:

```
print '<input type="submit"
→ name="submit" value=
→ "Register!"></form>';
```

The form needs a submit button in order to test the sticky feature.

Declaring Parameter Types

PHP 7 supports the ability to declare parameter types to indicate what kind of value must be passed. To use this feature, provide the type—**bool**, **float**, **int**, or **string**—before the parameter name:

```
function make_full_name(string
  $first, string $last) {
```

With that code in place, PHP will return an error if the function is called while provided with non-string arguments:

```
make_full_name(12, true);
  // Error!
```

Earlier versions of PHP supported *type hinting*, which was similar but did not support scalar variable types such as **string** and **int**. This type of stricter function definition is best when you want to guarantee the type of value passed to a function.

11. Complete the PHP and HTML:

```
?>
</body>
</html>
```

12. Save the file as **sticky1.php**, place it in the proper directory for your PHP-enabled server, and run it in your browser **C** and **D**.

> **TIP** You can define as many functions as you want, not just one per script as the examples in this chapter portray.

> **TIP** A function is not limited as to the number of arguments it can take.

> **TIP** Once you've defined your own functions like this, you can place them in an external file and then require that file when you need access to the functions.

Setting Default Argument Values

PHP allows functions to have *default argument values*: Just assign a value to the parameter in the function definition:

```
function greeting($who = 'world') {
    print "<p>Hello, $who!</p>";
}
```

Such a function will use the preset value unless it receives a value that then overwrites the default. In other words, by setting a default value for an argument, you render that particular argument optional when calling the function. You'd set an argument's default value if you wanted to assume a certain value but still allow for other possibilities **Ⓐ**:

```
greeting();
greeting('Zoe');
```

(Note: This isn't really a good use of a user-defined function, or a default argument value, but it's easily understood as an example.)

The parameters with default values must always be written after the other parameters (those without default values). This is because PHP directly assigns values to parameters in the order they're received from the call line. Thus, it isn't possible to omit a value for the first argument but include one for the second. For example, suppose you have

```
function calculate_total($qty,
→ $price = 20.00, $tax = 0.06) {...
```

If you call the function with the line

```
calculate_total(3, 0.07);
```

with the intention of setting **$qty** to 3, leaving **$price** at 20.00, and changing the **$tax** to 0.07, there will be problems.

The result will be that **$qty** is set to 3, **$price** is set to 0.07, and **$tax** remains at 0.06 **Ⓑ**, which isn't the desired outcome. The proper way to achieve that effect would be to code

```
calculate_total(3, 20.00, 0.07);
```

Let's rework the `make_text_input()` function to incorporate the notion of setting default argument values.

```
Hello, world!

Hello, Zoe!
```

Ⓐ Calling the function without any arguments uses the default value (the first greeting); calling it with an argument provided means that value will be used instead (the second).

```
function calculate_total($qty, $price = 20.00, $tax = 0.06) {
    // Make the calculations.
}

calculate_total(3, 0.07);
```

Ⓑ Because of the way function arguments work, you cannot "skip" an argument when calling a function.

Script 10.3 The function now takes three arguments, but only two of them are required. If no **$size** is passed to the function, its value will be 20.

```
1    <!doctype html>
2    <html lang="en">
3    <head>
4        <meta charset="utf-8">
5        <title>Sticky Text Inputs</title>
6    </head>
7    <body>
8    <?php // Script 10.3 - sticky2.php
9    /* This script defines and calls a
     function that creates a sticky text
     input. */
10
11   // This function makes a sticky text
     input.
12   // This function requires two arguments
     be passed to it.
13   // A third argument is optional (it has
     a default value).
14   function make_text_input($name,
     $label, $size = 20) {
15
16       // Begin a paragraph and a label:
17       print '<p><label>' . $label . ': ';
18
19       // Begin the input:
20       print '<input type="text" name="' .
         $name . '" size="' . $size . '" ';
21
22       // Add the value:
23       if (isset($_POST[$name])) {
24           print ' value="' .
             htmlspecialchars
             ($_POST[$name]) . '"';
25       }
26
27       // Complete the input, the label and
         the paragraph:
28       print '></label></p>';
29
30   } // End of make_text_input() function.
31
32   // Make the form:
33   print '<form action="" method="post">';
34
```

code continues on next page

To write a function that uses default values:

1. Open **sticky1.php** (**Script 10.2**) in your text editor or IDE, if it isn't open already.

2. Add a third argument with a default value to the **make_text_input()** function (**Script 10.3**):

   function make_text_input($name, $label, $size = 20) {

   Although I like the cleanliness of having all text inputs be the same size, a person's last name and email address is often longer than their first name, so an adjustable size would be better. By taking the input's size as an argument, this will be possible. But the size will have a default value, making it an optional argument. If three arguments are sent to the function, then **$size** will be set to the third value instead of the default.

3. Change the creation of the input so that it uses the **$size** variable:

   print '<input type="text" name="' . $name . '" size="' . $size . '" ';

   continues on next page

4. Change the function calls to vary the sizes:

```
make_text_input('first_name',
→'First Name');
make_text_input('last_name',
→'Last Name', 30);
make_text_input('email', 'Email
→Address', 50);
```

Now the first input will use the default size, and the others will be longer.

5. Save the script as **sticky2.php**, place it in the proper directory of your PHP-enabled server, and test it in your browser **C**.

TIP To pass no value to a function for a particular argument, use an empty string (' ') or the word NULL (without quotes). Either of these values will override the default value, if one is established.

TIP As mentioned way back in Chapter 1, "Getting Started with PHP," the PHP manual marks optional function arguments using square brackets. For example, when you use the number_format() function, the number of decimals to round to is optional:

```
string number_format(float number
→[, int decimals = 0])
```

Script 10.3 *continued*

```
35   // Create some text inputs:
36   make_text_input('first_name', 'First
     Name');
37   make_text_input('last_name', 'Last
     Name', 30);
38   make_text_input('email', 'Email
     Address', 50);
39
40   print '<input type="submit"
     name="submit" value="Register!"></
     form>';
41
42   ?>
43   </body>
44   </html>
```

C Now the function is capable of changing the size of the input, based on an argument. If no value is provided for that argument, the default size is used instead (the first input).

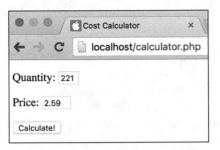

(A) This simple form takes two values on which calculations will be made.

(B) The result of the calculation, which takes place within a user-defined function.

Creating and Using Functions That Return a Value

Functions do more than take arguments; they can also return values. Doing so requires just two more steps. First, you use the **return** statement within the function. Second, you use the output somehow when you call the function. Commonly, you'll assign the returned value to a variable, but you can also, for example, directly print the output. Here is the basic format for a function that takes two arguments and returns a value:

```
function make_full_name
→ ($first, $last) {
  $name = $first . ' ' . $last;
  return $name;
}
```

This function could be used like so:

```
$full_name = make_full_name
→ ($fn, $ln);
```

There the returned value of the function is assigned to a variable. Here it's printed immediately:

```
print make_full_name($fn, $ln)
```

To best demonstrate this concept, let's create a function that performs a simple calculation and formats the result. This script will display an HTML form where a user enters a quantity and price **(A)**. When the form is submitted (back to this same page), a total value will be calculated and printed **(B)**.

To create and use a function that returns a value:

1. Create a new PHP document in your text editor or IDE, to be named `calculator1.php` (Script 10.4):

```
<!doctype html>
<html lang="en">
<head>
  <meta charset="utf-8">
  <title>Cost Calculator</title>
</head>
<body>
```

2. Begin the PHP code:

```
<?php // Script 10.4 -
calculator1.php
```

3. Define the function:

```
function calculate_total
→ ($quantity, $price) {
  $total = $quantity * $price;
  $total = number_format
  → ($total, 2);
  return $total;
}
```

This function takes two arguments—a quantity and a price—and multiplies them to create a total. The total value is then formatted before it's returned by the function.

Although this may seem like a silly use of a function, the benefits of putting even a one-step calculation into a function are twofold: First, the calculation will be easier to find and modify at a later date with your function located at the beginning of your script instead of hidden in the rest of the code, and second, should you want to repeat the action again in a script, you can do so without duplicating code.

4. Begin the conditional to see if the form was submitted:

```
if ($_SERVER['REQUEST_METHOD'] ==
→ 'POST') {
```

Because this page both displays and handles the HTML form, it has a conditional that checks how the page is being requested. If it's a POST request, that means the form has been submitted.

5. Validate the form data, and use the function:

```
if ( is_numeric($_POST
→ ['quantity']) AND is_numeric
→ ($_POST['price']) ) {
  $total = calculate_total
  → ($_POST['quantity'],
  → $_POST['price']);
  print "<p>Your total comes to
  → $<span style=\"font-weight:
  → bold;\">$total</span>.</p>";
```

This part of the PHP code—which handles the form if it has been submitted—first checks that a numeric quantity and price were entered. If so, the total is determined by calling the `calculate_total()` function and assigning the result to the **$total** variable. This result is then printed out.

continues on page 288

Script 10.4 This script both displays and handles an HTML form in order to perform some basic calculations. The script uses a function that takes two arguments and returns a single value.

```
1    <!doctype html>
2    <html lang="en">
3    <head>
4        <meta charset="utf-8">
5        <title>Cost Calculator</title>
6    </head>
7    <body>
8    <?php // Script 10.4 - calculator1.php
9    /* This script displays and handles an HTML form.
10   It uses a function to calculate a total from a quantity and price. */
11
12   // This function performs the calculations.
13   function calculate_total($quantity, $price) {
14
15       $total = $quantity * $price; // Calculation
16       $total = number_format($total, 2); // Formatting
17
18       return $total; // Return the value.
19
20   } // End of function.
21
22   // Check for a form submission:
23   if ($_SERVER['REQUEST_METHOD'] == 'POST') {
24
25       // Check for values:
26       if ( is_numeric($_POST['quantity']) AND is_numeric($_POST['price']) ) {
27
28           // Call the function and print the results:
29           $total = calculate_total($_POST['quantity'], $_POST['price']);
30           print "<p>Your total comes to $<span style=\"font-weight: bold;\">$total</span>.</p>";
31
32       } else { // Inappropriate values entered.
33           print '<p style="color: red;">Please enter a valid quantity and price!</p>';
34       }
35
36   }
37   ?>
38   <form action="" method="post">
39       <p>Quantity: <input type="text" name="quantity" size="3"></p>
40       <p>Price: <input type="text" name="price" size="5"></p>
41       <input type="submit" name="submit" value="Calculate!">
42   </form>
43   </body>
44   </html>
```

6. Complete the conditionals:

```
  } else {
    print '<p style="color:
    → red;">Please enter a valid
    → quantity and price!</p>';
  }
}
```

If either of the form variables was not properly submitted, a message is printed indicating that. The final brace closes the form submission conditional.

A little CSS is applied to both printed messages (here and in Step 5).

7. Display the HTML form:

```
?>
<form action="" method="post">
  <p>Quantity: <input type="text"
  → name="quantity" size="3"></p>
  <p>Price: <input type="text"
  → name="price" size="5"></p>
  <input type="submit"
  → name="submit"
  → value="Calculate!">
</form>
```

The form itself is quite simple, requesting two different values from the user **Ⓐ**. Because this form is created outside of the main submission conditional, the form will always be displayed by the page **Ⓑ**.

8. Complete the HTML page:

```
</body>
</html>
```

Returning Multiple Values

User-defined functions frequently return just a single value but can return multiple values by using arrays. Here's how you go about this:

```
function some_function($p1, $p2)
{
  // Do whatever.
  return [$a, $b];
  // Or: return array($v1, $v2);
}
```

Then, to call this function, use the `list()` function to assign the array elements to individual variables:

```
list($v1, $v2) = some_function
  ($a1, $a2);
```

The result is that **$a** from the function is assigned to **$v1** in the PHP script, and **$b** from the function is assigned to **$v2**.

Declaring Return Types

PHP 7 supports the ability to declare the type of value returned by a function. To use this feature, follow the function name with a colon and the type returned:

```
function make_full_name
 ($first, $last): string {
```

Or

```
function calculate_total
 ($quantity, $price): float {
```

This type of stricter function definition is best when you want to guarantee the type of value returned by a function.

9. Save the page as **calculator1.php**, place it in the proper directory for your PHP-enabled server, and test it in your browser **B**.

TIP You can have only one return statement *executed* in a function, but the same function can have multiple return statements. As an example, you may want to write a function that checks for a condition and returns a value indicating whether the condition was satisfied. In such a case, the function might contain

```
if (condition) {
   return true;
} else {
   return false;
}
```

TIP The result returned by the function is either **TRUE** or **FALSE**, indicating whether the stated condition was met.

Understanding Variable Scope

The concept of *variable scope* wasn't introduced in earlier chapters because without an understanding of functions, scope makes little sense. Now that you are acquainted with functions, this section revisits the topic of variables and discusses in some detail just how variables and functions work together.

As you saw in the second section of this chapter, "Creating and Calling Functions That Take Arguments," you can send variables to a function by passing them as arguments. However, you can also reference an external variable from within a function using the **global** statement. This is possible because of variable scope. The *scope* of a variable is the realm in which it exists.

By default, the variables you write in a script exist for the life of that lone script. Conversely, environment variables, such as **$_SERVER['PHP_SELF']**, exist throughout every PHP script on the server.

Functions, though, create a new level of scope. Function variables—the function's parameters as well as any variables defined within the function—exist only within that function and aren't accessible outside of it. Put another way, function variables are *local variables* with *local scope*. Likewise, a variable from outside a function is not available within the function, by default **A**. Even when a variable is used as an argument to a function call, that variable's *value* is being passed to the function, not the variable itself.

You can, however, make a variable external to a function available within the function by using the **global** statement. The **global** statement roughly means, "I want this variable within the function to refer to the same named variable outside of the function." In other words, the **global** statement turns a local variable with local scope into a global variable with global scope. Any changes made to the variable within the function are also reflected by the variable outside of the function, without using the **return** command (assuming the function is called, of course).

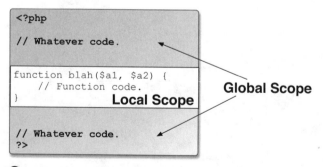

```php
<?php

// Whatever code.

function blah($a1, $a2) {
    // Function code.
}
```
Local Scope   **Global Scope**

```php
// Whatever code.
?>
```

A Adding function definitions to a script adds another area of variable scope.

The syntax of the **global** statement is simply

```
function function_name($args) {
   global $variable;
   statement(s);
}
```

There is another issue regarding functions and variables: Because of variable scope, a local variable within a function is a different entity—perhaps with a different value—than a variable outside of the function, *even if the two variables use the exact same name*. Let's look at this more explicitly...

Say you have:

```
function foo($param) {
   // Do whatever.
}
$var = 1;
foo($var);
```

When the function is called, the value of **$var** will be assigned **$param**, so their values are the same but their names are different and they are different variables.

Now if the name of the parameter in the function is also **$var**—

```
function bar($var) {
   // Do whatever.
}
$var = 1;
bar($var);
```

then the **$var** variable within the function is assigned the same value as the original **$var** outside of the function—but *they're still two separate variables*. The one has a scope within the function, and the other has a scope outside of it. This means that you can use the same name for variables in the function as exist outside of the function without conflict.

Just remember they aren't the same variable. What happens to a variable's value within a function only affects that variable within the function. Here's an example **B**:

```php
function add_one($n) {
    $n++;
    print 'Added one!<br>';
}
$n = 1;
print "\$n equals $n<br>";
add_one($n);
print "\$n equals $n<br>";
```

This is all true unless you use the **global** statement, which does make the two variables the same **C**:

```php
function add_one() {
    global $n; // Same!
    $n++;
    print 'Added one!<br>';
}
$n = 1;
print "\$n equals $n<br>";
add_one();
print "\$n equals $n<br>";
```

Note that in this case, the variable's value no longer needs to be passed to the function either.

To demonstrate variable scope, let's rework the **calculator1.php** script using the **global** statement.

$n equals 1
Added one!
$n equals 1

B Changes to a local variable inside a function have no effect on a similarly named global variable.

$n equals 1
Added one!
$n equals 2

C Changes made to a global variable inside of a function will change the variable outside of that function.

```
1    <!doctype html>
2    <html lang="en">
3    <head>
4        <meta charset="utf-8">
5        <title>Cost Calculator</title>
6    </head>
7    <body>
8    <?php // Script 10.5 - calculator2.php
     #2
9    /* This script displays and handles an
     HTML form.
10   It uses a function to calculate a total
     from a quantity, price, and tax rate. */
11
12   // Define a tax rate:
13   $tax = 8.75;
14
15   // This function performs the
     calculations.
16   function calculate_total ($quantity,
     $price) {
17
18       global $tax;
19
20       $total = $quantity * $price; //
         Calculation
21       $taxrate = ($tax / 100) + 1;
22       $total = $total * $taxrate; // Add
         the tax.
23       $total = number_format ($total, 2);
         // Formatting
24
25       return $total; // Return the value.
26
27   } // End of function.
28
29   // Check for a form submission:
30   if (isset($_POST['submitted'])) {
31
32       // Check for values:
33       if ( is_numeric($_POST['quantity'])
         AND is_numeric($_POST['price']) ) {
34
```

code continues on next page

To use the global statement:

1. Open **calculator1.php** (Script 10.4) in your text editor or IDE, if it is not already open.

2. Before the function definition, add the following (**Script 10.5**):

   $tax = 8.75;

   This line creates a **$tax** variable with a set value that will be used in the cost calculations. It's assigned a value outside of the function because it will be used later in the main body of the script.

3. Within the function definition, add a **global** statement:

   global $tax;

   This statement tells the function to incorporate the same **$tax** variable as the one that exists outside of the function.

4. Before the **$total** in the function is formatted, recalculate the value using the tax rate:

   $taxrate = ($tax / 100) + 1;
   $total = $total * $taxrate;

   To add the tax to the total value, you start by dividing the tax by 100 to create a percentage. Then you add 1 to this value to get a multiplier. This result is then multiplied by the total to come up with the new, final total.

   Notice that you use a **$taxrate** variable (based on **$tax**) to perform these calculations. This is because you'll print out the value of **$tax** later, and any changes made to it here will be reflected (because it's a global variable).

   continues on next page

5. Alter the main **print** line (after the function call) so that it prints the tax rate as well:

```
print "<p>Your total comes to
→ $<span style=\"font-weight:
→ bold;\">$total</span>,
→ including the $tax percent tax
→ rate.</p>";
```

The **$tax** variable defined at the beginning of the script is printed out at the end. If you hadn't used the **$taxrate** variable within the function and made the alterations to the global **$tax** instead, those calculations would be reflected in the value printed here.

6. Save the script, place it in the proper directory for your PHP-enabled server, and test it in your browser **D** and **E**.

TIP Constants and the superglobal arrays (**$_GET, $_POST, $_COOKIE, and $_SESSION**) have the added benefit that they're always available inside functions without requiring the **global** statement. This is why they are known as *superglobals*.

TIP Each function has its own, separate local scope.

Script 10.5 *continued*

```
35       // Call the function and print
         the results:
36       $total = calculate_
         total($_POST['quantity'],
         $_POST['price']);
37       print "<p>Your total comes
         to $<span style=\"font-
         weight: bold;\">$total</span>,
         including the $tax percent tax
         rate.</p>";
38
39   } else { // Inappropriate values
     entered.
40       print '<p style="color: red;">
         Please enter a valid quantity and
         price!</p>';
41   }
42
43 }
44 ?>
45 <form action="" method="post">
46     <p>Quantity: <input type="text"
       name="quantity" size="3"></p>
47     <p>Price: <input type="text"
       name="price" size="5"></p>
48     <input type="submit" name="submit"
       value="Calculate!">
49     <input type="hidden" name="submitted"
       value="true">
50 </form>
51 </body>
52 </html>
```

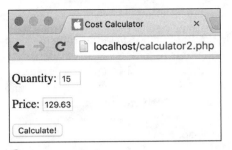

D Run the form again...

Your total comes to **$2,114.59**, including the 8.75 percent tax rate.

Quantity:

Price:

Calculate!

E ...and the calculation now makes use of a global **$tax** variable.

Function Design Theory

Understanding the syntax for defining your own functions is important, but you also need to understand good function design theory. A proper user-defined function should be easily reusable and be likely to be reused (that is, if a website only ever calls a function once, there's no need for it).

There should also be a "black box" mentality about the function: A programmer shouldn't need to know about the internals of a function in order to use it properly. As an example of this, think of any PHP function: You probably don't know what the underlying function code does specifically, but you can still tap into its power.

In support of the "black box" approach, proper function design suggests that you should be extremely cautious when using global variables. Arguably (pun!), a function should be passed all the information it needs, so that global variables—including the superglobals and constants—are not required.

Functions should also not make assumptions either, like **make_text_input()**, which assumes the form was submitted using the POST method.

By writing functions that neither rely on global variables nor make assumptions as to what outside of the function is true, you make the function more independent and portable—in short, better. Properly designing functions is a skill best learned by experience over time.

Review and Pursue

If you have any problems with the review questions or the pursue prompts, turn to the book's supporting forum (www.LarryUllman.com/forums/).

Review

- What is the basic syntax of a user-defined function?

- What naming rules must your own functions abide by?

- What naming rules must function parameters abide by?

- How do you provide a default value for a function argument?

- In the example code in the "Understanding Variable Scope" section of the chapter, why does the code use **\$n**? What would happen if that backslash weren't there?

- What is variable scope? What scope does a function argument variable have?

- What scope does a variable in an included file have? Note: This is a tricky one!

Pursue

- Make the function in **menus.php** take arguments to indicate the starting year and the number of years to generate. Make the later argument have a default value. Then rewrite the function body so that it uses these values in the year **for** loop.

- Rewrite the **make_text_input()** function so that it can be told whether to look for an existing value in either **$_POST** or **$_GET**.

- Create a variation on the **make_text_input()** function that can create a text input or a password input, depending on how the function is called.

- Modify the calculator script to also use the **make_text_input()** function.

- Come up with an idea for, create, and use your own custom function.

Files and Directories

Taking your web applications to the next level requires a method of storing and retrieving data. You have two primary options in PHP: using the filesystem or databases. This chapter will discuss the former, and the next chapter will introduce the latter. It's worth your time to learn both methods. Although a database can be more powerful and secure than a file-based system, you may be surprised at what's possible by writing and reading simple text documents on the server.

In this chapter, you'll learn about file permissions, a topic that you must grasp first. Then you'll learn to write, read from, and lock files. After that, you'll see how to handle file uploads with PHP, how to create directories, and an alternate method for reading data from a file. These last two examples will also demonstrate a simple file-based registration and login system that you can use in your web applications.

File Permissions

Before attempting to write to and read from a file, you must have an understanding of *file permissions*. The topic is large enough that you may want to pursue it further, but this quick introduction will get you started. Up front I will say that most of the information in this chapter applies only to non-Windows users. In my experience, the preparatory steps to be taken aren't necessary when running PHP on a Windows computer (although such things can change from one version of an operating system to the next). Still, having an understanding of permissions as a whole is a good idea, especially if you might later be running your PHP scripts on a non-Windows server.

Permissions identify who can do what with a file or directory. The options are *read*, *write*, and *execute* (actually, files can be designated *executable,* whereas directories are made *searchable*). Each of these options can be set for three types of users:

- The *owner* of the file (the person who created it or put it on the server)

- Members of a particular *group*, which a server administrator determines and which includes the owner

- *Others* (those who don't fall into the previous two categories)

There is also the implied *everyone* level, which includes all three user types.

As an example, if you use FTP to transfer a file to a server, the owner of the transferred file will be the account used to connect to the server. The default file permissions will likely be that everyone can read the file but that only the owner can modify it (for example, write to it).

The Web Root Directory

When discussing files, directories, and security, an important concept is that of the *web root directory*. To grasp this concept, first consider that a file on a web server is available in two ways. First, it exists in the filesystem. For example, this might be `C:\inetpub\wwwroot\filename.php` on your own computer, or `/var/web/sitename/htdocs/filename.php` on a remote server (that path would be applicable to *nix systems).

Second, files placed within the proper directories for a web server are also available through HTTP, such as `http://www.example.com/filename.php` or `http://localhost/filename.php`.

With this in mind, the web root directory is the folder in the filesystem where the base URL—such as `www.example.com`—points. Without further restrictions imposed, a browser can access all the files found within the web root directory and below (i.e., in subfolders). A browser cannot, however, access files found outside the web root directory.

When creating writable files and directories, it's more secure to place them outside the web directory. In other words, if your web pages go in `C:\inetpub\wwwroot` or `/Users/username/Sites`, then if you place items in `C:\inetpub` or `/Users/username`, they should be accessible to the locally running PHP but not to others over the Internet. The examples in this chapter follow this structure, and you should do so as well.

In general, the security concern here is more important for directories than for files.

A catch is that in most cases, PHP will be running through a web server application, which counts as a different server user. Therefore, PHP and the web server would be able to read files you put onto the server (and consequently make them available for viewing in a browser), but PHP would not, by default, be able to modify those files.

For the examples in this chapter, PHP needs to be able to write to some files and directories. This means that you must know how, and be able, to adjust the permissions a file or directory has. That being said, making a file or directory writable (i.e., making the permissions less restrictive) can be a security issue and should be done only when absolutely necessary.

Finally, a common point of confusion has to do with what, exactly, a "user" is. A user is an account created on a computer. On your own computer, there may be just one user—you—or several. Servers normally have multiple users, although most user accounts aren't associated with people who will log in, but rather with different programs running on the server. For example, there may be one user whose processes handle all web requests and another user through which the database application runs. Most importantly, know that a "user" is not a person on another computer and that "everyone" means "everyone on the server." Just because you've made a file or directory writable by any user doesn't mean it's writable by anyone over the Internet. The "user" must be a recognized account on the server.

Creating the text file

In the chapter's first example, you'll work with a text file, **quotes.txt**, that's located on the server. If the file doesn't have the correct permissions to do what your PHP script is asking it to, you might see an error message **Ⓐ**. Before proceeding, you should create **quotes.txt** on the server and establish its permissions.

(!)	Warning: file_put_contents(../quotes.txt): failed to open stream: Permission denied in /Users/larry/Sites/add_quote.php on line *20*			

Call Stack

#	Time	Memory	Function	Location
1	0.0001	370344	{main}( )	.../add_quote.php:0
2	0.0001	370400	file_put_contents ( )	.../add_quote.php:20

Ⓐ The *...failed to open stream: Permission denied...* message is the result of attempting to do something to a file that isn't allowed by the server. Here the server is denying the **fopen()** function that is attempting to open **quotes.txt** for the purpose of writing to it.

To create quotes.txt:

1. Open your text editor or IDE, and create a new, blank document.

2. Without typing anything into the file, save it as **quotes.txt**.

3. Move the file just outside the web root directory of your PHP-enabled server **B**.

The sidebar "The Web Root Directory" explains where you should put the file with respect to your web directory and why.

TIP The `file_exists()` function returns TRUE if a provided file or directory exists on the server. This can be used to test for the presence of a file before doing anything with it:

```
if (file_exists('somefile.ext'))
→ { ...
```

TIP Assuming that PHP has write permissions on a directory, you can create a blank document within that directory directly in PHP. This is accomplished using the `touch()` function:

```
touch('somefile.ext');
```

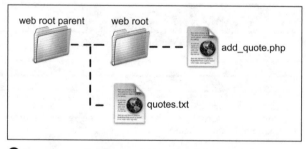

B The **quotes.txt** file should ideally be placed in the same directory as your web documents folder (i.e., not in the directory with the actual web documents).

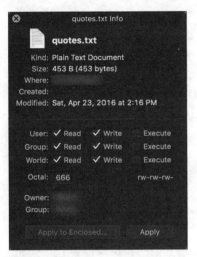

© This control panel, provided by a hosting company, lets users adjust a file's permissions.

D The Transmit FTP application uses this pop-up window to allow you to set a file's permissions.

Setting a file's permissions

The preceding sequence may seem like an odd series of steps, but in order to set the permission on a file, the file must first exist. You do want the file to be blank, though, because you'll use PHP to write data to it later.

The desired result for this example is to give either *others* or *everyone* permission to *read* and *write* (but not *execute*) `quotes.txt`. How you accomplish this depends on

- Whether you're running PHP on your own computer or on a remote server

- The operating system of the PHP-enabled computer

Unfortunately, it would be impossible to offer steps for how every user should set the permissions under any circumstances, but here are some rough guidelines and steps to get you going.

To set a file's permissions on a remote server:

- Most ISPs offer users a web-based control panel where they can set file permissions **©** as well as set other hosting parameters.

- You may be able to change a file's permissions using your FTP client **D**.

To set a file's permissions on your computer:

- If you're working on your own Windows computer, you may not need to change the permissions. To test this theory, try each example first. If a PHP script can't write to the file or directory in question, use the next suggestion to rework the permissions.

- Windows users who need to change the permissions can do so by viewing the file's or directory's properties. The resulting panel will differ for each version of Windows, but basically you just need to tweak who can access the file and how.

- Mac OS X users must select the file in the Finder and choose Get Info from the File menu. From there, use the Ownership & Permissions subpanel to adjust the file's permissions **E**.

- On Unix (including users of Linux and Mac OS X), you can also use the command line `chmod 0666 quotes.txt` in a terminal window, assuming you have authority to do so.

TIP Most operating systems have no *PHP* user. Instead, the *PHP* user is essentially the user the web server application (for example, Apache or IIS) is running as. In the Unix family, Apache often runs as *nobody*. On Windows, the web server frequently runs as the same user who is logged in (and who probably created the file), meaning there will be no need to alter a file's permissions.

TIP If you're already familiar with SSH and `chmod`, you probably also understand what the 0666 number means, but here's an explanation for those of you who aren't familiar with it. The 0 is just a prefix indicating the number is written in an *octal* format. Each 6 corresponds to *read* (4) plus *write* (2) permission—first assigning 6 to the owner, then to the group, and then to others. Comparatively, 0777 allows *read* (4) plus *write* (2) plus *execute* (1) permission to all three types of users. This numbering is applicable for Unix variant operating systems (Linux, Solaris, and Mac OS X).

TIP PHP has several functions for changing a file or directory's permissions, including `chgrp()`, `chmod()`, and `chown()`. However, they will only work if PHP already has permission to modify the file or directory in question.

TIP A website running on a shared hosting environment has greater security risks than one running on a dedicated server because there are literally more users. For example, if you make a file or directory writable by every user, then anyone with access to that server can manipulate that file (assuming they know it exists and that other restrictions are not in place).

E The Mac OS X Get Info panel lets you adjust a file's ownership and permissions, among other things.

File Paths

There are two ways of referring to any file or directory on the computer: using an *absolute* or *relative* path. An absolute path begins at the root of the computer:

- `C:\somedir\somefile.txt` (Windows)

- `/Users/`*username*`/somefile.txt` (Mac OS X)

A relative path will not start with the root of the computer—`C:\` or `/`. Instead, it will be relative to the current working directory:

- `fileA.txt` (in the same directory)

- `./fileA.txt` (in the same directory)

- `dirB/fileB.txt` (inside `dirB`)

- `../fileC.txt` (inside the parent directory)

- `../dirD/fileD.txt` (inside the parallel directory)

Two periods together represent the current directory's parent folder. A single period by itself represents the current directory. If a *file's name* begins with a single period, the file is hidden (on Unix, Linux, and Mac OS X).

It technically doesn't matter whether you use a relative or an absolute path to refer to a file, as long as the reference is accurate. An absolute path is easier for beginners to understand but will only be correct for that computer. A relative path can confound those new to the concept, but can continue to be correct even after moving the site from one server to another.

Writing to Files

Because you need to write something to a file in order to read something from it, this chapter explores writing first. The easiest way to write to a file is to use the `file_put_contents()` function:

`file_put_contents($file, $data);`

This function will open the file and write the data there. The first argument is the name of the file. This can be an *absolute* or *relative* path (see the sidebar "File Paths"). The second argument is the data, which can be a string, number, or array (one-dimensional, not multidimensional). Neither the file nor the data has to be represented by a variable, but it's common to do so.

If the file doesn't exist, the function will attempt to create it. If the file does exist, the file's current contents will be replaced with the new data. If you'd prefer to have the new data appended to what's already in the file, add the **FILE_APPEND** constant as a third argument:

`file_put_contents($file, $data,`
`→ FILE_APPEND);`

continues on next page

When appending data to a file, you normally want each piece of data to be written on its own line, so each submission should conclude with the appropriate line break for the operating system of the computer running PHP. This would be

- **\n** on Unix and Mac OS X
- **\r\n** on Windows

As with any meaningful escape sequence, these must be placed within double quotation marks in order to work.

Alternatively, you can use the special PHP constant **PHP_EOL**, which represents the correct end-of-line character sequence (e.g., **\n** or **\r\n**) for the current operating system:

```
file_put_contents($file,
→$data . PHP_EOL, FILE_APPEND);
```

With this in mind, let's create a form that stores user-submitted quotations in a plain-text file **A**. Later in this chapter, another PHP script will retrieve and randomly display these quotations. Before you get into the code, however, there's one more function to be introduced: **is_writable()**. This function returns a Boolean value indicating the writability of the named file:

```
if (is_writable($file)) {...
```

Invoking this function prior to attempting to write to a file (or directory) is a simple way to avoid permissions errors.

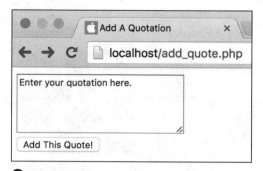

A This very simple form lets a user submit a quotation that will be written to a text file.

Legacy File Writing

Although you won't see examples in this book, you should also be familiar with the legacy approach to writing to files. First, open the file; second, write your data to it; and third, close the file:

```
$fp = fopen($file, mode);
fwrite($fp, $data . PHP_EOL);
fclose($fp);
```

To write to a file using this legacy approach, you must create a file pointer when opening it. The file pointer returned by the **fopen()** function will be used by PHP to refer to the open file.

The most important consideration when opening the file is what mode you use. Depending on what you intend to do with the file, the mode dictates how to open it. The most forgiving mode is **a+**, which allows you to read or write to a file. It creates the file if it doesn't exist, and it appends—hence *a*—new data to the end of the file automatically. Conversely, **r** only allows you to read from a file. **Table 11.1** lists all the possible modes. Each mode can also be appended with a **b** flag, which forces files to be opened in binary mode. This is a safer option for files that might be read on multiple operating systems.

TABLE 11.1 fopen() Modes

Mode	Meaning
r	Reading only; begin reading at the start of the file.
r+	Reading or writing; begin at the start of the file.
w	Writing only; create the file if it doesn't exist, and overwrite any existing contents.
w+	Reading or writing; create the file if it doesn't exist, and overwrite any existing contents (when writing).
a	Writing only; create the file if it doesn't exist, and append the new data to the end of the file (retain any existing data and add to it).
a+	Reading or writing; create the file if it doesn't exist, and append the new data to the end of the file (when writing).
x	Writing only; create the file if it doesn't exist, but do nothing (and issue a warning) if the file does exist.
x+	Reading or writing; create the file if it doesn't exist, but do nothing (and issue a warning) if the file already exists (when writing).

The modes that attempt to create the file if it doesn't exist can only do so if the PHP script has permission to create a file in the destination directory.

The **fwrite()** function writes the new data (sent as the second argument in the function call) to the file in accordance with the selected mode.

As the last step of the writing process, you close the file by once again referring to the file pointer while calling the **fclose()** function:

```
fclose($fp);
```

To write to an external file:

1. Create a new PHP document in your text editor or IDE, to be named **add_quote.php** (Script 11.1):

```
<!doctype html>
<html lang="en">
<head>
   <meta charset="utf-8">
   <title>Add A Quotation</title>
</head>
<body>
```

2. Create a section of PHP code, and identify the file to be used:

```
<?php // Script 11.1 -
→ add_quote.php
$file = '../quotes.txt';
```

This script will reference the same file twice, so it's a good idea to identify the file as a variable. This way, should you later need to change the name or location of the file, only one line of code will need to be edited.

The file identified is **quotes.txt**, which should be located in the directory above this script (which is presumably in the web directory root; see **B** in the previous section, "File Permissions," of this chapter). See the sidebar "File Paths" for more on this syntax.

3. Check if the form has been submitted:

```
if ($_SERVER['REQUEST_METHOD'] ==
→ 'POST') {
```

This page both displays and handles the HTML form. The conditional tests if the form has been submitted, in which case the quotation should be written to the text file.

4. Check that a quotation was entered:

```
if ( !empty($_POST['quote']) &&
→ ($_POST['quote'] != 'Enter your
quotation here.') ) {
```

Script 11.1 This script takes a user-submitted quotation and stores it in a text file.

```
1    <!doctype html>
2    <html lang="en">
3    <head>
4       <meta charset="utf-8">
5       <title>Add A Quotation</title>
6    </head>
7    <body>
8    <?php // Script 11.1 - add_quote.php
9    /* This script displays and handles an
     HTML form. This script takes text input
     and stores it in a text file. */
10
11   // Identify the file to use:
12   $file = '../quotes.txt';
13
14   // Check for a form submission:
15   if ($_SERVER['REQUEST_METHOD'] ==
     'POST') { // Handle the form.
16
17      if ( !empty($_POST['quote']) &&
        ($_POST['quote'] != 'Enter your
        quotation here.') ) { // Need
        something to write.
18
19         if (is_writable($file)) {
           // Confirm that the file is
           writable.
20
21            file_put_contents($file,
              $_POST['quote'] . PHP_EOL,
              FILE_APPEND); // Write the
              data.
22
23            // Print a message:
24            print '<p>Your quotation has
              been stored.</p>';
25
26         } else { // Could not open the
           file.
27            print '<p style="color:
              red;">Your quotation could
              not be stored due to a system
              error.</p>';
28         }
29
```

code continues on next page

```
30          } else { // Failed to enter a
            quotation.
31          print '<p style="color:
            red;">Please enter a quotation!
            </p>';
32      }
33
34  } // End of submitted IF.
35
36  // Leave PHP and display the form:
37  ?>

38  <form action="add_quote.php"
    method="post">
39      <textarea name="quote" rows="5"
        cols="30">Enter your quotation
        here.</textarea><br>
40      <input type="submit" name="submit"
        value="Add This Quote!">
41  </form>
42
43  </body>
44  </html>
```

This simple conditional validates the user-supplied data. The first part confirms that the **$_POST['quote']** variable isn't empty. The second part confirms that the variable doesn't still have the default value (as shown in Ⓐ).

5. Confirm that the file can be written to:

```
if (is_writable($file)) {
```

By placing this function call in a conditional, you make the PHP script attempt to write to the file only if the file is writable.

6. Write the data to the file, and then print a message:

```
file_put_contents($file,
→ $_POST['quote'] . PHP_EOL,
→ FILE_APPEND);
print '<p>Your quotation has been
→ stored.</p>';
```

The first line writes the user-submitted data to the file. The **PHP_EOL** constant is concatenated to the written data, so that each submission gets stored on its own line.

7. Complete the conditionals:

```
        } else { // Could not open
        → the file.
            print '<p style="color:
            → red;">Your quotation
            → could not be stored
            → due to a system error.
            → </p>';
        }
    } else { // Failed to enter
    → a quotation.
        print '<p style="color:
        → red;">Please enter a
        → quotation!</p>';
    }
} // End of submitted IF.
```

continues on next page

The first **else** completes the conditional that checks if PHP could open the file for writing **B**. If you see this message, there's likely a permissions issue or the file reference is incorrect. The second **else** completes the conditional that checks whether no quotation was entered **C**. The final closing brace marks the end of the main submission conditional.

If you'd rather, you can replace the inline CSS with an actual CSS class declaration.

Because this page handles the form and then displays it again (so that the user may keep entering quotations), the form isn't displayed as part of an **else** statement as it has been in other examples in this book.

8. Complete the PHP section:

```
?>
```

Because the rest of this script is standard HTML, exit out of the PHP code by closing the PHP tag.

9. Create the HTML form:

```
<form action="add_quote.php"
method="post">
    <textarea name="quote" rows="5"
    → cols="30">Enter your
    → quotation here.</textarea>
    → <br>
    <input type="submit"
    → name="submit" value="Add This
    → Quote!">
</form>
```

This HTML form presents a text box where the user can enter a quotation. The text box has a preset value of *Enter your quotation here.*, created by putting that text between the **textarea** tags.

B If the PHP script can't find the `quotes.txt` file, or if it's not writable, the user will see this message.

C The script includes basic form validation.

10. Complete the HTML page:

```
</body>
</html>
```

11. Save the file as **add_quote.php**, and place it in the proper directory for your PHP-enabled server.

Again, refer back to **B** in the previous section, "File Permissions," of this chapter for how **add_quote.php** and **quotes.txt** should be placed on your server relative to each other. If this arrangement isn't possible for you, or if it's just too confusing, then place both documents within the same directory (the one from which you can execute PHP scripts), and change the **$file** assignment line to

```
$file = 'quotes.txt';
```

12. Run the script several times in your browser **D** and **E**.

13. If you want, open the **quotes.txt** file in a text editor to confirm that the data has been written to it.

TIP Note that all of the file- and directory-related functions are usable only on files and directories on the same computer (i.e., server) on which PHP is running. A PHP script on a server has no access to a file on a client's computer (until the file is uploaded to the server).

TIP If you receive a permissions error when you run this script **B**, either the permissions aren't set properly or the PHP script couldn't access the data file. The latter can happen if you misspell the filename or incorrectly reference the file's path on the server.

TIP If your version of PHP is running in safe mode or has the **open_basedir** directive set, you may be limited in using PHP to access files and directories. Check your **phpinfo()** script to see these settings for your server.

D Filling out the form...

E ...and the result if all went well.

Locking Files

Although the last example worked fine (hopefully), it could be improved on. If only a single user were submitting the form at one time, there would be no problems. But what if two or more users submitted different quotations simultaneously? In such a case, there could be problems when multiple instances of the PHP script attempt to write to the same text file at once. The file could become corrupted.

When there's a risk of multiple scripts writing to the same file at once, the solution is to temporarily *lock* the file while PHP is writing to it. To do that, add the `LOCK_EX` constant as the third argument to `file_put_contents()`:

```
file_put_contents($file, $data,
→ LOCK_EX);
```

To use both the `LOCK_EX` and `FILE_APPEND` constants, separate them with the *bitwise* OR operator (|):

```
file_put_contents($file, $data,
→ FILE_APPEND | LOCK_EX);
```

It doesn't matter in which order you provide the two constants (see the sidebar "Bitwise Operators").

The different lock types are represented by the constants listed in **Table 11.2**. A shared lock, `LOCK_SH`, is for reading from a file, which means it's okay if multiple files use the file at the same time (all with shared locks). Conversely, the exclusive lock, `LOCK_EX`, means only the locking file should have access.

The `LOCK_UN` constant is for releasing any type of lock. It's provided to the `flock()` function, not used in this chapter (see the PHP manual for more information).

TABLE 11.2 flock() Lock Types

Lock	Meaning
LOCK_SH	Shared lock for reading purposes
LOCK_EX	Exclusive lock for writing purposes
LOCK_UN	Release of a lock
LOCK_NB	Nonblocking lock

Bitwise Operators

A lesser-known but often useful set of operators are the bitwise operators. Beginners will most likely use them in situations where constants are passed as arguments, as in the file locking example.

Bitwise operators work with *bits*—the smallest data type, also referred to as *binary digits*. The operators look and function like the standard ones: bitwise **&** instead of **&&**, bitwise | instead of ||.

Bitwise operators are often used with constants like **LOCK_EX** and **FILE_APPEND** because each constant represents a numeric value. The numeric value in turn is a type of flag indicating what's allowed. The code **FILE_APPEND | LOCK_EX** therefore says to apply whatever flags are represented by the **FILE_APPEND** or the **LOCK_EX** constants.

Note that you should unlock the file once the script is done with it, although PHP will kindly unlock it for you should you forget.

To demonstrate, let's update **add_quote.php** to lock the file during the writing process.

```
1   <!doctype html>
2   <html lang="en">
3   <head>
4       <meta charset="utf-8">
5       <title>Add A Quotation</title>
6   </head>
7   <body>
8   <?php // Script 11.2 - add_quote.php
9   /* This script displays and handles an
    HTML form. This script takes text input
    and stores it in a text file. */
10
11  // Identify the file to use:
12  $file = '../quotes.txt';
13
14  // Check for a form submission:
15  if ($_SERVER['REQUEST_METHOD'] ==
    'POST') { // Handle the form.
16
17      if ( !empty($_POST['quote']) &&
        ($_POST['quote'] != 'Enter your
        quotation here.') ) { // Need
        something to write.
18
19          if (is_writable($file)) { //
            Confirm that the file is writable.
20
21              file_put_contents($file,
                $_POST['quote'] . PHP_EOL,
                FILE_APPEND | LOCK_EX); //
                Write the data.
22
23              // Print a message:
24              print '<p>Your quotation has
                been stored.</p>';
25
26          } else { // Could not open the
            file.
27              print '<p style="color:
                red;">Your quotation could
                not be stored due to a system
                error.</p>';
28          }
29
```

code continues on next page

The **LOCK_NB** constant can be added to **LOCK_SH** or **LOCK_EX** using the bitwise OR. In normal situations, without using **LOCK_NB**, PHP will wait until it can lock the file; the script is blocked from proceeding until it can execute that lock. With **LOCK_NB**, the PHP script will just continue executing if no lock could be obtained.

To use file locks:

1. Open **add_quote.php** (Script 11.1) in your text editor or IDE, if it isn't already open.

2. Change the **file_put_contents()** line to the following (**Script 11.2**):

   ```
   file_put_contents($file,
   → $_POST['quote'] . PHP_EOL,
   → FILE_APPEND | LOCK_EX);
   ```

   This command places an exclusive lock on the file so that other scripts can't write to it at the same time.

   continues on next page

3. Save the file, place it in the proper directory for your PHP-enabled server, and test it again in your browser **(A)** and **(B)**.

TIP Technically, if a file is opened in an appending mode, as in this example, not locking it probably won't be a problem even if multiple scripts are writing to the file simultaneously. That said, better safe than sorry!

TIP For file locking to be reliable, every script that writes to a file needs to use locking.

Script 11.2 *continued*

```
30      } else { // Failed to enter a
        quotation.
31          print '<p style="color:
            red;">Please enter a quotation!</
            p>';
32      }
33
34   } // End of submitted IF.
35
36   // Leave PHP and display the form:
37   ?>
38
39   <form action="add_quote.php"
     method="post">
40       <textarea name="quote" rows="5"
         cols="30">Enter your quotation
         here.</textarea><br>
41       <input type="submit" name="submit"
         value="Add This Quote!">
42   </form>
43
44   </body>
45   </html>
```

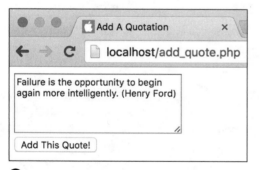

(A) Using the form once again...

(B) ...the quotation is still stored without a problem.

Reading from Files

Now that you've created a script that writes data to a file, it's time to create one that can read the information. There are a number of ways to read from a file; which approach you take depends on what your needs are. To read an entire file in as one string, use `file_get_contents()`:

```
$data = file_get_contents($file);
```

Alternatively, if the file has some data on each line, as is the case with **quotes.txt**, you're better off using the **file()** function:

```
$data = file($file);
```

The **file()** function is a valuable built-in tool in PHP. It reads everything from a file and, unlike **file_get_contents()**, returns that information as an array. Each array element contains one line from the file, where each line is terminated by a newline (**\n** or **\r\n**).

If the document represented by **$file** contains two lines of information, each of which ends with a newline, the corresponding array will contain two elements. The first element will be equal to the first line of **$file**, and the second element will be equal to the second line. Once the data is stored into an array, you can easily manipulate or print it, as you learned in Chapter 7, "Using Arrays."

Next, let's use this knowledge to create a script that randomly displays one of the stored quotations.

To read from a file:

1. Create a new PHP document in your text editor or IDE, to be named **view_quote.php** (Script 11.3):

```
<!doctype html>
<html lang="en">
<head>
  <meta charset="utf-8">
  <title>View A Quotation</title>
</head>
<body>
<h1>Random Quotation</h1>
```

2. Open a PHP code section:

```
<?php // Script 11.3 -
→ view_quote.php
```

3. Read the file contents, and store them in an array:

```
$data = file('../quotes.txt');
```

The function reads the file data into an array named **$data**. Each element of **$data** is a string, which is the submitted quotation.

If the **quotes.txt** file is not in the parent directory of this script, change the reference here accordingly.

4. Pick a random number based on the number of elements in **$data**:

```
$n = count($data);
$rand = rand(0, ($n - 1));
```

The first line counts how many elements (which is to say, how many quotations) are in the **$data** array. Then the **rand()** function selects a random number. In order for **rand()** to pick an appropriate number, a little logic is required.

Script 11.3 The `view_quote.php` file retrieves all the quotations from the text file and displays one at random.

```
1   <!doctype html>
2   <html lang="en">
3   <head>
4       <meta charset="utf-8">
5       <title>View A Quotation</title>
6   </head>
7   <body>
8   <h1>Random Quotation</h1>
9   <?php // Script 11.3 - view_quote.php
10  /* This script displays and handles an
    HTML form. This script reads in a file
    and prints a random line from it. */
11
12  // Read the file's contents into an
    array:
13  $data = file('../quotes.txt');
14
15  // Count the number of items in the
    array:
16  $n = count($data);
17
18  // Pick a random item:
19  $rand = rand(0, ($n - 1));
20
21  // Print the quotation:
22  print '<p>' . trim($data[$rand]) .
    '</p>';
23
24  ?>
25  </body>
26  </html>
```

A A random quotation is displayed each time the page is viewed.

B Subsequent viewings of the `view_quote.php` script display different quotations from the text file.

If `$data` has 10 elements, they're indexed between 0 and 9, so that's the range to use for `rand()`. Therefore, to calculate the range for a variable number of lines in the text file, use 0 and 1 less than the number of elements in `$data`.

5. Print out the quotation:

```
print '<p>' . trim($data
→[$rand]) . '</p>';
```

A simple `print` statement involving concatenation is used to print the random quotation. To retrieve the quotation, you refer to the `$data` array and use the generated `$rand` number as the index. The retrieved quotation is then trimmed to cut off the newline characters from the end of the quotation.

6. Complete the PHP code and the HTML page:

```
?>
</body>
</html>
```

7. Save the file as `view_quote.php`, place it on your web server (in the same directory as `add_quote.php`), and test it in your browser **A**.

8. Reload the page in your browser to view another random quote **B**.

> **TIP** If you want to be extra careful, you can use the `is_readable()` function to test that PHP can read a file before you call the `file()` function (although it's rare that a file isn't readable).

> **TIP** The `readfile()` function reads through a file and immediately sends the contents to the output buffer. This means that with output buffering enabled, the file's contents get added to the buffer. With output buffering disabled, the file's contents go straight to the browser.

> **TIP** Later in this chapter, you'll learn a more complex method of reading a file using `fgets()` and `fgetcsv()`.

Handling File Uploads

As this book has demonstrated, handling HTML forms using PHP is a remarkably easy achievement. Regardless of the data being submitted, PHP can handle it easily and directly. The same is true when the user uploads a file via an HTML form.

To give the user the option of uploading a file, you must make three changes to the standard HTML form. First, the initial **form** tag must include the code **enctype="multipart/form-data"**, which lets the browser know to expect different types of form data:

```
<form action="script.php"
→ enctype="multipart/form-data"
→ method="post">
```

The form must also always use the POST method.

Second, a special hidden input type should be added to the form:

```
<input type="hidden" name=
→ "MAX_FILE_SIZE" value="30000">
```

This tells the browser how large a file, in bytes, can be uploaded.

Third, the file input is used to create the necessary form field **A** and **B**:

```
<input type="file" name="picture">
```

The file type of form input allows users to select a file on their computer, which, upon submission, will be uploaded to the server. Note that the file input should be placed after the **MAX_FILE_SIZE** hidden input.

A This is how Chrome interprets the file input type (prior to selecting a file).

B This is how Internet Explorer interprets the file input type.

TABLE 11.3 FILE Error Codes

Code	Meaning
0	No error has occurred.
1	The file exceeds the `upload_max_filesize` setting in `php.ini`.
2	The file exceeds the `MAX_FILE_SIZE` setting in the HTML form.
3	The file was only partially uploaded.
4	No file was uploaded.
6	No temporary directory exists.
7	Failed write to disk.
8	Upload prevented by an extension.

Once you've configured the HTML form and the user has submitted a file through it, you can then use PHP to handle the file. In the PHP script, you refer to the **$_FILES** variable (think of it as the file equivalent of **$_POST**) to reference the uploaded file. The **$_FILES** array contains five elements:

- **name**, the name of the file as it was on the user's computer
- **type**, the MIME type of the file (for example, *image/jpg*)
- **size**, the size of the file in bytes
- **tmp_name**, the temporary name of the file as it's stored on the server
- **error**, an error code if something goes wrong (**Table 11.3**; note that, as strange as this may seem, there is no error code 5).

When a file is uploaded, the server first places it in a temporary directory. You should then use the **move_uploaded_file()** function to move the file to its final destination:

```
move_uploaded_file($_FILES
→ ['picture']['tmp_name'],
→ '/path/to/dest/filename');
```

The first argument is the temporary name of the file on the server, found in **$_FILES['input_name']['tmp_name']**. The second argument is the full path and name of the destination.

continues on next page

For PHP to be able to take these steps, you must set several configurations in the **php.ini** file (see the "Configuring PHP for File Uploads" sidebar), and the web server needs write access to both the temporary and the final destination directories. (PHP should have write access to the temporary directory by default.)

Next, you'll write a basic script that uploads a file and stores it on the server. Like the **add_quote.php** script, this example also both creates the HTML form 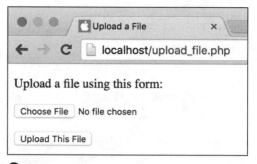 and processes it, all in one page. First, though, you'll create a writable directory as the destination point.

To create a writable directory:

1. Create a new folder named **uploads**, located outside the web directory root 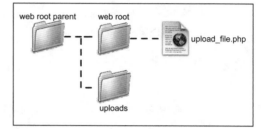.

2. Using the steps outlined in the first section of this chapter, "File Permissions," set the permissions so that everyone can write to, read from, and search (**0777** in Unix terms) the directory.

C This HTML form lets users select a file on their computer to upload to the server.

D For this example, a writable **uploads** directory must exist. Here, it's placed in the same directory as the web root folder. Thus, **uploads** is in the directory above the one in which the **upload_file.php** script resides and is not accessible via HTTP.

Configuring PHP for File Uploads

In order for file uploading to work, a number of settings in your **php.ini** configuration file must be set. These may or may not be enabled in your configuration, so you should check them by viewing the **php.ini** file or running a **phpinfo()** script.

For starters, **file_uploads** must be on. Second, the **upload_tmp_dir** value must be set to a directory on the server where PHP can place files (in other words, it must exist and be modifiable by the web server). If this setting has no value, that's probably fine (meaning that a hidden directory created expressly for purposes such as these will be used).

The **upload_max_filesize** and **post_max_size** settings dictate how large a file can be sent, such as 512 KB or 2 MB. Whereas the **MAX_FILE_SIZE** hidden form input is a recommendation to the browser, these two settings control whether the file is uploaded.

Finally, if really large files—many megabytes or larger—will be uploaded, you may need to increase the **memory_limit** and **max_execution_time** settings to give PHP the time and the resources to do what it needs to do.

Again, if you're running Windows you likely don't need to do anything (try the next script to see for sure). If you're running another operating system, check the list of bullet points in the first section of the chapter for the suggestion that works for your situation.

To use PHP for file uploads:

1. Create a new PHP document in your text editor or IDE, to be named **upload_file.php** (Script 11.4):

```
<!doctype html>
<html lang="en">
<head>
  <meta charset="utf-8">
  <title>Upload a File</title>
</head>
<body>
```

2. Create a section of PHP code:

```
<?php // Script 11.4 -
→ upload_file.php
```

3. Check whether the form has been submitted:

```
if ($_SERVER['REQUEST_METHOD'] ==
→ 'POST') {
```

Once again, this script both displays and handles the HTML form. If it has been submitted, the uploaded file should be addressed.

continues on page 321

Script 11.4 This script handles a file upload by first defining the proper HTML form and, second, invoking `move_uploaded_file()` to move the file to the desired location.

```
1   <!doctype html>
2   <html lang="en">
3   <head>
4       <meta charset="utf-8">
5       <title>Upload a File</title>
6   </head>
7   <body>
8   <?php // Script 11.4 - upload_file.php
9   /* This script displays and handles an HTML form. This script takes a file upload and stores
    it on the server. */
10
11  if ($_SERVER['REQUEST_METHOD'] == 'POST') { // Handle the form.
12
13      // Try to move the uploaded file:
14      if (move_uploaded_file ($_FILES['the_file']['tmp_name'], "../uploads/{$_FILES['the_
        file']['name']}")) {
15
```

code continues on next page

Script 11.4 *continued*

```php
16          print '<p>Your file has been uploaded.</p>';
17
18      } else { // Problem!
19
20          print '<p style="color: red;">Your file could not be uploaded because: ';
21
22          // Print a message based upon the error:
23          switch ($_FILES['the_file']['error']) {
24              case 1:
25                  print 'The file exceeds the upload_max_filesize setting in php.ini';
26                  break;
27              case 2:
28                  print 'The file exceeds the MAX_FILE_SIZE setting in the HTML form';
29                  break;
30              case 3:
31                  print 'The file was only partially uploaded';
32                  break;
33              case 4:
34                  print 'No file was uploaded';
35                  break;
36              case 6:
37                  print 'The temporary folder does not exist.';
38                  break;
39              default:
40                  print 'Something unforeseen happened.';
41                  break;
42          }
43
44          print '.</p>'; // Complete the paragraph.
45
46      } // End of move_uploaded_file() IF.
47
48  } // End of submission IF.
49
50  // Leave PHP and display the form:
51  ?>
52
53  <form action="upload_file.php" enctype="multipart/form-data" method="post">
54      <p>Upload a file using this form:</p>
55      <input type="hidden" name="MAX_FILE_SIZE" value="300000">
56      <p><input type="file" name="the_file"></p>
57      <p><input type="submit" name="submit" value="Upload This File"></p>
58  </form>
59
60  </body>
61  </html>
```

E If the file was uploaded and moved successfully, a message is printed and the form is displayed again.

4. Attempt to move the uploaded file to its final destination:

```
if (move_uploaded_file
→ ($_FILES['the_file']
→ ['tmp_name'], "../uploads/
→ {$_FILES['the_file']
→ ['name']}")) {
```

The `move_uploaded_file()` function attempts to move the uploaded file (identified by `$_FILES['the_file']['tmp_name']`) to its new location (`../uploads/{$_FILES['the_file']['name']}`). The location is the **uploads** directory, which is in the folder above the one this script is in. The file's name will be the same as it was on the user's computer.

Placing this function as a condition in an **if** statement makes it easy to respond based on whether the move worked.

Note that there is an implicit trust here that the user is uploading a file that's safe for you to put onto your server retaining the same name. See the tips for suggestions on how to make this process more secure.

5. Print messages indicating the success of the operation:

```
print '<p>Your file has been
→ uploaded.</p>';
} else { // Problem!
print '<p style="color: red;">
→ Your file could not be
→ uploaded because: ';
```

The first **print** statement is executed if the move worked **E**. The **else** applies if it didn't work, in which case an error message is begun. This message will be made more explicit in Step 6.

continues on next page

6. Print out the error message if the move didn't work:

```
switch ($_FILES['the_file']
['error']) {
    case 1:
        print 'The file exceeds the
        → upload_max_filesize setting
        → in php.ini';
        break;
    case 2:
        print 'The file exceeds the
        → MAX_FILE_SIZE setting in
        → the HTML form';
        break;
    case 3:
        print 'The file was only
        → partially uploaded';
        break;
    case 4:
        print 'No file was uploaded';
        break;
    case 6:
        print 'The temporary folder
        → does not exist.';
        break;
    default:
        print 'Something unforeseen
        → happened.';
        break;
}
```

If a move doesn't work, the **$_FILES['the_file']['error']** variable contains a number indicating the appropriate error message. When you use this in a **switch** conditional, the PHP script can print out the appropriate error message 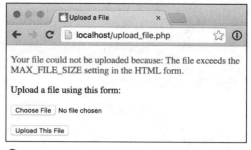.

You wouldn't normally place code like this in a public site—it's a little too much information—but it's exceptionally good for helping you debug a problem.

F If a problem occurred, the script indicates the cause.

7. Complete the error message, and close both conditionals:

```
      print '.</p>'; // Complete
      → the paragraph.
    } // End of move_uploaded_
    → file() IF.
  } // End of submission IF.
```

8. Exit out of PHP, and create the HTML form:

```
?>
<form action="upload_file.php"
enctype="multipart/form-data"
method="post">
  <p>Upload a file using this
  → form:</p>
  <input type="hidden"
  → name="MAX_FILE_SIZE"
  → value="300000">
  <p><input type="file"
  → name="the_file"></p>
  <p><input type="submit"
  → name="submit" value="Upload
  → This File"></p>
</form>
```

The HTML form is simple, containing only two visible elements: a file input type and a submit button. It differs from other HTML forms in this book in that it uses the **enctype** attribute and a **MAX_FILE_SIZE** hidden input type.

Be careful when giving your file input a name, because this value must exactly match the index used in the **$_FILES** variable. Here, you use a generic *the_file*.

9. Complete the HTML page:

```
</body>
</html>
```

continues on next page

10. Save the page as **upload_file.php**, place it in the proper directory for your PHP-enabled server relative to the **uploads** directory , and test it in your browser .

Only files smaller than about 300 KB should be allowed, thanks to the **MAX_FILE_SIZE** restriction.

11. Inspect the **uploads** directory to ensure that the file was placed there.

G Select a file on your computer to upload.

TIP If the file couldn't be moved and a permissions denied error is shown, check the permissions on the **uploads** directory. Then check that the path to the directory used in the script is correct and that there are no spelling errors.

TIP As you might discover, files uploaded through the browser are owned—in terms of permissions—by the web server application, which put them there.

TIP From a security standpoint, it's better to rename an uploaded file. To do so, you'll need to devise a system that generates a new, unique filename and stores both the original and new filenames in a text file or a database.

TIP A script can handle multiple file uploads as long as they have different names. In such a case, you need only one **MAX_FILE_SIZE** hidden input. In the PHP script, you'd apply the **move_uploaded_file()** function to **$_FILES['filename1']**, **$_FILES['filename2']**, and so on.

TIP You can limit a file upload to a specific size or type by referencing the appropriate index (for example, **$_FILES['the_file']['size']**) in your PHP script (after the file has been uploaded).

TIP Use **unlink()** to delete a file without moving or copying it.

TIP You can use the **copy()** function to make a copy of a file on the server.

Navigating Directories

The previous PHP scripts work with files, but you can also do many things with directories using PHP. In this example, you'll write a script that lists a directory's contents, but first you'll need to understand the usage and syntax of many of the functions you'll use.

To find all the contents of a directory, the easiest option is to use the **scandir()** function:

$stuff = scandir($dir);

This function returns an array of every item—directory or file—found within the given directory. As with the file-related functions, the value of **$dir** can be a relative or an absolute path to the directory in question.

This next example uses **scandir()**, but let's look at a couple more functions first. You'll use the **filesize()** function in this example; it determines how large a file is in bytes. This value can be assigned to a variable or be printed:

$size = filesize($file);

Similarly, the **filemtime()** function retrieves the modification time of a file. It returns a timestamp, which can be formatted using the **date()** function.

Finally, PHP includes several functions that identify attributes. This chapter has already mentioned **is_writable()** and **is_readable()**, but there are also **is_dir()** and **is_file()**. They return TRUE if the item in question is a directory or a file, respectively.

You'll put all of these capabilities together into one page, which will constitute a web-based control panel for viewing a directory's contents **Ⓐ**.

Directory Contents ✕

← → C 🔒 localhost/list_dir.php

Directories

- NetBoot
- css
- include
- larry.pub
- larryullman
- psu
- templates

Files

Name	Size	Last Modified
add_quote.php	1311 bytes	April 23, 2016
books.php	512 bytes	March 27, 2016
calculator.html	918 bytes	February 2, 2016
calculator.php	1275 bytes	April 9, 2016

Ⓐ The **list_dir.php** script shows the contents of a directory. The top part lists the subfolders, and the bottom table lists the files.

To create the directory control panel:

1. Create a new PHP document in your text editor or IDE, to be named `list_dir.php` (Script 11.5):

```
<!doctype html>
<html lang="en">
<head>
    <meta charset="utf-8">
    <title>Directory Contents</
    title>
</head>
<body>
```

Script 11.5 This script displays the contents of a directory. First the subdirectories are listed, followed by the files (with their sizes and modification dates) in a table.

```
1   <!doctype html>
2   <html lang="en">
3   <head>
4       <meta charset="utf-8">
5       <title>Directory Contents</title>
6   </head>
7   <body>
8   <?php // Script 11.5 - list_dir.php
9   /* This script lists the directories and files in a directory. */
10
11  // Set the time zone:
12  date_default_timezone_set('America/New_York');
13
14  // Set the directory name and scan it:
15  $search_dir = '.';
16  $contents = scandir($search_dir);
17
18  // List the directories first...
19  // Print a caption and start a list:
20  print '<h2>Directories</h2>
21  <ul>';
22  foreach ($contents as $item) {
23      if ( (is_dir($search_dir . '/' . $item)) AND (substr($item, 0, 1) != '.') ) {
24          print "<li>$item</li>\n";
25      }
26  }
27
28  print '</ul>'; // Close the list.
29
```

code continues on next page

Script 11.5 *continued*

```
30   // Create a table header:
31   print '<hr><h2>Files</h2>
32   <table cellpadding="2" cellspacing="2"
     align="left">
33   <tr>
34   <th>Name</th>
35   <th>Size</th>
36   <th>Last Modified</th>
37   </tr>';
38
39   // List the files:
40   foreach ($contents as $item) {
41       if ( (is_file($search_dir . '/' .
         $item)) AND (substr($item, 0, 1)
         != '.') ) {
42
43           // Get the file size:
44           $fs = filesize($search_dir .
             '/' . $item);
45
46           // Get the file's modification
             date:
47           $lm = date('F j, Y',
             filemtime($search_dir . '/' .
             $item));
48
49           // Print the information:
50           print "<tr>
51           <td>$item</td>
52           <td>$fs bytes</td>
53           <td>$lm</td>
54           </tr>\n";
55
56       } // Close the IF.
57
58   } // Close the FOREACH.
59
60   print '</table>'; // Close the HTML
     table.
61
62   ?>
63   </body>
64   </html>
```

2. Begin the PHP code, and set the time zone:

```
<?php // Script 11.5 -
→ list_dir.php
date_default_timezone_set
→ ('America/New_York');
```

Because this script will make use of the **date()** function, it needs to establish the time zone once. See Chapter 8, "Creating Web Applications," to learn more about using the **date_default_timezone_set()**.

3. Identify the directory to be opened, and scan in its contents:

```
$search_dir = '.';
$contents = scandir($search_dir);
```

By establishing this value as a variable at the top of the PHP script, it will be easy to find and change as needed. Here you use a single period to refer to the current directory. You could also use an absolute path to another directory (**/Users/larry/Documents** or **C:\\myfiles\\directory**) or a relative path (**../myfiles**), as long as PHP has permission to read the named directory.

The second line scans in the directory's contents and assigns them as an array to the variable **$contents**.

continues on next page

4. List the subdirectories of this directory:

```
print '<h2>Directories</h2>
<ul>';
foreach ($contents as $item) {
  if ( (is_dir($search_dir . '/'
→ . $item)) AND (substr($item,
→ 0, 1) != '.') ) {
    print "<li>$item</li>\n";
  }
}
print '</ul>';
```

This **foreach** loop accesses every item in the array, assigning each one to the **$item** variable. The script should first list every directory, so the **is_dir()** function is called to confirm the item's type. That same conditional also checks that the current item isn't the current directory or a hidden directory—both marked by a single period on Unix systems—or the parent directory, marked by a double period on Unix systems. If this conditional is TRUE, then the item's name is printed out, within list item tags, followed by a newline (to make for neater HTML source code).

So that the **is_dir()** function will work when dealing with items found in other directories, the **$search_dir** value, plus a slash, is appended to each item. If the code just referred to **$item** without adding the directory path, the code would only work for the current directory.

5. Create a new heading, and start a table for the files:

```
print '<hr><h2>Files</h2>
<table cellpadding="2"
→ cellspacing="2" align="left">
<tr>
<th>Name</th>
<th>Size</th>
<th>Last Modified</th>
</tr>';
```

The script also displays the files' sizes and modification dates. To make this look nicer, the results are placed in an HTML table.

6. Begin looping through the files in this directory:

```
foreach ($contents as $item) {
  if ( (is_file($search_dir . '/'
→ . $item)) AND (substr($item,
→ 0, 1) != '.') ) {
```

Another **foreach** loop is used to go through the directory contents again. This time, the conditional only wants items that are files, but not hidden files that begin with a single period.

Again, the **$search_dir** value and a slash is prepended to each item.

7. Calculate the file's size and modification date, and then print out the information:

```
$fs = filesize($search_dir . '/'
→ . $item);
$lm = date('F j, Y', filemtime
→ ($search_dir . '/' . $item));
print "<tr>
<td>$item</td>
<td>$fs bytes</td>
<td>$lm</td>
</tr>\n";
```

The first line calls the **filesize()** function to retrieve the file's size in bytes. The second line calls the **filemtime()** function, which returns a timestamp of the file's modification time. The timestamp is then fed into the **date()** function, along with the proper formatting, to return a string like *November 24, 2016*. Finally, these two items and the file's name are printed in the appropriate columns of the table.

For additional security, you can also apply **htmlspecialchars()** to the item's name when printing it.

Directories

- 01
- 02
- 03
- 04
- 05
- 06
- 07
- 08
- 09
- 10
- 11
- 12
- 13

Files

Name	Size	Last Modified
README.md	3275 bytes	January 15, 2016
license.txt	28 bytes	January 15, 2016

B The directory listing for another folder on the server.

8. Complete the conditional and the loop:

```
    }
}
```

9. Close the table:

```
print '</table>';
```

10. Complete the PHP code and the HTML page:

```
?>
</body>
</html>
```

11. Save the file as **list_dir.php**, place it in the proper directory for your PHP-enabled server, and test it in your browser **Ⓐ**.

12. If you want, change the value of **$search_dir**, and retest the script in your browser **Ⓑ**.

TIP Notice that you need to use double backslashes to create absolute path names on a Windows server. This is necessary because the single backslash, used in Windows path names, is the escape character. So, it must be escaped to be taken literally:

```
C:\\myfiles\\directory
```

TIP The glob() function lets you search a directory for files whose name matches a pattern (like *something*.jpg or *filename*.doc).

TIP Other file functions you might appreciate include fileperms(), which returns the file's permissions; fileatime(), which returns the last time a file was accessed; and fileowner(), which returns the user who owns the file.

TIP The basename() and dirname() functions are useful for finding subparts of a full directory or file path.

TIP The finfo_file() function is the best way to find a file's MIME type.

Creating Directories

Understanding how to read from and write to files on the server is only part of the data storage process. It's likely you'll want to read from and write to directories as well.

The command for creating a directory in PHP is `mkdir()`:

```
mkdir('directory_name',
→ permissions);
```

The directory name is the name of the directory to be created. This value can be relative to the current directory (i.e., the one the script is in), or it can be a full path:

```
mkdir('C:\\inetpub\\users\\rey');
```

On Windows servers, the permissions are ignored and therefore not required (as in the preceding example). On non-Windows servers, the permissions are **0777** by default (see the section "File Permissions" earlier in this chapter to learn what those numbers mean).

With this in mind, let's create a script that makes a new directory for a user when the user registers—the theory being that a user could upload files to that directory. This script also records the username and password to a text file so that the user can be validated when logging in. You'll begin by creating the parent directory, which must be writable so that PHP can create subdirectories in it, and the `users.txt` data file.

To create the directory and the data file:

1. Create a new folder named **users**, located outside of the web directory root.

   It could be created in the same directory as the **uploads** folder made earlier (see **D** in "Handling File Uploads").

2. Using the steps outlined in the first section of this chapter, "File Permissions," set the permissions so that everyone can write to, read from, and search (**0777** in Unix terms) the directory.

   If you're running Windows, this step will most likely not be necessary.

3. In your text editor, create a new, blank document.

4. Save this file in the **users** directory with the name **users.txt**.

5. Again using the steps outlined earlier in the chapter, set the permissions on **users.txt** so that everyone can write to and read from the file (**0666** in Unix terms).

   Again, this will probably not be necessary if you're running Windows on your PHP server.

> **TIP** Once you create a directory that PHP can write to, PHP should be able to automatically create a `users.txt` file in that directory to which PHP can write. However, it's best not to make assumptions about such things.

To create the registration script:

1. Begin a new PHP document in your text editor or IDE, to be named `register.php` (Script 11.6):

```
<!doctype html>
<html lang="en">
<head>
  <meta charset="utf-8">
  <title>Register</title>
  <style type="text/css"
→ media="screen">
    .error { color: red; }
  </style>
</head>
<body>
<h1>Register</h1>
```

In the page's head, a CSS class is defined that will be used to format errors.

continues on page 333

Script 11.6 The `register.php` script serves two purposes: It records the user's information in a text file and creates a new directory for that user's stuff.

```
1    <!doctype html>
2    <html lang="en">
3    <head>
4        <meta charset="utf-8">
5        <title>Register</title>
6        <style type="text/css" media="screen">
7            .error { color: red; }
8        </style>
9    </head>
10   <body>
11   <h1>Register</h1>
12   <?php // Script 11.6 - register.php
13   /* This script registers a user by storing their information in a text file and creating a
     directory for them. */
14
15   // Identify the directory and file to use:
16   $dir = '../users/';
17   $file = $dir . 'users.txt';
18
19   if ($_SERVER['REQUEST_METHOD'] == 'POST') { // Handle the form.
20
21       $problem = FALSE; // No problems so far.
22
```

code continues on next page

```
23      // Check for each value...
24      if (empty($_POST['username'])) {
25          $problem = TRUE;
26          print '<p class="error">Please enter a username!</p>';
27      }
28
29      if (empty($_POST['password1'])) {
30          $problem = TRUE;
31          print '<p class="error">Please enter a password!</p>';
32      }
33
34      if ($_POST['password1'] != $_POST['password2']) {
35          $problem = TRUE;
36          print '<p class="error">Your password did not match your confirmed password!</p>';
37      }
38
39      if (!$problem) { // If there weren't any problems...
40
41          if (is_writable($file)) { // Open the file.
42
43              // Create the data to be written:
44              $subdir = time() . rand(0, 4596);
45              $data = $_POST['username'] . "\t" . sha1(trim($_POST['password1'])) . "\t" .
                    $subdir . PHP_EOL;
46
47              // Write the data:
48              file_put_contents($file, $data, FILE_APPEND | LOCK_EX);
49
50              // Create the directory:
51              mkdir ($dir . $subdir);
52
53              // Print a message:
54              print '<p>You are now registered!</p>';
55
56          } else { // Couldn't write to the file.
57              print '<p class="error">You could not be registered due to a system error.</p>';
58          }
59
60      } else { // Forgot a field.
61          print '<p class="error">Please go back and try again!</p>';
62      }
63
64  } else { // Display the form.
65
66  // Leave PHP and display the form:
67  ?>
68
```

code continues on next page

```
68    <form action="register.php"
      method="post">
69        <p>Username: <input type="text"
          name="username" size="20"></p>
70        <p>Password: <input type="password"
          name="password1" size="20"></p>
71        <p>Confirm Password: <input
          type="password" name="password2"
          size="20"></p>
72        <input type="submit" name="submit"
          value="Register">
73    </form>
74
75    <?php } // End of submission IF. ?>
76    </body>
77    </html>
```

2. Begin the PHP code, and create two variables:

```
<?php // Script 11.6 -
→ register.php
$dir = '../users/';
$file = $dir . 'users.txt';
```

These two variables represent the directory and file being used by the example. The file will be in the directory, so its value starts with the directory's value. Change the value of **$dir** so that it's appropriate for your situation.

3. Check whether the form has been submitted:

```
if ($_SERVER['REQUEST_METHOD'] ==
→ 'POST') {
```

Once again, this page both displays and handles the HTML form. This is accomplished using a conditional that checks how the script is being requested.

4. Validate the registration information:

```
$problem = FALSE;
if (empty($_POST['username'])) {
  $problem = TRUE;
  print '<p class="error">Please
  → enter a username!</p>';
}
if (empty($_POST['password1'])) {
  $problem = TRUE;
  print '<p class="error">Please
  → enter a password!</p>';
}
if ($_POST['password1'] != $_POST
['password2']) {
  $problem = TRUE;
  print '<p class="error">Your
  → password did not match your
  → confirmed password!</p>';
}
```

continues on next page

The registration form is a simpler version of earlier registration forms developed in this book. The same validation process you previously developed is used to check the submitted username and passwords. The **$problem** variable is used as a flag to indicate whether a problem occurred.

5. Check for problems:

```
if (!$problem) {
```

Again, the **$problem** variable lets you know if it's okay to register the user. If no problems occurred, it's safe to continue.

6. Confirm that the **users.txt** file is writable:

```
if (is_writable($file)) {
```

Like before, the data file is first confirmed as writable in a conditional so that the script can respond accordingly.

7. Create the data to be written to the file, and then write it:

```
$subdir = time() . rand(0, 4596);
$data = $_POST['username'] .
→ "\t" . sha1(trim($_POST
→ ['password1'])) . "\t" .
→ $subdir . PHP_EOL;
file_put_contents($file, $data,
→ FILE_APPEND | LOCK_EX);
```

The name of the directory being created is a number based on the time the user registered and a random value. This system helps guarantee that the directory created is unique and has a valid name.

Register

You could not be registered due to a system error.

A The result if the `users.txt` file is not writable.

Register

Please enter a username!

Please enter a password!

Please go back and try again!

B The script reports any form validation errors.

Instead of storing a single string, as you previously have, this script stores three separate pieces of information: the user's name; an encrypted version of the password (using the **sha1()** function; see the "Encrypting Passwords" sidebar); and the directory name, created in the preceding line. The password is trimmed first, to get rid of any extraneous spaces.

To distinguish between the pieces of information, you insert a tab (created using the **\t** code). A newline is used to mark the end of the line, again using the **PHP_EOL** constant.

8. Create the user's directory, and print a message:

```
mkdir($dir . $subdir);
print '<p>You are now
→ registered!</p>';
```

The **mkdir()** function creates the directory in the **users** directory. The directory is named whatever random number was generated earlier.

9. Complete the conditionals:

```
  } else { // Couldn't write to
  the file.
    print '<p class="error">You
    → could not be registered due
    → to a system error.</p>';
  }
} else { // Forgot a field.
  print '<p class="error">Please
  → go back and try again!</p>';
}
```

The first **else** completes the conditional if the script couldn't open the **users.txt** file for writing **A**. The second **else** completes the conditional if the user failed to complete the form properly **B**.

10. Add an **else** clause to the main conditional, and exit out of PHP:

```
} else {
?>
```

Unlike the previous examples in this chapter, this PHP script first displays the form and then handles it. Whereas the other scripts would then display the form again, this one does not, because the form creation is part of an **else** statement. The rest of the page is just HTML, so you exit out of PHP to create the form.

11. Display the HTML form:

```
<form action="login.php"
method="post">
  <p>Username: <input type="text"
  → name="username" size="20">
  → </p>
  <p>Password: <input type=
  → "password" name="password"
  → size="20"></p>
  <input type="submit" name=
  → "submit" value="Login">
</form>
```

12. Complete the main conditional:

```
<?php } // End of submission IF.
?>
```

This final closing curly bracket closes the main submit conditional. For it to work, a new PHP section must first be created.

13. Complete the HTML page:

```
</body>
</html>
```

C The registration form is quite basic but serves its purpose.

D This is what the user sees if the registration process worked.

14. Save the file as **register.php**, place it in the proper directory for your PHP-enabled server, and test it in your browser **C** and **D**.

15. If you want, open the **users.txt** file in your text editor to see its contents (**Script 11.7**).

TIP You can also ensure that the page worked as it should by looking in the **users** directory for the new subdirectories.

TIP The **rmdir()** function deletes an existing directory, assuming PHP has permission to do so.

TIP When using a character, such as the tab, to separate stored values, you should additionally take measures to escape or strip that character from the stored values.

Script 11.7 The **users.txt** file lists three tab-delineated fields of information: the username, a scrambled version of the user's password, and the user's associated directory name.

```
1   larry    9d4e1e23bd5b727046a9e3b4b7db57bd8d6ee684    14615086124319
2   john     5baa61e4c9b93f3f0682250b6cf8331b7ee68fd8    14615086364092
3   paul     f0578f1e7174b1a41c4ea8c6e17f7a8a3b88c92a    14615086461481
4   george   81fe8bfe87576c3ecb22426f8e57847382917acf    14615252264106
5   ringo    c2543fff3bfa6f144c2f06a7de6cd10c0b650cae    1461525233328
```

Encrypting Passwords

The **sha1()** function creates a *hash*: a mathematically calculated representation of a string. So the registration script doesn't actually store the password but stores a representation of that password (in theory, no two strings would have the same **sha1()** value). You'll soon see how the hashed password is used by a login script.

That being said, the **sha1()** does not create a *secure* representation of the password. For modern computers, it's far too easy to perform the calculations necessary to crack passwords hashed with **sha1()**. But the book does use **sha1()** as an easy approach, with the expectation that you wouldn't replicate this in a real-life application.

The current, most secure solution for password management is to use PHP's built-in **password_hash()** and **password_verify()** functions. Although not overly complex, they are a bit involved for beginners, especially if you're not using at least PHP 5.5 or greater. When you're ready to implement your own login capability, see the PHP manual pages for these functions to learn how to use them.

Reading Files Incrementally

In the `view_quote.php` script (Script 11.3), an entire file was read into an array using the `file()` function. But what if you want to read in only a little of the file at a time? Then you need to use the `fgets()` function.

The `fgets()` function reads a string of a certain length. It's most often placed in a `while` loop that uses the `feof()` function to make sure the end of the file hasn't been reached. For example:

```
$fp = fopen($file, 'rb');
while (!feof($fp)) {
   $string = fgets($fp, 1024);
}
fclose ($fp);
```

With that code, 1,023 bytes of data at a time will be read in, as `fgets()` always reads 1 byte less than the length you specify. Or `fgets()` will stop reading once it reaches the end of the line or the end of the file. The second argument is optional, but if present, it should be a number larger than a single line of text in the file. If you want to just read to the end of the line, omit the length argument:

```
$string = fgets($fp);
```

In an example where the data is stored in a *delineated* format (commonly using a comma, hence a CSV—comma-separated values—format), you can use the `fgetcsv()` function instead. It breaks the string into parts, using the marked separator, and returns an array:

```
$array = fgetcsv($fp, length,
→ delimiter);
$array = fgetcsv($fp, 1024);
```

Again, the preceding function call returns 1023 bytes of data, but it breaks the string into an array using the default delimiter—a comma—as an indicator of where to make elements. This function is the equivalent of using the `fgets()` and `explode()` functions together. If you provide a delimiter argument, you can change what character is used to delineate the data.

Finally, because these functions rely on identifying the end of a line, it's a smart extra precaution to enable PHP's `auto_detect_line_endings` setting. You can do so using the `ini_set()` function:

```
ini_set('auto_detect_line_endings',
→ 1);
```

As an example, let's create a login script that uses the `users.txt` file created in the preceding example. It will continue to read a file until a matching username/password combination has been found.

To read a file incrementally:

1. Begin a new PHP document in your text editor or IDE, to be named `login.php` (**Script 11.8**):

   ```
   <!doctype html>
   <html lang="en">
   <head>
      <meta charset="utf-8">
      <title>Login</title>
   </head>
   <body>
   <h1>Login</h1>
   ```

2. Create the PHP section, and identify the file to use:

   ```
   <?php // Script 11.8 - login.php
   $file = '../users/users.txt';
   ```

   The value of `$file` should be the same as that in `register.php`.

3. Check whether the form has been submitted:

```
if ($_SERVER['REQUEST_METHOD'] ==
→ 'POST') {
```

4. Create a dummy variable to use as a flag:

```
$loggedin = FALSE;
```

The **$loggedin** variable is used to indicate whether the user entered the correct username/password combination. When the script first starts, it's assumed that the user has not entered the correct values.

continues on next page

Script 11.8 The `login.php` script uses the information stored in `users.txt` (created by Script 11.6) to validate a user.

```
1    <!doctype html>
2    <html lang="en">
3    <head>
4        <meta charset="utf-8">
5        <title>Login</title>
6    </head>
7    <body>
8    <h1>Login</h1>
9    <?php // Script 11.8 - login.php
10   /* This script logs a user in by check the stored values in text file. */
11
12   // Identify the file to use:
13   $file = '../users/users.txt';
14
15   if ($_SERVER['REQUEST_METHOD'] == 'POST') { // Handle the form.
16
17       $loggedin = FALSE; // Not currently logged in.
18
19       // Enable auto_detect_line settings:
20       ini_set('auto_detect_line_endings', 1);
21
22       // Open the file:
23       $fp = fopen($file, 'rb');
24
25       // Loop through the file:
26       while ( $line = fgetcsv($fp, 200, "\t") ) {
27
28           // Check the file data against the submitted data:
29           if ( ($line[0] == $_POST['username']) AND ($line[1] == sha1(trim($_
             POST['password']))) ) {
30
31               $loggedin = TRUE; // Correct username/password combination.
32
```

code continues on next page

5. Open the file for reading:

```
ini_set('auto_detect_line_
→ endings', 1);
$fp = fopen($file, 'rb');
```

Unlike the **file()** function, the **fgetcsv()** function requires a file pointer. Therefore, the **users.txt** file must be opened with the **fopen()** function, using the appropriate mode. Here, that mode is **rb**, meaning the file should be opened for reading in a binary safe mode.

First, though, just to be safe, PHP's **auto_detect_line_endings** setting is enabled. Stylistically, some developers prefer to adjust settings as the first line of code in the script, so feel free to move this up if you'd rather.

6. Loop through each line of the file:

```
while ( $line = fgetcsv($fp, 200,
→ "\t") ) {
```

This **while** loop reads another 200 bytes or one line of the file—whichever comes first—with each iteration. The data being read is broken into an array, using the tab to indicate the separate elements.

Because the **users.txt** file stores its data in the format *username tab password tab directory newline*, the **$line** array contains three elements indexed at 0 (*username*), 1 (*password*), and 2 (*directory*).

Script 11.8 *continued*

```
33          // Stop looping through the
            file:
34          break;
35
36      } // End of IF.
37
38  } // End of WHILE.
39
40  fclose($fp); // Close the file.
41
42  // Print a message:
43  if ($loggedin) {
44      print '<p>You are now logged in.
        </p>';
45  } else {
46      print '<p style="color: red;">The
        username and password you entered
        do not match those on file.</p>';
47  }
48
49  } else { // Display the form.
50
51  // Leave PHP and display the form:
52  ?>
53
54  <form action="login.php" method="post">
55      <p>Username: <input type="text"
        name="username" size="20"></p>
56      <p>Password: <input type="password"
        name="password" size="20"></p>
57      <input type="submit" name="submit"
        value="Login">
58  </form>
59
60  <?php } // End of submission IF. ?>
61
62  </body>
63  </html>
```

7. Check the submitted values against the retrieved values:

```
if ( ($line[0] == $_POST
→['username']) AND ($line[1] ==
→sha1(trim($_POST
→['password']))) ) {
```

This two-part conditional checks the submitted username against the stored username (**$line[0]**) and checks the submitted password against the stored password (**$line[1]**). However, because the stored password was scrambled using **sha1()**, apply **sha1()** to the submitted value and then make the comparison.

8. If a match was found, set **$loggedin** to TRUE, and exit the **while** loop:

```
$loggedin = TRUE;
break;
```

If the conditional is TRUE, the submitted username and password match those on file. In this case, the **$loggedin** flag is set to TRUE, and the **break** statement is used to exit the **while** loop. The benefit of this system is that only as much of the file is read as is required to find a match.

9. Close the conditional, the **while** loop, and the file:

```
    }
}
fclose ($fp);
```

10. Print a message to the user:

```
if ($loggedin) {
    print '<p>You are now logged
    →in.</p>';
} else {
    print '<p style="color: red;">
    →The username and password you
    →entered do not match those on
    →file.</p>';
}
```

Using the **$loggedin** flag, the script can now say whether the user is "logged in." You could add some functionality to this process by storing the user's directory in a session and then sending them to a file-upload page.

11. Continue the main submit conditional, and exit PHP:

```
} else {
?>
```

12. Create the HTML form:

```
<form action="login.php"
method="post">
    <p>Username: <input type="text"
    →name="username" size="20">
    →</p>
    <p>Password: <input
    →type="password"
    →name="password" size="20">
    →</p>
    <input type="submit"
    →name="submit" value="Login">
</form>
```

continues on next page

13. Return to PHP to complete the main conditional:

```php
<?php } // End of submission
→ IF. ?>
```

14. Finish the HTML page:

```html
</body>
</html>
```

15. Save the file as **login.php**, place it in the proper directory for your PHP-enabled server, and test it in your browser **Ⓐ**, **Ⓑ**, and **Ⓒ**.

TIP As of PHP 5.3, the `fgetcsv()` function takes another optional argument: the character used to escape problematic characters. Naturally, the default escape character is the backslash.

TIP If a line is blank, `fgetcsv()` returns an array containing a single null value.

Ⓐ The login form takes a username and password.

Ⓑ If the submitted username and password match those previously recorded, the user sees this message.

Ⓒ The result if the user submits a username and password combination that doesn't match the values previously recorded.

Review and Pursue

If you have any problems with the review questions or the pursue prompts, turn to the book's supporting forum (www.LarryUllman.com/forums/).

Review

- What version of PHP are you running?

- What steps did you need to take to make a file or directory writable for your server?

- What is the *web root directory* (as a concept)? What is the web root directory for your website (whether on your own computer or on a live server)?

- What are two ways you can write data to a file?

- How do you append new data to existing files (as opposed to replacing any existing data)?

- How do you ensure that new data is placed on its own line?

- In order for a form to accept file uploads, what attributes must the opening **form** tag have?

- In what variable will a PHP script be able to access an uploaded file? What function is used to move the file to its final destination on the server?

- How does the **fgetcsv()** function differ from **file()** or **file_get_contents()**?

- Is **sha1()** a secure method for hashing data?

Pursue

- Check out some of the other filesystem-related functions in the PHP manual (start at www.php.net/manual/en/ref.filesystem.php).

- Modify **add_quote.php** so that it confirms that the **quotes.txt** file exists prior to checking if it's writable.

- Make the text area in **add_quote.php** sticky.

- Change **add_quote.php** so that it takes the quotation and the attribution as separate inputs and writes them separately to the text file. Then modify **view_quote.php** so that it retrieves and displays both pieces of data.

- Modify **view_quote.php** so that it displays two random quotations.

- Update **upload_file.php**, making it confirm that the **uploads** directory is writable.

- View the PHP manual page for the **glob()** function to see what it can do and how to use it.

- Update **list_dir.php** to display other information about the files in a directory.

- Create a system to guarantee unique usernames in **register.php**. Hint: Before you attempt to create the directory, use PHP to check your list of existing usernames for a match to the just-registered name. If no match is found, the new name is acceptable. If the username is already in use, then PHP can create an error message requesting a new username.

- Use the combination of writing to and reading from text files, plus either sessions or cookies, to create a real registration and login system.

- When you're ready for a bigger challenge, rewrite **register.php** and **login.php** to use the **password_hash()** and **password_verify()** functions.

Intro to Databases

The Internet wouldn't be what it is today if not for the existence of databases. In fact, PHP probably wouldn't be as popular or as useful if not for its built-in support for numerous types of databases. This chapter will use MySQL as the example database management system (DBMS). Although MySQL—which is available for most platforms—may not be as powerful as the highest-end commercial database servers, it has enough speed and functionality for most purposes. And its price—free for most uses—makes it the common choice for web development.

This chapter walks through the development of a simple database for running a basic blog. Although you'll learn enough here to get started working with databases, you'll want to visit Appendix B, "Resources and Next Steps," once you've finished this chapter to find some references where you can learn more about the topic.

Introduction to SQL

A *database* is a collection of tables (made up of columns and rows) that stores information. Most databases are created, updated, and read using SQL (Structured Query Language). SQL has surprisingly few commands (**Table 12.1** lists the seven most important), which is both a blessing and a curse.

SQL was designed to be written a lot like the English language, which makes it very user friendly. But SQL is still extremely capable, even if it takes some thought to create more elaborate SQL statements with only the handful of available terms. In this chapter, you'll learn how to execute all the fundamental SQL commands.

For people new to PHP, confusion can stem from PHP's relationship to HTML (i.e., PHP can be used to generate HTML, but PHP code is never executed in the browser). When you incorporate a database, the relationships can become even fuzzier. The process is quite simple: PHP is used to send SQL statements to the database application, where they are executed. The result of the execution—the creation of a table, the insertion of a record, the retrieval of some records, or even an error—is then returned by the database to the PHP script **A**.

With that in mind, PHP's `mysqli_query()` function will be the most-used tool in this chapter. It sends an SQL command to MySQL:

```
$result = mysqli_query(database
→ connection, SQL command);
```

TABLE 12.1 Common SQL Commands

Command	Purpose
ALTER	Modifies an existing table
CREATE	Creates a database or table
DELETE	Deletes records from a table
DROP	Deletes a database or table
INSERT	Adds records to a table
SELECT	Retrieves records from a table
UPDATE	Updates records in a table

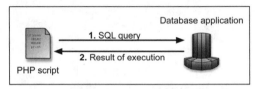

A PHP will be used to send an SQL statement to MySQL. MySQL will execute the statement and return the result to the PHP script.

MySQL Support in PHP

Support for the MySQL database server has to be built into PHP in order for you to use PHP's MySQL-specific functions. For most PHP installations, this should already be the case. You can confirm support for MySQL by calling the `phpinfo()` function, which reveals details of your installation.

When working through this chapter, if you see an error message saying ... *undefined function mysqli_...*, this means the version of PHP you're using doesn't have support for MySQL (or you misspelled the function name, which you should also check).

Enabling support for MySQL takes a little effort, but it can be done if you have administrative-level control over your server. For more information, see the PHP manual.

I start this chapter with this prologue because the addition of SQL and MySQL to the web development process will complicate things. When problems occur—and undoubtedly they will—you'll need to know how to solve them.

When a PHP script that interacts with a MySQL database does not perform as expected, the first step is to determine if the problem is in the query itself—number 1 in Ⓐ—or in the results of the query—number 2 in Ⓐ. To take this step, you can start by printing out the query being executed, using code such as the following:

```
print $query;
```

Assuming that **$query** represents the complete SQL command, often containing the values of PHP variables, this one simple line will reveal to you the actual SQL statement being run.

Next, you would take the printed query and execute it using another application. The two most common options are

- The MySQL client Ⓑ, a command-line tool for interacting with MySQL
- phpMyAdmin Ⓒ, a PHP-based MySQL interface

One or both of these should be provided to you by your hosting company or the software you installed on your own computer. For a demonstration of using each, see Appendix A, "Installation and Configuration."

TIP Technically, a DBMS, or database application, is the software that interfaces with the database proper. However, a lot of people use the terms *database* and *DBMS* synonymously.

TIP Lots of other applications are available for interacting with MySQL aside from the MySQL client and phpMyAdmin. Some are free, and others cost. A quick search using Google for *MySQL*, *admin*, and your operating system should turn up some interesting results.

Ⓑ The MySQL client comes with the MySQL database software and can be used to execute queries without the need for a PHP script.

Ⓒ phpMyAdmin is perhaps the most popular software written in PHP. It provides a web-based interface for a MySQL database.

Connecting to MySQL

When you worked with text files in Chapter 11, "Files and Directories," you saw that some functions, such as **fwrite()** and **fgets()**, require that you first create a file pointer using **fopen()**. This pointer then acts as a reference to that open file. You use a similar process when working with databases. First, you have to establish a connection to the database server—in this case, MySQL. This connection is then used as the access point for any future commands. The syntax for connecting to a database is

```
$dbc = mysqli_connect(hostname,
→ username, password,
→ database_name);
```

The database connection—assigned to **$dbc** in this example—is normally established using at least four arguments: the host, which is almost always *localhost*; the username; the password for that username; and the database name.

If you're using a database through a hosting company, the company will most likely provide you with all of these values. If you're running MySQL on your own computer, see Appendix A to learn how you create a user and a database before proceeding.

Once you're finished working with a database, you can close the connection, just as you'd close an open file:

```
mysqli_close($dbc);
```

The PHP script will automatically close the database connection when the script terminates, but it's considered good form to formally close the connection once it's no longer needed.

For the first example of this chapter, you'll write a simple script that attempts to connect to the MySQL database. Once you have this connection working, you can proceed through the rest of the chapter. Again, you'll need to already know the right hostname, username, password, and database values in order to execute this example. And the database will need to have been created!

To connect to a MySQL database:

1. Begin a new PHP document in your text editor or IDE, to be named **mysqli_connect.php** (Script 12.1):

```
<!doctype html>
<html lang="en">
<head>
  <meta charset="utf-8">
  <title>Connect to MySQL</title>
</head>
<body>
```

2. Start the section of PHP code:

```
<?php // Script 12.1 - mysqli_
connect.php
```

3. Connect to MySQL, and report on the results:

```
if ($dbc = mysqli_
connect('localhost', 'username',
'password', 'myblog')) {
  print '<p>Successfully
  → connected to the database!
  → </p>';
  mysqli_close($dbc);
} else {
  print '<p style="color:red;">
  → Could not connect to the
  → database.</p>';
}
```

Script 12.1 Being able to connect to the MySQL database is the most important step. This script tests that process.

```
1   <!doctype html>
2   <html lang="en">
3   <head>
4       <meta charset="utf-8">
5       <title>Connect to MySQL</title>
6   </head>
7   <body>
8   <?php // Script 12.1 - mysqli_connect.
    php
9   /* This script connects to the MySQL
    database. */
10
11  // Attempt to connect to MySQL and print
    out messages:
12  if ($dbc = mysqli_
    connect('localhost', 'username',
    'password', 'myblog')) {
13
14      print '<p>Successfully connected to
        the database!</p>';
15
16      mysqli_close($dbc); // Close the
        connection.
17
18  } else {
19
20      print '<p style="color: red;">Could
        not connect to the database.</p>';
21
22  }
23
24  ?>
25  </body>
26  </html>
```

By placing the connection attempt as the condition in an **if-else** statement, you make it easy to report on whether the connection worked.

This chapter will continue to use *username* and *password* as values. For your scripts, you'll need to replace these with the values provided by your web host or set them when you add a user using the steps outlined in Appendix A.

The database being used in this chapter is named *myblog*. It will need to be created prior to executing this script, either by your hosting company or by yourself (see Appendix A).

If a connection was established, a positive message is printed and then the connection is closed. Otherwise, a message stating the opposite is printed, and there is no need to close the database connection (because it wasn't opened).

4. Complete the PHP code and the HTML page:

```
?>
</body>
</html>
```

continues on next page

5. Save the file as `mysqli_connect.php`, place it in the proper directory of your PHP-enabled computer, and test it in your browser **Ⓐ**.

If you see results like those in **Ⓑ**, double-check the username and password values. They should match up with those provided to you by your web host or those you used to create the user. You can always test your connection username and password by using them in the MySQL client (again, see Appendix A).

If you see *call to undefined function mysqli_connect...*, your version of PHP doesn't support MySQL (see the "MySQL Support in PHP" sidebar).

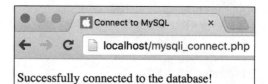

Successfully connected to the database!

Ⓐ If PHP has support for MySQL and the username/password/host/database combination you used was correct, you should see this simple message.

● ● ●	Connect to MySQL	×		
← → C	localhost/mysqli_connect.php			☆

(!) Warning: mysqli_connect(): (HY000/1045): Access denied for user 'username'@'localhost' (using password: YES) in /Users/larry/Sites/mysqli_connect.php on line *12*

Call Stack

#	Time	Memory	Function	Location
1	0.0001	366448	{main}( )	.../mysqli_connect.php:0
2	0.0001	366448	mysqli_connect ( )	.../mysqli_connect.php:12

Could not connect to the database.

Ⓑ If PHP couldn't connect to MySQL, you'll probably see something like this. The warning message may or may not appear, depending on your error management settings.

TIP The *localhost* value is used as the hostname when both the PHP script and the MySQL database reside on the same computer. You can use PHP to connect to a MySQL database running on a remote server by changing the hostname in the PHP script and creating the proper permissions in MySQL.

TIP PHP has built-in support for most databases, including MySQL, SQLite, MongoDB, Oracle, and PostgreSQL. If you're using a type of database that doesn't have direct support—for example, Access or SQL Server—you'll need to use PHP's ODBC (Open Database Connectivity) functions along with that database's ODBC drivers to interface with the database.

TIP The combination of using PHP and MySQL is so common that you may run across terms that identify servers configured with both PHP and MySQL: *LAMP*, *MAMP*, and *WAMP*. These stand for the operating system—Linux, Mac OS X, or Windows—plus the Apache web server, the MySQL DBMS, and PHP.

TIP You'll be working with MySQL, so all the functions you use in this chapter are MySQL specific. For example, to connect to a database in MySQL the proper function is `mysqli_connect()`, but if you're using PostgreSQL, you'd instead write `pg_connect()`. If you aren't using a MySQL DBMS, use the PHP manual (available through www.PHP.net) to find the appropriate function names.

TIP You don't have to select the database when connecting, but it's more common to do so. The most likely exception is if your application uses multiple databases.

TIP You haven't done so in these examples, but in general it's a good idea to set your database information—hostname, username, password, and database name—as variables or constants. Then you can plug them into the appropriate functions. By doing so, you can separate the database specifics from the functionality of the script, allowing you to easily port that code to other applications.

MySQL Error Handling

Before this chapter gets too deep into working with MySQL, it would be best to discuss some error-handling techniques up front. Common errors you'll encounter are

- Failure to connect to MySQL
- Inability to run a query
- No results returned by a query
- Data not inserted into a table

Experience will teach you why these errors normally occur, but immediately seeing what the problem is when running your scripts can save you much debugging time. To have your scripts give informative reports about errors that occur, use the `mysqli_error()` function. This function returns a textual version of the error that the MySQL server returned. It needs to be provided with the database connection: **$dbc** in this chapter:

```
print mysqli_error($dbc);
```

Connection errors are slightly different, however. To report upon those, invoke `mysqli_connect_error()`. This function does not take any arguments:

```
print mysqli_connect_error();
```

Along with these functions, you may want to use some PHP tools for handling errors. For beginners, you can start with the error suppression operator (@). When used preceding a function name, it suppresses any error messages or warnings the function might invoke:

```
@function_name();
```

Database Permissions

Database permissions are a bit more complicated than file permissions, but you need to understand this: Different types of users can be assigned different database capabilities. For example, one DBMS user may be able to create new databases and delete existing ones (you may have dozens of databases in your DBMS), but a lower-level user may only be able to create and modify tables within a single database. The most basic user may just be able to read from, but not modify, tables.

If you're using PHP and MySQL for a live hosted site, the hosting company will most likely give you the second type of access—control over a single database but not the DBMS itself—and establish the initial database for you. If you're working on your own server or have administrative access, you should have the capability to create new users and databases.

Script 12.2 By adding error control to the script (the @ symbol and the `mysqli_error()` function), you can more purposefully address problems that occur.

```
1   <!doctype html>
2   <html lang="en">
3   <head>
4       <meta charset="utf-8">
5       <title>Connect to MySQL</title>
6   </head>
7   <body>
8   <?php // Script 12.2 - mysqli_connect.
    php #2
9   /* This script connects to the MySQL
    database. */
10
11  // Attempt to connect to MySQL and print
    out messages:
12  if ($dbc = @mysqli_
    connect('localhost', 'username',
    'password', 'myblog')) {
13
14      print '<p>Successfully connected to
        the database!</p>';
15
16      mysqli_close($dbc); // Close the
        connection.
17
18  } else {
19
20      print '<p style="color:
        red;">Could not connect to the
        database:<br>' . mysqli_connect_
        error() . '.</p>';
21
22  }
23
24  ?>
25  </body>
26  </html>
```

Note that this operator doesn't stop the error from happening; it just prevents the message from being immediately displayed. You'd use it in situations where you intend to handle the error yourself, should one occur. This is an important point: The error still happens, so you should use the error suppression operator only when you're handling the error in another way.

To use error handling:

1. Open `mysqli_connect.php` (Script 12.1) in your text editor or IDE.

2. Suppress any PHP errors created by the `mysqli_connect()` function by changing the `if` conditional as follows (**Script 12.2**):

   ```
   if ($dbc = @mysqli_connect
   → ('localhost', 'username',
   → 'password', 'myblog')) {
   ```

   Rather than have PHP print out an error message when the `mysqli_connect()` function backfires (B in the previous section, "Connecting to MySQL"), the message will be suppressed here using the @ symbol. The errors still occur, but they're handled by the change made in the next step.

3. Add the `mysqli_error()` function to the `print` statement in the `else` section:

   ```
   print '<p style="color:
   → red;">Could not connect to
   → MySQL:<br>' . mysqli_connect_
   → error() . '.</p>';
   ```

   continues on next page

Instead of printing a message or relying on whatever error PHP kicks out (see **B** in the previous section, "Connecting to MySQL"), the script now prints the MySQL error within this context. You accomplish this by printing some HTML concatenated with the `mysqli_connect_error()` function.

You should note that the `mysqli_connect_error()` function is not provided with the database connection—`$dbc`—as an argument, since no database connection was made.

4. Save the file, and test it again in your browser **A**.

If there was a problem, this result now looks better than what would have been shown previously. If the script connected, the result is like that shown in **A** in the previous section, "Connecting to MySQL," because neither of the error-management tools is involved.

A Using PHP's error-control functions, you can adjust how errors are handled.

> **TIP** In this chapter, error messages are revealed to assist in the debugging process. Live websites should not have this level of explicit error messages shown to the user.

> **TIP** The error suppression operator should be used only in very limited situations—namely, when you're handling the error in other ways. As you build your PHP skills, you'll learn more sophisticated approaches for error management, such as using exceptions and writing your own error handler.

> **TIP** You may also see code where `die()`, which is an alias for `exit()`, is called when a connection error occurs. The thinking is that since a database connection cannot be made, there's no point in continuing. In my opinion, that's too heavy-handed an approach.

Creating a Table

Once you've created and selected the initial database, you can begin creating individual tables in it. A database can consist of multiple tables, but in this simple example you'll create one table in which all the chapter's data will be stored.

To create a table in the database, you'll use SQL—the language that databases understand. Because SQL is a lot like spoken English, the proper query to create a new table reads like this:

```
CREATE TABLE tablename (column1
→ definition, column2 definition,
→ etc.)
```

For each column, separated by commas, you first indicate the column name and then the column type. Common types are **TEXT**, **VARCHAR** (a variable number of characters), **DATETIME**, and **INT** (integer).

Because it's highly recommended that you create a column that acts as the *primary key* (a column used to refer to each row), a simple **CREATE** statement could be

```
CREATE TABLE my_table (
id INT PRIMARY KEY,
information TEXT
)
```

A table's primary key is a special column of unique values that is used to refer to the table's rows. The database makes an index of this column in order to more quickly navigate through the table. A table can have only one primary key, which you normally set up as an automatically incremented column of integers. The first row has a key of 1, the second has a key of 2, and so forth. Referring back to the key always retrieves the values for that row.

Finally, it's a good idea to establish the default character set when creating a table (or a database). This is accomplished by adding **CHARACTER SET** *name* at the end of the table creation statement:

```
CREATE TABLE my_table (
id INT PRIMARY KEY,
information TEXT
) CHARACTER SET utf8
```

Like the **charset** meta tag in HTML, this is merely an indication of what encoding to use for the stored characters. You almost certainly want to use **utf8** here.

You can visit the MySQL website for more information on SQL, column definitions, and character sets. By following the directions in this section, though, you should be able to accomplish some basic database tasks. The table that you'll create in this example is represented by **Table 12.2**.

In this example, you'll create the database table that will be used to store information submitted via an HTML form. In the next section of the chapter, you'll write the script that inserts the submitted data into the table created here.

To create the table with PHP, you use the **mysqli_query()** function to execute a **CREATE TABLE** SQL command:

```
mysqli_query($dbc, 'CREATE TABLE
→ entries...');
```

Alternatively, you can execute that same SQL command via another interface, such as the command-line MySQL client or the web-based phpMyAdmin.

TABLE 12.1 The ENTRIES Table

Column Name	Column Type
id	Positive, non-null, automatically incrementing integer
Title	Text up to 100 characters in length
Entry	Text of any length
date_entered	A timestamp including both the date and the time the row was added

```
1   <!doctype html>
2   <html lang="en">
3   <head>
4       <meta charset="utf-8">
5       <title>Create a Table</title>
6   </head>
7   <body>
8   <?php // Script 12.3 - create_table.php
9   /* This script connects to the MySQL
    server, selects the database, and
    creates a table. */
10
11  // Connect and select:
12  if ($dbc = @mysqli_connect('localhost',
    'username', 'password', 'myblog')) {
13
14      // Define the query:
15      $query = 'CREATE TABLE entries (
16  id INT UNSIGNED NOT NULL AUTO_
    INCREMENT PRIMARY KEY,
17  title VARCHAR(100) NOT NULL,
18  entry TEXT NOT NULL,
19  date_entered DATETIME NOT NULL
20  ) CHARACTER SET utf8 ';
21
22      // Execute the query:
23      if (@mysqli_query($dbc, $query)) {
24          print '<p>The table has been
            created!</p>';
25      } else {
26          print '<p style="color:
            red;">Could not create the
            table because:<br>' . mysqli_
            error($dbc) . '.</p><p>The
            query being run was: ' . $query
            . '.</p>';
27      }
28
29      mysqli_close($dbc); // Close the
        connection.
30
31  } else { // Connection failure.
32      print '<p style="color: red;">Could
        not connect to the database:<br>' .
        mysqli_connect_error() . '.</p>';
33  }
34  ?>
35  </body>
36  </html>
```

To create a new table:

1. Begin a new PHP document in your text editor or IDE, to be named **create_table.php** (Script 12.3):

   ```
   <!doctype html>
   <html lang="en">
   <head>
     <meta charset="utf-8">
     <title>Create a Table</title>
   </head>
   <body>
   ```

2. Begin a section of PHP code:

   ```
   <?php // Script 12.3 - create_
   table.php
   ```

3. Connect to the MySQL database:

   ```
   if ($dbc = @mysqli_connect
   → ('localhost', 'username',
   → 'password', 'myblog')) {
   ```

4. Define the query for creating the table:

   ```
   $query = 'CREATE TABLE entries (
   id INT UNSIGNED NOT NULL
   → AUTO_INCREMENT PRIMARY KEY,
   title VARCHAR(100) NOT NULL,
   entry TEXT NOT NULL,
   date_entered DATETIME NOT NULL
   ) CHARACTER SET utf8';
   ```

   First, to create a new table, you write **CREATE TABLE** *tablename* (where *table-name* is replaced by the desired table name). Then, within parentheses, you list every column you want, with each column separated by a comma. Your table and column names should be alphanumeric, with no spaces.

   continues on next page

The first column in the table is named **id;** it's an unsigned integer (**INT UNSIGNED**—which means that it can be only a positive whole number). By including the words **NOT NULL**, you indicate that this column must have a value for each row. The values automatically increase by 1 for each row added (**AUTO INCREMENT**) and stand as the primary key.

The next two columns consist of text. One, named **title**, is limited to 100 characters. The second, **entry**, can be vast in size. Each of these fields is also marked as **NOT NULL**, making them required fields.

Finally, the **date_entered** column is a timestamp that marks when each record was added to the table.

5. Execute the query:

```
if (@mysqli_query($query, $dbc))
{
  print '<p>The table has been
  → created.</p>';
} else {
  print '<p style="color:
  → red;">Could not create the
  → table because:<br>' . mysqli_
  → error($dbc) . '.</p><p>The
  → query being run was: ' .
  → $query . '</p>';
}
```

To create the table, call the **mysqli_query()** function using the database connection as the first argument and the query variable—**$query**—as the second. If a problem occurred, the MySQL error is printed, along with the value of the **$query** variable. This last step—printing the actual query being executed—is a particularly useful debugging technique 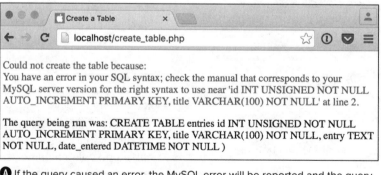.

Ⓐ If the query caused an error, the MySQL error will be reported and the query itself displayed (for debugging purposes).

The table has been created!

B If all went well, all you'll see is this message.

6. Close the database connection, and complete the **$dbc** conditional:

```
mysqli_close($dbc);
} else { // Connection failure.
  print '<p style="color:
  ⇢ red;">Could not connect to
  ⇢ the database:<br>' . mysqli_
  ⇢ connect_error() . '.</p>';
```

7. Complete the PHP code and the HTML page:

```
?>
</body>
</html>
```

8. Save the script as **create_table.php**, place it in the proper directory for your PHP-enabled server, and test it in your browser **B**.

> **TIP** It's not necessary to write your SQL keywords in all capital letters as I do here, but doing so helps distinguish the SQL terms from the table and column names.

> **TIP** On larger web applications, I highly recommended that you place the database connection code in a separate file, located outside the web directory. Then, each page that requires the database can include this external file. You'll see an example of this in Chapter 13, "Putting It All Together."

> **TIP** The mysqli_query() function returns TRUE if a query was successfully run on a database. That result doesn't necessarily mean the desired result occurred.

> **TIP** This chapter presents the basics of MySQL- and SQL-related knowledge (including column types). You'll want to check out other resources—listed in Appendix B—once you're comfortable with the fundamentals.

> **TIP** You wouldn't normally use a PHP script to create a table, just as you wouldn't normally create a database using a PHP script, but when you're just starting with MySQL, this is an easy way to achieve the desired results.

Inserting Data into a Database

As mentioned, this database will be used as a simple blog, an online journal. Blog entries—consisting of a title and text—will be added to the database using one page and then displayed on another page.

The last script created the table, which consists of four columns: **id**, **title**, **entry**, and **date_entered**. The process of adding information to a table is similar to creating the table itself in terms of which PHP functions you use, but the SQL query is different. To insert records, use the **INSERT** SQL command with either of the following syntaxes:

```
INSERT INTO tablename VALUES
→ (value1, value2, value3, etc.)
INSERT INTO tablename
→ (column1_name, column2_name)
→ VALUES (value1, value2)
```

The query begins with **INSERT INTO tablename**. Then you can either specify which columns you're inserting values for or not name the columns explicitly. The former is more specific and is therefore preferred, but it can be tedious if you're populating a slew of columns. In either case, you must be certain to list the right number of total values and the right type of value for each column.

The values are placed within parentheses, with each value separated by a comma. Non-numeric values—strings and dates—need to be quoted, whereas numbers do not:

```
INSERT INTO example (name, age)
→ VALUES ('Jonah', 1)
```

The query is executed using the **mysqli_query()** function. Because **INSERT** queries can be complex, it makes sense to assign each query to a variable and send that variable to the **mysqli_query()** function (as previously demonstrated).

To demonstrate, let's create a page that adds blog entries to the database. Like many of the examples in the preceding chapter, this one will both display and handle the HTML form. Before getting into the example, though, I'll say that this script knowingly has a security hole in it; it'll be explained and fixed in the next section of the chapter.

Building on This Example

The focus in this chapter is on explaining and demonstrating the basics of using PHP with MySQL. This also includes the core components of SQL. However, this chapter's examples do a few things that you wouldn't want to do in a real site, such as allow anyone to insert, edit, and delete database records.

In the next chapter, a different example will be developed that is also database driven. That example will use cookies to restrict what users can do with the site.

To enter data into a database from an HTML form:

1. Begin a new PHP document in your text editor or IDE, to be named **add_entry.php** (Script 12.4):

```
<!doctype html>
<html lang="en">
<head>
  <meta charset="utf-8">
  <title>Add a Blog Entry</title>
</head>
<body>
<h1>Add a Blog Entry</h1>
```

continues on next page

Script 12.4 The query statement for adding information to a database is straightforward enough, but be sure to match the number of values in parentheses to the number of columns in the database table.

```
1    <!doctype html>
2    <html lang="en">
3    <head>
4        <meta charset="utf-8">
5        <title>Add a Blog Entry</title>
6    </head>
7    <body>
8    <h1>Add a Blog Entry</h1>
9    <?php // Script 12.4 - add_entry.php
10   /* This script adds a blog entry to the database. */
11
12   if ($_SERVER['REQUEST_METHOD'] == 'POST') { // Handle the form.
13
14       // Validate the form data:
15       $problem = FALSE;
16       if (!empty($_POST['title']) && !empty($_POST['entry'])) {
17           $title = trim(strip_tags($_POST['title']));
18           $entry = trim(strip_tags($_POST['entry']));
19       } else {
20           print '<p style="color: red;">Please submit both a title and an entry.</p>';
21           $problem = TRUE;
22       }
23
24       if (!$problem) {
25
26           // Connect and select:
27           $dbc = mysqli_connect('localhost', 'username', 'password', 'myblog');
28
```

code continues on next page

2. Create the initial PHP section, and check for the form submission:

```php
<?php // Script 12.4 -
→ add_entry.php
if ($_SERVER['REQUEST_METHOD'] ==
→ 'POST') {
```

3. Validate the form data:

```php
$problem = FALSE;
if (!empty($_POST['title']) &&
!empty($_POST['entry'])) {
  $title = trim(strip_tags
  → ($_POST['title']));
  $entry = trim(strip_tags
  → ($_POST['entry']));
} else {
  print '<p style="color:
  → red;">Please submit both a
  → title and an entry.</p>';
  $problem = TRUE;
}
```

Before you use the form data in an **INSERT** query, it ought to be validated. Just a minimum of validation is used here, guaranteeing that some values are provided. If so, new variables are assigned those values, after trimming away extraneous spaces and applying **strip_tags()** (to prevent cross-site scripting attacks and other potential problems). If either of the values was empty, an error message is printed Ⓐ, and the **$problem** flag variable is set to TRUE (because there is a problem).

Script 12.4 *continued*

```
29        // Define the query:
30        $query = "INSERT INTO entries (id, title, entry, date_entered) VALUES (0,
          '$title', '$entry', NOW())";
31
32        // Execute the query:
33        if (@mysqli_query($dbc, $query)) {
34            print '<p>The blog entry has been added!</p>';
35        } else {
36            print '<p style="color: red;">Could not add the entry because:<br>' . mysqli_
              error($dbc) . '.</p><p>The query being run was: ' . $query . '</p>';
37        }
38
39        mysqli_close($dbc); // Close the connection.
40
41    } // No problem!
42
43  } // End of form submission IF.
44
45  // Display the form:
46  ?>
47  <form action="add_entry.php" method="post">
48      <p>Entry Title: <input type="text" name="title" size="40" maxsize="100"></p>
49      <p>Entry Text: <textarea name="entry" cols="40" rows="5"></textarea></p>
50      <input type="submit" name="submit" value="Post This Entry!">
51  </form>
52  </body>
53  </html>
```

Add a Blog Entry   ×

localhost/add_entry.php

Add a Blog Entry

Please submit both a title and an entry.

Entry Title:

Entry Text:

Post This Entry!

Ⓐ The PHP script performs some basic form validation so that empty records are not inserted into the database.

4. Connect to the database:

```
if (!$problem) {
  $dbc = mysqli_connect
  → ('localhost', 'username',
  → 'password', 'myblog');
```

Having basically valid data, it's safe to add the record to the database, so a connection must be established. At this point, if you're running these examples in order, I'll assume you have a working connection and selection process down, so I'll dispense with all the conditionals and error reporting (mostly to shorten the script). If you have problems connecting to and selecting the database, apply the code already outlined in the chapter.

5. Define the **INSERT** query:

```
$query = "INSERT INTO entries
→ (id, title, entry, date_
→ entered) VALUES (0, '$title',
→ '$entry', NOW())";
```

The query begins with the necessary **INSERT INTO** *tablename* code. Then it lists the columns for which values will be submitted. After that is **VALUES**, followed by four values—one for each column, in order—separated by commas. When assigning this query to the **$query** variable, use double quotation marks so that the values of the variables will be automatically inserted by PHP. The **$title** and **$entry** variables are strings, so they must be placed within single quotation marks in the query itself.

continues on next page

Because the **id** column has been set to **AUTO_INCREMENT**, you can use 0 as the value and MySQL will automatically use the next logical value for that column. You can also use the special keyword **NULL**. To set the value of the **date_entered** column, use the MySQL **NOW()** function. It inserts the current time as that value.

6. Run the query on the database:

```
if (@mysqli_query($dbc, $query)) {
  print '<p>The blog entry has
  → been added!</p>';
} else {
  print '<p style="color:
  → red;"> Could not add the
  → entry because:<br />' .
  → mysqli_ error($dbc) . '.
  → </p><p>The query being run
  → was: ' . $query . '</p>';
}
```

The query, once defined, is run using the **mysqli_query()** function. By calling this function as the condition of an **if-else** statement, you can print simple messages indicating the result of the query execution.

As an essential debugging tool, if the query didn't run properly, the MySQL error and the query being run are both printed to the browser **B**.

7. Close the database connection, the **$problem** conditional, and complete the main conditional and the PHP section:

```
    mysqli_close($dbc);

  } // No problem!
} // End of form submission IF.
?>
```

From here on out, the form will be displayed.

8. Create the form:

```
<form action="add_entry.php"
→ method="post">
  <p>Entry Title: <input type=
  → "text" name="title" size="40"
  → maxsize="100"></p>
  <p>Entry Text: <textarea
  → name="entry" cols="40"
  → rows="5"></textarea></p>
  <input type="submit" name=
  → "submit" value="Post This
  → Entry!">
</form>
```

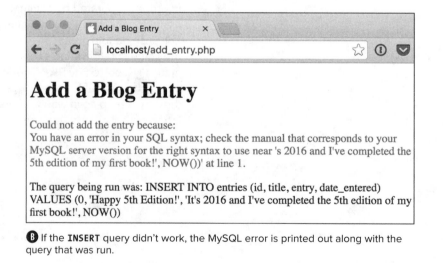

B If the **INSERT** query didn't work, the MySQL error is printed out along with the query that was run.

C This is the form for adding an entry to the database.

D If the **INSERT** query ran properly, a message is printed and the form is displayed again.

The HTML form is very simple, requiring only a title for the blog entry and the entry itself. As a good rule of thumb, use the same name for your form inputs as for the corresponding column names in the database. Doing so makes errors less likely.

9. Finish the HTML page:

   ```
   </body>
   </html>
   ```

10. Save the script as **add_entry.php**, place it in the proper directory for your PHP-enabled server, and test it in your browser **C** and **D**.

    You should probably avoid using apostrophes in your form values or you might see results like those in **B**. You'll find the explanation and solution in the next section.

TIP To retrieve the automatically incremented number created for an AUTO_INCREMENT column, call the `mysqli_insert_id()` function.

TIP Because of the way auto-incrementing primary keys work, this query is also fine:

```
INSERT INTO entries (title, entry,
→ date_entered) VALUES ('$title',
→ '$entry', NOW())";
```

TIP MySQL allows you to insert several records at once, using this format:

```
INSERT INTO tablename
→ (column1_name, column2_name)
→ VALUES (value1, value2), (value3,
→ value4);
```

Most other database applications don't support this construct, though.

Securing Query Data

As I mentioned in the introduction to the section "Inserting Data into a Database," the code as written has a pretty bad security hole in it. As it stands, if someone submits text that contains an apostrophe, that data will break the SQL query 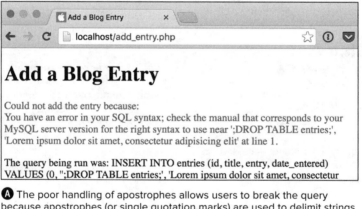 (security concerns aside, it's also a pretty bad bug). The result is obviously undesirable, but why is it insecure?

If malicious users know they can break a query by typing an apostrophe, they may try to run their own queries using this hole. If someone submitted *';DROP TABLE entries;* as the blog post title, the resulting query would be

```
INSERT INTO entries
→ (id, title, entry, date_entered)
→ VALUES (0, '';DROP TABLE
→ entries;', '<entry text>', NOW())
```

The initial apostrophe in the provided entry title has the effect of completing the blog title value part of the query. The semicolon then terminates the **INSERT** query itself. This will make the original query syntactically invalid. Then the database will be provided with a second query—**DROP TABLE entries**—with the hope that it will be executed when the original **INSERT** query fails.

A The poor handling of apostrophes allows users to break the query because apostrophes (or single quotation marks) are used to delimit strings used in queries.

This is known as an *SQL injection attack*, but fortunately it's easy to prevent.

To do so, send potentially insecure data to be used in a query through the `mysqli_real_escape_string()` function. This function will escape—preface with a backslash—any potentially harmful characters, making the data safe to use in a query:

```
$var = mysqli_real_escape_string
→ ($dbc, $var);
```

For this function to work properly, the character set needs to be established for the communications:

```
mysqli_set_charset($dbc, 'utf8')
```

This code effectively serves the same purpose as the **charset** meta tag in HTML: indicating the character set—or *character encoding*—of the data to follow. The previous code does assume your PHP script, database, and table are all using UTF-8, which they really ought to be by default (and was specifically established on the table when it was created, just to be certain).

Let's apply this function to the preceding script. Because both `mysqli_real_escape_string()` and `mysqli_set_charset()` require the database connection, the logic of the script must be tweaked a bit.

Showing MySQL Errors

Even if MySQL doesn't execute an injected SQL command (normally MySQL will only run a single SQL query sent through the `mysqli_query()` function), hackers will provide bad characters in form data in the hopes that the syntactically broken query generates a database error. By seeing the database error, the hacker seeks to gain knowledge about the database that can be used for malicious purposes. For this reason, it's imperative that a live site never reveal the actual MySQL errors or queries being executed. The scripts in this chapter do so only for your own debugging purposes.

To secure query data:

1. Open **add_entry.php** (Script 12.4) in your text editor or IDE, if it is not already open.

2. Update the assignment of the **$title** and **$entry** variables to read (**Script 12.5**) as follows:

```
$title = mysqli_real_escape_
→ string($dbc, trim(strip_tags
→ ($_POST['title'])));
$entry = mysqli_real_escape_
→ string($dbc, trim(strip_tags
→ ($_POST['entry'])));
```

These two lines will greatly improve the security and functionality of the script. For both posted variables, their values are first trimmed and stripped of tags, then sent through **mysqli_real_escape_string()**. The result will be safe to use in the query.

If the application of three functions to one variable is too confusing for you, you can separate the code into discrete steps:

```
$title = $_POST['title'];
$title = trim(strip_tags
→ ($title));
$title = mysqli_real_escape_
→ string($dbc, $title);
```

3. Move the database connection code—line 27 in Script 12.4—to above the validation lines.

The database connection should be established within the form handling code, but before **$problem = FALSE;**.

continues on page 370

Script 12.5 To better secure the web application and the database, the **mysqli_real_escape_string()** function is applied to the form data used in the query.

```
1    <!doctype html>
2    <html lang="en">
3    <head>
4       <meta charset="utf-8">
5       <title>Add a Blog Entry</title>
6    </head>
7    <body>
8    <h1>Add a Blog Entry</h1>
9    <?php // Script 12.5 - add_entry.php #2
10   /* This script adds a blog entry to the database. It now does so securely! */
11
12   if ($_SERVER['REQUEST_METHOD'] == 'POST') { // Handle the form.
13
```

code continues on next page

```
14          // Connect and select:
15      $dbc = mysqli_connect('localhost', 'username', 'password', 'myblog');
16
17      //Set the character set:
18      mysqli_set_charset($dbc, 'utf8');
20      // Validate and secure the form data:
21      $problem = FALSE;
22      if (!empty($_POST['title']) && !empty($_POST['entry'])) {
23          $title = mysqli_real_escape_string($dbc, trim(strip_tags($_POST['title'])));
24          $entry = mysqli_real_escape_string($dbc, trim(strip_tags($_POST['entry'])));
25      } else {
26          print '<p style="color: red;">Please submit both a title and an entry.</p>';
27          $problem = TRUE;
28      }
29
30      if (!$problem) {
31
32          // Define the query:
33          $query = "INSERT INTO entries (id, title, entry, date_entered) VALUES (0, '$title',
            '$entry', NOW())";
34
35          // Execute the query:
36          if (@mysqli_query($dbc, $query)) {
37              print '<p>The blog entry has been added!</p>';
38          } else {
39              print '<p style="color: red;">Could not add the entry because:<br>' . mysqli_
                error($dbc) . '.</p><p>The query being run was: ' . $query . '</p>';
40          }
41
42      } // No problem!
43
44      mysqli_close($dbc); // Close the connection.
45
46  } // End of form submission IF.
47
48  // Display the form:
49  ?>
50  <form action="add_entry.php" method="post">
51      <p>Entry Title: <input type="text" name="title" size="40" maxsize="100"></p>
52      <p>Entry Text: <textarea name="entry" cols="40" rows="5"></textarea></p>
53      <input type="submit" name="submit" value="Post This Entry!">
54  </form>
55  </body>
56  </html>
```

4. Move the database closing code—line 39 in Script 12.4—to just before the close of the form submission conditional.

Because the database connection is opened first thing within the form handling conditional, the database connection should be closed as the last step within that same block.

5. After opening the database connection, identify the character set in use:

```
mysqli_set_charset($dbc, 'utf8');
```

This needs to be done before `mysqli_real_escape_string()` is invoked.

6. Save the script, place it on your PHP-enabled server, and test it in your browser **B** and **C**.

TIP PHP's `addslashes()` function works similarly to `mysqli_real_escape_string()` but is not nearly as secure.

B Now apostrophes in form data...

C ...will not cause problems.

Retrieving Data from a Database

The next process this chapter demonstrates is retrieving data from a populated table. You still use the `mysqli_query()` function to run the query, but retrieving data is slightly different than inserting data—you have to assign the query result to a variable and then use another function to fetch the data.

The basic syntax for retrieving data is the **SELECT** query:

```
SELECT what columns FROM what table
```

The easiest query for reading data from a table is

```
SELECT * FROM tablename
```

The asterisk is the equivalent of saying *every column*. If you require only certain columns to be returned, you can limit your query, like so:

```
SELECT name, email FROM users
```

That query requests that only the information from two columns—**name** and **email**—be gathered. Keep in mind that this structure doesn't limit what rows (or records) are returned, just what columns for those rows.

Another way to alter your query is to add a conditional restricting which rows are returned, accomplished using a **WHERE** clause:

```
SELECT * FROM users WHERE name=
→ 'Larry'
```

Here you want the information from every column in the table, but only from the rows where the **name** column is equal to *Larry*. This is a good example of how SQL uses only a few terms effectively and flexibly.

The main difference in retrieving data from a database as opposed to inserting data into a database is that you need to handle the query differently. You should first assign the results of the query to a variable:

```
$result = mysqli_query($dbc,
→ $query);
```

Just as **$dbc** is a reference to an open database connection, **$result** is a reference to a query result set. This variable is then provided to the **mysqli_fetch_array()** function, which retrieves the query results:

```
$row = mysqli_fetch_array($result);
```

The function fetches one row from the result set at a time, creating an array in the process. The array will use the selected column names as its indexes: **$row['name']**, **$row['email']**, and so on. As with any array, you must refer to the columns exactly as they're defined in the database (the keys are case-sensitive). So, in this example, you must use **$row['email']** instead of **$row['Email']**.

If the query will return multiple rows, execute the **mysqli_fetch_array()** function within a loop to access them all:

```
while ($row = mysqli_fetch_
→ array($result)) {
   // Do something with $row.
}
```

continues on next page

With each iteration of the loop, the next row of information from the query (referenced by **$result**) is assigned to an array named **$row**. This process continues until no more rows of information are found. Within the loop, you would do whatever you want with **$row**.

The best way to understand this new code is to try it. You'll write a script that retrieves the posts stored in the **entries** table and displays them . You may want to run through **add_entry.php** a couple of more times to build up the table first.

To retrieve data from a table:

1. Begin a new PHP document in your text editor or IDE, to be named **view_entries.php** (Script 12.6):

```
<!doctype html>
<html lang="en">
<head>
  <meta charset="utf-8">
  <title>View My Blog</title>
</head>
<body>
<h1>My Blog</h1>
```

A This dynamic web page uses PHP to pull data from a database.

Script 12.6 The SQL query for retrieving all data from a table is quite simple, but in order for PHP to access every returned record, you must loop through the results one row at a time.

```
1    <!doctype html>
2    <html lang="en">
3    <head>
4        <meta charset="utf-8">
5        <title>View My Blog</title>
6    </head>
7    <body>
8    <h1>My Blog</h1>
9    <?php // Script 12.6 - view_entries.php
10   /* This script retrieves blog entries from the database. */
11
12   // Connect and select:
13   $dbc = mysqli_connect('localhost', 'username', 'password', 'myblog');
14
```

code continues on next page

2. Begin a PHP section, and connect to the database:

```php
<?php // Script 12.6 - view_
→ entries.php
$dbc = mysqli_connect
→ ('localhost', 'username',
→ 'password', 'myblog');
```

3. Define the SELECT query:

```php
$query = 'SELECT * FROM entries
ORDER BY date_entered DESC';
```

This basic query tells the database that you'd like to fetch every column of every row in the **entries** table. The returned records should be sorted, as indicated by the **ORDER BY** clause, by the order in which they were entered (recorded in the **date_entered** column), starting with the most recent first. This last option is set by **DESC**, which is short for *descending*. If the query was **ORDER BY date_entered ASC**, the most recently added record would be retrieved last.

4. Run the query:

```php
if ($r = mysqli_query($dbc,
→ $query)) {
```

The **SELECT** query is run like any other. However, the result of the query is assigned to a **$result** (or, more tersely, **$r**) variable, which will be referenced later.

continues on next page

Script 12.6 *continued*

```
15  // Define the query:
16  $query = 'SELECT * FROM entries ORDER BY date_entered DESC';
17
18  if ($r = mysqli_query($dbc, $query)) { // Run the query.
19
20      // Retrieve and print every record:
21      while ($row = mysqli_fetch_array($r)) {
22          print "<p><h3>{$row['title']}</h3>
23          {$row['entry']}<br>
24          <a href=\"edit_entry.php?id={$row['id']}\">Edit</a>
25          <a href=\"delete_entry.php?id={$row['id']}\">Delete</a>
26          </p><hr>\n";
27      }
28
29  } else { // Query didn't run.
30      print '<p style="color: red;">Could not retrieve the data because:<br>' . mysqli_
        error($dbc) . '.</p><p>The query being run was: ' . $query . '</p>';
31  } // End of query IF.
32
33  mysqli_close($dbc); // Close the connection.
34
35  ?>
36  </body>
37  </html>
```

5. Print out the returned results:

```
while ($row = mysqli_fetch_
→ array($r)) {
  print "<p><h3>{$row['title']}
  → </h3>
  {$row['entry']}<br />
  <a href=\"edit_entry.php?id=
  → {$row['id']}\">Edit</a>
  <a href=\"delete_entry.php?
  → id={$row['id']}\">Delete</a>
  </p><hr />\n";
}
```

This loop sets the variable **$row** to an array containing the first record returned in **$r**. The loop then executes the following command (the **print** statement). Once the loop gets back to the beginning, it assigns the next row, if it exists. It continues to do this until there are no more rows of information to be obtained.

Within the loop, the array's keys are the names of the columns from the table—hence, **id**, **title**, and **entry** (it's not printing out the **date_entered**).

At the bottom of each post, two links are created: to **edit_entry.php** and **delete_entry.php**. These scripts will be written in the rest of the chapter. Each link passes the posting's database ID value along in the URL. That information will be necessary for those other two pages to edit and delete the blog posting accordingly.

My Blog

This is the newest post!

This is so absolutely amazing that I'm downright speechless!
Edit Delete

It's Another Test!

"Will these quotes and apostrophes cause problems?", you ask. I don't think so!
Edit Delete

Everyone loves Latin!

B Thanks to the **SELECT** query, which orders the returned records by the date they were entered, the most recently added entry is always listed first.

6. Handle the errors if the query didn't run:

```
} else { // Query didn't run.
  print '<p style="color: red;">
  → Could not retrieve the
  → data because:<br>' .
  → mysqli_error($dbc) . '.
  → </p> <p>The query being run
  → was: ' . $query . '</p>';
} // End of query IF.
```

If the query couldn't run on the database, it should be printed out, along with the MySQL error (for debugging purposes).

7. Close the database connection:

```
mysqli_close($dbc);
```

8. Complete the PHP section and the HTML page:

```
?>
</body>
</html>
```

9. Save the script as **view_entries.php**, place it in the proper directory for your PHP-enabled server, and test it in your browser Ⓐ.

10. If you want, add another record to the blog using the **add_entry.php** page (Script 12.6), and run this page again Ⓑ.

11. Check the source code of the page to see the dynamically generated links Ⓒ.

> **TIP** The `mysqli_fetch_array()` function takes another argument, which is a constant indicating what kind of array should be returned. MYSQLI_ASSOC returns an associative array, whereas MYSQLI_NUM returns a numerically indexed array.

> **TIP** The `mysqli_num_rows()` function returns the number of records returned by a SELECT query.

> **TIP** It's possible to paginate returned records so that 10 or 20 appear on each page (like the way Google works). Doing so requires more advanced coding than can be taught in this book, though. See my book *PHP and MySQL for Dynamic Web Sites: Visual QuickPro Guide* (Peachpit Press, 2012), or look online for code examples and tutorials.

```
8   <h1>My Blog</h1>
9   <p><h3>This is the newest post!</h3>
10                   This is so absolutely amazing that I'm down
11                   <a href="edit_entry.php?id=3">Edit</a>
12                   <a href="delete_entry.php?id=3">Delete</a>
13                   </p><hr>
14  <p><h3>It's Another Test!</h3>
15                   "Will these quotes and apostrophes cause pr
    so!<br>
16                   <a href="edit_entry.php?id=2">Edit</a>
17                   <a href="delete_entry.php?id=2">Delete</a>
```

Ⓒ Part of the HTML source of the page. Note that the two links have *?id=X* appended to each URL.

Deleting Data in a Database

Sometimes you might also want to run a **DELETE** query on a database. Such a query removes records from the database. The syntax for a delete query is

```
DELETE FROM tablename WHERE
→ column=value
```

The **WHERE** clause isn't required, but if it's omitted, you'll remove every record from the table. You should also understand that once you delete a record, there's no way to recover it (unless you have a backup of the database).

As a safeguard, if you want to delete only a single record from a table, add the **LIMIT** clause to the query:

```
DELETE FROM tablename WHERE
→ column=value LIMIT 1
```

This clause ensures that only one record is deleted at most. Once you've defined your query, it's again executed using the **mysqli_query()** function, like any other query.

To see if a **DELETE** query worked, you can use the **mysqli_affected_rows()** function. This function returns the number of rows affected by an **INSERT**, **DELETE**, or **UPDATE** query. It takes the database connection as an argument.

As an example, let's write the **delete_entry.php** script, which is linked from the **view_blog.php** page. This page receives the database record ID in the URL. It then displays the entry to confirm that the user wants to delete it Ⓐ. If the user clicks the button, the record will be deleted Ⓑ.

Ⓐ When the user arrives at this page, the blog entry is shown, and the user must confirm deleting it.

Ⓑ If the delete query worked properly, the user sees this result.

To delete data from a database:

1. Begin a new PHP document in your text editor or IDE, to be named **delete_entry.php** (Script 12.7):

```
<!doctype html>
<html lang="en">
<head>
    <meta charset="utf-8">
    <title>Delete a Blog Entry
    → </title>
</head>
<body>
<h1>Delete an Entry</h1>
```

2. Start the PHP code, and connect to the database:

```
<?php // Script 12.7 -
→ delete_entry.php
$dbc = mysqli_connect
→ ('localhost', 'username',
→ 'password', 'myblog');
```

continues on page 379

Script 12.7 The **DELETE** SQL command permanently removes a record (or records) from a table.

```
1   <!doctype html>
2   <html lang="en">
3   <head>
4       <meta charset="utf-8">
5       <title>Delete a Blog Entry</title>
6   </head>
7   <body>
8   <h1>Delete an Entry</h1>
9   <?php // Script 12.7 - delete_entry.php
10  /* This script deletes a blog entry. */
11
12  // Connect and select:
13  $dbc = mysqli_connect('localhost', 'username', 'password', 'myblog');
14
15  if (isset($_GET['id']) && is_numeric($_GET['id']) ) { // Display the entry in a form:
16
17      // Define the query:
18      $query = "SELECT title, entry FROM entries WHERE id={$_GET['id']}";
19      if ($r = mysqli_query($dbc, $query)) { // Run the query.
20
```

code continues on next page

```
21          $row = mysqli_fetch_array($r); // Retrieve the information.
22
23          // Make the form:
24          print '<form action="delete_entry.php" method="post">
25          <p>Are you sure you want to delete this entry?</p>
26          <p><h3>' . $row['title'] . '</h3>' .
27          $row['entry'] . '<br>
28          <input type="hidden" name="id" value="' . $_GET['id'] . '">
29          <input type="submit" name="submit" value="Delete this Entry!"></p>
30          </form>';
31
32      } else { // Couldn't get the information.
33          print '<p style="color: red;">Could not retrieve the blog entry because:<br>' . mysqli_
            error($dbc) . '.</p><p>The query being run was: ' . $query . '</p>';
34      }
35
36  } elseif (isset($_POST['id']) && is_numeric($_POST['id'])) { // Handle the form.
37
38      // Define the query:
39      $query = "DELETE FROM entries WHERE id={$_POST['id']} LIMIT 1";
40      $r = mysqli_query($dbc, $query); // Execute the query.
41
42      // Report on the result:
43      if (mysqli_affected_rows($dbc) == 1) {
44          print '<p>The blog entry has been deleted.</p>';
45      } else {
46          print '<p style="color: red;">Could not delete the blog entry because:<br>' .
            mysqli_error($dbc) . '.</p><p>The query being run was: ' . $query . '</p>';
47      }
48
49  } else { // No ID received.
50      print '<p style="color: red;">This page has been accessed in error.</p>';
51  } // End of main IF.
52
53  mysqli_close($dbc); // Close the connection.
54
55  ?>
56  </body>
57  </html>
```

3. If the page received a valid entry ID in the URL, define and execute a **SELECT** query:

```
if (isset($_GET['id']) && is_
→ numeric ($_GET['id']) ) {
  $query = "SELECT title,
  → entry FROM entries WHERE
  → id={$_GET['id']}";
  if ($r = mysqli_query($dbc,
  → $query)) {
```

To display the blog entry, the page must confirm that a numeric ID is received by the page. Because that value should first come in the URL (when the user clicks the link in **view_blog.php**, see in the previous section, "Retrieving Data from a Database"), you reference **$_GET['id']**. The use of **is_numeric()** here does more than just ensure a record can be retrieved; it's also an important security measure. Because the **$_GET['id']** value is used directly in the query—without quotes—testing that value against **is_numeric()** prevents the query from breaking or being used in an attack.

The query is like the **SELECT** query used in the preceding example, except that the **WHERE** clause has been added to retrieve a specific record. Also, because only the two stored values are necessary—the title and the entry itself—only those are being selected.

This query is then executed using the **mysqli_query()** function.

4. Retrieve the record, and display the entry in a form:

```
$row = mysqli_fetch_array($r);
print '<form action="delete_
→ entry.php" method="post">
<p>Are you sure you want to
→ delete this entry?</p>
<p><h3>' . $row['title'] .
→ '</h3>' .
$row['entry'] . '<br>
<input type="hidden" name="id"
→ value="' . $_GET['id'] . '">
<input type="submit" name=
→ "submit" value="Delete this
→ Entry!"></p>
</form>';
```

Instead of retrieving all the records using a **while** loop, as you did in the previous example, use one call to the **mysqli_fetch_array()** function to assign the returned record to the **$row** variable. Using this array, the record to be deleted can be displayed.

The form first shows the blog entry details, much as it did in the **view_entries.php** script. When the user clicks the button, the form will be submitted back to this page, at which point the record should be deleted. In order to do so, the blog identification number, which is passed to the script as **$_GET['id']**, must be stored in a hidden input so that it exists in the **$_POST** array upon submission (because **$_GET['id']** won't have a value at that point).

continues on next page

5. Report an error if the query failed:

```
} else { // Couldn't get the
→ information.
   print '<p style="color: red;">
   → Could not retrieve the blog
   → entry because:<br>' . mysqli_
   → error($dbc) . '.</p> <p>The
   → query being run was: ' .
   $query . '</p>';
}
```

If the **SELECT** query failed to run, the MySQL error and the query itself are printed out.

6. Check for the submission of the form:

```
} elseif (isset($_POST['id']) &&
→ is_numeric($_POST['id'])) { //
→ Handle the form.
```

This **elseif** clause is part of the conditional begun in Step 3. It corresponds to the second usage of this same script (the form being submitted). If this conditional is TRUE, the record should be deleted.

7. Define and execute the query:

```
$query = "DELETE FROM entries
→ WHERE id={$_POST['id']} LIMIT
→ 1";
$r = mysqli_query($dbc, $query);
```

This query deletes the record whose **id** has a value of **$_POST['id']**. The ID value comes from the form, where it's stored as a hidden input. By adding the **LIMIT 1** clause to the query, you can guarantee that only one record, at most, is removed.

8. Check the result of the query:

```
if (mysqli_affected_rows($dbc)
→ == 1) {
   print '<p>The blog entry has
   → been deleted.</p>';
} else {
   print '<p style="color: red;">
   → Could not delete the blog
   → entry because:<br>' . mysqli_
   → error($dbc) . '.</p> <p>The
   → query being run was: ' .
   → $query . '</p>';
}
```

The **mysqli_affected_rows()** function returns the number of rows altered by the most recent query. If the query ran properly, one row was deleted, so this function should return 1. If so, a message is printed. Otherwise, the MySQL error and query are printed for debugging purposes.

9. Complete the main conditional:

```
} else { // No ID received.
   print '<p style="color: red;">
   → This page has been accessed
   → in error.</p>';
} // End of main IF.
```

If no numeric ID value was passed to this page using either the GET method or the POST method, then this **else** clause takes effect **C**.

Delete an Entry

This page has been accessed in error.

C If the script does not receive an **id** value in the URL, an error is reported.

10. Close the database connection, and complete the page:

```
mysqli_close($dbc);
?>
</body>
</html>
```

11. Save the script as **delete_entry.php**, place it in the proper directory for your PHP-enabled server, and test it in your browser **A** and **B**.

    To test this script, you must first run **view_entries.php**. Then, click one of the Delete links to access **delete_entry.php**.

> **TIP** You can empty a table of all of its records by running the query TRUNCATE TABLE *tablename*. This approach is preferred over using DELETE FROM *tablename*. TRUNCATE will completely drop and rebuild the table, which is better for the database.

> **TIP** It's a fairly common error to try to run the query DELETE * FROM *tablename*, like a SELECT query. Remember that DELETE doesn't use the same syntax as SELECT, because you aren't deleting specific columns.

Updating Data in a Database

The final type of query this chapter will cover is **UPDATE**. It's used to alter the values of a record's columns. The syntax is

```
UPDATE tablename SET
→ column1_name=value,
→ column2_name=value2 WHERE
→ some_column=value
```

As with any other query, if the values are strings, they should be placed within single quotation marks:

```
UPDATE users SET first_name=
→ 'Eleanor', age=7 WHERE user_id=142
```

As with a **DELETE** query, you should use a **WHERE** clause to limit the rows that are affected. If you don't do this, every record in the database will be updated.

To test that an update worked, you can again use the `mysqli_affected_rows()` function to return the number of records altered.

To demonstrate, let's write a page for editing a blog entry. It will let the user alter an entry's title and text, but not the date entered or the blog ID number (as a primary key, the ID number should never be changed). This script will use a structure like that in **delete_entry.php** (Script 12.7), first showing the entry Ⓐ and then handling the submission of that form Ⓑ.

Ⓐ When the user arrives at the edit page, the form is shown with the existing values.

Ⓑ Upon submitting the form, the user sees a message like this.

To update data in a database:

1. Begin a new PHP document in your text editor or IDE, to be named **edit_entry.php** (Script 12.8).

```
<!doctype html>
<html lang="en">
<head>
  <meta charset="utf-8">
  <title>Edit a Blog Entry</
   ⇥ title>
</head>
<body>
<h1>Edit an Entry</h1>
```

2. Start your PHP code and connect to the database:

```
<?php // Script 12.8 -
⇥ edit_entry.php
$dbc = mysqli_connect
⇥ ('localhost', 'username',
⇥ 'password', 'myblog');
mysqli_set_charset($dbc, 'utf8');
```

Because this script uses the **mysqli_ real_escape_string()** function, it also needs to set the character set (which you can do for all the scripts, if you want to be consistent).

continues on page 385

Script 12.8 You can edit records in a database table by using an **UPDATE** SQL command.

```
1   <!doctype html>
2   <html lang="en">
3   <head>
4       <meta charset="utf-8">
5       <title>Edit a Blog Entry</title>
6   </head>
7   <body>
8   <h1>Edit an Entry</h1>
9   <?php // Script 12.8 - edit_entry.php
10  /* This script edits a blog entry using an UPDATE query. */
11
12  // Connect and select:
13  $dbc = mysqli_connect('localhost', 'username', 'password', 'myblog');
14
15  //Set the character set:
16  mysqli_set_charset($dbc, 'utf8');
17
18  if (isset($_GET['id']) && is_numeric($_GET['id']) ) { // Display the entry in a form:
19
20      // Define the query.
21      $query = "SELECT title, entry FROM entries WHERE id={$_GET['id']}";
22      if ($r = mysqli_query($dbc, $query)) { // Run the query.
23
24          $row = mysqli_fetch_array($r); // Retrieve the information.
25
```

code continues on next page

```
26        // Make the form:
27        print '<form action="edit_entry.php" method="post">
28    <p>Entry Title: <input type="text" name="title" size="40" maxsize="100" value="' .
      htmlentities($row['title']) . '"></p>
29    <p>Entry Text: <textarea name="entry" cols="40" rows="5">' . htmlentities($row['entry'])
      . '</textarea></p>
30    <input type="hidden" name="id" value="' . $_GET['id'] . '">
31    <input type="submit" name="submit" value="Update this Entry!">
32    </form>';
33
34    } else { // Couldn't get the information.
35        print '<p style="color: red;">Could not retrieve the blog entry because:<br>' .
          mysqli_error($dbc) . '.</p><p>The query being run was: ' . $query . '</p>';
36    }
37
38  } elseif (isset($_POST['id']) && is_numeric($_POST['id'])) { // Handle the form.
39
40      // Validate and secure the form data:
41      $problem = FALSE;
42      if (!empty($_POST['title']) && !empty($_POST['entry'])) {
43          $title = mysqli_real_escape_string($dbc, trim(strip_tags($_POST['title'])));
44          $entry = mysqli_real_escape_string($dbc, trim(strip_tags($_POST['entry'])));
45      } else {
46          print '<p style="color: red;">Please submit both a title and an entry.</p>';
47          $problem = TRUE;
48      }
49
50      if (!$problem) {
51
52          // Define the query.
53          $query = "UPDATE entries SET title='$title', entry='$entry' WHERE
          id={$_POST['id']}";
54          $r = mysqli_query($dbc, $query); // Execute the query.
55
56          // Report on the result:
57          if (mysqli_affected_rows($dbc) == 1) {
58              print '<p>The blog entry has been updated.</p>';
59          } else {
60              print '<p style="color: red;">Could not update the entry because:<br>' .
              mysqli_error($dbc) . '.</p><p>The query being run was: ' . $query . '</p>';
61          }
62
63      } // No problem!
64
65  } else { // No ID set.
66      print '<p style="color: red;">This page has been accessed in error.</p>';
67  } // End of main IF.
68
69  mysqli_close($dbc); // Close the connection.
70
71  ?>
72  </body>
73  </html>
```

3. If the page received a valid entry ID in the URL, define and execute a **SELECT** query:

```
if (isset($_GET['id']) &&
→ is_numeric($_GET['id']) ) {
  $query = "SELECT title,
  → entry FROM entries WHERE
  → id={$_GET['id']}";
  if ($r = mysqli_query($dbc,
  → $query)) {
```

This code is exactly the same as that in the delete page; it selects the two column values from the database for the provided ID value.

4. Retrieve the record, and display the entry in a form:

```
$row = mysqli_fetch_array($r);
  print '<form action="edit_entry
  → php" method="post">
<p>Entry Title: <input type=
→ "text" name="title" size="40"
→ maxsize="100" value="' .
→ htmlentities($row['title']) .
→ '" /></p>
<p>Entry Text: <textarea name=
→ "entry" cols="40" rows="5">' .
→ htmlentities($row['entry']) .
→ '</textarea></p>
<input type="hidden" name="id"
→ value="' . $_GET['id'] . '">
<input type="submit" name=
→ "submit" value="Update this
→ Entry!">
</form>';
```

Again, this is almost exactly the same as in the preceding script, including the most important step of storing the ID value in a hidden form input. Here, though, the stored data isn't just printed but is actually used as the values for form elements. For security and to avoid potential conflicts, each value is run through **htmlentities()** first.

5. Report an error if the query failed:

```
} else { // Couldn't get the
→ information.
  print '<p style="color: red;">
  → Could not retrieve the blog
  → entry because: <br>' .
  → mysqli_error($dbc) . '.
  → </p><p>The query being run
  → was: ' . $query . '</p>';
}
```

6. Check for the submission of the form:

```
} elseif (isset($_POST['id']) &&
→ is_numeric($_POST['id'])) {
```

This conditional will be TRUE when the form is submitted.

7. Validate and secure the form data:

```
$problem = FALSE;
if (!empty($_POST['title']) &&
→ !empty($_POST['entry'])) {
  $title = mysqli_real_escape_
  → string($dbc, trim(strip_tags
  → ($_POST ['title'])));
  $entry = mysqli_real_escape_
  → string($dbc, trim(strip_tags
  → ($_POST ['entry'])));
} else {
  print '<p style="color: red;">
  → Please submit both a title
  → and an entry.</p>';
  $problem = TRUE;
}
```

This code comes from the page used to add blog postings. It performs minimal validation on the submitted data and then runs it through the **mysqli_real_escape_string()** function to be safe. Because the form data can be edited, the form should be validated as if it were a new record being created.

continues on next page

8. Define and execute the query:

```
if (!$problem) {
    $query = "UPDATE entries
    → SET title='$title',
    → entry='$entry' WHERE id=
    → {$_POST['id']}";
    $r = mysqli_query($dbc,
    → $query);
```

The **UPDATE** query sets the **title** column equal to the value entered in the form's title input and sets the **entry** column equal to the value entered in the form's entry text area. Only the record whose **id** is equal to **$_POST['id']**, which comes from a hidden form input, is updated.

9. Report on the success of the query:

```
if (mysqli_affected_rows($dbc)
→ == 1) {
print '<p>The blog entry has
→ been updated.</p>';
} else {
    print '<p style="color: red;">
    → Could not update the entry
    → because:<br>' . mysqli_ error
    → ($dbc) . '.</p><p>The query
    → being run was: ' . $query .
    → '</p>';
}
```

If one row was affected, then a success message is returned. Otherwise, the MySQL error and the query are sent to the browser.

10. Complete the conditionals:

```
    } // No problem!
} else { // No ID set.
    print '<p style="color: red;">
    → This page has been accessed
    → in error.</p>';
} // End of main IF.
```

If no numeric ID value was passed to this page using either the GET method or the POST method, then this **else** clause takes effect.

11. Close the database connection, and complete the page:

```
mysqli_close($dbc);
?>
</body>
</html>
```

12. Save the file as **edit_entry.php**, place it in the proper directory for your PHP-enabled server, and test it in your browser Ⓐ and Ⓑ.

As in the preceding example, to edit an entry, you must click its *Edit* link in the **view_blog.php** page.

C Reloading the `view_blog.php` script reflects the changes made to the entries.

13. Revisit `view_blog.php` to confirm that the changes were made **C**.

> **TIP** The `id` is a primary key, meaning that its value should never change. By using a primary key in your table, you can change every other value in the record but still refer to the row using that column.

> **TIP** The `mysqli_real_escape_string()` function does not need to be applied to the ID values used in the queries, because the `is_numeric()` test confirms they don't contain apostrophes or other problematic characters.

> **TIP** More thorough edit and delete pages would use the `mysqli_num_rows()` function in a conditional to confirm that the SELECT query returned a row prior to fetching it:
>
> `if (mysqli_num_rows($r) == 1) {...`

> **TIP** If you run an update on a table but don't change a record's values, `mysqli_affected_rows()` will return 0.

> **TIP** It can't hurt to add a LIMIT 1 clause to an UPDATE query, to ensure that only one row, at most, is affected.

> **TIP** A common beginner's mistake is to use the following erroneous syntax:
>
> `UPDATE tablename SET column1_name=`
> `→ value AND column2_name=value2 WHERE`
> `→ some_column=value`
>
> Note the improper AND in that example!

Review and Pursue

If you have any problems with the review questions or the pursue prompts, turn to the book's supporting forum (www.LarryUllman.com/forums/).

Review

- What version of MySQL are you using? What values do you personally use to connect to MySQL?

- How does a PHP script connect to a MySQL server? How does it disconnect?

- What is the error suppression operator? What does it do?

- What function returns MySQL-reported errors?

- What debugging techniques should you use when having problems with a PHP script that interacts with MySQL?

- What SQL command is used to create a table? To add new records? To retrieve records? To modify records? To remove records?

- What function should string values be run through to prevent SQL injection attacks?

Pursue

- Find the version of the MySQL manual that corresponds to your version of MySQL. Start reading!

- Move the code for connecting to the database to a separate script, then include that script in the PHP pages that interact with the database. Don't forget about setting the character set.

- Make the **add_entry.php** form sticky.

- Change the code in **view_entries.php** so that it converts newline characters in each entry into HTML break tags.

Putting It All Together

The 12 chapters to this point have covered all the fundamentals of using PHP for web development. In this chapter, you'll use your accumulated knowledge to create a complete and functional website. And even though the focus of this chapter is on applying your newfound knowledge, you'll still learn a few new tricks. In particular, you'll see how to develop a full-scale web application from scratch.

Getting Started

The first step when starting any project is identifying the site's goals. The primary goal of this chapter is to apply everything taught in the book thus far (a lofty aim, to be sure). The example for doing so combines ideas from the previous two chapters, creating a site that will store and display quotations. Instead of using a file to do so, as in Chapter 11, "Files and Directories," this site will use a MySQL database as the storage repository. But as with the blog example from Chapter 12, "Intro to Databases," the ability to create, edit, and delete quotations will be implemented. Further, the public user will be able to view the most recent quotation by default , or a random one, or a random quotation previously marked as a favorite.

For improved security, the site will have an administrator who can log in and log out. And only the logged-in administrator will be allowed to create, edit, or delete quotations 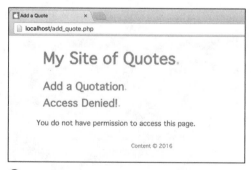.

The site will use a simple template to give every page a consistent look, with CSS handling all the formatting and layout. The site will also use one user-defined function, stored in an included file.

As in Chapter 12, you must first create the database and its one table. You can do so using the instructions in Appendix A, "Installation and Configuration."

The database will be named *myquotes* (or something else if you'd rather). You create its one table with this SQL command:

```
CREATE TABLE quotes (
    id INT UNSIGNED NOT NULL
    → AUTO_INCREMENT,
    quote TEXT NOT NULL,
    source VARCHAR(100) NOT NULL,
    favorite TINYINT(1) UNSIGNED NOT
    → NULL,
    date_entered TIMESTAMP NOT NULL
    → DEFAULT CURRENT_TIMESTAMP,
    PRIMARY KEY (id)
) CHARACTER SET utf8
```

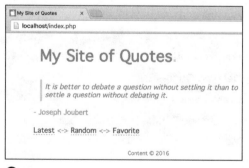

A The site's simple home page.

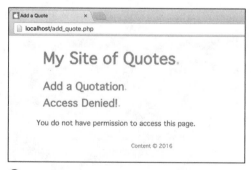

B Nonadministrators are denied access to certain pages.

The **id** is the primary key, and it will automatically be incremented to the next logical value with each new submission. The **quote** field stores the quote itself, with the **source** field storing the attribution (unlike in Chapter 11, where the quote and the source were stored together). The **favorite** field stores a 1 or a 0, marking the quote as a favorite or not. Finally, the **date_entered** column is a timestamp, automatically set to the current timestamp when a new record is created.

You can create this table using a PHP script, such as Script 12.3, or a third-party application (like the MySQL client or phpMyAdmin).

Finally, a word about how the site should be organized on the server **C**. Ideally the **mysqli_connect.php** script, which establishes a database connection, would be stored outside the web root directory. If that is not possible in your case, you can place it in the **includes** folder, then change the code in the other scripts accordingly.

Once you've created the database, the database table, and the necessary folders, you can begin coding.

TIP If you'd rather, you could move the **templates** and **includes** folders outside the web root directory as well. If so, you'll need to change all the references to them in the code to reflect the alternative structure.

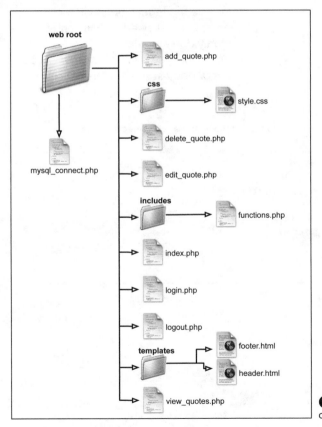

C The structure and organization of the files on the server.

Connecting to the Database

Unlike the scripts in Chapter 12, which connected to the database using code repeated in each script, this site will use the more common practice of placing the repeated code in a stand-alone file. Every script that interacts with the database—which will be most but not all of them—will then include this file. As you can see in **C** in the previous section, "Getting Started," this file should be stored outside the web root directory or, if that's not possible, within the **includes** folder.

To create mysqli_connect.php:

1. Begin a new PHP script in your text editor or IDE, to be named **mysqli_connect.php** (Script 13.1):

   ```php
   <?php
   ```

2. Connect to the database:

   ```php
   $dbc = mysqli_connect
   →('localhost', 'username',
   →'password', 'myquotes');
   ```

   Naturally, you'll need to change the values used here to be appropriate for your server.

3. Set the character set:

   ```php
   mysqli_set_charset($dbc, 'utf8');
   ```

   It's a best practice to establish the character set being used for interactions. Also, it's a requirement when using **mysqli_real_escape_string()**, as this chapter will do.

4. Save the file as **mysqli_connect.php**.

   You may notice that the script does not include the terminating PHP tag. This omission is allowed by PHP, and is commonly done for included files like this one. (Doing so can help prevent *headers already sent* errors from occurring.)

Script 13.1 The **mysqli_connect.php** script connects to the database server and selects the database to be used.

```
1   <?php // Script 13.1 - mysqli_connect.php
2   /* This script connects to the database
3   and establishes the character set for communications. */
4
5   // Connect:
6   $dbc = mysqli_connect('localhost', 'username', 'password', 'myquotes');
7
8   //Set the character set:
9   mysqli_set_charset($dbc, 'utf8');
```

Privacy Alert

The website "192.168.0.107" has requested to save a file on your computer called a "cookie." This file may be used to track usage information. Do you want to allow this?

☐ Apply my decision to all cookies from this website

[Allow Cookie] [Block Cookie] [More Info] [Help]

Cookie Information

Name	Samuel
Domain	192.168.0.107
Path	/
Expires	Wednesday, May 11, 2016 2:58:06 AM Secure No
Data	Clemens

3rd Party	No	Session	No

A This cookie will be used to identify the administrator.

Writing the User-Defined Function

The site will have a single user-defined function. As discussed in Chapter 10, "Creating Functions," the best time to create your own functions is when a script or a site might have repeating code. In this site there are a couple of such instances, but the most obvious one is this: Many scripts will need to check whether or not the current user is an administrator. In this next script, you'll create your own function that returns a Boolean value indicating if the user is an administrator. But what will be the test of administrative status?

Upon successfully logging in, a cookie will be sent to the administrator's browser, with a name of *Samuel* and a value of *Clemens* **A**. This may seem odd or random, and it is. When using something simple, like a cookie, for authentication, it's best to be obscure about what constitutes verification. If you went with something more obvious, such as a name of *admin* and a value of *true*, that'd be quite easy for anyone to guess and falsify. With this cookie in mind, this next function simply checks if a cookie exists with a name of *Samuel* and a value of *Clemens*.

To create functions.php:

1. Begin a new PHP script in your text editor or IDE, to be named **functions.php** (Script 13.2):

   ```
   <?php // Script 13.2 -
   → functions.php
   ```

   Even though, as written, the script defines only a single function, I'm naming the file using the plural—*functions*—with the understanding that more user-defined functions might be added to the script in time.

Script 13.2 The **is_administrator()** function, defined in an includable script, will be called on any page that needs to verify administrator status.

```
1   <?php // Script 13.2 - functions.php
2   /* This page defines custom functions. */
3
4   // This function checks if the user is an administrator.
5   // This function takes two optional values.
6   // This function returns a Boolean value.
7   function is_administrator($name = 'Samuel', $value = 'Clemens') {
8
9       // Check for the cookie and check its value:
10      if (isset($_COOKIE[$name]) && ($_COOKIE[$name] == $value)) {
11          return true;
12      } else {
13          return false;
14      }
15
16  } // End of is_administrator() function.
```

2. Begin defining a new function:

```
function is_administrator
→ ($name = 'Samuel', $value =
→ 'Clemens') {
```

The function takes two arguments: the cookie's name and its value. Both have default values.

Since the function checks only a single cookie with a single expected value, it doesn't need to take arguments at all, let alone default ones. But by having the function take arguments, it can be used in different ways should the site's functionality expand (for example, if you had multiple types of authentication to perform). Still, by using default values for those arguments, function calls don't need to provide argument values when the assumed cookie name and value are being checked.

3. Return a Boolean value based on the cookie's existence and value:

```
if (isset($_COOKIE[$name]) &&
→ ($_COOKIE[$name] == $value)) {
   return true;
} else {
   return false;
}
```

If the cookie exists and has the appropriate value, the Boolean TRUE is returned. Otherwise, the function returns FALSE.

4. Complete the function and the script:

```
} // End of is_administrator()
→ function.
```

Again, the closing PHP tag is being omitted.

5. Save the file as **functions.php**, stored in the **includes** directory.

TIP Checking for the presence of a specific cookie with a specific value is a fairly minimal level of security, although not totally inappropriate for a site such as this. For better security, create a session element that reflects administrative status:

```
$_SESSION['admin'] = true;
```

Then check this value on each page.

Creating the Template

Now that the two helper files have been created, it's time to move on to the template. As introduced in Chapter 8, "Creating Web Applications," the site's layout will be controlled by two includable files: a header and a footer. Both will be stored in the **templates** directory. The header also references a style sheet, to be stored in the **css** folder. You can find the style sheet by downloading the book's code from www.LarryUllman.com (the file will be in the **ch13** folder of the download).

Besides generating the primary HTML for the site, the header file must include the functions script. The footer file should also display some administration links **A**, should the current user be an administrator.

To create header.html:

1. Begin a new HTML document in your text editor or IDE, to be named **header.html** (Script 13.3).

```php
<?php // Script 13.3 -
→ header.html
include('includes/functions.php');
→ ?>
```

The header will start with a PHP section in order to include the **functions.php** script, which will be required by multiple pages on the site. The reference to the script is relative to the pages that will be including the header: files in the main directory.

Site Admin.

Add Quote <-> View All Quotes <-> Logout

Content © 2016

A If the person viewing any page is an administrator, additional links appear.

2. Begin the HTML document:

```
<!doctype html>
<html lang="en">
<head>
   <meta charset="utf-8">
   <link rel="stylesheet" media=
 → "all" href="css/style.css">
```

Again, the style sheet needs to be down-loaded from the book's corresponding website. And the reference to that style sheet is relative to the scripts that include the header, all found within the main directory.

3. Print the page's title:

```
<title><?php
if (defined('TITLE')) {
   print TITLE;
} else {
   print 'My Site of Quotes';
}
?></title>
```

This code also comes from Chapter 8, printing either the default title or a custom one, if set as a constant.

4. Complete the head:

```
</head>
```

5. Begin the page's body:

```
<body>
   <div id="container">
      <h1>My Site of Quotes</h1>
      <br>
      <!-- BEGIN CHANGEABLE
 → CONTENT. -->
```

6. Save the file as **header.html**, stored in the **templates** directory.

Script 13.3 The header file includes the **functions.php** script and begins the HTML page.

```
1    <?php // Script 13.3 - header.html
2
3    // Include the functions script:
4    include('includes/functions.php'); ?>
5    <!doctype html>
6    <html lang="en">
7    <head>
8       <meta charset="utf-8">
9       <link rel="stylesheet" media="all" href="css/style.css">
10      <title><?php // Print the page title.
11      if (defined('TITLE')) { // Is the title defined?
12         print TITLE;
13      } else { // The title is not defined.
14         print 'My Site of Quotes';
15      }
16      ?></title>
17   </head>
18   <body>
19      <div id="container">
20         <h1>My Site of Quotes</h1>
21         <br>
22         <!-- BEGIN CHANGEABLE CONTENT. -->
```

To create footer.html:

1. Begin a new HTML document in your text editor or IDE, to be named **footer.html (Script 13.4)**:

   ```
   <!-- END CHANGEABLE CONTENT. -->
   ```

2. Check if it's appropriate to display general administration links:

   ```php
   <?php
   if ((is_administrator() &&
   → (basename($_SERVER['PHP_SELF'])
   → != 'logout.php'))
   OR (isset($loggedin) &&
   → $loggedin) ) {
   ```

   This conditional is a bit complicated. To start, most pages can confirm that the current user is an administrator by just invoking the **is_administrator()** function. But because of how cookies work, that function will return inappropriate results on two pages: **login.php** and

logout.php. On **logout.php**, the script will have received the administrative cookie prior to deleting it. So on that page, it will seem like the user is an administrator (as was just the case), but links to the administrative pages should not be shown, as the user will be blocked from using them (because when the user gets to those pages, the cookie will no longer exist). Hence, the first part of the conditional requires that **is_administrator()** return TRUE and that the current page not be **logout.php**. The code **basename($_SERVER['PHP_SELF'])** is a reliable way to get the current script (and because the footer file is included by another script, **$_SERVER['PHP_SELF']** will have the value of the *including* script).

Script 13.4 The footer file displays general administrative links, when appropriate, and completes the HTML page.

```
1    <!-- END CHANGEABLE CONTENT. -->
2    <?php // Script 13.4 - footer.html
3
4    // Display general admin links...
5    // - if the user is an administrator and it's not the logout.php page
6    // - or if the $loggedin variable is true (i.e., the user just logged in)
7    if ( (is_administrator() && (basename($_SERVER['PHP_SELF']) != 'logout.php'))
8    OR (isset($loggedin) && $loggedin) ) {
9
10       // Create the links:
11       print '<hr><h3>Site Admin</h3><p><a href="add_quote.php">Add Quote</a> <->
12       <a href="view_quotes.php">View All Quotes</a> <->
13       <a href="logout.php">Logout</a></p>';
14
15   }
16
17   ?>
18       </div><!-- container -->
19       <div id="footer">Content &copy; 2016</div>
20   </body>
21   </html>
```

The second part of the conditional, after the **OR**, checks if the **$loggedin** variable is set and has a TRUE value. This will be the case on the **login.php** page, after the user successfully logged in. The **is_administrator()** function won't return a TRUE value at that juncture, because the cookie will have been just sent by the script and therefore won't be available to be read.

3. Create the links:

```
print '<hr><h3>Site Admin</h3>
→ <p><a href="add_quote.php">
→ Add Quote</a> <->
<a href="view_quotes.php">
→ View All Quotes</a> <->
<a href="logout.php">Logout</a>
→ </p>';
```

Three links are created: to a page for adding new quotes, to a page for viewing every quote, and to the logout page.

4. Complete the conditional and the PHP section:

```
}
?>
```

5. Complete the HTML page:

```
</div><!-- container -->
<div id="footer">Content &copy;
→ 2016</div>
</body>
</html>
```

6. Save the file as **footer.html**, stored in the **templates** directory.

Logging In

Next, it's time to create the script through which the administrator can log in. The result will be very similar to the scripts in Chapter 9, "Cookies and Sessions," with one structural difference: That chapter used *output buffering*, allowing you to lay out your script however you want. This site does not use output buffering, so the handling of the form must be written in such a way that the cookie can be sent without generating *headers already sent* errors (see Chapter 9 if this isn't ringing a bell for you). In other words, the script must check for a form submission prior to including the header. To still be able to reflect errors and other messages within the context of the page, you must use variables.

To create login.php:

1. Begin a new PHP document in your text editor or IDE, to be named **login.php** (Script 13.5):

   ```php
   <?php // Script 13.5 - login.php
   ```

2. Define two variables with default values:

   ```php
   $loggedin = false;
   $error = false;
   ```

   These two variables will be used later in the script. Here they are given default values, indicating that the person is not logged in and no errors have yet occurred.

3. Check if the form has been submitted:

   ```php
   if ($_SERVER['REQUEST_METHOD'] ==
   → 'POST') {
   ```

Script 13.5 The login script both displays and handles a form, sending a cookie upon a successful login attempt.

```php
1   <?php // Script 13.5 - login.php
2   /* This page lets people log into the
    site. */
3
4   // Set two variables with default
    values:
5   $loggedin = false;
6   $error = false;
7
8   // Check if the form has been submitted:
9   if ($_SERVER['REQUEST_METHOD'] ==
    'POST') {
10
11      // Handle the form:
12      if (!empty($_POST['email']) &&
        !empty($_POST['password'])) {
13
14          if ( (strtolower($_POST['email'])
            == 'me@example.com') &&
            ($_POST['password'] ==
            'testpass') ) { // Correct!
15
16              // Create the cookie:
17              setcookie('Samuel', 'Clemens',
                time()+3600);
18
19              // Indicate they are logged in:
20              $loggedin = true;
21
22          } else { // Incorrect!
23
24              $error = 'The submitted email
                address and password do not
                match those on file!';
25
26          }
27
28      } else { // Forgot a field.
29
30          $error = 'Please make sure you
            enter both an email address and a
            password!';
31
32      }
33
34  }
35
```

code continues on next page

4. Handle the form:

```
if (!empty($_POST['email']) &&
→ !empty($_POST['password'])) {
  if ( (strtolower
  → ($_POST['email']) ==
  → 'me@example.com') &&
  → ($_POST ['password'] ==
  → 'testpass') ) {
```

Similar to examples in Chapter 9, this script first confirms that **$_POST['email']** and **$_POST['password']** are not empty. The second conditional compares the submitted values against what they need to be.

5. Create the cookie:

```
setcookie('Samuel', 'Clemens',
→ time()+3600);
```

The cookie has a name of *Samuel* and a value of *Clemens*. It's set to expire in an hour. Again, you could alternatively use sessions to track the user and indicate whether that user is an administrator.

6. Indicate that the user is logged in:

```
$loggedin = true;
```

This variable will be used later in this same script, and in the footer file (see Script 13.4).

continues on next page

Script 13.5 *continued*

```
36   // Set the page title and include the header file:
37   define('TITLE', 'Login');
38   include('templates/header.html');
39
40   // Print an error if one exists:
41   if ($error) {
42       print '<p class="error">' . $error . '</p>';
43   }
44
45   // Indicate the user is logged in, or show the form:
46   if ($loggedin) {
47
48       print '<p>You are now logged in!</p>';
49
50   } else {
51
52       print '<h2>Login Form</h2>
53       <form action="login.php" method="post">
54       <p><label>Email Address <input type="email" name="email"></label></p>
55       <p><label>Password <input type="password" name="password"></label></p>
56       <p><input type="submit" name="submit" value="Log In!"></p>
57       </form>';
58
59   }
60
61   include('templates/footer.html'); // Need the footer.
62   ?>
```

7. Create error messages for the two other conditions:

```
    } else { // Incorrect!
        $error = 'The submitted
        → email address and
        → password do not match
        → those on file!';
    }
} else { // Forgot a field.
    $error = 'Please make sure
    → you enter both an email
    → address and a password!';
    }
}
```

The first **else** clause applies if an email address and password were provided but were wrong. The second **else** clause applies if no email address or password was submitted. In both cases, the message is assigned to a variable so that it may be used later in the script.

8. Set the page title, and include the header file:

```
define('TITLE', 'Login');
include('templates/header.html');
```

9. Print an error if one exists:

```
if ($error) {
  print '<p class="error">' .
  → $error . '</p>';
}
```

The error itself will be determined in Step 7, but it can't be printed at that point because the HTML header will not have been included. The solution is to have this code check for a non-FALSE **$error** value and then print **$error** within some HTML and CSS **A**.

A Error messages are displayed after the header is included but before the HTML form.

My Site of Quotes.

You are now logged in!

Site Admin.

Add Quote <-> View All Quotes <-> Logout

B The result upon successfully logging in.

My Site of Quotes.

Login Form.

Email Address [   ]

Password [   ]

[Log In!]

C The basic login form.

10. Indicate that the user is logged in, or display the form:

```
if ($loggedin) {
    print '<p>You are now logged
    → in!</p>';
} else {
    print '<h2>Login Form</h2>
    <form action="login.php"
    → method="post">
    <p><label>Email Address <input
    → type="email" name="email">
    → </label></p>
    <p><label>Password
    → <input type="password"
    → name="password"></label></p>
    <p><input type="submit"
    → name="submit" value=
    → "Log In!"></p>
    </form>';
}
```

If the **$loggedin** variable has a TRUE value—its value is FALSE by default—then the user just successfully logged in to the site and a message saying so is displayed **B**. If the **$loggedin** variable still has its default value, then the form should be shown **C**.

11. Include the footer, and complete the page:

```
include('templates/footer.html');
?>
```

12. Save the file as **login.php**.

13. Test the file in your browser (**A**, **B**, and **C**).

I purposefully omitted creating a link to the login section (as a security measure), so you'll need to enter the correct URL in your browser's address bar.

TIP Note that, as written, the script requires administrators to log back in after an hour, whether or not they continue to be active in the site.

Logging Out

If you write a login process, there must be a logout process too. In this case, just using cookies, it's a very simple script.

To create logout.php:

1. Begin a new PHP document in your text editor or IDE, to be named **logout.php** (**Script 13.6**):

   ```php
   <?php // Script 13.6 - logout.php
   ```

2. Destroy the cookie, but only if it already exists:

   ```php
   if (isset($_COOKIE['Samuel'])) {
     setcookie('Samuel', FALSE,
     → time()-300);
   }
   ```

   As an extra security measure, the script attempts to delete the cookie only if it exists. By making this check, the script prevents hackers from discovering the name of the cookie used by the site by accessing the logout script without having first logged in.

   To delete the existing login cookie, another cookie is sent with the same name, a value of FALSE, and an expiration time in the past.

3. Define a page title, and include the header:

   ```php
   define('TITLE', 'Logout');
   include('templates/header.html');
   ```

4. Print a message:

   ```php
   print '<p>You are now logged
   → out.</p>';
   ```

5. Include the footer:

   ```php
   include('templates/footer.html');
   ?>
   ```

6. Save the file as **logout.php**.

7. Test the file in your browser **A**.

Script 13.6 The logout script deletes the administrator-identifying cookie.

```php
1   <?php // Script 13.6 - logout.php
2   /* This is the logout page. It destroys
    the cookie. */
3
4   // Destroy the cookie, but only if it
    already exists:
5   if (isset($_COOKIE['Samuel'])) {
6       setcookie('Samuel', FALSE,
        time()-300);
7   }
8
9   // Define a page title and include the
    header:
10  define('TITLE', 'Logout');
11  include('templates/header.html');
12
13  // Print a message:
14  echo '<p>You are now logged out.</p>';
15
16  // Include the footer:
17  include('templates/footer.html');
18  ?>
```

A The resulting logout page.

My Site of Quotes.

Add a Quotation.

> Work finally begins when the fear of doing nothing exceeds the fear of doing it badly.

Quote

Source Alain de Botton

Is this a favorite? ☑

[Add This Quote!]

A The form for adding quotations to the database.

Script 13.7 The `add_quote.php` script allows only administrators to add new quotations to the database.

```
1   <?php // Script 13.7 - add_quote.php
2   /* This script adds a quote. */
3
4   // Define a page title and include the
    header:
5   define('TITLE', 'Add a Quote');
6   include('templates/header.html');
7
8   print '<h2>Add a Quotation</h2>';
9
10  // Restrict access to administrators
    only:
11  if (!is_administrator()) {
12      print '<h2>Access Denied!</h2><p
        class="error">You do not have permission
        to access this page.</p>';
13      include('templates/footer.html');
14      exit();
15  }
16
17  // Check for a form submission:
18  if ($_SERVER['REQUEST_METHOD'] ==
    'POST') { // Handle the form.
19
20      if ( !empty($_POST['quote']) &&
        !empty($_POST['source']) ) {
21
```

code continues on next page

Adding Quotes

Now that the administrator has the ability to log in, she or he should be able to start adding quotations. The script for doing so is a lot like the one for adding blog postings (from Chapter 12), but the form will have an additional checkbox for marking the quotation as a favorite **A**.

Because this script creates records in the database, security must be a primary concern. As an initial precaution, the script will make sure that only the administrator can use the page. Second, values to be used in the SQL command will be sanctified to prevent invalid queries.

To create add_quote.php:

1. Begin a new PHP document in your text editor or IDE, to be named **add_quote.php** (Script 13.7):

   ```
   <?php // Script 13.7 -
   → add_quote.php
   define('TITLE', 'Add a Quote');
   include('templates/header.html');
   print '<h2>Add a Quotation</h2>';
   ```

2. Deny access to the page if the user is not an administrator:

   ```
   if (!is_administrator()) {
     print '<h2>Access Denied!
     → </h2><p class="error">
     → You do not have permission to
     → access this page.</p>';
     include('templates/
     → footer.html');
     exit();
   }
   ```

continues on next page

By invoking the **is_administrator()** function, the script can quickly test for that condition. If the user is not an administrator, an *Access Denied* error is displayed, the footer is included, and the script is terminated **B**.

3. Check for a form submission:

```
if ($_SERVER['REQUEST_METHOD'] ==
→ 'POST') {
```

Note that this check comes after confirming that the user is an administrator.

My Site of Quotes.

Add a Quotation.

Access Denied!.

You do not have permission to access this page.

B Any user not logged in as an administrator is denied access to the form.

Script 13.7 *continued*

```
22        // Need the database connection:
23        include('../mysqli_connect.php');
24
25        // Prepare the values for storing:
26        $quote = mysqli_real_escape_string($dbc, trim(strip_tags($_POST['quote'])));
27        $source = mysqli_real_escape_string($dbc, trim(strip_tags($_POST['source'])));
28
29        // Create the "favorite" value:
30        if (isset($_POST['favorite'])) {
31           $favorite = 1;
32        } else {
33           $favorite = 0;
34        }
35
36        $query = "INSERT INTO quotes (quote, source, favorite) VALUES ('$quote', '$source',
          $favorite)";
37        mysqli_query($dbc, $query);
38
39        if (mysqli_affected_rows($dbc) == 1){
40           // Print a message:
41           print '<p>Your quotation has been stored.</p>';
42        } else {
43           print '<p class="error">Could not store the quote because:<br>' . mysqli_error($dbc)
             . '.</p><p>The query being run was: ' . $query . '</p>';
44        }
45
46        // Close the connection:
47        mysqli_close($dbc);
48
49     } else { // Failed to enter a quotation.
50        print '<p class="error">Please enter a quotation and a source!</p>';
51     }
52
53  } // End of submitted IF.
54
```

4. Check for values:

```
if ( !empty($_POST['quote']) &&
→ !empty($_POST['source']) ) {
```

This script performs a minimum of validation, checking that the two variables aren't empty. With large blocks of text, such as a quotation, there's not much more that can be done in terms of validation.

5. Prepare the values for use in the query:

```
include('../mysqli_connect.php');
$quote = mysqli_real_escape_string
→ ($dbc, trim(strip_tags($_POST
→ ['quote'])));
$source = mysqli_real_escape_string
→ ($dbc, trim(strip_tags($_POST
→ ['source'])));
```

To make the two textual values safe to use in the query, they're run through the `mysqil_real_escape_string()` function (see Chapter 12). Because this function requires a database connection, that file must first be included.

To make the values safe to later display in the web page, the `strip_tags()` function is applied too (see Chapter 5, "Using Strings").

6. Create the *favorite* value:

```
if (isset($_POST['favorite'])) {
  $favorite = 1;
} else {
  $favorite = 0;
}
```

In the database, a quotation's status as a favorite is indicated by a 1. Non-favorites are represented by a 0. To determine which number to use, all the PHP script has to do is check for a `$_POST['favorite']` value. If that variable is set, regardless of what its value is, it means the user checked the favorite checkbox. If the user didn't do that, then the variable won't be set, and the `$favorite` variable will be assigned the value 0.

7. Define and execute the query:

```
$query = "INSERT INTO quotes
→ (quote, source, favorite)
→ VALUES ('$quote', '$source',
→ $favorite)";
mysqli_query($dbc, $query);
```

The query specifies values for three fields and uses the variables already defined. The remaining two table columns—**id** and **date_entered**—will automatically be assigned values, thanks to the table's definition.

continues on next page

Script 13.7 *continued*

```
55   // Leave PHP and display the form:
56   ?>
57
58   <form action="add_quote.php" method="post">
59       <p><label>Quote <textarea name="quote" rows="5" cols="30"></textarea></label></p>
60       <p><label>Source <input type="text" name="source"></label></p>
61       <p><label>Is this a favorite? <input type="checkbox" name="favorite" value="yes"></label></p>
62       <p><input type="submit" name="submit" value="Add This Quote!"></p>
63   </form>
64
65   <?php include('templates/footer.html'); ?>
```

8. Print a message based on the results:

```
if (mysqli_affected_rows($dbc)
→ == 1){
  // Print a message:
  print '<p>Your quotation has
  → been stored.</p>';
} else {
  print '<p class="error">
  → Could not store the quote
  → because:<br>' .
  → mysqli_error($dbc) . '.
  → </p><p>The query being run
  → was: ' . $query . '</p>';
}
```

If the **INSERT** query created one new row in the database, a message indicating that is displayed. Otherwise, debugging information is shown so that you can try to figure out what went wrong.

9. Complete the validation conditional:

```
} else { // Failed to enter a
→ quotation.
  print '<p class="error">
  → Please enter a quotation and
  → a source!</p>';
}
```

10. Complete the submission conditional and the PHP block:

```
} // End of submitted IF.
?>
```

11. Create the form:

```
<form action="add_quote.php"
→ method="post">
  <p><label>Quote <textarea
  → name="quote" rows="5"
  → cols="30"></textarea>
  → </label></p>
  <p><label>Source <input type=
  → "text" name="source"></label>
  → </p>
  <p><label>Is this a favorite?
  → <input type="checkbox"
  → name="favorite" value="yes">
  → </label></p>
  <p><input type="submit" name=
  → "submit" value="Add This
  → Quote!"></p>
</form>
```

The form has one text area, one text input, and a checkbox (plus the submit button, of course). It is not designed to be sticky—that's a feature you could add later, if you wanted.

12. Include the footer:

```
<?php include('templates/footer.
→ html'); ?>
```

13. Save the file as **add_quote.php**, and test in your browser **C**.

> **TIP** The ability to create (**INSERT**), retrieve (**SELECT**), update, and delete database records is collectively referred to as CRUD.

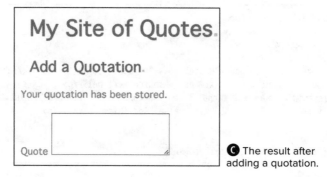

C The result after adding a quotation.

My Site of Quotes.

All Quotes.

Work finally begins when the fear of doing nothing exceeds the fear of doing it badly.

- Alain de Botton Favorite!

Quote Admin: **Edit** <-> **Delete**

It is better to debate a question without settling it than to settle a question without debating it.

- Joseph Joubert

Quote Admin: **Edit** <-> **Delete**

If you can't explain it simply, you don't understand it well enough.

- Albert Einstein

Quote Admin: **Edit** <-> **Delete**

Ⓐ The full list of stored quotations, with links to edit or delete each.

Script 13.8 This script lists every quotation currently stored, providing links for the administrator to edit or delete them.

```
1    <?php // Script 13.8 - view_quotes.php
2    /* This script lists every quote. */
3
4    // Include the header:
5    define('TITLE', 'View All Quotes');
6    include('templates/header.html');
7
8    print '<h2>All Quotes</h2>';
9
10   // Restrict access to administrators
     only:
11   if (!is_administrator()) {
12       print '<h2>Access Denied!</h2><p
         class="error">You do not have permission
         to access this page.</p>';
13       include('templates/footer.html');
14       exit();
15   }
16
17   // Need the database connection:
18   include('../mysqli_connect.php');
19
20   // Define the query:
21   $query = 'SELECT id, quote, source,
         favorite FROM quotes ORDER BY date_
         entered DESC';
22
```

code continues on next page

Listing Quotes

The administrative side of the site will have a page that lists every quote stored in the database Ⓐ. Although the same script could easily be adapted for the public side, its primary purpose is to provide quick links for the administrator to edit or delete any quote (as opposed to searching randomly through the public side for the right quote to manage).

Like the **add_quote.php** script, this page will restrict access to just administrators.

To create view_quotes.php:

1. Begin a new PHP document in your text editor or IDE, to be named **view_quotes.php** (Script 13.8):

   ```
   <?php // Script 13.8 -
   ↪ view_quotes.php
   define('TITLE', 'View All
   ↪ Quotes');
   include('templates/header.html');
   print '<h2>All Quotes</h2>';
   ```

2. Terminate the script if the user isn't an administrator:

   ```
   if (!is_administrator()) {
     print '<h2>Access Denied!
     ↪ </h2><p class="error">You do
     ↪ not have permission to access
     ↪ this page.</p>';
     include('templates/
     ↪ footer.html');
     exit();
   }
   ```

   This is the exact same code as that in **add_quote.php**. Except for the browser's title, the result for nonadministrators will be the same as in Ⓑ in the previous section, "Adding Quotes."

continues on next page

3. Include the database connection, and define the query:

```
include('../mysqli_connect.php');
$query = 'SELECT id, quote,
→ source, favorite FROM quotes
ORDER BY date_entered DESC';
```

The query returns four columns—all but the date entered—from the database for every record. The results will be returned in order by the date they were entered.

4. Execute the query, and begin retrieving the results:

```
if ($r = mysqli_query
→ ($dbc, $query)) {
  while ($row =
  → mysqli_fetch_array($r)) {
```

The **while** loop code was explained in Chapter 12, even though it wasn't used in that chapter. This construct is how you fetch every record returned by a query.

5. Begin printing out the record:

```
print "<div><blockquote>
→ {$row['quote']}</blockquote>-
→ {$row['source']}\n";
```

This code starts a DIV, places the quotation itself within blockquote tags, and then shows the quote's attribution.

Script 13.8 continued

```
23   // Run the query:
24   if ($result = mysqli_query($dbc,
     $query)) {
25
26       // Retrieve the returned records:
27       while ($row = mysqli_fetch_
         array($result)) {
28
29           // Print the record:
30           print "<div><blockquo
             te>{$row['quote']}</
             blockquote>- {$row['source']}\n";
31
32           // Is this a favorite?
33           if ($row['favorite'] == 1) {
34               print ' <strong>Favorite!</
                 strong>';
35           }
36
37           // Add administrative links:
38           print "<p><b>Quote Admin:</
             b> <a href=\"edit_quote.
             php?id={$row['id']}\">Edit</a>
             <->
39           <a href=\"delete_quote.
             php?id={$row['id']}\">Delete</
             a></p></div>\n";
40
41       } // End of while loop.
42
43   } else { // Query didn't run.
44       print '<p class="error">Could not
         retrieve the data because:<br>' .
         mysqli_error($dbc) . '.</p><p>The
         query being run was: ' . $query . '</
         p>';
45   } // End of query IF.
46
47   mysqli_close($dbc); // Close the
     connection.
48
49   include('templates/footer.html'); //
     Include the footer.
50   ?>
```

6. Indicate that the quotation is a favorite, if applicable:

```php
if ($row['favorite'] == 1) {
  print ' <strong>Favorite!
  ↪ </strong>';
}
```

The value of **$row['favorite']** will be either 1 or 0. If it's 1, the word *Favorite!*, emphasized, is displayed along with the record.

7. Add administrative links for editing and deleting the quote:

```php
print "<p><b>Quote Admin:</b>
↪ <a href=\"edit_quote.php?id=
↪ {$row['id']}\">Edit</a> <->
<a href=\"delete_quote.php?id=
↪ {$row['id']}\">Delete</a></p>
↪ </div>\n";
```

For each quote, two links must be created. The first is to **edit_quote.php** and the second to **delete_quote.php**. Each link must also pass the **id** value along in the URL, as the code in Chapter 12 does **B**.

The end of the **print** statement closes the DIV for the specific quotation (begun in Step 5).

8. Complete the **while** loop and the **mysqli_query()** conditional:

```php
  } // End of while loop.
} else { // Query didn't run.
  print '<p class="error">
  ↪ Could not retrieve the
  ↪ data because:<br>' .
  ↪ mysqli_error($dbc) . '.
  ↪ </p><p>The query being run
  ↪ was: ' . $query . '</p>';
} // End of query IF.
```

9. Close the database connection:

```php
mysqli_close($dbc);
```

10. Complete the page:

```php
include('templates/footer.html');
?>
```

11. Save the view as **view_quotes.php**, and test in your browser.

TIP As some of the queries in this chapter demonstrate, you can use a column or value in an **ORDER BY** clause even if it's not selected by the query.

```
14              <a href="delete_quote.php?id=5">Delete</a></p></div>
15  <div><blockquote>It is better to debate a question without settling it than to settle a ques
    </blockquote>- Joseph Joubert
16  <p><b>Quote Admin:</b> <a href="edit_quote.php?id=1">Edit</a> <->
17              <a href="delete_quote.php?id=1">Delete</a></p></div>
18  <div><blockquote>If you can't explain it simply, you don't understand it well enough.</block
19  <p><b>Quote Admin:</b> <a href="edit_quote.php?id=2">Edit</a> <->
20              <a href="delete_quote.php?id=2">Delete</a></p></div>
21  <div><blockquote>It is useless to attempt to reason a man out of a thing he was never reason
    Swift
22  <strong>Favorite!</strong><p><b>Quote Admin:</b> <a href="edit_quote.php?id=3">Edit</a> <->
23              <a href="delete_quote.php?id=3">Delete</a></p></div>
24  <div><blockquote>The best way to become acquainted with a subject is to write a book about i
25  <p><b>Quote Admin:</b> <a href="edit_quote.php?id=4">Edit</a> <->
```

B The HTML source code for the page shows how the **id** value is passed in the URL to the linked pages.

Editing Quotes

The **view_quotes.php** page (and later, **index.php**) has links to **edit_quote.php**, where the administrator can update a quote. Functionally, this script will be very similar to **edit_entry.php** from Chapter 12:

1. The script needs to receive an ID value in the URL.

2. Using the ID, the record is retrieved and used to populate a form Ⓐ.

3. Upon form submission, the form data will be validated (even if only slightly).

4. If the form data passes validation, the record will be updated in the database.

For the most part, this script is just another application of what you've already seen. But one new thing you'll learn here is how to select or not select a form's checkbox element based on a preexisting value.

To create edit_quote.php:

1. Begin a new PHP document in your text editor or IDE, to be named **edit_quote.php** (Script 13.9):

   ```php
   <?php // Script 13.9 -
   → edit_quote.php
   define('TITLE', 'Edit a Quote');
   include('templates/header.html');
   print '<h2>Edit a Quotation </h2>';
   ```

2. Terminate the script if the user isn't an administrator:

   ```php
   if (!is_administrator()) {
     print '<h2>Access Denied!
   → </h2><p class="error">You do
   → not have permission to access
   → this page.</p>';
     include('templates/
   → footer.html');
     exit();
   }
   ```

My Site of Quotes.

Edit a Quotation.

Quote [It is useless to attempt to reason a man out of a thing he was never reasoned into.]

Source [Jonathan Swift]

Is this a favorite? ☑

[Update This Quote!]

Ⓐ The form's elements are prepopulated, and preselected, using the record's existing values.

Script 13.9 The **edit_quote.php** script gives the administrator a way to update an existing record.

```php
1   <?php // Script 13.9 - edit_quote.php
2   /* This script edits a quote. */
3
4   // Define a page title and include the
    header:
5   define('TITLE', 'Edit a Quote');
6   include('templates/header.html');
7
8   print '<h2>Edit a Quotation</h2>';
9
10  // Restrict access to administrators
    only:
11  if (!is_administrator()) {
12      print '<h2>Access Denied!</h2><p
        class="error">You do not have permission
        to access this page.</p>';
13      include('templates/footer.html');
14      exit();
15  }
16
17  // Need the database connection:
18  include('../mysqli_connect.php');
19
20  if (isset($_GET['id']) && is_numeric($_
    GET['id']) && ($_GET['id'] > 0) ) { //
    Display the entry in a form:
21
```

code continues on next page

3. Include the database connection:

```
include('../mysqli_connect.php');
```

Both phases of the script—displaying the form and handling the form—require a database connection, so the included file is incorporated at this point.

4. Validate that a numeric ID value was received in the URL:

```
if (isset($_GET['id']) &&
→ is_numeric($_GET['id']) &&
→ ($_GET['id'] > 0) ) {
```

This conditional is like one from Chapter 12, with the addition of checking that the ID value is greater than 0. Adding that clause doesn't do anything

for the security of the script—the `is_numeric()` test confirms that the value is safe to use in a query, but prevents the query from being executed if the ID has an unusable value.

5. Define and execute the query:

```
$query = "SELECT quote, source,
→ favorite FROM quotes WHERE
→ id={$_GET['id']}";
if ($result = mysqli_query($dbc,
→ $query)) {
```

The query returns three columns for a specific record.

continues on page 415

Script 13.9 *continued*

```
22     // Define the query.
23     $query = "SELECT quote, source, favorite FROM quotes WHERE id={$_GET['id']}";
24     if ($result = mysqli_query($dbc, $query)) { // Run the query.
25
26         $row = mysqli_fetch_array($result); // Retrieve the information.
27
28         // Make the form:
29         print '<form action="edit_quote.php" method="post">
30             <p><label>Quote <textarea name="quote" rows="5" cols="30">' .
                 htmlentities($row['quote']) . '</textarea></label></p>
31             <p><label>Source <input type="text" name="source"value="' .
                 htmlentities($row['source']) . '"></label></p>
32             <p><label>Is this a favorite? <input type="checkbox" name="favorite" value="yes"';
33
34         // Check the box if it is a favorite:
35         if ($row['favorite'] == 1) {
36             print ' checked="checked"';
37         }
38
39         // Complete the form:
40         print '></label></p>
41             <input type="hidden" name="id" value="' . $_GET['id'] . '">
42             <p><input type="submit" name="submit" value="Update This Quote!"></p>
43     </form>';
44
```

code continues on next page

```
45      } else { // Couldn't get the information.
46          print '<p class="error">Could not retrieve the quotation because:<br>' . mysqli_
            error($dbc) . '.</p><p>The query being run was: ' . $query . '</p>';
47      }
48
49  } elseif (isset($_POST['id']) && is_numeric($_POST['id']) && ($_POST['id'] > 0)) { // Handle
    the form.
50
51      // Validate and secure the form data:
52      $problem = FALSE;
53      if ( !empty($_POST['quote']) && !empty($_POST['source']) ) {
54
55          // Prepare the values for storing:
56          $quote = mysqli_real_escape_string($dbc, trim(strip_tags($_POST['quote'])));
57          $source = mysqli_real_escape_string($dbc, trim(strip_tags($_POST['source'])));
58
59          // Create the "favorite" value:
60          if (isset($_POST['favorite'])) {
61              $favorite = 1;
62          } else {
63              $favorite = 0;
64          }
65
66      } else {
67          print '<p class="error">Please submit both a quotation and a source.</p>';
68          $problem = TRUE;
69      }
70
71      if (!$problem) {
72
73          // Define the query.
74          $query = "UPDATE quotes SET quote='$quote', source='$source', favorite=$favorite WHERE
            id={$_POST['id']}";
75          if ($result = mysqli_query($dbc, $query)) {
76              print '<p>The quotation has been updated.</p>';
77          } else {
78              print '<p class="error">Could not update the quotation because:<br>' . mysqli_
                error($dbc) . '.</p><p>The query being run was: ' . $query . '</p>';
79          }
80
81      } // No problem!
82
83  } else { // No ID set.
84      print '<p class="error">This page has been accessed in error.</p>';
85  } // End of main IF.
86
87  mysqli_close($dbc); // Close the connection.
88
89  include('templates/footer.html'); // Include the footer.
90  ?>
```

6. Begin creating the form:

```
print '<form action="edit_quote.
php" method="post">
  <p><label>Quote
  → <textarea name="quote"
  → rows="5" cols="30">' .
  → htmlentities($row['quote']) .
  → '</textarea></label></p>
  <p><label>Source <input type=
  → "text" name="source"value=
  → "' . htmlentities($row
  → ['source']) . '"></label></p>
  <p><label>Is this a favorite?
  → <input type="checkbox"
  → name="favorite" value="yes"';
```

The form is posted back to this same page. It starts with a text area, whose value will be prepopulated with the quote value retrieved from the database. That value is run through **htmlentities()** as a safety precaution.

Next, a text input is created, pre-populated with the quotation's source. Finally, the checkbox for the indication of the favorite is begun. Note that this checkbox element is not completed, because the script needs to next determine whether or not to select the box (in Step 7).

7. Select the box if it is a favorite:

```
if ($row['favorite'] == 1) {
  print ' checked="checked"';
}
```

If the record's **favorite** value equals 1, then the administrator previously marked this quotation as a favorite. In that case, additional HTML needs to be added to the checkbox input to prese-lect it. After this point in the code, the favorite checkbox's underlying HTML will be either

```
<input type="checkbox"
→ name="favorite" value="yes"
```

or **B**

```
<input type="checkbox"
→ name="favorite" value="yes"
→ checked="checked"
```

continues on next page

```
<p><label>Quote <textarea name="quote" rows="5" cols="30">It is useless to attempt to reason a man o
reasoned into.</textarea></label></p>
<p><label>Source <input type="text" name="source"value="Jonathan Swift"></label></p>
<p><label>Is this a favorite? <input type="checkbox" name="favorite" value="yes" checked="checked">

<input type="hidden" name="id" value="3">
```

B The HTML source code for the page, upon first arriving, shows how the favorite checkbox can be preselected.

8. Complete the form:

```
print '></label></p>
  <input type="hidden" name="id"
→ value="' . $_GET['id'] . '">
  <p><input type="submit"
→ name="submit" value="Update
→ This Quote!"></p>
</form>';
```

The **print** statement starts by closing the checkbox. Then the form must also store the ID value in a hidden input, so that it's available to the script upon the form submission.

Note that it's safe to print out **$_GET['id']** here without using **htmlentities()** because the **is_numeric()** function already confirmed that it has a numeric value.

9. Create an error if the record could not be retrieved:

```
} else { // Couldn't get the
→ information.
  print '<p class="error">Could
→ not retrieve the quotation
→ because:<br>' . mysqli_error
→ ($dbc) . '.</p><p>The query
→ being run was: ' . $query .
→ '</p>';
}
```

10. Check for a form submission:

```
} elseif (isset($_POST['id']) &&
→ is_numeric($_POST['id']) &&
→ ($_POST['id'] > 0)) {
```

This conditional begins the second phase of the script: handling the submission of the form. The validation is the same as in Step 4, but now **$_POST['id']** is referenced instead of **$_GET['id']**.

11. Validate the form data:

```
$problem = FALSE;
if (!empty($_POST['quote']) &&
→ !empty($_POST['source']) ) {
```

The form validation for the edit page mirrors that in the **add_quote.php** script (Script 13.7).

12. Prepare the values for use in the query:

```
$quote = mysqli_real_escape_string
→ ($dbc, trim(strip_tags($_POST
→ ['quote'])));
$source = mysqli_real_escape_string
→ ($dbc, trim(strip_tags($_POST
→ ['source'])));
if (isset($_POST['favorite'])) {
  $favorite = 1;
} else {
  $favorite = 0;
}
```

This code is also taken straight from **add_quote.php**.

13. Indicate a problem if the form wasn't completed:

```
} else {
  print '<p class="error">
→ Please submit both a
→ quotation and a source.</p>';
  $problem = TRUE;
}
```

14. If no problem occurred, update the database:

```
if (!$problem) {
  $query = "UPDATE quotes
→ SET quote='$quote',
→ source=$source',
→ favorite=$favorite WHERE
→ id={$_POST['id']}";
  if ($r = mysqli_query($dbc,
→ $query)) {
  print '<p>The quotation has
→ been updated.</p>';
```

My Site of Quotes.

Edit a Quotation.

The quotation has been updated.

C The result upon successfully editing a record.

The **UPDATE** query updates the values of three of the record's columns. The two string values are enclosed in single quotation marks (within the query); the numeric **$favorite** value is not.

The **WHERE** clause, which dictates the record to be updated, is the critical piece.

Finally, a simple message indicates the success of the operation **C**.

15. Indicate a problem if the query failed:

```
} else {
  print '<p class="error">
  → Could not update the
  → quotation because:<br>' .
  → mysqli_error($dbc) . '.
  → </p><p>The query being run
  → was: ' . $query . '</p>';
}
```

16. Complete the conditionals:

```
  } // No problem!
} else { // No ID set.
  print '<p class="error">
  → This page has been accessed
  → in error.</p>';
} // End of main IF.
```

The **else** clause applies if no valid ID value is received by the page via either GET or POST.

17. Close the database connection, and complete the page:

```
mysqli_close($dbc);
include('templates/footer.html');
?>
```

18. Save the file, and test in your browser (by clicking a link on **view_quotes.php**).

Deleting Quotes

The script for deleting existing quotations mimics **delete_entry.php** from Chapter 12.

Upon first arriving, assuming that a valid record ID was passed along in the URL, the quote to be deleted is displayed **A**. If the administrator clicks the submit button, the form will be submitted back to this same page, at which point the record will be removed from the database **B**.

To create delete_quote.php:

1. Begin a new PHP document in your text editor or IDE, to be named **delete_quote.php** (Script 13.10):

   ```
   <?php // Script 13.10 -
   → delete_quote.php
   define('TITLE', 'Delete a
   → Quote');
   include('templates/header.html');
   print '<h2>Delete a Quotation
   → </h2>';
   ```

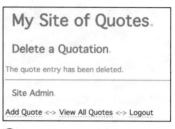

A The first step for deleting a record is confirming the record to be removed.

My Site of Quotes.

Delete a Quotation.

The quote entry has been deleted.

Site Admin.

Add Quote <-> View All Quotes <-> Logout

B Upon submission of the form, the quotation is deleted and a message is printed.

Script 13.10 The **delete_quote.php** script provides the administrator with a way to delete an existing record.

```
1    <?php // Script 13.10 - delete_quote.php
2    /* This script deletes a quote. */
3
4    // Define a page title and include the header:
5    define('TITLE', 'Delete a Quote');
6    include('templates/header.html');
7
8    print '<h2>Delete a Quotation</h2>';
9
10   // Restrict access to administrators only:
11   if (!is_administrator()) {
12       print '<h2>Access Denied!</h2><p class="error">You do not have permission to access this
         page.</p>';
13       include('templates/footer.html');
14       exit();
15   }
16
```

code continues on next page

2. Terminate the script if the user isn't an administrator:

```
if (!is_administrator()) {
    print '<h2>Access Denied!
    → </h2> <p class="error">You do
    → not have permission to access
    → this page.</p>';
    include('templates/
    → footer.html');
    exit();
}
```

continues on next page

Script 13.10 *continued*

```
17    // Need the database connection:
18    include('../mysqli_connect.php');
19
20    if (isset($_GET['id']) && is_numeric($_GET['id']) && ($_GET['id'] > 0) ) { // Display the
      quote in a form:
21
22        // Define the query:
23        $query = "SELECT quote, source, favorite FROM quotes WHERE id={$_GET['id']}";
24        if ($result = mysqli_query($dbc, $query)) { // Run the query.
25
26            $row = mysqli_fetch_array($result); // Retrieve the information.
27
28            // Make the form:
29            print '<form action="delete_quote.php" method="post">
30            <p>Are you sure you want to delete this quote?</p>
31            <div><blockquote>' . $row['quote'] . '</blockquote>- ' . $row['source'];
32
33            // Is this a favorite?
34            if ($row['favorite'] == 1) {
35                print ' <strong>Favorite!</strong>';
36            }
37
38            print '</div><br><input type="hidden" name="id" value="' . $_GET['id'] . '">
39            <p><input type="submit" name="submit" value="Delete this Quote!"></p>
40            </form>';
41
42        } else { // Couldn't get the information.
43            print '<p class="error">Could not retrieve the quote because:<br>' . mysqli_error($dbc)
               . '.</p><p>The query being run was: ' . $query . '</p>';
44        }
45
46    } elseif (isset($_POST['id']) && is_numeric($_POST['id']) && ($_POST['id'] > 0) ) { // Handle
      the form.
47
```

code continues on next page

3. Include the database connection:

```
include('../mysqli_connect.php');
```

4. Validate that a numeric ID value was received in the URL:

```
if (isset($_GET['id']) &&
→ is_numeric($_GET['id']) &&
→ ($_GET['id'] > 0) ) {
```

This is the same conditional used in `edit_quote.php`.

5. Retrieve the record to be deleted:

```
$query = "SELECT quote, source,
→ favorite FROM quotes WHERE
→ id={$_GET['id']}";
if ($r = mysqli_query($dbc,
→ $query)) {$row =
→ mysqli_fetch_array($r);
```

The standard three fields are retrieved from the database for the record. Because only one record is being addressed in this script, the `mysqli_fetch_array()` function is called once, outside of any loop.

6. Begin creating the form:

```
print '<form action=
→ "delete_quote. php"
→ method="post">
<p>Are you sure you want to
→ delete this quote?</p>
<div><blockquote>' . $row
→ ['quote'] . '</blockquote>- ' .
→ $row['source'];
```

The form, for the most part, just displays the quotation.

7. Indicate if the quotation is a favorite:

```
if ($row['favorite'] == 1) {
   print ' <strong>Favorite!
     → </strong>';
}
```

This code is the same as that on the `view_quotes.php` page, indicating that the quote is, in fact, a favorite.

Script 13.10 *continued*

```
48     // Define the query:
49     $query = "DELETE FROM quotes WHERE id={$_POST['id']} LIMIT 1";
50     $result = mysqli_query($dbc, $query); // Execute the query.
51
52     // Report on the result:
53     if (mysqli_affected_rows($dbc) == 1) {
54         print '<p>The quote entry has been deleted.</p>';
55     } else {
56         print '<p class="error">Could not delete the blog entry because:<br>' . mysqli_
           error($dbc) . '.</p><p>The query being run was: ' . $query . '</p>';
57     }
58
59 } else { // No ID received.
60     print '<p class="error">This page has been accessed in error.</p>';
61 } // End of main IF.
62
63 mysqli_close($dbc); // Close the connection.
64
65 include('templates/footer.html');
66 ?>
```

8. Complete the form:

```
print '</div><br>
<input type="hidden" name="id"
→ value="' . $_GET['id'] . '">
<p><input type="submit" name=
→ "submit" value="Delete this
→ Quote!"></p>
</form>';
```

The form must contain a hidden input that will pass the quote ID back to the page upon form submission.

9. Complete the `mysqli_query()` conditional:

```
} else { // Couldn't get the
→ information.
  print '<p class="error">
  → Could not retrieve the quote
  because:<br>' .
  → mysqli_error($dbc) . '.
  → </p><p>The query being run
  → was: ' . $query . '</p>';
}
```

If the query failed, the MySQL error and the query itself are displayed for debugging purposes.

10. Check for a form submission:

```
} elseif (isset($_POST['id']) &&
→ is_numeric($_POST['id']) &&
→ ($_POST['id'] > 0) ) {
```

This conditional begins the second phase of the script: handling the submission of the form. The validation is the same as in Step 4, but now `$_POST['id']` is referenced instead of `$_GET['id']`.

11. Delete the record:

```
$query = "DELETE FROM quotes
→ WHERE id={$_POST['id']} LIMIT
→ 1";
$r = mysqli_query($dbc, $query);
```

The **DELETE** query will remove the record. The **WHERE** conditional indicates which specific record is to be removed, and the **LIMIT 1** clause is applied as an extra precaution.

12. Report on the result:

```
if (mysqli_affected_rows($dbc)
→ == 1) {
  print '<p>The quote entry has
  → been deleted.</p>';
} else {
  print '<p class="error">
  → Could not delete the blog
  → entry because:<br>' .
  → mysqli_error($dbc) . '.
  → </p><p>The query being run
  → was: ' . $query . '</p>';
}
```

If the query succeeded, then one record will have been affected and a message is displayed to the user **Ⓑ**.

13. Complete the conditionals:

```
} else { // No ID received.
  print '<p class="error">
  → This page has been accessed
  → in error.</p>';
} // End of main IF.
```

The **else** clause applies if no valid ID value is received by the page via either GET or POST.

14. Close the database connection, and complete the page:

```
mysqli_close($dbc);
include('templates/footer.html');
?>
```

15. Save the file, and test in your browser (by clicking a link on **view_quotes.php**).

Creating the Home Page

Last, but certainly not least, there's the home page. For this site, the home page will be the only page used by the public at large. The home page will show a single quotation, but the specific quotation can be one of the following:

- The most recent (the default)
- A random quotation
- A random favorite quotation

To achieve this effect, links will pass different values in the URL back to this same page .

The script should also display administrative links—edit and delete—for the currently displayed quote, if the user is an administrator .

A Values passed in the URL trigger the execution of different queries.

B When an administrator views the home page, extra links are displayed.

Script 13.11 The home page of the site shows a single quotation at a time, plus administrative links (when appropriate).

```
1    <?php // Script 13.11 - index.php
2    /* This is the home page for this site. It displays:
3    - The most recent quote (default)
4    - OR, a random quote
5    - OR, a random favorite quote */
6
7    // Include the header:
8    include('templates/header.html');
9
10   // Need the database connection:
11   include('../mysqli_connect.php');
12
13   // Define the query...
14   // Change the particulars depending upon values passed in the URL:
15   if (isset($_GET['random'])) {
16       $query = 'SELECT id, quote, source, favorite FROM quotes ORDER BY RAND() DESC LIMIT 1';
17   } elseif (isset($_GET['favorite'])) {
18       $query = 'SELECT id, quote, source, favorite FROM quotes WHERE favorite=1 ORDER BY RAND()
         DESC LIMIT 1';
```

code continues on next page

To create index.php:

1. Begin a new PHP document in your text editor or IDE, to be named **index.php** (Script 13.11):

   `<?php // Script 13.11 - index.php`

2. Include the header:

   `include('templates/header.html');`

   The home page does not need a custom title, so no constant is defined before including the header.

3. Include the database connection:

   `include('../mysqli_connect.php');`

4. Begin defining the query to be run:

   ```
   if (isset($_GET['random'])) {
     $query = 'SELECT id, quote,
   → source, favorite FROM quotes
   → ORDER BY RAND() DESC LIMIT 1';
   ```

   If a **$_GET['random']** variable is set, the user clicked a link requesting a random quotation. It doesn't matter what value this variable has, as long as it is set.

   For all the queries, four columns—**id**, the **quote**, the **source**, and **favorite**—from one row will be returned. To retrieve only one row, a **LIMIT 1** clause is used.

continues on next page

Script 13.11 *continued*

```
19   } else {
20       $query = 'SELECT id, quote, source, favorite FROM quotes ORDER BY date_entered DESC LIMIT
         1';
21   }
23       // Run the query:
24   if ($result = mysqli_query($dbc, $query)) {
25
26       // Retrieve the returned record:
27       $row = mysqli_fetch_array($result);
28
29       // Print the record:
30       print "<div><blockquote>{$row['quote']}</blockquote>- {$row['source']}";
31
32       // Is this a favorite?
33       if ($row['favorite'] == 1) {
34           print ' <strong>Favorite!</strong>';
35       }
36
37       // Complete the DIV:
38       print '</div>';
39
40       // If the admin is logged in, display admin links for this record:
41       if (is_administrator()) {
42           print "<p><b>Quote Admin:</b> <a href=\"edit_quote.php?id={$row['id']}\">Edit</a> <->
43           <a href=\"delete_quote.php?id={$row['id']}\">Delete</a>
44           </p>\n";
45       }
46
```

code continues on next page

To select a random row in MySQL, use the **ORDER BY RAND()** clause. This code uses MySQL's **RAND()** function, short for *random*, to return the records in a random order. So this query first selects every record in random order, and then returns only the first in that set.

5. Define the query that selects a random favorite record:

```
} elseif (isset
→ ($_GET['favorite'])) {
  $query = 'SELECT id, quote,
  → source, favorite FROM quotes
  → WHERE favorite=1 ORDER BY
  → RAND() DESC LIMIT 1';
```

This query is similar to that in Step 4, but it uses a **WHERE** clause to restrict the pool of possible quotations to just those whose **favorite** value equals 1.

6. Define the default query:

```
} else {
  $query = 'SELECT id, quote,
  → source, favorite FROM quotes
  → ORDER BY date_entered DESC
  → LIMIT 1';
}
```

If no value was passed in the URL, then the home page should display the most recently added quotation. To do that, the query orders all the quotes in descending order of date entered and then limits the results to just a single record.

7. Execute the query, and fetch the returned record:

```
if ($r = mysqli_query($dbc,
→ $query)) {
  $row = mysqli_fetch_array($r);
```

8. Print the quotation:

```
print "<div><blockquote>
→ {$row ['quote']}</blockquote>-
→ {$row['source']} ";
```

This code is similar to that in **view_quotes.php**, but needs to be used only once.

9. Indicate if the quotation is a favorite, and complete the DIV:

```
if ($row['favorite'] == 1) {
  print ' <strong>Favorite!
  → </strong>';
}
print '</div>';
```

The conditional is the same as in **delete_quote.php** and **view_quotes.php**.

Script 13.11 *continued*

```
47   } else { // Query didn't run.
48     print '<p class="error">Could not retrieve the data because:<br>' . mysqli_error($dbc) .
       '.</p><p>The query being run was: ' . $query . '</p>';
49   } // End of query IF.
50
51   mysqli_close($dbc); // Close the connection.
52
53   print '<p><a href="index.php">Latest</a> <-> <a href="index.php?random=true">Random</a> <-> <a
     href="index.php?favorite=true">Favorite</a></p>';
54
55   include('templates/footer.html'); // Include the footer.
56   ?>
```

10. If the user is an administrator, create links to edit or delete this record:

```
if (is_administrator()) {
  print "<p><b>Quote Admin:
  → </b> <a href=\"edit_quote.
  → php? id={$row['id']}\">Edit
  → </a> - + | + -
  <a href=\"delete_quote.php?
  → id={$row['id']}\">Delete</a>
  </p>\n";
}
```

If the user is an administrator, links to the edit and delete scripts will be added to the page. The links themselves have values just like those in `view_quotes.php`.

11. If the query didn't run, print out an error message:

```
} else { // Query didn't run.
  print '<p class="error">
  → Could not retrieve the data
  because:<br>' .
  → mysqli_error($dbc) . '.
  → </p><p>The query being run
  → was: ' . $query . '</p>';
} // End of query IF.
```

This code is for your own debugging purposes. You would not display a MySQL error, or the query that caused it, to the general public.

As a precaution, you could only show the MySQL error if `is_administrator()` returns TRUE.

12. Close the database connection:

```
mysqli_close($dbc);
```

The database connection will no longer be needed, so it can be closed at this point.

13. Create links to other pages:

```
print '<p><a href="index.php">
→ Latest</a> <-> <a href=
→ "index.php?random=true">
→ Random</a> <-> <a href=
→ "index.php?favorite=true">
→ Favorite</a></p>';
```

Three public links are added to the page, each back to this same script. The first link, which passes no values in the URL, will always show the most recent quotation. The second, which passes a *random* value in the URL, will trigger the query in Step 4, thereby retrieving a random record. The third link, which passes a *favorite* value in the URL, will trigger the query in Step 5, thereby retrieving a random favorite record.

14. Include the footer, and complete the page:

```
include('templates/footer.html');
?>
```

15. Save the file, and test in your browser **C**.

TIP Normally the home page is one of the first scripts written, not the last. But in this case I wanted to build up to this point in the example.

C The latest quotation (note the URL).

Review and Pursue

If you have any problems with the review questions or the pursue prompts, turn to the book's supporting forum (www.LarryUllman.com/forums/).

Review

- How would the `is_administrator()` function be called to check for the same cookie—named *Samuel*—with a different value? A different cookie—not named *Samuel*—with a different value?

- Why is the reference to the style sheet in the header file `css/style.css` instead of `../css/style.css`? How else could the style sheet be referenced?

- Why is the `login.php` script structured the way it is? How could that script be organized more linearly?

- What would be some other good ideas for user-defined functions with this site? Hint: Look for repeated code.

Pursue

- Make the login form sticky.

- Define the login credentials—the cookie name and value—as constants in a configuration file. Then include that configuration file on every page, and use those constants for creating, deleting, and confirming the value of the cookie.

- Limit the cookie's expiration to only 15 minutes, and then re-send the cookie on each page, if appropriate (i.e., if the cookie exists).

- Use sessions instead of a cookie.

- Make the `add_quote.php` and `edit_quote.php` forms sticky.

- Change `view_quotes.php` so that the administrator can list the quotes in different order. Hint: Create links back to the page like those on `index.php`, and change the query accordingly.

- Before putting this site on a live server (should you do that), update all the code so that no MySQL error is ever shown to a nonadministrative user.

- See what other repetitive code could also be moved into your own functions.

Installation and Configuration

The three technical requirements for executing all of this book's examples are PHP, the scripting language; the web server application that PHP runs through; and MySQL, the database application. This appendix describes the installation of these tools on two different platforms—Windows 10 and Mac OS X. If you are using a hosted website, all of this will already be provided for you, but these products are all free and easy enough to install, so putting them on your own computer still makes sense.

After the installation section, this appendix demonstrates some basics for working with MySQL and configuring PHP. The PHP and MySQL manuals cover installation and configuration in a reasonable amount of detail. You may want to also peruse them, particularly if you encounter problems.

Installation on Windows

Although you can certainly install a web server (such as Apache, Nginx, or IIS), PHP, and MySQL individually on a Windows computer, I strongly recommend you use an all-in-one installer instead. It's simply easier and more reliable to do so.

Several all-in-one installers are out there for Windows. The four that I see mentioned most frequently are

- XAMPP (www.apachefriends.org)
- WAMP (www.wampserver.com)
- AMPPS (www.ampps.com)
- Bitnami (www.bitnami.com), which also partners with XAMPP

For this appendix, I'll use XAMPP, which runs on Windows 2008, 2012, Vista, 7, and 8. (The XAMPP site makes no mention of Windows 10, but you should be able to use XAMPP on that version of Windows too.)

On Firewalls

A firewall prevents communications in many ways, the most common of which being over *ports*: an access point to a computer. Versions of Windows starting with Service Pack 2 of XP include a built-in firewall. You can also download and install third-party firewalls. Firewalls improve the security of your computer, but they may also interfere with your ability to run Apache, MySQL, and some of the other tools used by XAMPP because they all use ports.

When running XAMPP for the first time, or during the installation process, if you see a security prompt indicating that the firewall is blocking Apache, MySQL, or the like, choose *Unblock* or *Allow access*. Otherwise, you can configure your firewall manually through the operating system settings.

The ports that need to be open are as follows: 80 for Apache, 3306 for MySQL, and 25 for the Mercury mail server. If you have any problems starting or accessing one of these, disable your firewall and see if it works then. If so, you'll know the firewall is the problem and that it needs to be reconfigured.

Just to be clear, firewalls aren't found just on Windows, but in terms of the instructions in this appendix, the presence of a firewall will more likely trip up a Windows user than any other.

Along with Apache, PHP, and MySQL, XAMPP also installs the following:

- phpMyAdmin, the web-based interface to a MySQL server
- OpenSSL, for secure connections
- A mail server (for sending email)
- Several useful extensions

As of this writing, XAMPP (Version 7.0.6) installs PHP 7.0.6, Apache 2.4.18, and phpMyAdmin 4.5.1. There is one catch, however!

As of XAMPP 5.5.30, the installer includes MariaDB (www.mariadb.com) instead of MySQL. MariaDB is an open source fork of MySQL that is functionally equivalent. Despite the fact that XAMPP installs MariaDB instead of MySQL, you shouldn't have any problems following all the MySQL-specific instructions or code in this book.

I'll run through the installation process in these next steps. Note that if you have any problems, you can use the book's supporting forum (www.LarryUllman.com/forums/), but you'll probably have more luck turning to the XAMPP site (it is their product, after all). Also, the installer works really well and isn't that hard to use, so rather than detail every single step in the process, I'll highlight the most important considerations.

To install XAMPP on Windows:

1. Download the latest release of XAMPP for Windows from www.apachefriends.org .

   I suggest that you grab the latest version of PHP available, although you'll be fine with this book's content if you use a PHP 5 version instead.

2. On your computer, double-click the downloaded file to begin the installation process.

3. When prompted **B**, install all the components.

   Admittedly, you don't need Tomcat—a Java server—or Perl, but it's fine to install them too.

4. When prompted **C**, install XAMPP somewhere other than in the Program Files directory.

   You shouldn't install it in the Program Files directory because of a permissions issue in Windows. I recommend installing XAMPP in your root directory (e.g., **C:**).

   Wherever you decide to install the program, make note of that location, because you'll need to know it several other times as you work through this appendix.

XAMPP for Windows 5.5.35, 5.6.21 & 7.

Version		Checksum		
5.5.35 / PHP 5.5.35	What's Included?	md5	sha1	Download (32 bit)
5.6.21 / PHP 5.6.21	What's Included?	md5	sha1	Download (32 bit)
7.0.6 / PHP 7.0.6	What's Included?	md5	sha1	Download (32 bit)

Requirements   Add-ons   More Downloads »

Windows XP or 2003 are not supported. You can download a compatible version of XAMPP platforms here.

A From the Apache Friends website, grab the latest installer for Windows.

B The XAMPP components that can be installed.

C Select where XAMPP should be installed.

D The installation of XAMPP is complete!

E The XAMPP Control Panel, used to manage the software.

5. After the installation process has done its thing **D**, opt to start the XAMPP Control Panel.

6. To start, stop, and configure XAMPP, use the XAMPP Control Panel **E**.

   Apache has to be running for every chapter in this book. MySQL must be running for Chapter 12, "Intro to Databases," and Chapter 13, "Putting It All Together." Mercury is the mail server that XAMPP installs. It needs to be running in order to send email using PHP (see Chapter 8, "Creating Web Applications").

7. Immediately set a password for the root MySQL user.

   How you do this is explained in the "Managing MySQL Users" section later in this appendix.

continues on next page

TIP The XAMPP Control Panel's various admin links will take you to different web pages (on your server) and other resources 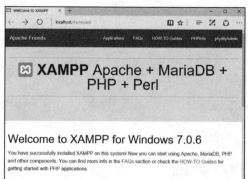.

TIP See the "Configuring PHP" section to learn how to configure PHP by editing the `php.ini` file.

TIP Whenever you restart your computer, you'll need to restart the XAMPP services.

TIP Your web root directory—where your PHP scripts should be placed in order to test them— is the `htdocs` folder in the directory where XAMPP was installed. Following my installation instructions, this would be `C:\xampp\htdocs`.

F The web-based splash page for XAMPP, linked from its Control Panel.

Installation on Mac OS X

Mac OS X is at its heart a version of Unix, and because PHP and MySQL were originally written for Unix-like systems, numerous options are available for installing them on Mac OS X. In fact, Mac OS X already comes with Apache installed, saving you that step.

Seasoned developers and those at home in the Terminal will likely want to install PHP and MySQL using package installers such as http://php-osx.liip.ch/ and Homebrew (http://brew.sh/). But for beginners, I recommend using an all-in-one installer such as

- XAMPP (www.apachefriends.org)
- AMPPS (www.ampps.com)
- Bitnami (www.bitnami.com), which also partners with XAMPP
- MAMP (www.mamp.info)

Not only are these installers relatively foolproof, but they also won't leave you scrambling when an operating system update overwrites your Apache configuration file. For this appendix, I'll use XAMPP, which runs on Mac OS X 10.6 and later.

Along with Apache, PHP, and MySQL, XAMPP also installs the following:

- phpMyAdmin, the web-based interface to a MySQL server
- OpenSSL, for secure connections
- Several useful extensions

As of this writing, XAMPP (Version 7.0.6) installs PHP 7.0.6, Apache 2.4.18, and phpMyAdmin 4.5.1. There is one catch, however!

As of XAMPP 5.5.30, the installer includes MariaDB (www.mariadb.com) instead of MySQL. MariaDB is an open source fork of MySQL that is functionally equivalent. Despite the fact that XAMPP installs MariaDB instead of MySQL, you shouldn't have any problems following all the MySQL-specific instructions or code in this book.

I'll run through the installation process in these next steps. Note that if you have any problems, you can use the book's supporting forum (www.LarryUllman.com/forums/), but you'll probably have more luck turning to the XAMPP site (it is their product, after all). Also, the installer works really well and isn't that hard to use, so rather than detail every single step in the process, I'll highlight the most important considerations.

To install XAMPP on Mac OS X:

1. Download the latest release of XAMPP for Mac OS X from www.apachefriends.org **A**.

   I suggest you grab the latest version of PHP available, although you'll be fine with this book's content if you use a PHP 5 version instead.

2. On your computer, double-click the downloaded file to mount the disc image.

3. In the mounted disk image, double-click the package installer to begin the installation process.

4. When prompted **B**, install all the components.

   You'll see only two, broad options; install both.

5. After the installation process has done its thing **C**, opt to launch XAMPP.

6. To start, stop, and configure XAMPP, use the XAMPP Control Panel **D**.

   Apache has to be running for every chapter in this book. MySQL must be running for Chapters 12 and 13. You probably won't ever need the FTP application, because you can just move your files directly.

7. Immediately set a password for the root MySQL user.

   How you do this is explained in the "Managing MySQL Users" section later in this appendix.

A From the Apache Friends website, grab the latest installer for Mac OS X.

B The XAMPP components that can be installed.

C The installation of XAMPP is complete!

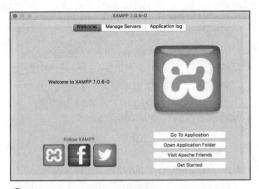

D The XAMPP Control Panel, used to manage the software.

TIP See the "Configuring PHP" section to learn how to configure PHP by editing the `php.ini` file.

TIP Whenever you restart your computer, you'll need to restart the XAMPP services.

TIP Your web root directory—where your PHP scripts should be placed in order to test them—is the `htdocs` folder in the directory where XAMPP was installed. This would be `/Applications/XAMPP/xamppfiles/htdocs`.

Configuring PHP

One of the benefits of installing PHP on your own computer is that you can configure it however you prefer. How PHP runs is determined by the **php.ini** file, which is normally created when PHP is installed.

Two of the most important settings you may want to consider adjusting are **display_errors** and **error_reporting** (both are discussed in Chapter 3, "HTML Forms and PHP"). To change any setting, open the PHP configuration file, edit it as needed, then save it and restart the web server.

To alter PHP's configuration:

1. In your browser, execute a script that invokes the **phpinfo()** function **A**.

   The **phpinfo()** function, discussed in Chapter 1, "Getting Started with PHP," reveals oodles of information about the PHP installation.

2. In the browser's output, search for *Loaded Configuration File*.

   The value next to this text is the location of the active configuration file. This will be something like **C:\xampp\php\php.ini** or **/Applications/XAMPP/xamppfiles/etc/php.ini**.

   If there is no value for the *Loaded Configuration File*, your server has no active **php.ini** file. This is highly uncommon, but you'd need to download the PHP source code, from www.php.net, to find a sample configuration file.

3. Open the **php.ini** file in any text editor.

4. Change the settings as you wish.

   Depending on your operating system, you may need to be an administrator or enter a password to make changes to this file.

   Many instructions are included in the file. Lines are commented out (made inactive) by preceding them with a semicolon.

5. Save the **php.ini** file.

PHP Version 7.0.6	php
System	Windows NT WIN10-MAR2016 10.0 build 10586 (Windows 10) i586
Build Date	Apr 28 2016 13:44:25
Compiler	MSVC14 (Visual C++ 2015)
Architecture	x86
Configure Command	cscript /nologo configure.js "--enable-snapshot-build" "--enable-debug-pack" "--with-pdo-oci=c:\php-sdk\oracle\x86\instantclient_12_1\sdk,shared" "--with-oci8-12c=c:\php-sdk\oracle\x86\instantclient_12_1\sdk,shared" "--enable-object-out-dir=../obj/" "--enable-com-dotnet=shared" "--with-mcrypt=static" "--without-analyzer" "--with-pgo"
Server API	Apache 2.0 Handler
Virtual Directory Support	enabled
Configuration File (php.ini) Path	C:\Windows
Loaded Configuration File	C:\xampp\php\php.ini

A Some of the output from calling the **phpinfo()** function.

Enabling Mail

The `mail()` function works only if the computer running PHP has access to sendmail or another mail server. One way to enable the `mail()` function is to set the `smtp` value in the `php.ini` file (for Windows only). This approach works if, for example, your Internet provider has an SMTP address you can use. Unfortunately, you can't use this value if your ISP's SMTP server requires authentication.

For Windows, a number of free SMTP servers, such as Mercury, are available. It's installed along with XAMPP, or you can install it yourself if you're not using XAMPP.

Mac OS X comes with a mail server installed—postfix and/or sendmail—that needs to be enabled. Search Google for instructions on manually enabling your mail server on Mac OS X.

Alternatively, you can search some of the PHP code libraries to learn how to use an SMTP server that requires authentication.

6. Restart your web server.

   You don't need to restart the entire computer, just the web server (e.g., Apache). In XAMPP, simply click Stop and then Start for Apache.

TIP You can also use the `phpinfo()` function to confirm that your configuration changes have taken effect.

TIP If you edit the `php.ini` file and restart the web server but your changes don't take effect, make sure you're editing the proper `php.ini` file (you may have more than one on your computer).

MySQL Interfaces

In Chapters 12 and 13, a PHP script will be used to interact with a MySQL database. As I explain in Chapter 12, being able to interact with MySQL independent of your PHP scripts is the most valuable debugging tool there is. Knowing how to use a separate MySQL interface is therefore critical information. I'll quickly introduce the two most common options.

Using the MySQL client

The MySQL software comes with an important tool known as the MySQL *client*. This application provides a simple interface for communicating with the MySQL server. It's a command-line tool that must be accessed using the Terminal application on Linux and Mac OS X or through the command (DOS) prompt on Windows.

To use the MySQL client:

1. Make sure the MySQL server is running.

   If you're using XAMPP on Windows, you can start MySQL there and then skip ahead to Step 3.

2. Find the MySQL **bin** directory.

   To connect to the client, you'll need to know where it's located. The MySQL client is found within the **bin** directory for your installation (*bin* is short for "binary," which is to say an executable). I'll run through the common possibilities.

   If you installed MySQL yourself, the client's location depends on where you installed the software, but it's most likely

   `C:\mysql\bin\mysql` (Windows)

   or

   `/usr/local/mysql/bin/mysql` (Mac OS X and Unix)

Using Semicolons

Within the MySQL client, a semicolon indicates the completion of a statement to be executed. This allows you to write a complicated command or SQL query over multiply lines, and MySQL won't attempt to run that command until it meets a semicolon. This is only a requirement within the MySQL client, though. Queries run through PHP scripts or phpMyAdmin do not need to be terminated by semicolons. And you don't need to use a semicolon after **exit** to leave the MySQL client.

A Use the Run dialog to access a console window on Windows.

B The Shell button in the XAMPP Control Panel takes you straight to a command prompt.

If you used XAMPP on Windows, it's
`C:\xampp\mysql\bin\mysql` (assuming you installed XAMPP in `C:\`). If you installed XAMPP on Mac OS X, it's
`/Applications/XAMPP/xamppfiles/bin`.

3. Access a command prompt.

   On Mac OS X and Unix, you can accomplish this by running the Terminal application. On Mac OS X, it's found within the `/Applications/Utilities` folder.

   On Windows, press Command+R to open the Run dialog, and at the prompt, type **cmd** and press Enter or click OK **A**.

   If you're using XAMPP on Windows, click the Shell button in the Control Panel **B** to access a command prompt.

4. Attempt to connect to the MySQL server.

   To connect, enter the pathname identified in Step 2 plus **-u** *username* **-p**. So, the command might be

   `C:\mysql\bin\mysql -u username -p`
   (Windows)

   or

   `/usr/local/mysql/bin/mysql`
   → **-u** *username* **-p** (Unix and Mac OS X)

   or

   `/Applications/XAMPP/xamppfiles/`
   → `bin/mysql -u` *username* **-p** (Mac OS X)

   For XAMPP on Windows, you can just use **mysql -u** *username* **-p** (assuming you clicked the Shell button in Step 3).

   Replace *username* with the username you want to use. If you haven't yet created any other users, this will be *root* (root is the supreme MySQL user). If you haven't yet established a root user password (the default behavior for XAMPP), you can omit the **-p** flag.

continues on next page

5. Enter the password at the prompt **C**.

   The password requested is the MySQL password for the user named during the connection. You'll see this prompt only if you used the **-p** option in Step 4.

   If you installed MAMP on Mac OS X, the password for the root user will be root. If you installed XAMPP on Windows, no password is set initially.

6. List the available databases **D**:

   SHOW DATABASES;

   The **SHOW DATABASES** command is a SQL query that lists every database hosted on that MySQL installation that the connected user can see.

7. Exit the MySQL client.

   To do so, type **exit** or **quit**.

TIP If you see a **Can't connect to local MySQL server through socket...** error message, it normally means MySQL isn't running.

TIP The MySQL client is one of the best tools for debugging PHP scripts that work with MySQL. You can use the MySQL client to check user permissions and to run queries outside of the PHP script.

```
◻ mysql -u root -p

Setting environment for using XAMPP for Windows.
user@WIN10-MAR2016 c:\xampp
# mysql -u root -p
Enter password:
Welcome to the MariaDB monitor.  Commands end with ; or \g.
Your MariaDB connection id is 6
Server version: 10.1.13-MariaDB mariadb.org binary distribution

Copyright (c) 2000, 2016, Oracle, MariaDB Corporation Ab and others.

Type 'help;' or '\h' for help. Type '\c' to clear the current input statement.

MariaDB [(none)]> ▁
```

C Successfully accessing the MySQL client on Windows.

```
MariaDB [(none)]> SHOW DATABASES;
+--------------------+
| Database           |
+--------------------+
| information_schema |
| mysql              |
| performance_schema |
| phpmyadmin         |
| test               |
+--------------------+
5 rows in set (0.00 sec)

MariaDB [(none)]>
```

D After a fresh MySQL installation, there will only be a couple of databases.

Using phpMyAdmin

phpMyAdmin (www.phpmyadmin.net) is a web-based interface for interacting with a MySQL server, allowing you to create tables, import and export records, and much more, without having to use a command-line interface. It is arguably the most popular web software written in PHP, as every PHP hosting company provides it. In fact, the all-in-one XAMPP installer includes it too. phpMyAdmin is well documented and easy to use, but I'll highlight a couple of quick points.

To use phpMyAdmin:

1. Access phpMyAdmin in your browser **E**.

   When using XAMPP, phpMyAdmin is available at http://localhost/phpmyadmin/. On Windows, you can also get to this page by clicking the MySQL admin link in the Control Panel.

2. Click a database name in the left column to select that database.

continues on next page

E The phpMyAdmin front page.

3. Click a table name in the left column to select that table **F**.

You don't always have to select a table, but by doing so you can simplify some tasks.

4. Use the tabs and links (on the right side of the page) to perform common tasks.

For the most part, the tabs and links are shortcuts to common SQL commands. For example, the Browse tab performs a **SELECT** query and the Insert tab creates a form for adding new records.

5. Use the SQL tab to execute any SQL command.

You can alternatively use the SQL Query Window, linked just above the list of database or table names. Using either interface, you can test queries that your PHP scripts are using, without the added complication of the script itself.

TIP Many other clients are available for interacting with a MySQL database, but the MySQL command-line client and phpMyAdmin are the two most common.

F Selecting a database or a table, from the left column, changes the options on the right side of the page.

Managing MySQL Users

Once you've successfully installed MySQL, you can begin creating MySQL users. A MySQL user is a fundamental security concept, limiting access to, and influence over, stored data. Just to clarify, your databases can have several different users, just as your operating system might. But MySQL users are different from operating system users. While learning PHP and MySQL on your own computer, you don't necessarily need to create new users, but live production sites need to have dedicated MySQL users with appropriate permissions.

The initial MySQL installation comes with one user (named *root*) with no password set. At the very least, you should create a new, secure password for the root user after installing MySQL.

After that, you can create other users with more limited permissions. As a rule, you shouldn't use the root user for normal, day-to-day operations.

While you're creating new users, you'll also see how to create new databases, which will be necessary for Chapters 12 and 13.

Setting the root user password

When you install MySQL, no value—or no secure password—is established for the root user. This is certainly a security risk that should be remedied before you begin to use the server (because the root user has unlimited powers).

You can set any user's password using either phpMyAdmin or the MySQL client, as long as the MySQL server is running. If MySQL isn't currently running, start it now using the steps outlined earlier in this appendix.

You must be connected to MySQL as the root user in order to be able to change the root user's password.

To assign a password to the root user via the MySQL client:

1. Connect to the MySQL client.

   See the set of steps in "To use the MySQL client" for detailed instructions.

2. Enter the following command, replacing *thepassword* with the password you want to use **A**:

   ```
   SET PASSWORD FOR
   → 'root'@'localhost' =
   → PASSWORD('thepassword');
   ```

   Keep in mind that passwords in MySQL are case-sensitive, so *Kazan* and *kazan* aren't interchangeable. The term **PASSWORD** that precedes the actual quoted password tells MySQL to encrypt that string using the MySQL **PASSWORD()** function. You cannot have a space between **PASSWORD** and the opening parenthesis.

   continues on next page

```
MariaDB [(none)]> SET PASSWORD FOR 'root'@'localhost' = PASSWORD('thepassword');
Query OK, 0 rows affected (0.00 sec)

MariaDB [(none)]>
```

A Updating the root user's password using SQL within the MySQL client.

3. Exit the MySQL client:

```
exit
```

4. Test the new password by logging in to the MySQL client again.

   Now that a password has been established, you need to add the **-p** flag to the connection command. You'll see an Enter password prompt, where you enter the just-created password.

To assign a password to the root user via phpMyAdmin:

1. Open phpMyAdmin in your browser.

   See the set of steps in the section "To use phpMyAdmin" for detailed instructions.

2. On the home page, click the User accounts tab.

   You can always click the home icon, in the upper-left corner, to get to the phpMyAdmin home page.

3. In the list of users, click the *Edit Privileges* icon on the root user's row **B**.

4. On the next page, click *Change Password*.

5. Use the Change Password form **C**, found further down the resulting page, to change the password.

User accounts overview

	User name	Host name	Password	Global privileges	Grant	Action
☐	mysql.sys	localhost	Yes	USAGE	No	🔧 Edit privileges Export
☐	root	localhost	Yes	ALL PRIVILEGES	Yes	🔧 Edit privileges Export
☐	username	localhost	Yes	USAGE	No	🔧 Edit privileges Export

B The list of MySQL users, as shown in phpMyAdmin.

Change password

○ No Password

⦿ Password: ●●●●●●●●   Re-type: ●●●●●●●●

Password Hashing: Native MySQL authentication ▾

Generate password [Generate] [_____]

C The form for updating a MySQL user's password within phpMyAdmin.

6. Change the root user's password in phpMyAdmin's configuration file, if necessary.

The result of changing the root user's password will likely be that phpMyAdmin is denied access to the MySQL server. This is because phpMyAdmin, on a local server, normally connects to MySQL as the root user, with the root user's password hard-coded into a configuration file. After following Steps 1–4, find the `config.inc.php` file in the phpMyAdmin directory—likely **/Applications/XAMPP/ xamppfiles/phpmyadmin** (Mac OS X with XAMPP) or **C:\xampp\phpMyAdmin** (Windows with XAMPP). Open that file in any text editor or IDE and change this next line to use the new password:

```
$cfg['Servers'][$i]['password'] =
→ 'thepassword';
```

Then save the file, and reload phpMy-Admin in your browser.

Creating a database, users, and privileges

After you have MySQL successfully up and running, and after you've established a password for the root user, you can add other users. This is commonly done as part of creating new databases: To improve the security of your databases, you should always create new users to access your databases rather than using the root user at all times.

To create a database, simply run a CREATE DATABASE command:

```
CREATE DATABASE database_name
```

The database name can contain numbers, letters, a dollar sign, and an underscore, but not spaces. You can run this command only if you are connected as a user with **CREATE DATABASE** permissions.

The MySQL privileges system was designed to ensure proper authority for certain commands on specific databases. This technology is how a web host, for example, can let several users access several databases without concern. Each user in the MySQL system can have specific capabilities on specific databases from specific hosts (computers). The root user—the MySQL root user, not the system's—has the most power and is used to create subusers, although subusers can be given rootlike powers (inadvisably so).

When a user attempts to do something with the MySQL server, MySQL first checks to see if the user has permission to connect to the server at all (based on the username, the user's host, the user's password, and the information in the `mysql` database's `user` table). Second, MySQL checks to see if the user has permission to run the specific SQL statement on the specific databases—for example, to select data, insert data, or create a new table. Table A.1 lists most of the various privileges you can set on a user-by-user basis.

You can set users and privileges in MySQL in a handful of ways, but I'll start by discussing the **GRANT** command. The syntax goes like this:

```
GRANT privileges ON database.*
→ TO 'username'@'hostname'
→ IDENTIFIED BY 'password'
```

For the *privileges* aspect of this statement, you can list specific privileges from Table A.1, or you can allow for all of them by using **ALL** (which isn't prudent). The *database.** part of the statement specifies which database and tables the user can work on. You can name specific tables using the *database.tablename* syntax or allow for every database with *.* (again, not prudent). Finally, you can specify the username, hostname, and a password.

The username has a maximum length of 32 characters (as of MySQL 5.7.8; it was 16 in earlier versions). When you're creating a username, be sure to avoid spaces—use the underscore instead, and note that usernames are case-sensitive.

TABLE A.1 MySQL Privileges

PRIVILEGE	ALLOWS
SELECT	Read rows from tables.
INSERT	Add new rows of data to tables.
UPDATE	Alter existing data in tables.
DELETE	Remove existing data from tables.
INDEX	Create and drop indexes in tables.
ALTER	Modify the structure of a table.
CREATE	Create new tables or databases.
DROP	Delete existing tables or databases.
RELOAD	Reload the grant tables (and therefore enact user changes).
SHUTDOWN	Stop the MySQL server.
PROCESS	View and stop existing MySQL processes.
FILE	Import data into tables from text files.
GRANT	Create new users.
REVOKE	Remove users' permissions.

The hostname is the computer from which the user is allowed to connect. This could be a domain name, such as www.example.com, or an IP address. Normally, *localhost* is specified as the hostname, meaning that the MySQL user must be connecting from the same computer that the MySQL database is running on. To allow for any host, use the hostname wildcard character (%):

```
GRANT privileges ON database.* TO
→ 'username'@'%' IDENTIFIED BY
→ 'password'
```

But that is also not recommended. When it comes to creating users, it's best to be explicit and confining.

The password has no length limit but is also case-sensitive. The passwords are encrypted in the MySQL database, meaning they can't be recovered in a plain text format. Omitting the **IDENTIFIED BY** '*password*' clause results in that user not being required to enter a password (which, once again, should be avoided).

As an example of this process, you'll create two new users with specific privileges on a new database named *myblog*. Keep in mind that you can grant permissions only to users on existing databases. This next sequence will also show how to create a database.

To create new users using GRANT:

1. Log in to the MySQL client as a root user.

   Use the steps already explained to do this. You must be logged in as a user capable of creating databases and other users.

2. Create a new database **D**:

   ```
   CREATE DATABASE myblog;
   ```

   This particular database will be used in Chapter 12.

3. Create a user with administrative-level privileges on the **myblog** database **E**:

   ```
   GRANT SELECT, INSERT, UPDATE,
   → DELETE, CREATE, DROP, ALTER,
   → INDEX ON myblog.* TO 'llama'@
   → 'localhost' IDENTIFIED BY
   → 'camel';
   ```

   This user, *llama*, can create tables, alter tables, insert data, update data, and so forth, on the temp database. This essentially includes every administrative-level capability aside from creating new users. Be certain to use a password—perhaps more clever than the one used here.

continues on next page

```
MariaDB [(none)]> CREATE DATABASE myblog;
Query OK, 1 row affected (0.00 sec)

MariaDB [(none)]>
```

D Creating a new database.

```
MariaDB [(none)]> GRANT SELECT, INSERT, UPDATE, DELETE, CREATE, DROP, ALTER,
INDEX ON myblog.* TO 'llama'@'localhost' IDENTIFIED BY 'camel';
Query OK, 0 rows affected (0.00 sec)

MariaDB [(none)]> _
```

E Creating an administrative-level user for a single database.

4. Create a user with basic access to the database **F**:

```
GRANT SELECT, INSERT, UPDATE,
→ DELETE ON myblog.* TO 'webuser'@
→ 'localhost' IDENTIFIED BY
→ 'BroWs1ng';
```

Now the generic *webuser* can browse through records (**SELECT** from tables) as well as add, edit, and delete them, but this user can't alter the structure of the database. When you're establishing users and privileges, work your way from the bottom up, allowing the bare minimum of access at all times.

5. Apply the changes **G**:

```
FLUSH PRIVILEGES;
```

The changes just made won't take effect until you've told MySQL to reset the list of acceptable users and privileges, which is what this command does. Forgetting this step and then being unable to access the database using the newly created users is a common mistake.

TIP Any database whose name begins with test_ can be modified by any user who has permission to connect to MySQL. Therefore, be careful not to create a database named this way unless it truly is experimental.

TIP The **REVOKE** command removes users and permissions.

```
MariaDB [(none)]> GRANT SELECT, INSERT, UPDATE, DELETE ON myblog.* TO
  'webuser'@'localhost' IDENTIFIED BY 'BroWs1ng';
Query OK, 0 rows affected (0.00 sec)

MariaDB [(none)]>
```

F This user has more restricted rights to the same database.

```
MariaDB [(none)]> FLUSH PRIVILEGES;
Query OK, 0 rows affected (0.00 sec)

MariaDB [(none)]>
```

G Don't forget this step before you try to access MySQL using the newly created users.

Resources
and Next Steps

This book was written to give beginning PHP programmers a good foundation on which to base their learning. A few topics have been either omitted or glossed over, because the book focuses on covering the absolute fundamentals. This appendix lists a number of useful resources, briefly discusses where to obtain more information for databases and some uncovered topics, and includes a few tables, both old and new.

Along with those sites included here, you should check out the book's companion website at www.LarryUllman.com. There you'll find all of the book's code, a support forum, an errata page, and more.

The PHP Manual

All PHP programmers should familiarize themselves with, and possibly acquire, some version of the PHP manual before beginning to work with the language. The manual is available from the official PHP site—www.php.net/docs.php—as well as from a number of other locations.

You can download the manual in nearly a dozen languages in different formats. The official website also has an annotated version of the manual available at www.php.net/manual/en/ (in English), where users have added helpful notes and comments. If you're having problems with a particular function, reading the manual's page for that function will likely provide an answer.

A trick pointed out in Chapter 1, "Getting Started with PHP," is that you can quickly access the documentation page for any specific function by going to www.php.net/*functionname*. For example, the page for the `number_format()` function is www.php.net/number_format.

Database Resources

Which database resources will be most useful to you depends, obviously, on which database management system (DBMS) you're using. The most common database used with PHP is probably MySQL, but PHP supports all the standard database applications.

To learn more about using MySQL, begin with the official MySQL website (www.mysql.com). You can download the MySQL manual to use as a reference while you work.

If you're using MySQL, don't forget to download and install phpMyAdmin (www.phpmyadmin.net). Written in PHP, this is an invaluable tool for working with a database and much more approachable for beginners than some other interfaces.

Another area of database resources you should delve into is SQL. Websites discussing SQL, the language used by every database application, include the following:

- SQL Course (www.sqlcourse.com)
- A Gentle Introduction to SQL (www.sqlzoo.net)
- W3Schools' SQL Tutorial (www.w3schools.com/sql/)
- SQL.org (www.sql.org)

(All of the above are a bit dated in appearance, but the content still applies.)

My *PHP and MySQL for Dynamic Web Sites: Visual QuickPro Guide* (Peachpit Press, 2012) also discusses SQL and MySQL in much greater detail than this book.

Top 10 Frequently Asked Questions (or Problems)

Debugging is a valuable skill that takes time and experience to fully develop. But rather than send you off on that journey ill-equipped, I've included the 10 most frequently seen problems in PHP scripts, along with the most likely causes. First, though, here are five of my best pieces of advice when it comes to debugging a problem:

- **Know what version of PHP you're running.**

  Some problems are specific to a version of PHP. Use the `phpinfo()` function to test the version in use whenever you use a server for the first time. Also make sure you know what version of MySQL you're using, if applicable; the operating system; and the web server (e.g., Apache 2.4).

- **Run all PHP scripts through a URL.**

  If you don't run a PHP script through a URL—and this includes the submission of a form to a PHP script—the web server will not handle the request, meaning that PHP will never execute the code.

- **Trust the error message!**

  Many beginners have more difficulty than they should in solving a problem because they don't pay attention to the error message they see. Although some of PHP's error messages are cryptic and a few can even be misleading, if PHP says there's a problem on line 22, the problem is probably on line 22. With a parse error, maybe the actual problem was a missing semicolon on line 21.

- **Avoid "trying" things to fix a problem!**

  If you're not sure what's causing the problem and what the proper fix is, avoid trying random things as a solution. You'll likely create new issues this way and only further confuse the original problem.

- **Take a break!**

  The best piece of advice I can offer is to step away from the computer and take a break. I've solved many, many problems this way. Sometimes a clear head is what you need.

Moving on, here are the top 10 likely problems you'll encounter in PHP:

- **Blank pages**

  If you see a blank screen in your browser after submitting a form or loading a PHP script, it's most likely because an error occurred that terminated the execution of the page. First check the HTML source code to see if it's an HTML problem. Then turn on `display_errors` in your `php.ini` configuration file or PHP script to see what PHP problem could be occurring.

- *Undefined variable* or *undefined index* error Ⓐ

  These errors occur when error reporting is set on its highest level, and they may or may not indicate a problem. Check the spelling of each variable or array index to make sure it's correct. Then make sure you initialize variables prior to referring to them. Also make sure, of course, that variables that should have a value actually do!

- **Variables that don't have a value**

  Perhaps you referred to a variable by the wrong name. Double-check your capitalization and spelling of variable names, and then be certain to use `$_GET`, `$_POST`, `$_COOKIE`, and `$_SESSION` as appropriate. If need be, use the `print_r()` function to see the value of any variable.

- *Call to undefined function...* error

  Such an error message means you're attempting to use a function that PHP doesn't have. This problem can be caused by a misspelling of a function name, failure to define your own function before calling it, or using a function that's not available in your version of PHP. Check your spelling and the PHP manual for a non-user-defined function to find the problem.

⚠ Notice: Undefined variable: Street in /Users/larry/Sites/variables.php on line *17*

Call Stack

#	Time	Memory	Function	Location
1	0.0001	362024	{main}( )	.../variables.php:0

The address is:

State College PA 16801

Ⓐ Errors complaining about undefined variables or indexes often come from spelling or capitalization mistakes.

- *Headers already sent* error **B**

  This error message indicates that you've used an HTTP header-related function—**header()**, **setcookie()**, or **session_start()**—after the browser has already received HTML or even a blank space. Double-check what occurs in a script before you call any of these functions. You can also use output buffering to prevent these errors from occurring.

- *Access denied* error **C**

  If you see this message while attempting to work with a database, then the username, password, and host combination you're using doesn't have permission to access the database. This isn't normally a PHP issue. Confirm the values that are being used, and attempt to connect to the database using a different interface (such as the MySQL client).

- *Supplied argument is not a valid MySQL result resource* error

  This is another database-related error message. The message means that a query result is being used inappropriately. Most frequently, this is because you're trying to fetch rows from a query that didn't return any records, commonly due to badly formed SQL. To solve this problem, print out the query being run, and test it using another tool (such as the MySQL client or phpMyAdmin). Also check that you've been consistent with your variable names.

  continues on next page

Warning: Cannot modify header information - headers already sent by (output started at /Users/larry/Sites/templates/header.html:8) in /Users/larry/Sites/login.php on line *22*

B Some functions create *headers already sent* errors if called at the wrong time.

Connect to MySQL

localhost/mysqli_connect.php

Warning: mysqli_connect(): (HY000/1045): Access denied for user 'username'@'localhost' (using password: YES) in /Users/larry/Sites/mysqli_connect.php on line *12*

Call Stack				
#	Time	Memory	Function	Location
1	0.0001	366448	{main}( )	.../mysqli_connect.php:0
2	0.0001	366448	mysqli_connect ( )	.../mysqli_connect.php:12

Could not connect to the database.

C If the MySQL access information is incorrect, you'll see a message saying that database access has been denied.

- **Preset HTML form values are cut off**

  You must put the value attribute of an HTML form input within double quotation marks. If you fail to do so, only the part of the value up to the first space will be set as that input's value.

- **Conditionals or loops behave unpredictably**

  These logical errors are quite common. Check that you haven't used the wrong operator (such as = instead of ==) and that you refer to the proper variables. Then use **print** statements to let you know what the script is doing.

- **Parse errors**

  Parse errors are the most ubiquitous problems you'll deal with. Even the most seasoned PHP programmer sees them occasionally. Check that every statement concludes with a semicolon and that all quotation marks, parentheses, braces, and brackets are evenly paired. If you still can't find the parse error, comment out large sections of the script using the **/*** and ***/** characters. Uncomment a section at a time until you see the parse error again. Then you'll know where in the script the problem is (or most likely is).

Parse error: syntax error, unexpected 'page' (T_STRING) in /Users/larry/Sites/test.php on line 11

D Parse errors are all too common and prevent scripts from executing.

Next Steps

This book will get you started using PHP, but you might want to investigate a few topics further. Before taking on more topics, however, you should get more experience. If you need a good library of problems to work through, check out Project Euler (https://projecteuler.net/archives).

Security

Web servers, operating systems, databases, and PHP security are all topics that merit their own books. Although this book demonstrates writing secure web applications, there's always room for you to learn more in this area. Start by checking out these sites:

- A Study in Scarlett (www.securereality.com.au/studyinscarlett/)

  This is an article about writing secure PHP code. It's old but still has fundamental concepts.

- The Open Web Application Security Project (www.owasp.org)

  This is a standard resource for web security, and its Top Ten list (www.owasp.org/index.php/Category:OWASP_Top_Ten_Project) is a must-read.

You should also read the relevant sections of the PHP manual and the manual for the database you're using. Searching the Internet for *PHP* and *security* will turn up many interesting articles as well. Pay attention to the dates of articles you read, though, so you do not pick up outdated habits!

Object-oriented programming

The subject of objects and object-oriented programming (OOP) is not covered in this book for two reasons:

- It's well beyond the scope of a beginner's guide.
- You won't be restricted as to what you can do in PHP by not understanding objects.

When you decide you want to learn the subject, you can search the PHP sites for tutorials, check out a framework (see the next section of this appendix), or read my *PHP Advanced and Object-Oriented Programming: Visual QuickPro Guide* (Peachpit Press, 2013). I dedicate around 150 pages of that book just to OOP (and there are still aspects of OOP that I didn't get to)!

Frameworks

A framework is an established library of code that you can use to develop sophisticated web applications. By reusing someone else's proven code, you can quickly build parts or all of a website.

There are many PHP frameworks available, starting with the Zend Framework (http://framework.zend.com). This framework was created by some of the key people behind PHP and is well documented.

My personal favorite PHP framework, as of this writing, is Yii (www.yiiframework.com). I write about Yii extensively on my site. Many developers are fans of Laravel (https://laravel.com/), which you ought to consider.

This book's esteemed technical editor, Paul Reinheimer, is a big fan of *microframeworks*, such as Slim (www.slimframework.com).

Many people love frameworks and what they offer. On the other hand, it does take some time to learn how to use a framework, and customizing the framework's behavior can be daunting.

JavaScript

JavaScript is a client-side technology that runs in the browser. It can be used to add various dynamic features to a website, from simple eye candy to interactive menus and forms. Because it runs within the browser, JavaScript provides some functionality that PHP cannot. And, like PHP, JavaScript is relatively easy to learn and use. For more, see

- JavaScript.com (www.javascript.com)
- Mozilla Developer Network (https://developer.mozilla.org/en-US/docs/Web/JavaScript)
- W3School's JavaScript pages (www.w3schools.com/js/)

I highly recommend you consider learning jQuery (www.jquery.com) to help you with your JavaScript needs. jQuery is a JavaScript framework that's easy to use, powerful, and pretty well documented. It's on the verge of being overly used, but it's a great and reliable way to get started with JavaScript.

Other books

It is my hope that after reading this book you'll be interested in learning more about PHP and web development in general. Although I could recommend books by other writers, there's an inherent conflict there and my opinion as a rival writer would not be the same as yours as a reader. So, instead, I'll just quickly highlight a couple of my other books and how they compare to this one.

PHP and MySQL for Dynamic Web Sites: Visual QuickPro Guide, Fourth Edition (Peachpit Press, 2012) is kind of a companion to this book. There is some overlap in content, particularly in the early chapters, but the examples are different, and it goes at a faster pace. MySQL and SQL in particular get a lot more coverage, and there are three different example chapters: a multilingual forum, a user registration and login system, and an e-commerce setup.

My *PHP Advanced and Object-Oriented Programming: Visual QuickPro Guide, Third Edition* (Peachpit Press, 2013) is kind of a companion to the PHP and MySQL book just mentioned. This book is much more advanced, spending a lot of time on topics such as OOP. It's not intended to be read as linearly as this one, but rather each chapter focuses on a specific topic.

My book *Effortless E-Commerce with PHP and MySQL* (New Riders, 2014) covers everything you need to know to create fully functioning e-commerce sites. The book uses two specific examples for doing so, and incorporates two different payment systems. Complete comfort with PHP and MySQL is assumed, however.

Finally, my *Modern JavaScript: Develop and Design* (New Riders, 2012) teaches you this very important programming language using today's modern techniques. There's even a chapter dedicated to using PHP and JavaScript together!

Tables

This book has a handful of tables scattered about, the three most important of which are reprinted here as a convenient reference. You'll also find one new table that lists operator precedence (**Table B.1**). This partial list goes from highest to lowest (for example, multiplication takes precedence over addition).

Table B.2 lists PHP's main operators and their types. It's most important to remember that a single equals sign (=) assigns a value to a variable, whereas two equals signs (==) are used together to check for equality.

TABLE B.1 Operator Precedence

++ --
!
* / %
+ - .
< <= > >=
== != === !== <=>
&&
||
= += -= *= /= .= %=
and
xor
or

TABLE B.2 PHP's Operators

Operator	Usage	Type
+	Addition	Arithmetic
-	Subtraction	Arithmetic
*	Multiplication	Arithmetic
/	Division	Arithmetic
%	Modulus (remainder of a division)	Arithmetic
++	Incrementation	Arithmetic
--	Decrementation	Arithmetic
=	Assigns a value to a variable	Assignment
==	Equality	Comparison
!=	Inequality	Comparison
<	Less than	Comparison
>	Greater than	Comparison
<=	Less than or equal to	Comparison
>=	Greater than or equal to	Comparison
!	Negation	Logical
AND	And	Logical
&&	And	Logical
OR	Or	Logical
||	Or	Logical
XOR	Exclusive or	Logical
<=>	Null coalescing	Logical
.	Concatenation	String
.=	Concatenates to the value of a variable	Combined concatenation and assignment
+=	Adds to the value of a variable	Combined arithmetic and assignment
-=	Subtracts from the value of a variable	Combined arithmetic and assignment

The various formats for the **date()** function may be one of the hardest things to remember. Keep **Table B.3** nearby when you're using the **date()** function.

TABLE B.3 Date() Function Formatting

Character	Meaning	Example
Y	Year as 4 digits	2017
y	Year as 2 digits	17
L	Is it a leap year?	1 (for yes)
n	Month as 1 or 2 digits	2
m	Month as 2 digits	02
F	Month	February
M	Month as 3 letters	Feb
j	Day of the month as 1 or 2 digits	8
d	Day of the month as 2 digits	08
l (lowercase L)	Day of the week	Monday
D	Day of the week as 3 letters	Mon
w	Day of the week as a single digit	0 (Sunday)
z	Day of the year: 0 to 365	189
t	Number of days in the month	31
S	English ordinal suffix for a day, as 2 characters	rd as in 3rd
g	Hour; 12-hour format as 1 or 2 digits	6
G	Hour; 24-hour format as 1 or 2 digits	18
h	Hour; 12-hour format as 2 digits	06
H	Hour; 24-hour format as 2 digits	18
i	Minutes	45
s	Seconds	18
u	Microseconds	1234
a	am or pm	am
A	AM or PM	PM
U	Seconds since the epoch	1154523600
e	Timezone	UTC
I (capital i)	Is it daylight savings?	1 (for yes)
O	Difference from GMT	+0600

Index

' (single quotation marks)
  using, 44
  versus double quotation marks ("), 169
<=> (spaceship) operator, 135, 138, 457
- (subtraction) operator, 79, 135, 457
_ (underscore)
  using with forms, 51
  using with functions, 270
  using with variables, 37

A

absolute paths, 203, 303, 329
access to pages, denying and
      troubleshooting, 405, 453
action attribute, including in forms, 50,
      53, 57
add_entry.php document
  creating, 361–365
  opening, 368
add_quote.php document
  creating, 306–309, 405–408
  opening, 311–312
addition (**+**) operator, 79, 135, 457
addslashes() function, 370
administrator. *See* **is_administrator()**
      function
Adobe Dreamweaver, 4
alphabetical sort, performing on
      arrays, 184
ALTER privileges, 446
ALTER SQL command, 346
AM or PM, formatting with **date()** function,
      211, 458
am or pm, formatting with **date()** function,
      211, 458
ampersand (**&**), using with forms, 68
AMPPS website, 428, 433
And (**&&**) logical operator, 135, 139, 457
AND logical operator, 135, 139, 457
Apache, 10
Aptana Studio, 4
arguments
  passing, 277
  setting default values, 282–284
  using with functions, 276–281
arithmetic, performing, 79–82

arithmetic operators, 89, 135, 457
array elements
  accessing, 161, 163, 170–172, 177
  adding, 167–168
  deleting, 166
  entering, 165
  pointing to, 173
array() function, 162–163
array values, printing, 171–172
arrays. *See also* multidimensional arrays
  adding items to, 166–169
  creating, 162–165
  creating from HTML forms, 186–190
  deleting, 166
  explained, 160
  indexes and keys in, 161
  merging, 169
  parse errors, 170
  printing, 164
  versus scalar variable types, 160
  sorting, 178–181
  syntactical rules, 161
  transforming between strings, 182–185
  using, 40
asort() functions, using with arrays,
      178–180
.aspx extension, 9
assignment operator, 89, 135
associative arrays, 40
Atom, 4

B

backslash (****), using with strings, 39
basename() function, 329
binary digits, 310
birth year, creating input for, 123
Bitnami website, 428, 433
bitwise (**&**), 310
blank pages, troubleshooting, 452
<body> section, creating, 5
$books multidimensional array, 174–176
books.php document, creating, 174–176,
      208–209
bool type, 281
Boolean TRUE and FALSE, 121, 125, 131, 139,
      395. *See also* **false** value

braces (**{}**)
    versus parentheses (**()**), 172
    using with conditionals, 143
    using with **if** conditional, 125
brackets (**[]**), using with keys in arrays, 161
break language construct, 148
buffer size, setting, 236

C

calculations, performing, 76–78
calculator1.php document
    creating, 286–289
    opening, 293
calculator.html script, creating, 76–78
camel-hump and camel-case
    conventions, 37
case-sensitive searches, performing, 117
character set, setting for database, 392
characters, escaping, 62
checkboxes
    confirming, 142
    creating for HTML form, 124
    presetting status of, 227
closing tag, adding, 5
combined operators, 457
comments, adding to scripts, 24–26
comparison operators, 135–138, 457
concatenating strings, 97–100
concatenation (**,**) operator, 97, 135, 457
conditionals. *See also* nesting conditionals
    best practices, 143
    explained, 121
    nesting, 139
    troubleshooting, 454
    using functions in, 131
configuration changes, confirming, 437
configuring PHP, 436–437
constants. *See also* predefined constants
    benefits, 210
    header.html file, 209
    naming, 210
    printing, 209–210
    and superglobal arrays, 294
    using, 207–210
control panel
    creating for directory, 326–329
    viewing file permissions in, 301

control structures
    comparison operators, 135–138
    default action, 132
    die language construct, 150
    else statement, 132–134
    elseif statement, 144–147
    HTML form for, 122–124
    if conditional, 125–127
    logical operators, 138–143
    for loop, 152–156
    switch conditional, 148–151
    validation functions, 128–131
    while loop, 156
$_COOKIE array, 251
cookie data, retrieving with PHP, 251–253
cookies
    adding parameters to, 254–256
    checking for presence of, 395
    comparing to sessions, 260–261
    creating, 246–250
    data limitation, 250
    debugging, 244
    deleting, 257–259
    encoding values of, 253
    expiration value, 254–255
    explained, 244–245
    httponly argument, 255
    path and **domain** arguments, 254–256
    reading from, 251–253
    security issues, 245, 252, 255
    sending, 247–250
    setting expiration date, 255–256
    testing safety of, 250
    transmitting and receiving, 245
    using tabs and newlines with, 252
    using to identify administrators, 393
copying files on servers, 324
count() function, using with arrays, 167
CREATE DATABASE command, 445, 447
CREATE privileges, 446
CREATE SQL command, 346
CREATE TABLE SQL command, 356–357
create_table.php document, creating,
    357–359
creating documents, 4
CSS (Cascading Style Sheets)
    basics, 3
    font size and color, 251

E

Edit menu, accessing for templates, 199
edit_entry.php document, creating, 383–387
edit_quote.php document, creating, 412–417
else statement, 132–134
elseif statement, 144–147
email, sending, 228–232
email address
    creating inputs for, 123
    validating, 129
empty() function, 128, 131
empty string (' '), using with functions, 284. *See also* strings
encoding
    explained, 5
    external files, 206
encrypting
    data, 112
    passwords, 337
ENTRIES table, columns in, 356
equality (/ and ==) operator, 135, 457
equals sign (=), using with variables, 41
error codes for files, 317
Error level, 65
error messages. *See also* parse errors; troubleshooting
    Add a Blog Entry, 364
    arguments, 277
    connection attempt refused, 10
    Could not connect to the database, 350
    Could not create the table, 358
    Delete an Entry, 381
    displaying in scripts, 63–64
    double quotation marks ("), 21
    email address and password, 402
    foreach loop, 176
    functions, 275
    header() call, 233
    include() function, 201
    nonexisting variables, 61
    Not Found, 14
    output buffering, 233
    permission denied, 299
    for registration results, 142
    related to color selection, 147
    related to external files, 201, 206

related to header() call, 233
require() function, 201
setcookie() function, 246
trusting, 28, 451
unassigned value, 72
undefined function call, 275
Undefined variable, 43
error reporting, 65–67
error suppression operator, 354
error_reporting levels and constants, 65–67
event.html document, creating, 186–187
event.php document, creating, 188–190
everyone permission, 298, 301
exclusive or (XOR) logical operator, 139
execute permission, 298
exit() and die() functions, 237, 354
explode() function
    and fgets(), 338
    using with arrays, 182, 184
external files. *See also* file extensions
    benefits, 206
    closing PHP tag, 206
    using, 201–206
    writing to, 306–309

F

FALSE and TRUE, 121
false value, 19. *See also* Boolean TRUE and FALSE
fclose() function, 305
feedback.html document
    creating, 51
    opening, 56
feof() function, 338
fgetcsv() function, 338, 342
fgets() function, 338, 348
file error codes, 317
file extensions. *See also* external files
    being aware of, 9
    and included files, 206
file() function, 313, 338
file navigation, 203
file paths, 303
file permissions, 298–302, 352
FILE privileges, 446
file uploads, handling, 316–324

FILE_APPEND constant, 303–304
file_exists() function, 300
file_get_contents() function, 313
fileatime() function, 329
filemtime() function, 328
filename() function, 325
fileperms() function, 329
files. *See also* saving documents and scripts
   copying on servers, 324
   deleting, 324
   locking, 310–312
   organizing, 204
   reading from, 313–315
   reading incrementally, 338–342
   writing to, 303–309
$_FILES array, elements of, 317
filesize() function, 328
filter() function, 131
finfo_file() function, 329
firewalls, 429
first name, checking entry of, 223
flag variable, creating for sticky form, 222
float type, 281
floating-point numbers, 38
flock() lock types, 310
folders and files, organizing, 204
font size and color, setting in CSS, 251
footer, adding to template, 197
footer file, creating for template, 200
footer.html document
   creating, 398–399
   opening, 212
fopen() function, 305, 348
for loop, 152–156
   using with functions, 272
   using with numerically indexed arrays, 172
foreach loop
   error generated by, 176, 189
   using with array elements, 170–172
   using with directory control panel, 328
   using with functions, 272
   using with multidimensional arrays, 177
form data. *See also* HTML forms; sticky forms
   accessing, 62
   displaying, 62
   processing, 217
   receiving in PHP, 58–62

sending to pages manually, 68–72
   validating, 128–131
form methods, choosing, 54–57
form submission, determining, 214–215
form tags, 50
   creating, 122
   using with functions, 274
formatting numbers, 83–85
forms. *See* HTML forms
forums, 96
frameworks, 455–456
function keyword, 271
function_exists() function, 275
functions. *See also* PHP functions; undefined functions; user-defined functions
   accessing, 281
   arguments, 276–281
   with arguments and value, 287
   best practice, 275
   calling without arguments, 282
   creating and calling, 272–275
   default argument values, 282–285
   defining with parameters, 276–277
   design theory, 295
   error related to, 65
   invoking, 271
   looking up definitions of, 18–20
   naming conventions, 270
   return statement, 285
   returning values, 285–289
   syntax, 275–276
   user-defined syntax, 270–271, 275
   using spaces with, 85
   using within conditionals, 131
functions.php script
   code, 397
   creating, 394–395
fwrite() function, 305, 348

G

garbage collection, 267
A Gentle Introduction to SQL website, 450
$_GET and $_POST, 55–62, 68
$_GET array, 161
GET method, using with HTTP headers, 240
getrandmax() function, explained, 91

Git version control software, 11
glob() function, 329
global statement, 290–294
GMT difference, formatting with date()
    function, 211–212, 458
GRANT privileges, 446–448
greater than (>) operator, 135, 457
greater than or equal to (>=) operator,
    135, 457
$greeting variable, 97
grocery list array, 160

H

handle_form.php document
    creating, 59
    opening, 66
handle_post.php document
    creating, 79–82, 98–99
    opening, 84, 86, 88, 101, 106, 109, 115, 118
handle_reg.php document
    creating, 126–127
    opening, 129, 132, 136, 140, 145, 149
hash, 40
<head> tag, creating, 5
header file, creating for template, 198–199,
    203
header() function
    and HTTP headers, 237–240
    and output buffering, 233
    using **exit** with, 150
header lines, creating, 4
header.html document
    creating, 396–397
    opening, 209, 234
headers already sent error, troubleshooting,
    453
headers_sent() function, 240
Hello, World! greeting, sending to browser,
    2, 16–17
hello1.php document
    creating, 16–17
    opening, 21
hello2.php document
    creating, 21-22
    opening, 25
hello.html script, creating, 69–70
hidden extensions, being aware of, 9

hidden input, checking for, 219
home page, creating, 422–425
hours, formatting with **date()** function,
    211, 458
HTML (Hypertext Markup Language)
    current version, 2
    resources, 6
    sending to browsers, 21–23
    syntax, 2
HTML comments, accessing, 26
.html extension, 9
HTML forms. *See also* form data; sticky
    forms
    control structures, 122–124
    for cookies, 249
    creating, 50–53
    creating arrays from, 186–190
    displaying and handling, 214, 216–219
    event.php page, 187–190
    handling, 59–61
    handling with PHP, 214–219
    hidden type of input in, 62
    making sticky, 220–227
    for numbers, 76–78
    radio-button value, 62
    re-displaying, 219
    for strings, 94–96
    for strings and arrays, 183–185
HTML pages
    creating, 4–6
    example, 6
    versus PHP scripts, 7
    viewing source, 23
HTML source code, checking, 28
HTML tags
    addressing in PHP, 106–107
    using PHP functions with, 104–107
</html> tag, adding, 5
HTML5, 2
htmlentities() function, 384–385
htmlspecialchars() function, 328
HTTP (Hypertext Transfer Protocol), 237
HTTP headers, manipulating, 237–240

I

id primary key, 387, 391
if conditional, 121, 125–127, 140

if-else conditional, 132–134, 143

if-elseif conditionals, simplifying, 148–150

if-elseif-else conditional, 144–147

IIS (Internet Information Server), 10

implode() function, using with arrays, 182, 184

include() function
failure of, 201
and parentheses (**()**), 206
using with constants, 207
using with external files, 202

increment (**++**) operator, 88–89, 135, 457

index errors, troubleshooting, 452

INDEX privileges, 446

indexed arrays, 40, 165

index.php document, creating, 202–205, 423–425

inequality (**%**) operator, 135

inequality (**!=**) operator, 457

ini_set() function, 263

INSERT INTO *tablename* SQL command, 360, 363

INSERT privileges, 446

INSERT SQL command, 346

installation
on Mac OS X, 433–435
on Windows, 428–432

int type, 281

integers, 38

invalid MySQL argument error, troubleshooting, 453

is_administrator() function, 394, 406

is_array conditional, 189

is_dir() function, 325

is_file() function, 325

is_numeric() function, 128, 131

is_readable() function, 315

isset() function, 128, 131

J

JavaScript, 105, 456

join() function, 185

JQuery website, 456

K

keyboard shortcuts
Cut and Paste, 199
Edit menu, 199

ksort() functions, using with arrays, 178–180

L

language constructs, 150

languages. *See* multilingual web pages

Laravel PHP framework, 455

leap year, formatting, 458

legacy file writing, 305

less than (**<**) operator, 135, 457

less than or equal to (**<=**) operator, 135, 457

linking strings, 100

links
using to pass values, 68–69
using with multiple values, 72

list() function
using with array elements, 189
using with functions, 288

list_dir.php document, creating, 326–329

list_dir.php script, 325

list.html document, creating, 183

list.php document, creating, 184–185

local variables, 97, 290

locking files, 310–312

$loggedin variable, 339, 341

logical operators, 135, 138–143, 457

login form, displaying, 218–219

login page
HTTP headers added to, 240
purpose of, 216–217

login.php document
creating, 216–219, 266–267, 338–342, 400–404
opening, 238, 262

loops
nesting, 156
troubleshooting, 454

ltrim() function, 119

M

Mac OS X
    Get Info panel, 302
    installation on, 433–435
    installing XAMPP on, 434–435
Magic Quotes, 62
`mail()` function, 228–230, 232, 437
`make_date_menus()` function, 274
`make_text_input()` function, 279, 295
MAMP website, 433
MariaDB, installation by XAMPP, 429
math. See arithmetic
memory allocation, error related to, 65
`menus.php` document, creating, 272–274
merging arrays, 169
messages, printing, 16
`meta` tags, using for encoding, 5
`method` attribute, using with forms, 54–57
microseconds, formatting with `date()`
    function, 211
microseconds parameters, formatting with
    `date()` function, 458
minutes, formatting with `date()` function, 211
modulus (%) operator, 135, 457
`money_format()` function, using with
    numbers, 85
month pull-down menu, creating, 272
month values, formatting, 458
monthly payment, calculating, 81
months, formatting with `date()` function, 211
`move_uploaded_file()` function, 317,
    319–320
Mozilla Developer Network website, 456
`mtrand()` function, using, 90–91
multidimensional arrays, creating, 40,
    173–177. See also arrays
multilingual forums, 96
multilingual web pages, creating, 5
multiplication (*) operator, 79, 135, 457
myblog database, 349
myquotes database, 390
MySQL client
    debugging PHP scripts, 440
    using, 438–440
    using semicolon (;) in, 438
    on Windows, 440
MySQL database management system
    (DBMS), 345

MySQL databases. See also databases;
    tables
    apostrophes (') in form data, 370
    connecting to, 348–351
    creating, 445, 447
    creating tables, 355–359
    error handling, 352–354
    inserting records into, 365
    `localhost` value, 351
    myblog, 349
    queries and query results, 347
    sending SQL statements to, 346
    support in PHP, 346
    username and password values, 349
MySQL users
    creating, 445–448
    privileges, 445–448
    root user password, 443–445
`mysqli_affected_rows()` function, 380, 387
`mysqli_connect.php` document
    creating, 348–350, 392
    opening, 353
`mysqli_error()` function, 352–354
`mysqli_fetch_array()` function, 371–372,
    375
`mysqli_num_rows()` function, 375, 387
`mysqli_query()` function, 346, 357, 371, 379
`mysqli_real_escape_string()` function,
    367–370, 383, 385, 387

N

`name` value, using to print greetings, 70–72
`$name` variable, creating via concatenation, 99
names, concatenating, 100
`natsort()` functions, using with strings, 181
navigating
    directories, 325–329
    files, 203
negation (!) logical operator, 135, 457
nesting conditionals, 139, 217–218. See also
    conditionals
nesting loops, 156
newlines (\n)
    converting to breaks, 101–103, 107
    using, 22
    using with cookies, 22, 252
Nginx, 10

nl2br() function
  looking up, 19
  using concatenation with, 100
  using with newlines, 102
nobody permission, 302
Not Found response, receiving, 14
Notice error level, 65
NULL, using with functions, 284
null coalescing (**??**) logical operator, 135, 143
null coalescing (**<=>**) logical operator, 457
number_format() function, using, 83–85
numbers. *See also* random numbers
  creating HTML form for, 76–78
  formatting, 83–85
  incrementing and decrementing, 88–89
  types of, 38
  valid and invalid, 38
numeric indexes
  setting, 165
  using **for** loop with, 172

O

ob_clean() function, 234, 236
ob_end_flush() function, 234–237
ob_flush() function, 236
ob_get_contents() function, 236
ob_get_length() function, 236
ob_start() function, invoking, 233–234
octal format, 302
$okay variable, using with control structures, 126–127, 129–130
OOP (object-oriented programming), 455
The Open Web Application Security Project website, 455
operator precedence table, 457
operators
  for arithmetic, 79
  table, 457
or (**| |**) logical operator, 135, 139, 457
OR logical operator, 135, 139, 457
ORDER BY RAND() clause, 424
ordinal suffix, 458
organizing files and folders, 204
others permission, 301
output buffering, 233–236, 250
owner of file, explained, 298

P

pages. *See* HTML pages
parameters, defining functions with, 276–277
parent folder (**..**), 303
parentheses (**()**)
  versus braces (**{}**), 172
  using in calculations, 86–87
  using with conditionals, 143
Parse error level, 65
parse errors. *See also* error messages; troubleshooting
  avoiding, 170
  double quotation marks (**"**), 58
  receiving, 43
  troubleshooting, 454
password values, validating, 136–137
password_hash() function, 112, 337
password_verify() function, 337
passwords
  encrypting, 337
  entering in HTML form, 123
  managing, 124
  validating, 130, 224
permissions, 298–302, 309, 352
PHP
  configuring, 436–437
  configuring for file uploads, 318–319
PHP code, storing, 236
.php extension, 9
PHP functions, using with HTML tags, 104–107. *See also* functions
PHP manual, using, 18–20, 449
PHP scripts
  accessing, 14
  adding comments to, 24–26
  creating, 8, 70–71
  debugging, 28, 440
  executing, 9
  versus HTML pages, 7
  requesting, 215
  running through URLs, 451
  testing, 12–14
  testing in browsers, 12–14
<?php tag, 8
PHP version, verifying, 451
phpinfo() function, 8–9, 436

phpinfo.php document, creating, 8–9
php.ini file
   editing, 437
   saving, 436
   session settings, 263
phpMyAdmin, using, 347, 441–442
PhpStorm, 4
pipe (|), explained, 67
$_POST and **$_GET**, 58–62, 68
POST and GET, using with **method** attribute, 54–57
$_POST array, 161
$_POST elements, using with cost calculator, 80
postfix mail server, 437
posting.html document, creating, 94–96
precedence
   managing, 86–87
   table, 457
predefined constants, 210. *See also* constants
predefined variables, printing, 33–35. *See also* variables
predefined.php document, creating, 33
preset HTML form values cut off error, troubleshooting, 454
primary keys, 365, 387
print language construct, using, 15–16, 21, 32–33
print statement
   control variables, 129–130
   forms, 61
   HTML form tags, 274
   str_ireplace() and **trim()**, 118–119
   substrings, 115–116
   urlencode() function, 109–111
   variables, 41
printf() function, using with numbers, 85
printing
   $ (dollar sign), 82
   arrays, 164
   constants, 209–210
   greetings, 70–71
   multidimensional arrays, 176
   predefined variables, 33–35
   results from cost calculator, 81–82
   values of arrays, 171–172
   values of constants, 207

printing messages, 16
$problem variable
   creating, 222
   using, 224
   using with databases, 362, 364
PROCESS privileges, 446
Project Euler, 455
pull-down menus
   creating, 272–274
   preselecting, 227

Q

query data, securing, 366–770. *See also* databases
quotation marks ("). *See* double quotation marks ("); single quotation marks (')
   using with constants, 207
quotes
   adding, 304, 405–408
   deleting, 418–421
   editing, 412–417
   listing, 409–411
   storing in text file, 306–307
quotes.php script, creating, 45
quotes.txt file
   creating, 300
   opening, 300

R

radio buttons, presetting status of, 227
RAND() function, 424
rand() function, using, 90–91
random numbers, 90–91. *See also* numbers
random.php document, creating, 90–91
read permission, 298, 301–302
readfile() function, 315
reading
   from files, 313–315
   files incrementally, 338–342
register.html directory, 122, 130
register.html document
   creating, 122–124
   opening, 153
register.php script, 331–337
   creating, 331–337
   opening, 229

Sublime Text, 4

submit button, creating for HTML form, 124

substrings, finding, 113–116. *See also* strings

subtraction (-) operator, 79, 135, 457

superglobals and constants, 161, 294

switch conditional, 121, 148–151

T

tab (**\t**), using with cookies, 252

tables. *See also* MySQL databases
creating, 355–360
primary keys, 355
using primary keys in, 387

tags. *See* HTML tags

tax rate, calculating, 81

$tax variable, 293

template.html document
creating, 195–197
opening, 198, 200

templates. *See also* CSS templates
creating, 194
footer file, 200
header file, 198–199
layout model, 195–197
website project, 396–399

testing
PHP scripts, 12–14
safety of sending cookies, 250

text, sending to browsers, 15–17

text area, presetting value of, 227

text file, creating for file permissions, 299–300

text input type, checking, 138

textarea form element
adding to forms, 53
using with newlines, 101–102

time() and **date()** functions
table, 458
using, 211–213, 254
using with sessions, 265

time zones
formatting with **date()** function, 211–212, 458
setting for servers, 213

tokens, substrings as, 113

Transmit FTP application, 301

trim() function
using in comparisons, 138
using with strings, 117–119

troubleshooting. *See also* error messages; parse errors
access denied, 453
advice, 451
blank pages, 452
calls to undefined functions, 452
conditionals and loops, 454
headers already sent, 453
invalid MySQL argument, 453
parse errors, 454
preset HTML form values cut off, 454
undefined variable and index errors, 452
variables without values, 452

TRUE and FALSE, 121, 395

true value, 19. *See also* Boolean TRUE and FALSE

TRUNCATE TABLE *tablename* query, 381

types, declaring, 289

U

uasort() functions, using with arrays, 181

undefined functions, troubleshooting calls to, 452. *See also* functions

Undefined index notice, 170

Undefined offset notice, 170

Undefined variable error, 43

underscore (_)
forms, 51
functions, 270
variables, 37

unlink() function, 324

UPDATE privileges, 446

UPDATE SQL command, 346, 382–387

upload_file.php document, creating, 319–324

uploaded files, renaming, 324

uploads folder, creating, 318

urlencode() function, 108–112

"user," defining, 299

user-defined functions, 270–271, 275, 278, 288, 393–395. *See also* functions

username, using on registration pages, 124